FoxPro® Programming
2nd Edition

Les Pinter
Foreword by Walter Kennamer, COO, Fox Software

Windcrest®/McGraw-Hill

FoxPro®   Fox Software

SECOND EDITION
FIRST PRINTING

© 1992 by **Les Pinter**. First edition © 1990 by Les Pinter.
Published by Windcrest Books, an imprint of TAB Books.
TAB Books is a division of McGraw-Hill, Inc.
The name "Windcrest" is a registered trademark of TAB Books.

Printed in the United States of America. All rights reserved. The publisher takes no responsibility for the use of any of the materials or methods described in this book, nor for the products thereof.

Library of Congress Cataloging-in-Publication Data

Pinter, Les.
    FoxPro programming / by Les Pinter. — 2nd ed.
      p.   cm.
    Includes index.
    ISBN 0-8306-2586-0 (P)
    1. Data base management. 2. FoxPro (Computer program) I. Title.
QA76.9.D3P52   1992
005.75'65—dc20   92-764
                                                                                   CIP

TAB Books offers software for sale. For information and a catalog, please contact TAB Software Department, Blue Ridge Summit, PA 17294-0850.

Acquisitions Editor: Ron Powers
Book Editor: John C. Baker
Director of Production: Katherine G. Brown
Book Design: Jaclyn J. Boone
Cover: Sandra Blair Design and Brent Blair Photography, Harrisburg, PA   WP1

This book is dedicated to people who love FoxPro: to José Rodriguez, who's a doctor when he's not programming; to Stephen Simpson, another former economist; to Jack Knell, who made his fortune and retired and now works harder writing programs for fun than he ever did making T-shirts; to Louis Castro, who changed my life with his generated application that first showed me how a database program works; to Pei-shan Van Zoeren of Anthology Software, who came to America and did good; to Drew Verret, who taught me that "When life hands you a lemon, make lemonade;" and to my personal angel, Ying-Ying, who finds my keys for me every morning.

Contents

Foreword — x

Acknowledgments — xi

Introduction — xii
   Programming in FoxPro 2.0 xiv
   Systems analysis xv
   Event loops versus foundation reads xvi

1 *What is FoxPro?* — 1
   Database files 1
   Commands and functions 5
   Special files 9
   The workbench 11
   Programming in FoxPro 18
   Writing applications 21
   Optimization 25
   Summary 30

2 *Data: files, indexes, variables, & arrays* — 32
   FoxPro file structures 32
   Creating files from within programs 33
   Primary/secondary files 33
   Multiple child files 35
   Data modeling 35
   Special files 38
   Memo files 38

    Importing and exporting data 39
    Memory variables 39
    The case of the disappearing variables 39
    Assignment within procedures 40
    MEM files 40
    Memory availability 41
    Public, private, and regional variables 41
    Arrays 43
    Summary 46

3 Functions and procedures   47

    Passing parameters 47
    Built-in functions 48
    User-defined functions 48
    API library functions 48
    Ways to call functions 51
    Special procedures 57
    Procedure libraries 63
    Summary 64

4 Control structures and techniques   65

    DO WHILE...ENDDO 65
    Using DO WHILE to read through a file 67
    SCAN...ENDSCAN 68
    FOR...ENDFOR 69
    DO CASE...ENDCASE 71
    Menus 73
    A hybrid case 78
    Event handlers 80
    Summary 88

5 Windows   89

    The DEFINE WINDOW and ACTIVATE WINDOW
      commands 90
    Window commands and functions 92
    Ordering of windows 93
    Use of windows in programs 94
    Principles of operation 94
    Using the mouse 95
    Moving among windows 98
    Windows in screen design 100
    Browse windows 101
    Browses as table lookups 105

Dialog boxes   106
Validation pop-up windows   115
Moving and resizing windows   116
Limiting access to windows   118
Summary   118

6 The screen builder and @...SAY/GET — 119
A simple example   119
@...SAY/GET controls   125
A complex example   130
Are code generators dead?   142
Summary   142

7 Menus — 143
Theory of menus   143
New ways to use menus   144
Traditional menus   145
Another approach to menus   146
A sample menu builder session   149
Generating the code   151
Using parts of the FoxPro system menu   153
Summary   159

8 More on the screen builder — 160
A simple screen   160
Adding a menu   164
How it works   164
Summary   178

9 Pop-ups and pulldowns — 179
Fixed length versus variable length pop-ups   179
Fixed length lists   180
The MENU command   180
The DEFINE POPUP command   182
Prompts   183
Color control in pop-ups   184
Specialty pop-ups   185
Scrolling information displays   188
Variable length pop-ups   189
Finding and popping up only the near misses   191
Special effects   193
Pop-ups that display several fields   206
Selecting multiple values from a pop-up   207
Summary   207

10 Advanced screen building — 208

The LaserDisk library example   208
The screen builder   210
The screen builder code   213
Placement of your functions and procedures   219
Other screens   222
The GOTO screen   222
The REPORT screen   231
The menu builder   237
Report forms   246
The project builder   246
Summary   247

11 Reports — 248

FoxPro's report form   248
A simple example   248
Reports for one-to-many relationships   251
Printer drivers   253
RQBE and the report writer   259
Reports for laser printers   260
Printing data "two up"   267
A LaserJet invoice   271
Summary   276

12 Color — 277

The raw materials   277
Detecting color monitors   278
Intensity and blink   278
Putting color pairs together   278
Monochrome screens   279
Detecting monochrome VGA   279
The color picker and assigned color schemes   280
Commands with COLOR   281
Color schemes   283
User-selectable colors   289
A manifestly beautiful screen   295
Summary   304

13 Searching and selecting — 305

Desperately seeking records   305
Indexed searches   306
Notes and observations   307
Non-indexed (Sequential) searches   308
Simple searches   308
Tabling near-matches   311

Databases with multiple keys   315
Sequential (non-indexed) searches   322
Continue loops   325
A potpourri of searches   333
Selecting records   353
Rushmore   353
Building a filter expression   357
Roll your own expression builders   357
The GETEXPR command   358
Copying to a work file   358
Scope and condition selection   359
SQL Select   359
Summary   360

Index 361

Foreword

The past six months have been an exciting time for Fox. FoxPro 2.0 has taken off in the market and our business has increased significantly. At the same time, the level of support from book authors, newsletter publishers, training firms, and other software vendors also has increased. There are many more books for FoxPro 2.0 than there were for earlier releases, for example.

Les Pinter is a Fox "old-timer" and has written about Fox products for many years. I think this book is one of his best efforts. I particularly like the large amount of FoxPro code that he includes in his book. In my experience, it is easiest to learn a new product by taking actual working code and modifying it to add new features and explore new commands. Les' book provides a host of tools for getting up and running quickly.

Additionally, as a FoxPro veteran, Les also has useful tips for experienced FoxPro users. I was particularly impressed with his explanation of printer drivers. I plan to make use of his ideas in programs I write myself.

Congratulations to Les for completing this book. It is obvious that he has invested a lot of time in it, but the time pays off in a book that should be helpful to all FoxPro users.

Walter Kennamer
Chief Operating Officer
Fox Software
Perrysburg, Ohio

Acknowledgments

I want to thank my son John Pinter, who taught me courage. Also, I want to thank Dave Fulton and Walt Kennamer of Fox Software, who wrote the examples analyzed in this book. I owe the correct use of my mother tongue to my mother and father and my excellent editor, John Baker of TAB Books. I also would like to thank the various contributors to my Newsletter, especially Galen Hall, for setting a higher standard than I felt like as many a deadline approached.

Introduction

FoxPro, like most database programs, is two products. On one hand, it's a product for end users, who don't need to know anything about programming. This is sometimes referred to as the *command line* or *user interface*. Alternatively, it can be used as a programming language, without recourse to the command line.

Command line FoxPro is controlled via a pulldown menu or by typing commands into the command window. Some features are accessible only through commands, while others are selectable only through the menus.

This book is not about command line FoxPro. There are a lot of things that you can do from the command line, but systems involve complex sequences of events that require a program structure to organize and remember. Also, as a woefully large number of my newsletter readers can attest to, you can get yourself into a world of hurt with a single command. You don't always want your average user to have access to the full power of the user interface. FoxPro can index a million records in less than a minute and also can delete them forever in about the same period of time. Programming also is a way of limiting users' access to the power of the language.

Programming in FoxPro 2.0

If you learn to program, you'll discover a fantastic world of power and enjoyment. I'd like everyone, in this last decade of the twentieth century, to experience that pleasure. Realistically, however, programming takes a long time to master. I started programming about 20 years ago and, in my estimation, I got really good about two years ago. That's not to say that it will take you 18 years to learn to program. Tools like FoxPro 2.0 weren't available. It used to require assembly language just to clear the screen.

If you're a newcomer to writing software, you might find programming a bit challenging at first. Programming is a lot harder than non-programmers imagine. In the case of FoxPro 2.0 in particular, event driven programming is intrinsically harder than traditional techniques. More things can go wrong. You also must protect against those potential problems. Suddenly, nothing is simple.

However, once you've made the commitment to write programs, the programmer's workbench built into FoxPro—which consists of the editor, the trace and debug windows, the 50-line display, and a host of other features—will make the job a pleasure.

My newsletter has given me an opportunity to make a difference in the working lives of many programmers and would-be programmers. Techniques like the LaserPro library take weeks of coding and testing to perfect. For the working programmer who needs to use such a tool, a library of code like this is just what the doctor ordered. For beginners, a simple working model is the starting point; Fox Software's examples are not simple. I hope that this book contains enough different examples of how to write code so that one will speak to you.

Systems analysis

Programming used to be 90% of the job in producing software. In the world of mainframes, there was pretty much one way of doing things. It took tons of COBOL to accomplish the same tasks over and over again. There were no choices to make, so systems analysis consisted of data normalization and little else.

With FoxPro 1.02, programming was reduced to about 30% of the job. Programming got easier and the need for design effort increased. FoxPro is a procedural language, with commands like APPEND FROM *filename* that let the programmer spend less time coding and more time designing the software. The availability of increasingly sophisticated display monitors and faster screen I/O added to the ability to design attractive and functional software, so that task demanded more time. FoxPro's use of windows and pop-ups opened up immense new design possibilities, further challenging database software designers.

FoxPro 2.0 stands to reduce the time required to program software to possibly no more than the time it took to design it. That is, if you spend 40 hours designing a product, you can have it running in reasonably complete form in another 40 hours. That's especially true for programmers who make use of good software engineering principles, build smart library modules that don't harm the software that calls them, and make use of third-party sources of software modules and ideas.

Systems analysis is not programming. Universities are turning out many new graduates who've taken a dozen courses in computer languages, but perhaps one software design course. Even students who've taken a design course often find that the textbook techniques are so theoretical or are so couched in terms of a mainframe environment that they just don't apply to the FoxPro world.

I don't know of any better way to prototype software than to get into a few examples and see how they work. This book is top-heavy with design examples for that very purpose. I don't doubt that some users will have seen many of these techniques before. However, if you see just a half-dozen new ideas with the code to implement them already laid out for you, you'll be well served. If you're a novice, run every single program. The differences might seem subtle, but my consulting clients want what they want when they want it. Every technique shown in this book was paid for by a former client. They pay you to do what they ask for, not what you want to do.

Event loops versus foundation reads

There are two ways to write applications in FoxPro. The first is the traditional method, involving a menu loop from which users choose what they want to do next. That technique continues to work just fine in FoxPro 2.0. Both you and your users will understand it.

With FoxPro 2.0, you also can write applications that allow your users to interrupt themselves and go elsewhere, then come back to where they were. This event-driven approach, which is widely used in the Macintosh world, is implemented using the foundation read technique described at the end of this book. The event-driven paradigm permits your users to skip keystrokes in moving from one menu selection to another and really is spectacular when properly implemented.

I can state unequivocally that foundation reads are harder, more time-consuming, more expensive, and harder to understand than menu loop programs. The programmers at Fox Software really are brilliant, but I think they might not understand what it's like to have a production deadline from someone who threatens to fire you if you take twice as long and cost twice as much as you could have, simply to implement a new technique. The good news is that, if your users want to pay for it, you don't have to tell them that it just can't be done or write endless workarounds for nonexistent features. However, you can write pretty good software without using a foundation read.

If you don't understand foundation reads, don't use them. The time to master the "Mother of all Reads" is when your employer or client wants you to write one or in the evenings on your own time. Try to master this technique on someone else's budget and you'll hurt them and yourself, because it will take longer and cost more than you thought it would. This is like the emperor's new clothes. If no one else will say it, I will. I'm not implying that the results aren't worth it. I just want you to know that it's not just your imagination; foundation reads really are more difficult than traditional techniques.

I'm sorry to say that there are some elitists out there who believe that, if you're not writing event-driven code in FoxPro 2.0, you don't deserve to use the product. Ignore them. If you can write programs that you and your users like, you don't have to please self-serving critics.

Having said that, I have no doubt that learning to design and write software using the richness of FoxPro 2.0 will be one of the most satisfying experiences of your life.

1
What is FoxPro?

FoxPro 2.0 consists of

- A characteristic data file and index file structure
- Over 600 commands and functions and the syntax that binds them together
- Several other specialized file structures for storing screens, reports, labels, and project information
- A programmer's workbench within which programs are written, compiled, and tested.

In most languages, you build data structures, then use an editor to write programs that display and read from the screens, do internal manipulations, and read and write files and reports. In FoxPro, you build file structures, design screens and reports, generate code, and then run it, often without recourse to an external editor. It's possible to do all of your work within the development environment.

Database files

Your FoxPro data files are based on the X-base standard, with some internal differences. A data file consists of a header containing a 32-byte definition block, plus 32 bytes for each field name, plus one more byte, followed by the data records without delimiters, followed by a hex 1A (Ctrl–Z). You can peek inside your file by using a hex viewer like Vern Buerg's LIST.COM program (available from your local weekend computer swap for practically nothing) or the Norton Utilities. The header contains record length and record count information in an internal binary format that will look pretty strange at first, but it's readable.

Unlike just about any other computer language on Earth, your programs don't necessarily need to be recompiled if you change a file structure. FoxPro reads the header at run time, then calculates the offset needed to find the record you want as you ask for it.

Unlike non-database languages, there is no need to explicitly write a record. Once you move past the buffer area containing the current record, the program puts the record back on the disk for you. You can flush the buffers and force a write to disk (sometimes it's a good idea to do so), but you don't have to.

USE and USE AGAIN

To open a data file, say, FAMILY, you write:

    USE FAMILY IN A

The IN A part means that you want FAMILY.DBF to occupy select area A. There are 25 select areas.

Once a file is opened, it can be referred to using SELECT plus the file's alias or by prefixing field name references with *alias-*> or *alias*, where *alias* is the alias string. The default work area aliases are A through J for the first 10 files and W11 through W25 for the next 15. SELECT 1 or SELECT A or SELECT *alias* gets you the first file. SELECT W11 or SELECT *alias* (but not SELECT K) will get you to the file in area 11. You can declare an alias different from the filename either to produce a shorter prefix or when you're using a temporary file that's name might vary (for example, a filename generated by the SYS(3) function).

FoxPro allows you to use the same DBF file in more than one area using the AGAIN parameter. If you want to allow a hot key search of a file that you already are positioned within, USE AGAIN will reopen the file for searching the same file without losing your place in the original select area.

Index files

There are two types of index files in FoxPro 2.0. The .IDX extension is used by files containing a single index expression. The .CDX extension designates compound index files containing as many index tags as you want to have for the data file. You'll probably want to use .CDX files exclusively, but .IDX files are supported for compatibility. Actually, you can use the COMPACT keyword to create smaller and faster index files that still use the .IDX extension.

Structural index files are .CDX files that have the same name as their corresponding database file. Index files created using a TAG statement with no index filename supplied are called *structural index files* and are opened automatically every time you USE the file thereafter. When you

USE *databasename*, its structural index file is opened automatically with no index tag order selected. To open a file in a particular order, use:

USE *filename* ORDER *tagname*

It's a peculiarity of .CDX files that if you index on every field in your data file—an operation called *fully inverting the file*—the resulting .CDX file will be only about one half the size of the data file from whence it came.

Index expressions can be of any type; however, if there are several parts to an index expression, they must all be of type Character. If several numeric components exist, they will be algebraically summed and lead to unpredictable results. For example, the expression shown in LISTING 1-1 is valid.

Listing 1-1

```
USE CUSTOMER

INDEX ON ;
  LEFT(name,10) + DTOC(date,,1) + STR(amount,10) ;
  TAG namedate
```

The use of TAG implies a .CDX extension. Because no index filename is given, FoxPro will attach this file to the DBF of the same name.

You use SEEK *memvar* to locate the first record that matches the contents of *memvar*. With EXACT set to OFF, a match is found if the key matches up to the length of *memvar*; with EXACT set to ON, the key and the contents of *memvar* must be of the same length. For most purposes, you probably will want to SET EXACT OFF and provide your own handler for multiple matches.

Alternatively, you might want to SET RELATION TO *key expression* INTO *filename*. This produces a one-to-one relationship, provided the key expression is exactly matched in the index expression—length and all. Corresponding fields used in the SET RELATION statement must be of exactly the same length.

For complex one-to-many relations, you probably won't use SET RELATION. It can be used to advantage with REPORT FORM but less frequently in programs. Besides, I like to be in control.

Indexes can be created in ascending or descending order and can be accessed either way thereafter. That is, an ascending index can be used to access records in descending order simply by adding the descending keyword: SET ORDER TO STATE DESCENDING.

Rushmore and index files

Rushmore is Fox Software's trademark for the technique of reading the index file, instead of the data file, whenever possible. The precise nature of Rushmore is a trade secret, but its speed is no secret.

The FoxPro Rushmore technology means that any operations that use indexes to search for records will be very fast. If you do a LOCATE FOR *expression* that involves an index field, the LOCATE actually will do the equivalent of a SEEK internally, so that the speed will be comparable to an indexed search, as opposed to a sequential search. However, LOCATE FOR "XYZ" $ NAME will not be any faster, even if NAME is an indexed field, because the dollar sign in-string operator can't take advantage of the index.

Limitations

FoxPro 2.0 permits up to 25 open data files. If you have 25 open databases in your application, there probably is a better way to do whatever you're doing.

FoxPro limits you to a total of 99 open files overall. Files in this context means open databases, index files, programs in the calling chain (A does B does C and so on), and several file handles used by FoxPro itself. You probably will never see this limit.

If possible, it's very useful to open all of your data files at the start of your application. For one thing, movement from one part of the application to another can be done very quickly and smoothly if all files are open already. Otherwise, considerable delays can ensue, especially in multi-user environments.

Memo fields

In FoxPro, most field types (including numeric fields) contain ASCII data. The MEMO field, on the other hand, actually is a pointer to the corresponding record in a related file with the FPT extension. Memo fields have a default block size of 512 bytes, but you can set any size from 16 bytes up to 32K bytes.

Memo fields can be dealt with in precisely the same way as any other string field. This lets your programs do in-string searching and replacing, as well as some other string functions available only on memo fields. It's hard to imagine anything that you'd have to add for yourself.

Memo fields can be used to store anything. You can store binary picture images, program source code, or whatever in memo fields. When you compile to an .APP file, the compiled results are stored in memo fields to minimize directory clutter.

Packing files

When you delete records from a FoxPro data file, they don't go anywhere. FoxPro marks them for deletion. If you SET DELETED ON, the deleted files aren't displayed with LIST or BROWSE and your programs will treat them as if they didn't exist. They actually disappear only if and when you issue the PACK command. PACK MEMO is required to remove similar unused space from associated FPT files.

Use of DELETE and PACK is an area of some controversy. PACK requires locking the database, which is a no-no in multiuser installations. You can't lock files when other users might need them. That pretty much precludes the use of PACK, which precludes the use of DELETE under normal circumstances. I recommend a technique called *record recycling*, which is described in chapter 8 (BOOKS.SPR) and chapter 13 (AIRCRAFT.PRG). Please, take the time to master this technique. It only takes a few minutes and will change your life—at least with regard to writing multiuser applications.

Commands and functions

At the annual Fox Developer's Conference, one of the programmers was asked about the possibility of adding a new command to the language. The new command was up and running in the demonstration salon the next day. This ability to respond to user requests for commands is apparent in the product. There are over 500 commands and functions in FoxPro 2.0 and more are certain to be added. (A few anachronisms might disappear eventually but are retained for downward compatibility.)

Some commands have no operands (for example, CLEAR clears the screen). Others, like BROWSE, have a wealth of operands. You could write a book about nothing but the BROWSE command, if you didn't need to earn a living. Some commands begin with special characters, like @ or \, but most are more or less English.

Functions take a parameter, which might be optional. For example, InsMode( ) returns .T. (true) if the keyboard is in insert mode, but =Ins Mode(.T.) turns insert mode on (the equals sign operator forces the function to be acted upon immediately). Functions are followed by parentheses, even when there's nothing inside them.

Only the first four characters of FoxPro commands and functions are significant. A command like RECCOUNT( ) often is abbreviated RECC( ). Unfortunately, this leads to code that can be very difficult to read. You should adopt a standard for coding. I try to use uppercase for commands and functions, lowercase for variables, and mixed case for procedure names. I indent in increments of 3 spaces and don't use tabs. There's nothing sacrosanct about these standards, but you should stick with something; it makes code more readable. Interpersonal communications are hard enough as it is without ugly code.

Commands do whatever their mission in life is the moment they're encountered in a program or in the command window. Functions generally are expected to return a value to the variable at the left of an assignment statement or to a command like ? (print).

Metacommands: BROWSE, RQBE, and others

Some FoxPro commands are so preponderant that they can comprise major elements of an application. BROWSE and Relational Query By Example (RQBE), FoxPro's SQL implementation, are two such animals.

BROWSE presents data in tabular form. The EDIT command, which has fallen into disfavor, presents one record at a time on the screen. BROWSE presents one record per line, thus allowing up to 43 lines of detail depending on the display mode.

The Open Query option under the DataBase menu begins an RQBE session that builds an SQL SELECT statement for either immediate use or inclusion in a program. SQL is regarded in some circles as the greatest thing a database user could ask for. Your own range of applications and users will determine that for you.

If you include RQBE in your applications, you can use the FoxPro RQBE window to allow your users to build search or filter expressions. FoxPro extracts the data that matches either to a temporary browse area or to a predetermined output file. Your users will need some training to use this facility—knowing that you have to enclose literal strings in quotes is not part of the GED requirements as of this writing.

If you prefer and if you're able to predetermine what search expressions your users are likely to want to use, you can use the RQBE screen to generate the pattern SQL SELECT statements, then save them in your own library routines. Then, after asking your users what values to search for, you can patch them into your saved RQBE expressions and execute them directly. This might be preferable to training, if you can get away with it.

Windows

Since the first days of addressable screen locations, programmers have fought with the 25×80 screen. It's a very small canvas on which to build substantial software designs. User-defined windows permit the construction of a world of mirrors and trap doors, by means of which a huge set of data structures can communicate with the outside world. It's a bit like looking at the Pacific Ocean through a periscope sometimes, but it's all we've got for now. FoxPro windows do make it easy.

The commands DEFINE WINDOW» and ACTIVATE WINDOW can be used to create scratchpad areas on the screen that clean up after themselves. If you write:

```
DEFINE WINDOW XYZ FROM 5,15 TO 20,55
ACTIVATE WINDOW XYZ
```

your subsequent @ SAY...GET statements will appear in the defined rectangle. When you issue the command RELEASE WINDOW (or HIDE or DEACTIVATE WINDOW), the window disappears and the underlying screen or window reappears. The ease of use opens up a whole world of design possibilities.

FoxPro does windows like nobody's business. A number of features are available as windows: the command, debug, trace, and desktop features and more. In addition, you can define and activate huge numbers of your own windows within your programs. The Ctrl–F1 key combination skips from window to window. You can use Alt–W to pull down a list of all available windows and pick from the list.

If you issue GETs that span several windows, FoxPro cycles among the windows as you move from the last GET in one window to the first GET in the next one. For example, try the code fragment in LISTING 1-2.

Listing 1-2

```
DEFINE WINDOW FIRST  FROM  5,10 TO 20, 60
DEFINE WINDOW SECOND FROM 15,15 TO 22, 650
ACTIVATE WINDOW FIRST
@ 1,10 GET A
@ 3,10 GET B
ACTIVATE WINDOW SECOND
@ 1,10 GET C
@ 3,10 GET D
READ CYCLE
```

Window FIRST would become the active window. Once you left field B for field C, window SECOND would become the top window. I introduced the CYCLE keyword of the READ command to further stress the point. Once you leave field D, window FIRST would pop up again to let you back into field A. You also can use the mouse to click on the edge of the window that's not on top and bring it to the front, activating its first GET at the same time.

In the user interface, the command window is the only window that is opened initially. Others can be selected by pressing Alt plus the first letter of the six choices listed in the system menu bar at the top of the screen. Each edited program file appears in its own window, as do the calculator, calendar, ASCII chart, puzzle, and more. The Windows pulldown menu is shown in FIG. 1-1.

One of the major changes in the use of windows in FoxPro 2.0 is the ability to use event handlers to go anywhere from anywhere. This places complete responsibility for knowing where you are and getting where you want to go on the programmer. Users like programs that let you go anywhere from anywhere. FoxPro's windows are the way to write such software. However, they're not trivial to write. You probably will find that the new window functions will be invaluable in playing the game of *if it's Tuesday, it must be Belgium*.

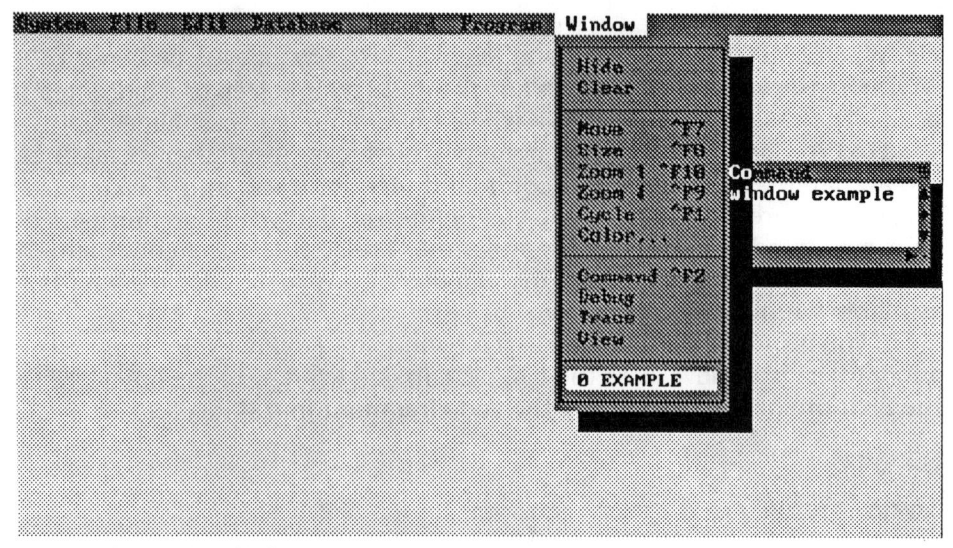

1-1 FoxPro's WINDOWS menu pulldown.

User-defined functions

You can write your own functions, then use them pretty much anywhere in your programs. For example, you can write a function to index a file on the second word in a particular character string. This ill-advised function would be called as shown in LISTING 1-3.

Listing 1-3

```
USE TEXTFILE
*   Structure for TEXTFILE.DBF
*   1  TEXT        Character     80
*..

INDEX ON WordTwo() TAG SecondWord
LIST


FUNCTION WordTwo

txt = ALLTRIM(TEXT)
FirstBlank = AT ( [ ] , txt )
Word1 = LEFT     ( txt , FirstBlank - 1 )
txt   = ALLTRIM ( txt , FirstBlank + 1 ))
RETURN txt
```

You also can call your UDFs using the equal sign operator. Don't forget the requisite trailing parentheses:

=Header( ) && print page header

Calling programs and functions

Programs are run by typing the command:

DO *program-name*

If the program or procedure starts with a PARAMETERS statement, the syntax is:

DO *program-name* WITH *parameter1* [...*parameter2*] ...

In the case of a UDF (User-defined function), if all RETURN statements return a value, you can use:

varname = FUNCTIONNAME( )

or, if there are parameters:

varname = FUNCTIONNAME (*Parameter1* [...*Parameter2*])

If the function's returned values are not needed, you can just use:

= FUNCTIONNAME ( )

Note that you can invoke FoxPro functions in the same way:

= InsMode(.T.) && turn insert mode on

The double ampersand indicates a comment; it tells FoxPro to ignore the rest of the line.

You can write a FoxPro statement of up to 2048 characters on a single line if your editor and your personal value system permit it. More common is the practice of typing a semicolon and continuing on the next line. In that case, you can't use the && comment feature after the semicolon. If the length of your program statements approaches this limit, there probably is a better way to do whatever it is you're doing.

Special files

When you create a screen, a menu, a report, a label, or a project, FoxPro creates a database for each, with the extensions .SCX, .MNX, .FRX, .LBX, and .PJX respectively. These files also are FoxPro databases, which can be opened and viewed at your own risk.

There also is a special file called FOXUSER.DBF, which contains user preferences, color sets, printer drivers, and other such goodies. You actually can buy color sets done by experts in screen aesthetics—Wayne Harless and the Harless Color Sets come to mind—or design and save your own.

The screen builder

You probably will want to design your input screens using the new screen builder feature. The screen builder gives you a visual workplace to do screen design, much like FoxView and other application generators. Beyond that, however, the variety of new screen I/O features is so extensive (especially the new GET parameters) that the screen builder might be the best way to remember what's available. Figure 1-2 is an example.

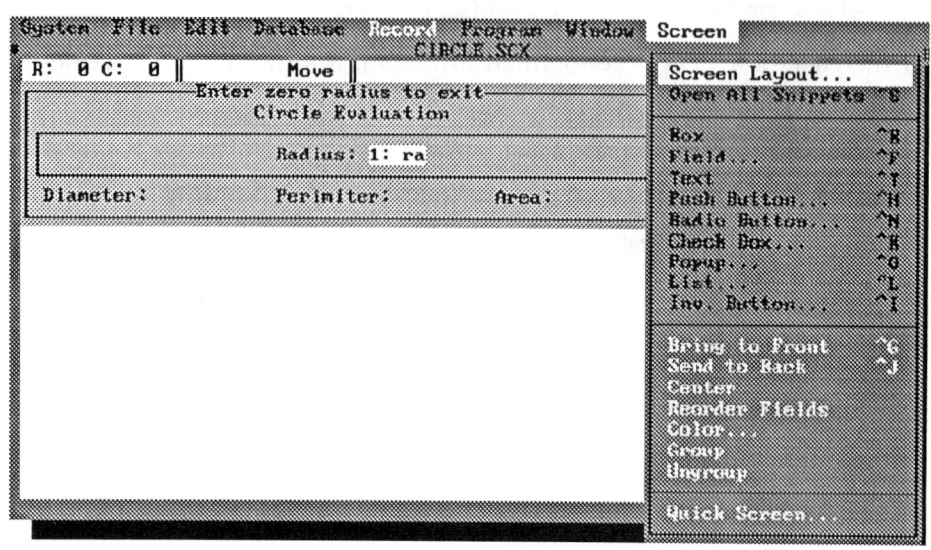

1-2 The screen builder pulldown.

    Even though it's unfamiliar at first, you should develop screen builder skills as quickly as your work load permits. The screen builder creates screen (SCX) files that the project builder can operate on. It enforces a unified approach and standardizes your screens. With the newest @ GET commands, you might be able to do almost all of your screens with this tool alone. If your goal is to integrate the mouse into screen use, this feature is definitely the place to start. One of the examples demonstrates what it takes to make a mouse work on a read loop screen, and it's a bear.

The menu builder

FoxPro's menu builder (FIG. 1-3) functions as a design center for your application. By defining all of your menus and their relationships to one another in an interactive, visual environment, you can prototype from within FoxPro. Getting users to understand and sign off on your designs is terribly important for a successful programming project. This feature might help you get organized and present your ideas before any coding has been done. Once you've mastered the menu builder, you might be able to assemble fairly complete applications without leaving its borders.

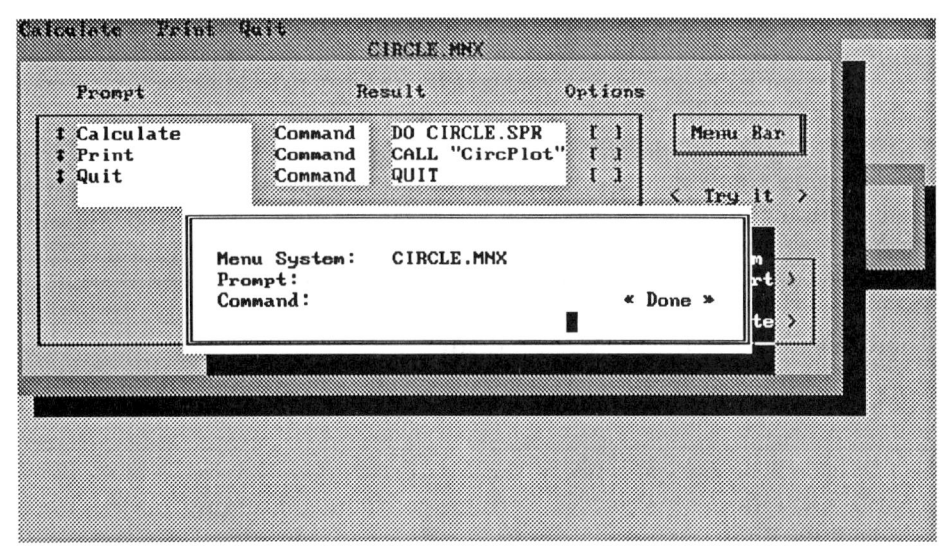

1-3 The menu builder pulldown.

FoxPro redefines the FoxPro System Menu _MSYSMENU. Generally, you PUSH _MSYSMENU (which saves a copy of the FoxPro menu), redefine _MSYSMENU (so that the Alt key can bring it down any time), then ACTIVATE MENU _MSYSMENU. After you're done, use POP _MSYSMENU or SET SYSMENU TO DEFAULT to get FoxPro's menu back. You can include any and all of FoxPro's menu functions into your own. Type ?SYS(2013) for the names to put in the menu bar slots in the menu builder.

The project builder

Designing reports is very easy. With just a little practice, you might find yourself designing most, if not all, reports using FoxReport. System variables, including some new ones, are directly accessible. As part of the report's setup code snippets, you can define memory variables that your report will need. The project manager binds your label programs and reports into a single .APP or .EXE file.

These file formats are completely accessible to the programmer. I've written a program that reads FoxPro 1.02 programs and writes out .SCX files. So, if you don't feel like redesigning all of your screens, give me a call at the Newsletter.

The workbench

FoxPro starts up with its characteristic sign-on screen, then positions a little window at the lower right corner of the screen. That's the command window. If you type commands there, they'll execute immediately. You can even type several lines that end with a semicolon. These lines will be evaluated as a single line—very handy for testing BROWSE and other long command strings.

You'll notice a series of words across the top of the screen: System, File, Edit, Database, Record, Program, and Window. If the system menu isn't showing, the F10 key will display it. This is the FoxPro System menu—referred to as _MSYSMENU within your programs. If you press the Alt key plus the first letter of one of these keywords, you'll get a pulldown menu of options. Some of the options have a trailing function key with or without a special character prefix. The pulldown menu indicates what you can do within that menu. The function keys are shortcuts that can do the indicated choices without pulling down the menu.

You can write your own menus and make them act exactly like _MSYSMENU. That's because your menu *is* _MSYSMENU, if you define it that way.

By selecting components of these pulldown menus, you can do all of your work within FoxPro 2.0. Editing, compiling, building project files, and relating databases—all of the elements needed to write, test, and package your programs—are contained within this environment. I tried to cling stubbornly to my old ways, but it drew me in. I suspect it will do the same to you.

In addition, you can write your own macros, redefine function keys (and other keys, for that matter), and customize the workbench to work however you want.

Keyboard macros

Keyboard macros are memorized keystrokes. If you have an operation that you do frequently, you might want to store those keystrokes so that they can be recalled with a pair of keys pressed simultaneously. For example, you're editing a program and want to change all fields referred to with the prefix of B-> (which means to look in select area B for this field) with the more easily understandable prefix INVOICES->. Make sure you're in insert rather than overstrike mode and use Shift–F10 (define macro) to save the keystrokes:

- Find the string B->
- Delete one character
- Insert the string INVOICES

You could save the keystrokes as, say, Alt–P (for *prefix*). You then can repetitively apply the commands simply by holding down the Alt key and pressing P.

Figure 1-4 shows the beginning of the Store Macro dialog. Shift–F10 is used to begin and to end this dialog.

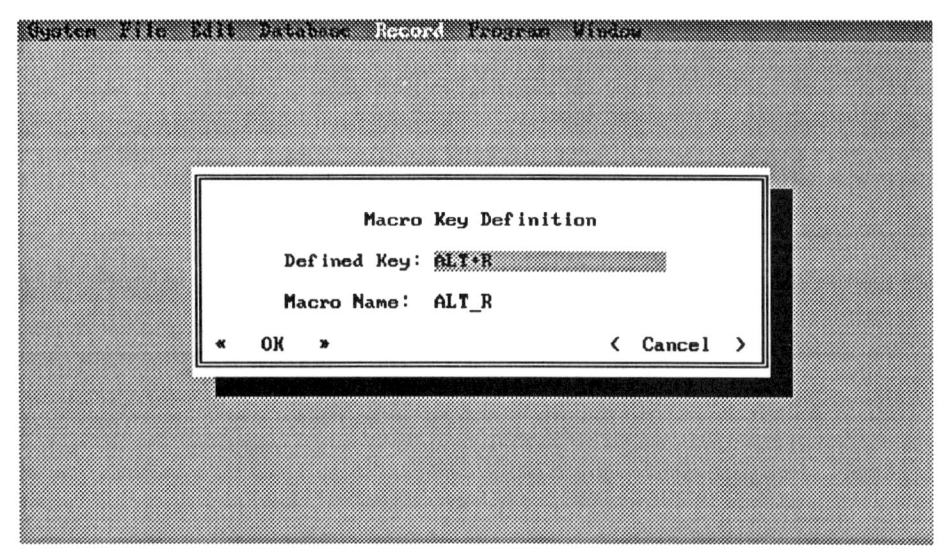

1-4 The Store Macro dialog box.

Function key definitions

Initially, FoxPro assigns common single-word commands to the function keys F2 through F10. By typing the command DISPLAY STATUS (or DISP STAT), you can see what these settings are. You can change the setting of, say, the F4 key by typing:

SET FUNCTION 4 TO [BRAVO;]

Thereafter, every time you pressed F4, the word BRAVO and a carriage return would be entered—presumably, into a data entry field. This might be one way of speeding up data entry.

Key label definitions

ON KEY LABEL is another way to assign values to specific keystroke combinations. If you enter the command:

ON KEY LABEL Alt-F4 DO XYZ

the program XYZ will be run every time you hold down the Alt key and press the F4 key. Because there are hundreds of combinations of Alt, Ctrl, Shift, and unshifted keys on the keyboard, you can create a monster if you've a mind to.

This is arguably the most powerful design feature in FoxPro 2.0 (with system menu redefinition running a close second). Attaching triggers to function keys allows you to use events to drive your application, instead of relying exclusively on menus. You're watching a new day dawn in the history of software design. The approach is probably different from anything you've done before and might seem alien at first. I urge you in the strongest terms to force yourself to make this approach your own. Once you get past that moment where you hit your forehead and say "Now I get it," you'll enter into a new world of interface design.

Testing and debugging

Unlike most computer languages, FoxPro and the other X-Base dialects are interactive, interpreted languages. In FoxPro, you can pause a program at any time, inspect the contents of any memory variable, or just watch the code scroll by as the program executes. The implications for programmers are immense. Debugging is simple, straightforward and fast. Figure 1-5 shows a sample debugging screen with the trace and debug windows opened.

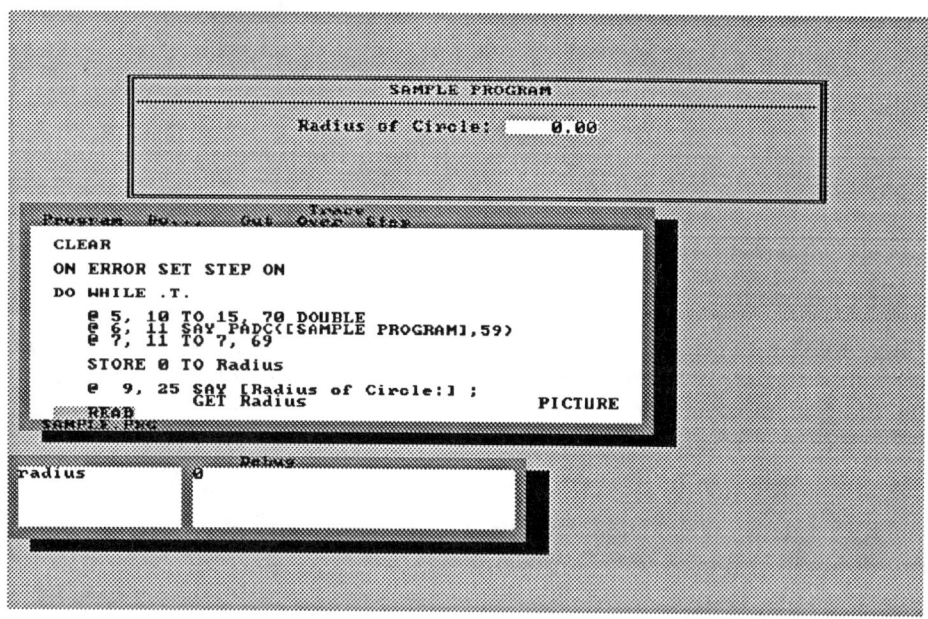

1-5 The Trace and Debug windows.

Debugging in FoxPro is a pleasure. If your program blows up, a good error trapping routine (see chapter 3) will tell you where you were when it happened, what line you were on, and what statement caused the error. When you get an error message, pop up the editor, open the program file, and insert the following code a few lines before the place where your error happened:

```
SET DISPLAY TO VGA50
SET STEP ON
```

Then, re-run your program. When it gets to these statements, the program TRACE window appears and the command window opens up and waits for your command. Press Alt–W to open the Windows pulldown, select Debug, press Ctrl–F1 to cycle back to the TRACE window, and press R to resume. The program will cycle through, one line at a time, as you press S (for *step*). By cycling to the DEBUG window using Ctrl–F1 and entering the names of the variables of interest, you can check on their values. Return to the TRACE window and continue pressing R. The reason for the blow-up should become apparent in no time.

If you're not creating .APP or .EXE files, you don't need to ask FoxPro to recompile every time the program code has been changed. The instant FoxPro runs the modified program, it compares the date/time stamp. If it finds that the source code is newer than the .FXP file of the same name, it recompiles right then and there. This feature can be suppressed (using SET DEVELOPMENT OFF), but you probably won't want to suppress it.

The program in LISTING 1-4 will blow up if you've got more than two .PRG or .FXP files in your directory. I've inserted SET DISPLAY TO VGA50 and SET STEP ON where you can watch the action. Note that there are other (and better) ways to table a list of files than the way used in LISTING 1-4.

Listing 1-4

```
* Program-ID....: BUGGY.PRG
* Purpose.......: Demonstrates use of SET STEP ON to debug...

numfiles = 2
DIMENSION FYLES ( NumFiles )

SET DISPLAY TO VGA50            && DEBUGGING
SET STEP ON                     && STATEMENTS

I = 1
name = SYS(2000,[*.PRG])

IF LEN ( name ) > 0
  fyles( I ) = name
    DO WHILE .T.
    name   = SYS(2000,[*.PRG],1)
    IF LEN ( name ) = 0
      EXIT
    ENDIF
    I = I + 1
    fyles( I ) = name
  ENDDO
ENDIF
name = SYS(2000,[*.FXP])

IF LEN ( name ) > 0
  I = I + 1
  fyles ( I ) = name
  DO WHILE .T.
    name   = SYS(2000,[*.FXP],1)
    IF LEN ( name ) = 0
      EXIT
```

Listing 1-4 Continued
```
      ENDIF
      I = I + 1
      FYLES( I ) = name
   ENDDO
ENDIF

@ 5,5 MENU FYLES , I TITLE [PRGS and FXPS]
z = 1
READ MENU TO 1
```

The compiler

The Build Application dialog can produce a single .APP file from your programs and reports. All of your .FXP code is stored in the memo fields of the project file, so that your production directory is kept free of clutter.

With the optional Run-time Distribution Kit, FoxPro also can compile your programs into .EXE files. The Build Application dialog presents a range of options. You can compile to compact .EXE files, which use the FoxPro Distribution Kit files in conjunction with your program, or to standalone .EXE files. If you use the compact .EXE format, the FoxPro Support Library files (FOXPRO.ESL and FOXPRO.ESO, the standard library, or FOXPROX.ESL, the Extended Support Library) will have to go out with your program. (This is analogous to MicroSoft BASIC compiled programs, which require BASCOM.EXE.)

You also can write your own functions in C and build a library, which is attached using the SET LIBRARY TO *LibraryName* command. Your programs can refer to the functions defined in your library as if they were FoxPro functions. To use the applications Program Interface (API), you will need the Library Construction Kit. You have access to FoxPro's internal functions and variables, as well as to your own program's data and functions. To get a quick idea of what you can do with this, run the SWATCH program that comes with FoxPro, then press Alt–S to pull down the system menu and select the new StopWatch command that SWATCH added. Korenthal Associates already has marketed a library of phonetic search routines. Many more products in LIBRARY format will undoubtedly follow.

The project manager

Within a project, you can define menus, screens, reports, and labels, which can all be used to generate a complete application at the press of a button. FoxPro will create either an .APP file, which you execute as you would an .FXP file, or an .EXE file. You might or might not feel compelled to use SQL, or even the menu builder, right away; however, I urge you to start using the project manager from day one. (Some of the options are shown in FIG. 1-6.)

The project manager knows which programs, screens, and/or menus have been changed and automatically recompiles them when rebuilding

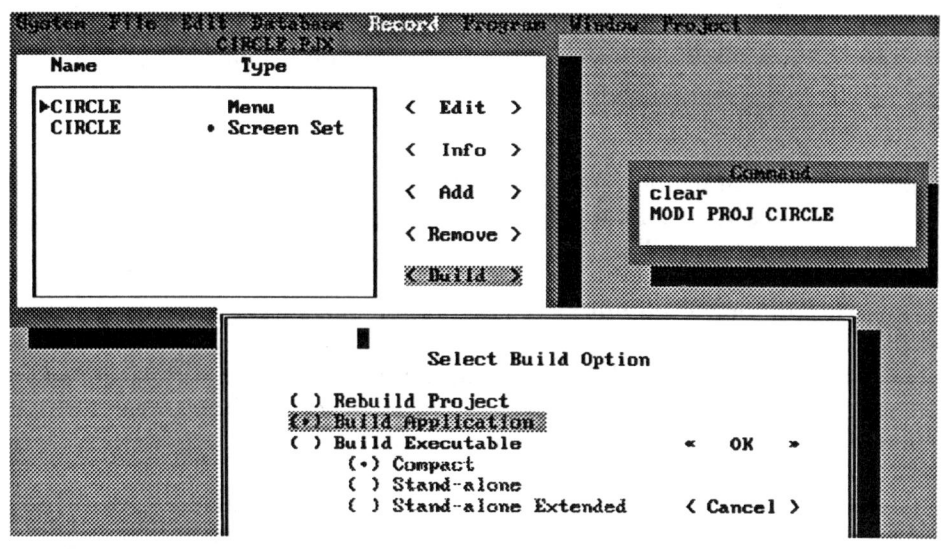

1-6 The FoxPro project manager.

your .APP or .EXE file. That alone would make it worth the effort in my book. By the way, don't bother to type in all of your program names from your already-built programs into the project builder screen. Just give it the name of the top program and the project builder will build the rest of the list for you. This might be your chance to dump all of those abortive .PRGs that you wrote during testing but forgot to erase from the production directory.

The project manager is really handy. I can imagine working on screens without using the screen builder and I can certainly whip out a little menu without using the menu builder; however, I can't imagine writing applications without using the project manager.

The editor

FoxPro's built-in editor might be all the editor you need. It easily handles very large programs, has excellent cut and paste capabilities, and works in a simple, intuitive manner. Also, it's very fast. MODIFY FILE brings up the editor with word-wrapping, while MODIFY COMMAND assumes program files and doesn't word wrap.

To invoke the editor, type:

MODIFY COMMAND *program-name*

Because all FoxPro commands can be shortened to the first four letters, you could type:

MODI COMM *program-name*

The program name does not need the extension .PRG, which is the default

The workbench   17

for all FoxPro programs. You can use Ctrl–F2 to return to the Command Window, then open yet another program file in a second editor window. Alternatively, the command:

    MODI COMM *.PRG

opens up one edit window for each and every .PRG file in the current directory. There might seldom be a reason to do such a thing, but you should do it just once for the thrill of watching it.

Program text can be highlighted by holding down the Shift key and using the cursor movement keys to highlight the text. While highlighted, text can be copied with Ctrl–C or cut with Ctrl–X, then pasted into a new destination using Ctrl–V. So, copying some useful code from the Help screens, from another one of your programs, or from the source code disk to accompany this book (see the order form at the end of this book) is quick and easy.

Note that the invisible carriage return, CHR(13), can be included or excluded in cut and paste operations, yielding quite different results. Experiment a time or two to make sure you know how to get only what you want.

Programming in FoxPro

FoxPro programming consists of designing control structures and program modules to do what you want. The best way to design programs is to find a program that looks like something you'd like to have, then read the source code until you understand every line of it. I don't know of any faster way to get up to speed.

Program structure

Within a program, control flows from top to bottom unless a control structure determines otherwise. Control structures consist of:

    DO WHILE...ENDDO
    DO CASE...ENDCASE
    SCAN...ENDSCAN
    IF...ENDIF

Traditionally, programs generally consist of *modules* (either procedures or functions—the latter can return a value, although it's not required) that call each other in a hierarchy called the *command tree*. Lotus 1-2-3 is typical of this sort of program design. The mechanism of control usually is the DO WHILE .T. loop, within which a menu is presented. Once a selection is made from the menu, the program uses a DO CASE...ENDCASE construct to determine what to do based on which key was pressed.

In FoxPro 2.0, additional commands and functions have been added to enable you to program in a style that's called *event-driven*. The event is the pressing of a function or other hot key. The trick is to do whatever the hot key was supposed to do, then come back to where you were before. Under this scenario, the main controls become:

- Your menu, which can be pulled down at any time
- A hot key, set with the ON KEY LABEL statement
- Selection of a different window or control.

Windows can be selected by pointing and clicking with the mouse or by cycling to the desired window using the Ctrl–F1 key. FoxPro knows when a new window is selected. Your programs can take advantage of that fact.

With this wide variety of methods for controlling your programs, you probably can do just about anything you've seen in any other program.

Macros

Generally, if you want to print the contents of a variable, you write ? x. Sometimes, however, x might contain the name of a variable. This is called *indirection*. FoxPro permits indirection in two ways. If you store an expression to a string named banana, the statement:

```
&banana
```

will result in the execution-time evaluation of the expression contained in the variable banana. For example:

```
cmd = [REPORT FORM ] + RPTNAME ( MONTH ( DATE() ) ) + [ TO PRINT]
&cmd
```

will print the report name contained in the fourth element of array RPTNAME if today's date is in the month of April.

If you store the name of a file or a variable into a variable, say, banana, the following expressions are legal:

```
banana = [MYFILE]
USE ( banana )     && opens the file "MYFILE"
```

or

```
banana = "X"
STORE 1.23 TO ( banana ) && Assigns 1.23 to X
```

I personally hope the latter doesn't catch on. Macro substitution is perhaps the slowest command in FoxPro, so if you must use it, don't do so inside of a looping structure that gets evaluated over and over again.

The EVALUATE function

If you build an expression called, say, expr, and want to see what result it produces, the function:

```
myresult = EVALUATE ( 'expr' )
```

will do what you might be tempted to do using macro expansion in FoxPro 1.02 or other X-base dialects. EVALUATE is faster, although you can't use it every place you now might use macro expansion.

Complex logical expressions

Complex logical expressions can be formed in FoxPro by connecting together simple expressions with parentheses and/or with the connectors AND, OR, and NOT. The pair of periods around these three connectors is no longer required in FoxPro 2.0. The maximum expression length is over 2,000 characters. If your expressions tend to get that long, you probably should be doing things a different way.

There are three types of truly complex expressions. The first is the kind that users who have many fields and want to simulate crosstabulation do. These can involve so many expressions and so many levels of parentheses that you might want to can their most likely requests to eliminate the confusion that is likely to result.

Another type of search is the kind that SQL is intended to deal with, where the purpose is to select matching records with maximum efficiency. If you have a million patient records, selecting the females would take, let's say, one minute using a physical sequential read of the file. If the first 500,000 records were the females, on the other hand, you would have to read only the first half of the file; you could stop when you encountered the first male. Clearly, you can accomplish the same thing (more or less) just by indexing on gender, then doing a SEEK 'F' and DO WHILE gender = 'F', followed by some tabling, tagging, or copying mechanism.

FoxPro 2.0 goes one better. When determining what records to select, it only reads the index. Because index files are even smaller than the data they contain, the resulting disk access speed is spectacular even when dealing with a fully inverted index file. If the index contains only the gender tag, representing only one or two percent of the size of the original data file, the results are even more spectacular.

A third type of complex search is perfect for RQBE. In some searches, you might want to select only those patients who have at least two female children between 12 and 18. If the file structure has patients in one file and children (one per record) in the other, for each patient, you'll have to count all of their child records in which (DATE( )-Child->Birthday) > = (365*12) .AND. (DATE( )-Child->Birthday) < = (365*18). Then, you'll have to tell your program what to do when the count is nonzero in the child file. It's a pain in the neck—I've done it. SQL can find these little rug rats faster than you can, even if you write your own search algorithm.

Arrays and array-specific functions

FoxPro 2.0 contains a full set of array manipulation functions of the type that have been supplied by third-party vendors like Tom Rettig and Galen

Hall in the past. For example, the MENU command can be used to pop up a list of values. So can the ACTIVATE POPUP command. However, unless the data is alphabetized already in the file where it resides, DEFINE BAR *n* OF POPUP will create POPUP bars in the order in which they're read. To read, alphabetize, and sort the array before using @ *coord* MENU to display them, you'll want to use the ASORT command. You can even tell ASORT to sort only the elements of the array that were read in, skipping the uninitialized .T. values in the tail of the array. You also can redimension the array to drop the unused tail end.

Use of arrays in procedures

FoxPro now permits passing an array name to a procedure in either of two ways. You can either SET UDFPARMS TO REFERENCE or prefix the array name with an at sign. In FoxPro 1.02, you had to use macro substitution (LISTING 1-5). In 2.0, you use the code shown in LISTING 1-6. Note that this syntax requires the use of parentheses around the parameters. DO *XXX* WITH @*Arrayname* doesn't work.

Listing 1-5

```
DO PROC1 WITH 'Array1',3

PROCEDURE PROC1
PARAMETERS ArrayName,element
? &ArrayName(element)
```

Listing 1-6

```
DO PROC1 ( @Array , 3 )

PROCEDURE PROC1
PARAMETERS ArrayName,element

? ArrayName(element)
```

Writing applications

You can write all of your code in .PRG file format. FoxPro will cheerfully compile them on the fly. Generally, you compile your programs. Available formats include:

- .FXP (tokenized)
- .APP
- compact .EXE
- standalone .EXE

Which of these you choose generally depends on the target audience and what stage you're at in the life cycle of the program. I use .FXP format while debugging a function or subroutine. I use .APP files when developing or testing within the project manager. I use .APP or compact .EXE files when distributing the application to end users. Until the application is stable, I ship in compact .EXE format, so that patches or upgrades are as small as possible. If the product is stable and absolutely bug-free, I use standalone .EXE format.

Internal program structure

FoxPro programs usually are written in the form of a main program, followed by all other programs in the system with the title statement PROCEDURE *program-name* or FUNCTION *program-name*. When you DO a program, FoxPro will search that program for any programs that the program calls. If you've SET PROCEDURE TO *Procedure-File-Name*, that's the next place FoxPro will look for your program. You also can use the new syntax:

> DO *progname* IN *filename*

FoxPro uses this extensively in generated code to refer to generated functions and procedures within screen and menu programs.

In the project manager, you can designate any of your project's components to be the main program, using the SET MAIN option. Thus, you can let a .MPR (menu) program run your .APP, or an .SPR (screen) program, or a .PRG.

Tokenized FoxPro (.FXPs and .APPs)

When you issue the command COMPILE *.PRG, FoxPro converts all commands to *tokens*, which are shortened versions of your original source code. It also builds tables of what's where, so that it can find variables and internal functions and procedures easier. You can encrypt while tokenizing and can strip out debugging information using the NODEBUG keyword. Tokenizing makes your programs run faster and also permits you to distribute programs without releasing the original source code.

Compiled FoxPro

In addition to .FXP and .APP formats, you can ask the project manager to build an .EXE file. To run an .FXP or an .APP, you get into FoxPro and type DO *program name*. To run an .EXE file, you type it's name from the DOS prompt. All your program code goes into a single .EXE file, which can be very large (often more than 1 Mb). You might wonder how DOS can run a 1 Mb program in something less than 640 K of memory. Before, you would've had to build an overlay. If you don't know what overlays are, you're fortunate. FoxPro uses a loader technology that makes overlays unnecessary.

You can get either compact .EXE output or standalone .EXE output. The former relies on the FOXPRO.ESO and FOXPRO.ESL (or the corresponding Extended version) at run-time. Compact .EXE files can be quite small—the *Hello, World* program is about 7 K. Standalone, it's 750 K.

Using the screen builder as a design tool

FoxPro 2.0 has abandoned the FoxView application generator in favor of a very powerful screen builder. Using this tool, you can design elegant screens, then let FoxPro write the source code to support them. By writing code snippets, which the screen builder lets you insert at various points in your screen files, the code then can be handcrafted to include elements of your personal style. Figure 1-7 shows the screen builder dialog.

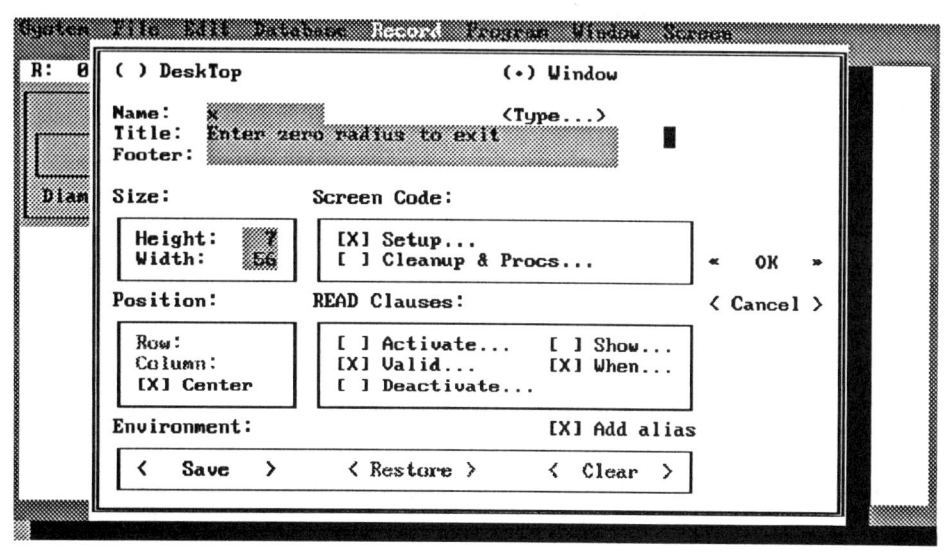

1-7 The Screen Builder dialog.

The screen builder enforces a particular look and feel. You'll see some of that approach in this book. However, much of what you do here involves designing and managing your own screens.

When it comes to handing designs to my clients and gaining their approval painlessly, I've had limited success in my consulting practice. Most of my clients want to be involved in designing their own screens, sometimes in excruciating detail. There are at least three reasons for this.

Part of the reason might be simple ego-involvement. I have a friend who started with nothing and has become a millionaire. He's feeling his oats and sincerely believes that he's a better systems analyst than his contractors are. His designs never work, so he throws the work away, blames the contractor, hires someone else, and starts over.

Another part of it is a firm conviction on the part of the client that the screen will be usable only if it looks a certain way. I've seen thousands of input screens, so I usually see several ways to solve any given problem. My customers, on the other hand, might have experience with only one or two programs. Based on that limited experience, they might well ask me to design a database that looks and acts just exactly like Quattro or 1-2-3. If I do what they ask, it won't work or will cost a fortune. If I don't do what they ask, they won't pay me. The resulting moral dilemma can be very stressful.

Finally, part of the reason clients want to help design their own screens is that they aren't too crazy about the current screen design paradigm. Programmers get caught up in a wave of enthusiasm for the latest and greatest. Customers, however, might not share their enthusiasm. Ideas that might be intuitively obvious to programmers can appear unfathomable to unsophisticated users. For example, I've seen a few screen generator products that seem to favor single-screen flat files with a dozen hot keys. That scenario might be ideal for advanced users, but it's very frustrating for novices, because they can't really use the program until they've understood what all of the hot keys do.

So, the screen builder can help you manage your client relationships by involving them in the interface from the start. It cuts down the that-isn't-what-I-said complaints to a minimum. However, don't agree to a client's design if it's not workable. You might ask him to show you a little more of how clever his design is and continue along that path until he's the first one to realize that his design's unworkable. I've done that.

The screen builder is a very powerful tool, but it doesn't guarantee usable screens. It just produces the underlying code very quickly. If you haven't settled on a design methodology for your applications, poke around some popular commercial software first. Then, once you've seen what software can look like, use the screen builder to make FoxPro do what you want it to do. Don't assume that, just because something can be done, it should be done. There's some bad code floating around out there.

Directory structure

Because of the way the project manager pulls components into a unit, it often is convenient to design your applications directory structure to look something like this:

```
MYAPP─┬─DBFS
      ├─PRGS
      ├─REPORTS
      └─DOCS
```

I generally keep production source in the MYAPP\PRGS subdirectory. If I want to modify one of the programs, I copy it up one level to the MYAPP directory and tell the project manager to loop at the test copy of the source. Once it's working properly, I can copy it down to production and change the project manager reference to look for the program back in MYAPP\PRGS.

Pathing

FoxPro needs to be on the DOS path. Somewhere in your AUTOEXEC.BAT file, you should have something like this:

PATH=C:\;D:\DOS;D:\FOXPRO;C:\UTIL....

Within your CONFIG.FP you should include a FoxPro PATH statement to tell FoxPro where your data and index files are:

PATH=D:\DATFILES

FoxPro can read and update your data files anywhere on the FOX path. Because DOS gets grumpy if there are more than about 127 files in a single directory, you really can speed things up by putting .DBFs in one area, .FXPs in another, source in yet another, and so forth. If you use the project manager, you won't have any .FXPs cluttering up your directories.

The program in LISTING 1-7 shows how to look for a particular file, find where it's located, then tell FoxPro to look for other files in that same path. Variations on this theme can be used to make applications easier to maintain on diverse customers' systems. In this example, I have two different files called STATES.DBF. One is on the DOS path; the other is on one of my client paths. This dual example shows how to extract the path information after finding the data file on either the FOX path or the DOS path.

Listing 1-7

```
* Program-ID....: FIND_DIR.PRG
* Purpose.......: Find a file and make it's path the default path

SET PATH TO D:\BILLING    && use your own paths here...
* Search fox path for file and make it's directory the default...
w = FULLPATH('STATES.DBF')
w = LEFT ( w , RAT ( [\], w ) - 1 )
SET PATH TO &w
? [Path set to: ] + w
WAIT WINDOW

* Search DOS path for file and make it's directory the default...
w = FULLPATH('STATES.DBF', 1 ) && The number parameter can be anything
w = LEFT ( w , RAT ( [\], w ) - 1 )
SET PATH TO &w
WAIT WINDOW [Path set to: ] + w
RETURN
```

Optimization

FoxPro is very complex and powerful. There are trade-offs implicit in power and complexity; you'll run into them immediately. The main comment I hear is that FoxPro 2.0 is very fast if you're set up properly and a little slow if you're not. So, I should cover what constitutes a proper setup before doing much else.

The configuration file

FoxPro uses a text file called CONFIG.FP to tell it which side of the bed to get out of when it starts up. You can use any text editor (or MODIFY FILE CONFIG.FP within FoxPro) to change it. The new values take effect as soon as you start FoxPro from the DOS prompt.

CONFIG.FP can be pointed to in any of three ways. It can be:

- Present in the current directory
- Pointed to by the environmental variable FOXPROCFG
- Pointed to on the DOS command line following the -c flag.

The contents of CONFIG.FP can radically change the way FoxPro works. In addition, you might want to release a single version of your software, but use the CONFIG.FP file to designate the multiuser version. Other uses include memory allocation and fine-tuning, defining the location of programs and data using the PATH parameter, and saving individual users' preferences in multiuser settings.

Some useful settings include the following:

```
TALK = off    Don't echo changed values
STATUS = off    Don't display file status on line 25
SCORE = off    Don't display record pointer info on top line
EXCLUSIVE = off    Multiuser file access
MVARSIZ = 64    64 K of memory variables allowed
MVCOUNT = 500    Total of 500 memory variable names
TMPFILES = F:    USE RAM disk F: for all work areas
```

For networked environments, the single most important thing you can do to enhance performance is to define a RAM disk using your CONFIG.SYS, then use the CONFIG.FP command TMPFILES= to tell FoxPro to use it for work files, index manipulation, and so forth. At the same time, you should use an EMS driver to give FoxPro some expanded memory to work with. I made one application of mine run about five times faster by including the following statement in CONFIG.FP:

```
TMPFILES = F:
```

where F: is my RAM disk.

The same should be done with the FoxPro OVERLAY file, if you have the space. FoxPro loads the routines that it needs when it needs them. Giving it a faster place to find its overlay can't hurt. The CONFIG.FP statement is:

```
OVERLAY = F:
```

where F: is a RAM disk. If that's not available, a directory on the workstation's hard drive would be good as well. Avoid using the root directory of any drive; it can get cluttered.

Customizing FoxPro

If you don't like FoxPro straight out of the box, you can do several things to change the way it works using keyboard macros or key label redefinition. In addition, you can add or change statements in the file CONFIG.FP to change the way FoxPro acts. Finally, there is a file called FOXUSER, which contains settings or preferences that you can change from time to time. FoxPro remembers how it was configured at the end of your last session and does the same thing the next time. You might want to add color sets or printer drivers to FOXUSER to jazz up your environment.

There are a number of SET functions that determine how FoxPro handles certain events in all programs. SET BELL ON, for example, provides an annoying little beep whenever a user tries to type past the end of a field. SET BELL OFF usually is welcome. You might want to provide a bell on/off switch somewhere in your application. It can either be done in a menu or using a function key. For example, if you display:

F3 - BELL ON   F4 - BELL OFF

then ON KEY LABEL F3 SET BELL ON and ON KEY LABEL F4 SET BELL OFF will do the trick.

A toggle is handled a little differently. SET CONFIRM ON/OFF is a good example. It often is preferable to require users to press the Enter key when selecting menu items or exiting input fields until they truly understand the implications of selecting an operation. The command SET CONFIRM ON does just that, with no additional coding required. Experienced users probably will not appreciate the extra keystrokes that CONFIRM ON requires and will want a way to turn the feature off. A very short UDF to toggle a switch on or off might look like LISTING 1-8.

Listing 1-8

```
* Program-ID.....: Expert.prg
* Uses F3 function key to toggle expert/novice mode

SET TALK OFF

expertmode = .F.
ON KEY LABEL F3 DO chg_mode
CLEAR

DO WHILE .T.

   ModeSet = GetMode()
   SET CONFIRM &modeset            && contains either "ON" or "OFF"

   @ 22, 0 TO 22, 79
   @ 23,       0 PROMPT ' First '
   @ 23, COL()+1 PROMPT ' Second '
```

Listing 1-8 Continued

```
  MENU TO option

  option = IIF ( option = 0 , [ ] , SUBSTR ( [FS] , option , 1 ) )

  IF option = [ ]
     EXIT
  ENDIF

  WAIT option + [ pressed ] WINDOW TIMEOUT 1
ENDDO


PROCEDURE getmode
RETURN IIF ( expertmode , 'OFF' , 'ON' )


PROCEDURE chg_mode
ExpertMode = .NOT. expertmode
@ 24, 35 SAY IIF ( expertmode , [ expert ] , [ novice ] ) + [mode]
RETURN
```

Here, the command ON KEY LABEL F3 DO Chg_Mode means that your users press the F3 key to determine whether to require pressing Enter when a menu option is selected by first letter.

EMS usage

FoxPro 2.0 comes in several configurations. The extended version includes its own mechanisms for managing expanded memory. With the normal version of FoxPro, you need to use your own memory manager.

FoxPro runs at least twice as fast on my machine under QuarterDeck's QEMM-386 program. Other expanded memory managers should yield similar improvement in performance. There are a lot of good reasons for using EMS in conjunction with FoxPro. Many video cards use a part of memory that can be moved to high memory. The BIOS can be moved to speed I/O operations and space required for FILES and BUFFERS can be gotten from high memory. You definitely will notice an improvement if you use just about anyone's drivers. Read the latest release notes from Fox Software to see what they recommend.

Files and buffers

FoxPro uses one file for each program in the current calling sequence, one more for each open data and index file, and another five for internal purposes. FILES=nn must be declared in CONFIG.SYS in your boot directory. A value of 99 might be a good minimum setting; I never use less than 60. Because they only take 64 bytes each, feel free. I've included a little routine that reads CONFIG.SYS and informs your user if the setting for FILES is too low. You probably should give it a pretty high value (say, FILES=60).

Buffers, on the other hand, are 512 byte work areas used by DOS. Under QEMM, files and buffers are handled in expanded memory. Files take a very small amount of memory compared to buffers. My QEMM386 moves buffers to high memory. I generally use 40 of them. I've heard that BUFFERS=75 is needed on networks under some circumstances and that BUFFERS=10 is the best workstation setting for some networks. You'll notice that those two pieces of advice appear to conflict; they both came from a very famous expert on the subject. It will take you about 10 minutes to experiment with your network and configuration to determine optimal settings for you. In my experience, more is better.

Memory usage

FoxPro 2.0 needs only about 280 K to start up. That doesn't mean the end of the need to manage memory, but it certainly removes it from the critical list. If you allow plenty of EMS (4 Mb is a good number) and use a RAM disk for TMPFILES as mentioned earlier, you should be fine. Also, you might want to fine-tune the MVARSIZ parameter in CONFIG.FP. FoxPro allows about a zillion memory variables and all the string space you want, but you have to tell CONFIG.FP if you want more than 6 K of string memory.

FoxPro version 1.02, on the other hand, likes at least 500 K. If you're running on a Novell network, the network TSRs (60 K) and DOS (40 K) will get you down to 540 K with no files or buffers. If you add any number of either, you can't run FoxPro/LAN 1.02 unless you move the TSRs to high memory using LOADHI, NETROOM, or a similar product. FoxPro 1.02 is faster than 2.0 for most operations, so there still will be a call for it; however, be advised that memory management is a bigger issue with FoxPro 1.02.

Disk usage

FoxPro creates work files in the current directory or in the directory you designate as the work file directory. If there isn't enough disk space remaining on the active drive, FoxPro won't run. You'll get a message that reads unable to create workspace. Also, if your user powers down or reboots without exiting FoxPro, these work files (which can be identified by their characteristic names consisting of 8 hexadecimal—mainly numeric—digits, plus the extension .TMP) will build up on the disk. Eventually, they can occupy all available disk space.

You might want to consider using some of your extended memory—the memory above 1 Mb—as a RAM disk for your temporary files. Your programs will run faster and no directory management is required. If your users insist on turning off the computer and going home without exiting their screens, the temporary files in RAM disk will simply disappear. However, so will some of their data and their file allocation table's integrity.

Upgrading to 2.0

If you already have FoxPro 1.02, you'll need to do a few things to transition smoothly to version 2.0:

- Install the new product.
- Recompile all of your .PRG files—the new .FXP format is different.
- Run the FIXUSER program located in the FOXPRO2 \ GOODIES \ MISC directory. This program will translate various files to the new formats.
- Be prepared to explain to your users why their programs have slowed down.

The last item is the hardest to deal with, because all you've heard about FoxPro is how fast it is. Actually, file access is amazingly fast and probably overshadows slowdowns in other areas. However, data entry screens, particularly cursor movement from field to field, is demonstrably slower. I'll mention a few techniques for speeding up data entry in subsequent chapters, but you might have to live with it for a revision or two.

I don't apologize for the slowdown in some FoxPro functions. In this book, you'll see some programs written in 1.02, then in 2.0, so that you can appreciate how much less code it takes to accomplish the same things that were nearly impossible in 1.02. For heads-down data entry, you probably will want to write a very lean style of code, perhaps avoiding BROWSE and leaving many validations for a batch screening process. I think the gain is worth the pain.

Standard versus extended FoxPro

FoxPro comes with two versions of the program: Standard FoxPro, for use with databases of normal proportions, and Extended FoxPro, for use with systems having an aggregate record count of more than a half-million or so. The extended version uses some very sophisticated memory management techniques and will effectively use all of the memory it finds on your board. Because additional power comes at additional expense in terms of time and resources, you probably will use the standard version unless file size dictates use of the extended FoxPro. There might be power users who prefer the Extended version, but standard is best for development. Anyway, it loads faster.

Summary

FoxPro is an ideal environment for program development. The environment is visual and easy to learn; the internal editor and automatic recompiler speed up the edit/compile/test cycle; and testing and debugging is made much easier via the TRACE and DEBUG windows. If you start with straightforward functional designs, you'll be producing software faster than you ever thought possible. You'll find immediate use for the menu and screen builders and the project manager.

All of the example programs that ship with FoxPro 2.0 are heavily invested in the event-driven paradigm. You might take a little longer to warm up to event-driven programming. I find it more difficult to plan and execute than event loop code and can't tell if it's going to become as ubiquitous as menu-driven programs are today. Everyone will know a lot more about this in a year. However, I do look forward to the 20/20 hindsight that I'm sure will be widely available a few months down the road.

2
Data:
files, indexes,
variables, & arrays

FoxPro keeps information in files on disk and in memory variables (scalars and arrays) in memory. The structure and usage of these elements determines how you write applications in FoxPro.

FoxPro file structures

FoxPro files are *flat files*. That is, a file consists of multiple occurrences of a single record structure. In some environments, a database can consist of a number of related record types in a single file. We don't do that.

One of the brilliant insights of Wayne Ratliff was that programming in an environment with completely uncomplicated file structures would be vastly simplified. That simple wisdom has been validated in the growth in popularity of the X-base family of languages. In developing software, the smallest price you pay is the cost of the programming language. The cost of programmers' time and training is by far the greatest cost in software implementation.

In a typical file structure, any field or combination of fields can be a key; there's nothing in the database itself that designates fields as keys.

The name *flat file* derives from the fact that the data, if printed out, would be flat on the right margin. That is, all records have the same length, because they're all the same data structure. If we permitted multiple record types, you might see a structure like the one shown in TABLE 2-1.

Note that the right margin is ragged, because different type records inhabit the file. This is not a flat file structure. The 001 and 002 values are sometimes called *segment IDs* and indicate which kind of record you're reading. When you get to the next *001*, you're starting at a new person.

In FoxPro, each type record is put in its own file. The structure shown previously would be rearranged so that the individuals would occupy one

Table 2-1   A hierarchical sequential data structure.

Key	Data
001	Smith, John, 1014 Ridgecrest, Houston, TX 77055
002	Houston Community College 1984–1986
002	University of Houston 1986–1989
001	Jones, Fred, 2202 Nantucket, Houston, TX 77024
002	University of Texas 1978–1982

file and their education would occupy another. The first file is sometimes referred to as the *parent file*; the second is the *child file*. Key fields are used to tell your programs how to find related records. This process is not automatic, but neither is it difficult. Segment IDs are no longer meaningful, so they aren't used in these files.

Creating files from within programs

It now is very easy to create a file structure from within a program. The CREATE TABLE command in LISTING 2-1 will create an empty file.

Listing 2-1
```
CREATE TABLE MYFILE ;
( NAME C(30), ADDRESS C(30), CITY C(15), STATE C(2), ZIP C(10),;
  DATEPAID D(8), AMOUNT N(10,2), NOTES M(10) )
```

Structure of file: MYFILE.DBF

NAME	Character	30
ADDRESS	Character	30
CITY	Character	15
STATE	Character	2
ZIP	Character	10
DATEPAID	Date	8
AMOUNT	Numeric 10	2
NOTES	Memo	10

Primary/secondary files

In FoxPro, you would restructure the example shown previously into two files (see TABLE 2-2). If your data was exactly as shown in the table, you'd have no way to see which education records went with which people. So, you add fields that contain the same values for those records that refer to the same people (see TABLE 2-3). Now, you can locate the records for John Smith in both files.

One way to do this is shown in the following code:

```
SELECT SCHOOLS
LIST FOR NAME = PEOPLENAME
```

Table 2-2 Primary and secondary file structures.

People:

FIELD_NAME	FIELD_TYPE	FIELD_LENGTH
NAME	Character	16
ADDRESS1	Character	20
ADDRESS2	Character	20
Smith, John	1014 Ridgecrest	Houston, TX 77055
Jones, Fred	2202 Nantucket	Houston, TX 77024

Schools:

FIELD_NAME	FIELD_TYPE	FIELD_LENGTH
SCHOOL	Character	30
YEARS	Character	9
Houston Community College		1984–1986
University of Houston		1986–1989
University of Texas		1978–1982

Table 2-3 Schools with NAME key field added.

FIELD_NAME	FIELD_TYPE	FIELD_LENGTH
NAME	Character	16
SCHOOL	Character	30
YEARS	Character	9
Smith, John	Houston Community College	1984–1986
Smith, John	University of Houston	1986–1989
Jones, Fred	University of Texas	1978–1982

which says *go to the SCHOOLS file and list all records where the person's name is the same as the name in the record currently pointed to in the PEOPLE file.* Absent an index, FoxPro will read every record in the database, testing each one to see if name matches. This sequential access is very slow. The more records that there are in the file, the slower it is. (Note that, if the file is indexed on NAME, the FOR expression will be optimized by Rushmore and will be very fast.)

The preferred mechanism for doing this is to index the child file on the field containing the key:

SELECT SCHOOLS
INDEX ON name TO SCHOOLS

Now, you can print all matches by typing:

SELECT SCHOOLS

```
SEEK PEOPLE.NAME
LIST WHILE NAME = PEOPLE.NAME
```

which says *go to the SCHOOLS file, find the first record where the person's name is the same as the name in the record currently pointed to in the PEOPLE file and list matching records until the name changes.* (This is the clumsiest possible way, but it's early yet.)

Note that under Rushmore, you can accomplish exactly the same thing using:

```
LIST FOR NAME = PEOPLE.NAME
```

Multiple child files

In real life, there might be many related bits of information, not just two or three. To the non-computer-literate, a file probably consists of a manila folder with 27 different forms in it relating to John Smith. That would be 27 related child files in the FoxPro world. That simple misunderstanding is one of the reasons why you occasionally meet clients who want you to take their files and put them on the computer this afternoon. Other than taking the manila folder and physically placing it on top of the computer case, it can't be done in an afternoon.

The actual process of determining how many files you need, what fields they should contain, what key structures will allow you to find and report on related information, is called *data modeling*. It probably is the most important part of systems analysis.

Data modeling

There are a number of technical approaches to data modeling. Books by Gane and Sarsen, Codd, Warnier-Orr, and others, have become best-sellers. They train students in the process of reducing data structures to third normal form.

First normal form: eliminate repetition

First normal form involves creating a separate table (DBF) for groups of related fields. For example, beginners often structure invoice records something like TABLE 2-4. For first normal form, this should be separated into two files (TABLE 2-5).

Second normal form: eliminate redundancy

Second normal form involves the creation of a separate table for all fields that depend on the value of a multi-value key. In the last example, customers might have the same store name, but several store numbers. The key is STORE ID + STORE NUMBER (see TABLE 2-6).

Table 2-4 Unnormalized file structure.

FILE: INVOICES

INVOICE #
CUSTOMER ID
CUSTOMER NAME
STORE NUMBER
CUSTOMER ADDRESS
TAX_CODE
TAX_RATE
DESCRIPTION 1
QUANTITY 1
PRICE 1
EXTENSION 1
DESCRIPTION 2
QUANTITY 2
PRICE 2
EXTENSION 2
DESCRIPTION 3
QUANTITY 3
PRICE 3
EXTENSION 3

Table 2-5 Reduction to first normal form.

FILE: INVOICES

INVOICE #
CUSTOMER ID
CUSTOMER NAME
STORE NUMBER
CUSTOMER ADDRESS
TAX_CODE
TAX_RATE

FILE: INVOICE LINES

INVOICE #
DESCRIPTION
QUANTITY
PRICE
EXTENSION

Third normal form: eliminate secondary dependencies

Finally, because TAX_CODE uniquely identifies TAX_RATE, you can take it out and put it in its own file (TABLE 2-7). The reduction of data structures to third normal form is a technical procedure for file design. You don't want a

Table 2-6 Second normal form.

FILE: INVOICES

INVOICE #
CUSTOMER ID
STORE NUMBER
FILE: INVOICE LINES

INVOICE #
DESCRIPTION
QUANTITY
PRICE
EXTENSION

FILE: CUSTOMERS

CUSTOMER ID
STORE NUMBER
CUSTOMER NAME
CUSTOMER ADDRESS
TAX_CODE
TAX_RATE

Table 2-7 Third normal form.

FILE: CUSTOMERS

CUSTOMER ID
STORE NUMBER
CUSTOMER NAME
CUSTOMER ADDRESS
TAX_CODE
TAX_FILE

TAX_CODE
TAX_RATE

guy's address to appear in two different files. If it does, you'll have to edit it in two places if it changes. That's not new. It's just common sense.

In actual fact, the most important requirement of data modeling is extracting the whole truth from your users. If they attempt to spare you the complexity of their reality, everyone involved is going to be hurt.

My rich friend who would be a systems analyst is particularly guilty of this. A former intelligence specialist in the military, he really believes in operating on a need-to-know basis. As far as he's concerned, anyone who has information is dangerous. Unfortunately, a systems analyst with incomplete information is even more dangerous. If you find out that something was left out after you've finished programming, you might just have to throw away everything you've done and start over.

You generally can get to the heart of the matter by starting with output requirements and working backwards. By knowing exactly what printed reports, sorting and selecting requirements, screen displays, and instantaneous totals will be needed, you can infer data structure requirements without knowing exactly what third normal form is. People were doing this right before it acquired a new name.

Normalio ad absurdum

There are cases where blindly applying rules to file structures can produce unnecessary complexity. A common example is one where a master file for a customer is designed to have up to, say, three contact names. Rigorous normalization says to build a related child file with CUSTOMER CODE as the key and contact names and phones in the record structure. Actually, by adding tags for all three contact names in the .CDX file and seeking all three of them until a hit is made, you can permit very fast searching of the customer file by contact name with only a tiny bit of programming.

This is a case where I probably wouldn't build and maintain a separate record structure, especially if the client decided to spring this on me late in the project. If you have a case where strict application of the rules would add excessively to the cost of the project, back off. Getting the biggest bang for the buck generally is the goal. So much for purism.

Special files

In addition to data and index files, FoxPro 2.0 also uses database files to store report forms (.FRX files), label forms (.LBX files), screens (.SCX files), menu structures (.MNX files), and projects (.PJX files). These are database files and can be USEd like any .DBF file.

Memo files

If your file structure contains one or more fields of type MEMO, FoxPro will create a parallel file with the extension .FPT. Memo fields have a fixed block size that you can set at the time of creation and that can be packed to remove deleted space using the PACK MEMO command. Each memo field contains a 10-byte pointer field in your .DBF, while the actual contents of the memo fields reside in the .FPT file.

Memo fields are extremely accessible in FoxPro 2.0, compared to their ancestors in other dialects. You can search for substrings embedded within the memo text. Line-by-line manipulation and extraction is very simple. Extensive use is made of memo fields in .FRX, .SCX, .PJX, and .MNX files (that is, in their associated .FRT, .SCT, .PJT, and .MNT files).

If you lose your .FPT file, just copy and rename another .FPT file to replace it. Your data will be gone; however, at least, FoxPro will let you back in.

Importing and exporting data

FoxPro also can import and export data between most important data formats, including the following:

DIF	Data Interchange Format
FW2	Framework
MOD	Multiplan
RPD	RapidFile database
SYLK	Symbolic Link interchange format
WK1	Lotus 1-2-3 Release 2.*xx*
WK2	Lotus 1-2-3 Release 3.0
WKS	Lotus 1-2-3 Release 1A
WR1	Symphony version 1.1 and above
WRK	Symphony versions under 1.1
XLS	MicroSoft Excel Version 2

As of this date, it also can read from (but not write to) Paradox files.

Memory variables

FoxPro permits the same types of memory variables as it does field types in file structures, with the exception of memo fields (which can be stored in memory as character variables):

- Character
- Numeric
- Date
- Logical

In addition, SCREEN type memory variables can be created by the SAVE SCREEN command.

The command SCATTER MEMVAR creates a copy of every field in the active database as a memory variable of the same name. FoxPro can create databases containing FLOAT type fields using the CREATE TABLE command, but these become numeric when scattered to MEMVARs. For example, the code fragment in LISTING 2-2 creates the variables M.NAME, M.ADDRESS1, M.ADDRESS2, M.PHONE, and M.BALANCE. (You also can refer to memory variables using the M−> prefix.) To include copies of memo fields, add the MEMO keyword: SCATTER MEMVAR MEMO. The inverse function GATHER MEMVAR also can take the MEMO keyword.

The case of the disappearing variables

When you call a procedure using one or more memory variables as parameters, they become hidden while you're within the called procedure. That is, your program can't refer to them by the names with which they were called.

Listing 2-2

```
USE DENTISTS

* Structure of file: DENTISTS.DBF
* NAME                  Character     40
* ADDRESS1              Character     40
* ADDRESS2              Character     40
* PHONE                 Character     14
* BALANCE               Float         10      2
* MyMemo                Memo          10

SCATTER MEMVAR
```

For example, you use the code shown in LISTING 2-3 and get a variable not found error, so you try to display it in the DEBUG window and, lo and behold, it's gone. Don't panic. You just have to know where to look.

Listing 2-3

```
xyz = [Fred]
DO PROC2 WITH xyz

PROCEDURE PROC2
PARAMETERS delta

? xyz             && can't be found!!!!
```

Assignment within procedures

Memory variables can be updated by storing new values to the corresponding parameter names in called procedures, provided that the statement SET UDFPARMS TO REFERENCE has preceded it. Otherwise, the code in LISTING 2-4 will print the value Fred.

Listing 2-4

```
Name = 'Fred'
DO PROC2 WITH Name
? Name
.
.
PROCEDURE PROC2
PARAMETERS xNAME
STORE 'Joe' TO xNAME
RETURN
```

MEM files

Some or all of your memory variables can be stored to .MEM files. This technique can be useful for color management (see chapter 8). MEM files overwrite memory unless the word ADDITIVE is included. Thus, the unexpected result in LISTING 2-5 is correct.

Listing 2-5

```
001 * Program-Id....: Memory.PRG -Demonstrates RESTORE FROM MEMfile
002 X = 1                       && without ADDITIVE.
003 Y = 2
004 Z = 3
005 DISPLAY MEMORY

           X            Priv   N        1
           Y            Priv   N        2
           Z            Priv   N        3

006 SAVE TO MEMTEST
007 W = 4                       && New variable created and assigned a value.
008 RESTORE FROM MEMTEST        && Without keyword ADDITIVE, W will be erased.
009 DISPLAY MEMORY

           X            Priv   N        1    && Note that W has
           Y            Priv   N        2    && disappeared. The
           Z            Priv   N        3    && RESTORE FROM .MEM file>
                                             && overwrites memory unless
010 QUIT                                     && ADDITIVE is appended.
```

Memory availability

FoxPro uses the setting in the CONFIG.FP file to determine how much space to allocate for memory variables. The amount of space available for string variables is limited by the CONFIG.FP setting for MVARSIZ (there's no *E* at the end), while the total number of variables is limited by MVCOUNT. I usually use the following:

MVARSIZ = 48
MVCOUNT = 600

Public, private, and regional variables

Variables are assumed to be public for all routines below the procedure in which they are first assigned a value and are nonexistent above the originating procedure. If you want to use a called procedure to allocate variables, you have to use the PUBLIC statement to tell FoxPro that these variables can be used anywhere thereafter. You can dimension and declare public in one fell swoop—for example, PUBLIC OXEN(24). Also, for completeness, the statements DECLARE X(10) and DIMENSION X(10) are equivalent to each other, although they aren't equivalent to PUBLIC. If you try to PUBLIC a variable that already exists, FoxPro will object strenuously.

Declaring PUBLIC variables generally is done only in initialization routines called by the main routine. By moving all such initial definitions to another procedure, you improve readability of the main program.

One use of the PUBLIC statement is in the invocation of optional procedures that are passed the names of memory variables that are to be passed back. For example, the PICKLIST routine returns an array containing the keys of multiple selected records. The program can be called from anywhere. One if its parameters is the name of the array in which to store the selected records' keys. At the moment the PICKLIST is called, the array doesn't exist. Upon return, the named array is available for post-processing. To avoid any error message resulting from an attempt to re-declare an array PUBLIC, you test for the value of the first array element. If TYPE('&varname(1)') = "U", you can safely PUBLIC the array name. Otherwise, it already has been declared PUBLIC and you assume the programmer intends to reuse it.

Private declarations

Private declarations, on the other hand, are done for purely defensive reasons. If you reuse a variable in a lower-level procedure, figuring out why it's trashed when you get back up to the main procedure can be next to impossible. If you have a local procedure in which you intend to use the statements (LISTING 2-6), then, if the previous value of i was supposed to be preserved for use at a higher level, it's been reassigned the value max count+1 at this point and its former value is long gone. By including the declaration:

```
PRIVATE i
```

at the top of the called procedure, your original value of i still is whatever it was before you called this procedure.

Listing 2-6

```
I = 2
sum = 0
DO SUMMBAL
? i, sum          && sum is correct, but i is changed.
.
PROCEDURE SUMMBAL

sum = 0
FOR i = 1 TO maxcount
   sum = sum + balance ( i )
ENDFOR
```

Regional declarations

The screen builder in FoxPro allows you to define regional variables that are used within different parts of the generated code. Because you might use the same memory variable name in several screens that are all accessed in the same program, FoxPro uses regions to keep things straight in its mind. For now, you can think of regional variables as variables to which FoxPro appends the number of the region as a suffix so that references to them won't be confused with references to similar names in other

.SPR programs. For an example, see LISTING 2-7. Region directives are used by the screen builder, which might be the only place you see or use them.

Listing 2-7

```
* IN FIRST.SPR

#REGION 1
REGIONAL x

x = 3

* IN SECOND.SPR

#REGION 1
REGIONAL x

x = [A]
```

Arrays

Arrays can be of either one or two dimensions in FoxPro. A single array can have up to 65,000 elements, given sufficient memory. After dimensioning, all elements of the array have a value of .F., but the code:

```
DIMENSION x(100)
STORE 0 TO x
```

causes all 100 elements of x to contain the value 0.

Array functions

The new array functions in FoxPro include:

- ACOPY( )—Copies elements from one array to another.
- ADEL( )—Deletes array elements.
- ADIR( )—Puts file names into an array.
- AELEMENT( )—Returns an array element's number from its row and column number.
- AFIELDS( )—Puts field names into an array.
- AINS( )—Inserts elements into an array.
- ALEN( )—Returns the number of elements in an array.
- ASCAN( )—Searches an array for an expression.
- ASORT( )—Sorts an array.
- ASUBSCRIPT( )—Returns a row or column elements from an array element.

Commands that operate on arrays include:

- APPEND FROM ARRAY—Moves data from a database to an array.
- DECLARE/DIMENSION—Creates a one- or two-dimensional array.

- GATHER FROM array—Stores array elements into database fields.
- SCATTER FROM array—Moves database fields into an array.

Uses for arrays

Arrays are used for several purposes in FoxPro. The MENU command makes certain types of pop-up selection menus very easy to create. Record contents and summary statistics can be stored in arrays. The new ASORT command operates on arrays to sort array elements in either ascending or descending order quickly and easily. Also, SCATTER TO ARRAY X copies the fields in the current record to a similar number of elements in the named array, creating it if it doesn't exist already. It's very fast, although not always as convenient as SCATTER MEMVAR.

Looping

One of the most important reasons for loading data to an array is to permit loop processing. The construct:

```
FOR i = 1 TO NElements
    x ( i ) = x ( i ) / 100
ENDFOR
```

is a simple way of dealing with a large number of values in a small amount of code. However, this isn't the only use for arrays in FoxPro.

Menu arrays

Listing 2-5 displays a menu of all tabled choices stored in an array and returns the element number of the selected element. This program produces the pop-up menu shown in FIG. 2-1. The NumOnScr parameter, while not required, can be used to limit the height of the pop-up on the screen. This isn't essential, but sometimes it's esthetically desirable.

Generally, such menu displays consist of data loaded from a file. In FoxPro 1.02, no more than 128 elements could be included in the menu and the menu elements couldn't exceed screen width. In 2.0, you're limited only by memory in both dimensions. I've menued arrays of 300 elements 100 characters wide with no trouble. (Only the first 78 or so characters appear on the screen.) If your data already is in an array, this is one easy way to pop it up. For some purposes, MENU is just what the doctor ordered.

Scatter/gather arrays

The command SCATTER TO X takes the contents of the current record and puts one field's value in each element of the array X. X is created if it doesn't exist already. This syntax might be preferable to SCATTER MEMVAR for some types of utility functions.

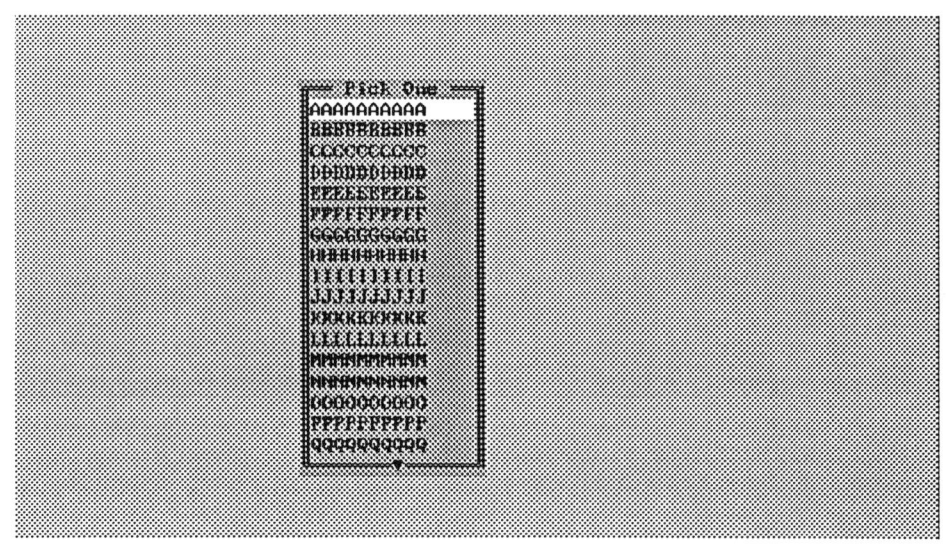

2-1 The menu produced by program MENUTEST.

Arrays for sorting

The new ASORT command makes it simple to sort array-based data. You can sort all array elements or start anywhere and include only as many elements as you want. The data in the array is sorted in ascending order.

The code fragments in LISTINGS 2-8 and 2-9 table and sort the names of all .PRG files in the current directory, then sort the names alphabetically and display them in a menu for selection. Figure 2-2 shows the screen this program produces in my directory.

Listing 2-8

```
* PROGRAM-ID.....: MenuTest.PRG

DIMENSION mylist(26)
FOR i = 1 TO 26
   mylist ( i ) = REPLICATE ( CHR(64+i), 10 )   && ASC(65) = "A", etc...
ENDFOR
TotalNum  = 26
NumOnScrn = IIF ( TotalNum <= 17 , TotalNum , 17 )  && max 17 on scrn
@ 3, 25 MENU mylist, TotalNum, NumOnScrn TITLE " Pick One "
READ MENU TO x
? IIF ( x > 0 , ;
  'You selected number ' + STR ( x , 2 ) + ', ' + mylist ( x ) ,;
  'None selected' )
WAIT WINDOW
```

Note that the ability to limit the array elements to be sorted is critical, because ASORT gets sick if asked to sort elements of disparate types. The uninitialized elements still have the value of .F. Even if ASORT didn't get sick, the uninitialized elements would sort to the top and appear in the menu, a situation up with which you cannot put.

Arrays   45

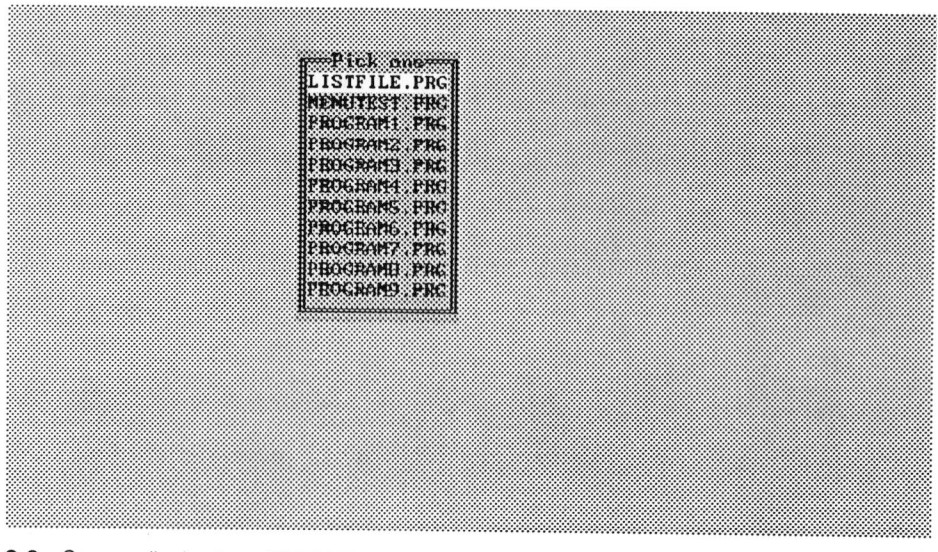

2-2 Screen display from FILELIST.PRG.

Listing 2-9

```
* Program-ID......: ListFile.PRG

DIMENSION fils( 128 )
fils ( 1 ) = SYS ( 2000 , "*.PRG" )
i = 2
DO WHILE [] <> fils ( i ) AND i < 128
  fils ( i ) = SYS ( 2000 , "*.PRG" , 1 )
  i = i + 1
ENDDO
NumFiles = i - 1
= ASORT ( fils , 1 , NumFiles )
NumOnScrn = IIF ( NumFiles <= 17 , NumFiles , 17 )
@ 2, 25 MENU fils, NumFiles, NumOnScrn TITLE 'Pick one'
READ MENU TO z
? IIF ( z = 0 , ;
  ' None selected ' , ;
  fils ( z ) + ' selected'
WAIT WINDOW
```

Summary

FoxPro data and index file structures are simple, straightforward and versatile. This, together with the menuing options, the powerful array functions, pop-ups, and the ability to import and export data in various file formats, provide the programmer with a full complement of powerful tools for building applications.

3
Functions and procedures

Functions are the workhorses of the programming world. You'll be happy to know that there are very few limitations on the use of functions in FoxPro. You can use one of the over 200 built-in functions included in the language or write your own. When you write your own, you have a choice of techniques, depending on how you want the functions to take action or return values.

If included within another file, functions consist of the PROCEDURE or FUNCTION header followed by the function name, which can contain up to 10 characters. Unless you want to pass a return value back, the terminating statement RETURN is optional. RETURN implies RETURN .T., which can be very important when terminating a READ VALID clause. RETURN .F. means *keep reading*; RETURN .T. (and hence RETURN by itself) means *stop*. The absence of RETURN implies RETURN .T.

Passing parameters

If you need to give values to the function to work with, you probably will want to follow the FUNCTION/PROCEDURE statement with a PARAMETERS statement, giving a name for each parameter to be passed. The main reason is that it's too hard to keep track of which variable names are global and which are local and you start making mistakes of a kind that are relatively hard to track down. Generally, all of the variables in your functions should be either private or parameters.

Parameters are passed to functions either by listing them following the WITH token or by listing them in parentheses (see LISTING 3-1). If you intend to modify one of the parameters within the function, use SET UDF PARMS TO REFERENCE before calling the function.

Listing 3-1

```
DO MyFunct WITH Amount, Date, Name
a = MyFunct ( Amount, Date, Name )
FUNCTION MyFunct
PARAMETERS one, two, three
```

An unusual feature of functions in FoxPro is that, if a PARAMETER statement exists, you don't have to supply as many parameters as the number of variables on the PARAMETERS statement. Thus, one or more trailing parameters can be left off if they are not needed. Your code can be written to ignore the missing parameters and to look only at the ones passed.

Built-in functions

FoxPro functions return a value or perform a service. Most, but not all, accept parameter values that determine the value returned by the function. The over 200 functions can be grouped into 16 functional categories (FIG. 3-1). Some of these functions are new to FoxPro 2.0. Note especially the array functions and those related to windows.

User-defined functions

In FoxPro, you can write your own functions. UDFs are extremely useful. For one thing, you can write libraries of functions that reflect your style and frequent requirements. In addition, several special uses add tremendous power to FoxPro:

- VALID and WHEN clauses in GET statements
- Indexing expressions

As of FoxPro 2.0, UDFs don't have to return a value; that is, the RETURN statement doesn't have to have a spurious .T. or 3 or whatever placed after it just to avoid an error message.

FoxPro 2.0's screen painter generates a function or procedure name for every action that requires one. For example, your code snippets are placed within a UDF generated by the screen painter. The names of generated functions are letter and number sequences like _A123B11XP.

API library functions

Using the Applications Programming Interface (or API) Library Construction Kit available from Fox Software, you can write functions in C or assembler, then attach them to FoxPro using the SET LIBRARY TO *libraryname* command. After that, you can refer to these functions as if they were part of FoxPro. The C routines have to be compiled in WatCom C. As usual, anything written in C will take a lot longer to perfect than it would if written in FoxPro. FoxPro wasn't made to do graphics, screen special effects, and a lot of other normal computer things. With this new capability, the dividing lines blur considerably. A strong after-market of hopeful software developers is sure to result from this welcome addition.

3-1 FoxPro 2.0 functions.

Class: Char
 ALLTRIM( )
 ASC( )
 AT( )
 ATC( )
 ATCLINE( )
 ATLINE( )
 DIFFERENCE( )
 LEFT( )
 LEN( )
 LIKE( )
 LTRIM( )
 OCCURS( )
 PADC( ) | PADL( ) | PADR( )
 RAT( )
 RATLINE( )
 REPLICATE( )
 RIGHT( )
 RTRIM( )
 SOUNDEX( )
 SPACE( )
 STR( )
 STUFF( )
 SUBSTR( )
 TRIM( )
 TYPE( )
 UPPER( )

Class: Char, Data Convrt
 CHR( )
 CHRTRAN( )
 LOWER( )
 PROPER( )
 STRTRAN( )

Class: Char, Data Convrt, Interface
 TRANSFORM( )

Class: Char, Date
 DTOC( )
 EMPTY( )
 INLIST( )
 SYS( )

Class: Char, Date Data Convrt
 CTOD( )

Class: Char, Logical
 ISALPHA( )
 ISLOWER( )
 ISUPPER( )

Class: Char, Menus/Prompts
 PAD( )

Class: Char, Numeric
 INT( )

Class: Char, Numeric, Date
 BETWEEN( )
 EVALUATE( )

Class: Database
 ALIAS( )
 DBF( )
 FCOUNT( )
 FIELD( )
 FILTER( )
 FSIZE( )
 LUPDATE( )
 MEMLINES( )
 MLINE( )
 RECCOUNT( )
 RECNO( )
 RECSIZE( )
 RELATION( )
 SELECT( )
 TARGET( )
 USED( )
 VARREAD( )

Class: Database, Interface
 UPDATED( )

Class: Database, Index
 KEY( )
 NDX( )
 ORDER( )

Class: Database Index   * NEW *
 CDX( )
 MDX( )

Class: Database Index
 TAG( )

API library functions 49

3-1 Continued.

Class: Date
  CDOW( )
  CMONTH( )
  DATE( )
  DAY( )
  DMY( )
  DOW( )
  DTOC( )
  GOMONTH( )
  MDY( )
  MONTH( )
  SECONDS( )
  TIME( )

Class: Environment
  ERROR( )
  FKLABEL( )
  FKMAX( )
  GETENV( )
  LINENO( )
  MEMORY( )
  MESSAGE( )
  OS( )
  PROGRAM( )
  SCHEME( )
  SET( )
  VERSION( )

Class: Environment, File Mgmt
  GETFILE( )
  LOCFILE( )
  PUTFILE( )

Class: Environment, Interface
  COL( )
  READKEY( )
  ROW( )
  SCOLS( )
  SROWS( )

Class: Environment, Keybd/Mouse
  CAPSLOCK( )
  INSMODE( )
  NUMLOCK( )
  INKEY( )

Class: Environment, Print
  PCOL( )
  PROW( )

Class: File Mgmt
  CURDIR( )
  DISKSPACE( )
  FULLPATH( )
  PARAMETERS( )

Class: Interface   * NEW *
  OBJNUM( )

Class: Keybd/Mouse
  CHRSAW( )
  LASTKEY( )
  MCOL( )
  MDOWN( )
  MROW( )

Class: Low Lvl I/O
  FCHSIZE( )
  FCLOSE( )
  FCREATE( )
  FEOF( )
  FERROR( )
  FFLUSH( )
  FGETS( )
  FOPEN( )
  FPUTS( )
  FREAD( )
  FSEEK( )
  FWRITE( )
  HEADER( )

Class: Logical, Database
  BOF( )
  DELETED( )
  EOF( )
  FOUND( )
  SEEK( )

Class: Logical, Environment
  ISCOLOR( )

Class: Logical, File Mgmt
  FILE( )
  IIF( )

Class: Logical, Print
  PRINTSTATUS( )

Class: Menus/Prompts
  BAR( )
  MENU( )
  POPUP( )
  PROMPT( )

Class: Menus/Prompts   * NEW *
  CNTBAR( )

CNTPAD( )
GETBAR( )
GETPAD( )
MRKBAR( )
MRKPAD( )
PRMBAR( )
PRMPAD( )

Class: MultiUser
FLOCK( )
LOCK( )
NETWORK( )
RLOCK( )

Class: Mem Var   * NEW *
ACOPY( )
ADEL( )
ADIR( )
AELEMENT( )
AFIELDS( )
AINS( )
ALEN( )
ASCAN( )
ASORT( )
ASUBSCRIPT( )

Class: Numeric
ABS( )
ACOS( )
ASIN( )
ATAN( )
ATN2( )
CEILING( )
COS( )
DTOR( )
EXP( )
FLOOR( )
FV( )

ISDIGIT( )
LOG( )
LOG10( )
MAX( )
MIN( )
MOD( )
PAYMENT( )
PI( )
PV( )
RAND( )
ROUND( )
RTOD( )
SIGN( )
SIN( )
SQRT( )
TAN( )
VAL( )

Class: Numeric, Date
YEAR( )

Class: Numeric, Environment
RDLEVEL( )

Class: Windows
WCOLS( )
WEXIST( )
WLCOL( )
WLROW( )
WONTOP( )
WOUTPUT( )
WROWS( )
WVISIBLE( )

Class: Windows   * NEW *
WBORDER( )
WCHILD( )
WPARENT( )

Ways to call functions

Functions can be invoked in any of five ways:

- In a regular expression
- By executing them as programs
- By returning a value (UDF)
- By evaluating the function using the equal sign operator
- In VALID, WHEN, ACTIVATE/DEACTIVATE, and SHOW clauses

In a regular expression

The first type is the one you probably are most familiar with. You simply use one of the FoxPro functions in a regular expression (LISTING 3-2). Fox-Pro evaluates it and returns a value.

Listing 3-2

```
amt = 123.45                           && Insert leading zeros...
a = STR ( 1000000 + amt , 7 , 2 )      && Convert to string
? RIGHT ( a , 6 )                      && Drop leftmost character
```

By executing them as programs

Listing 3-3 uses a previously-defined variable, Pay_Amount, which was given a new value within the function. It also is possible to name the value to be returned as a parameter, provided that the statement SET UDFPARMS TO REFERENCE has been included.

FoxPro defaults to SET UDFPARMS TO VALUE. That means that the values passed as parameters are viewed by the called procedure as constants and can't be changed. That is, you can assign values to their counterparts in the called procedure; however, when you return, the original parameters will not have changed. Based on that, I'd rewrite LISTING 3-3 as shown in LISTING 3-4.

Listing 3-3

```
Principal    = 250000
Interest     = 10.5
Years        = 30
Pay_Amount   = 0

DO Payment with Principal, Interest, Months

? Pay_Amount

PROCEDURE Payment
PARAMETERS prin, int, yrs

Pay_Amount = PAYMENT ( prin , int/12, yrs * 12 )

RETURN
```

By returning a value (UDF)

By using the third format, that of returning a value directly, you create what is called a *user-defined function*. The resulting code is shorter and, once you get used to it, more straightforward. You can reduce the code in LISTING 3-5 to a single line by typing:

```
? ' Payment is ' + STR(Payment(Principal,Interest,Years),10,2)
```

Listing 3-4

```
Principal    = 250000
Interest     = 10.5
Years        = 30
Pay_Amount = 0
SET UDFPARMS TO REFERENCE

DO Payment with Principal, Interest, Months, Pay_Amount
? Pay_Amount

PROCEDURE Payment
PARAMETERS prin, int, yrs, pmt

Pmt = PAYMENT ( prin , int/12, yrs * 12 )
RETURN
```

Listing 3-5

```
Principal    = 250000
Interest     = 10.5
Years        = 30

a = PAYMENT ( Principal, Interest, Years )
? 'Payment is ' + TRANSFORM(a,"@Z 999,999.99")

PROCEDURE Payment
PARAMETERS prin, int, yrs
Pay_Amount = PAYMENT ( prin , int/12, yrs * 12 )
RETURN Pay_Amount
```

A very useful function of this type is a function to center text in the current window or screen (LISTING 3-6). Unlike the FoxPro PADC function, which centers within blanks, this version doesn't overwrite whatever might be to the left and right of the centered text. It also clears the line if no parameter is passed.

Listing 3-6

```
* PROGRAM-ID...: CenTest.PRG
*
= center ( 23 , 'Processing your report request' )
= center ( 24 , 'Press ESCAPE to cancel the report' )
*
DEFINE      WINDOW LITTLE FROM 5, 20 TO 7, 60 DOUBLE SHADOW
ACTIVATE    WINDOW LITTLE
= center ( 0, 'Report is printing')
* DO REPORT
DEACTIVATE WINDOW LITTLE
= center ( 23 )      && clear line 23
= center ( 24 )      && clear line 24
*
*
PROCEDURE center
PARAMETERS line, text
```

Listing 3-6 Continued

```
IF PARAMETERS() = 1      && No message - just clear the line
   @ line, 0 CLEAR
   RETURN .T.
ENDIF

length    = LEN ( ALLTRIM ( text ) )
width     = WCOLS()                       && works with windows or screen
msg       = text
IF length > width
   msg    = LEFT ( text , WCOLS() )
   length = LEN ( ALLTRIM ( text ) )
ENDIF

start = ( width / 2 ) - ( length / 2 )

@ line, start SAY ALLTRIM ( msg )

RETURN .T.
```

Figure 3-2 shows what the results of the function look like. Note that the window size is taken into account by the function.

An example of a function that returns a value for a purpose is shown in LISTING 3-7, which inserts leading zeros in front of an integer.

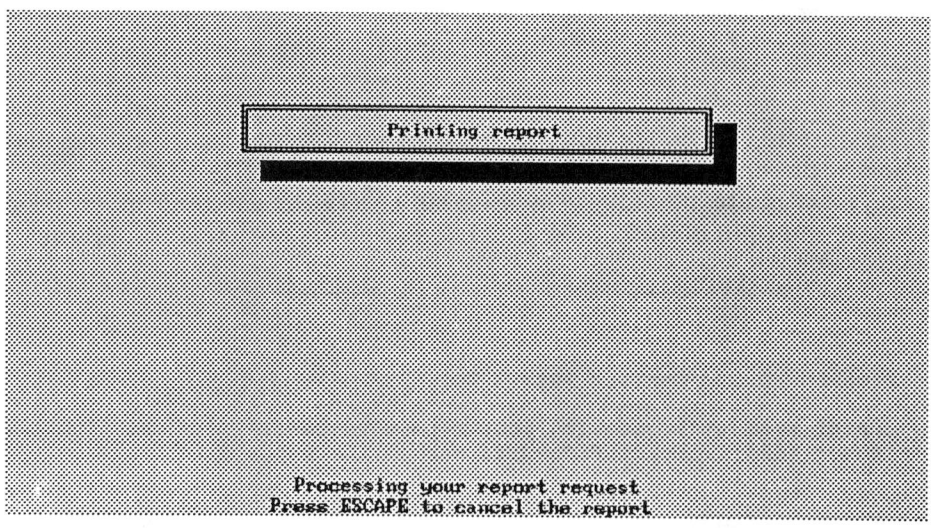

3-2 Screen display from CENTEST.PRG.

Listing 3-7

```
amt = 114
? lead(amt,7)
.
.
.
FUNCTION Lead
PARAMETERS val, length

RETURN RIGHT(STR(10^(length+1)+val,length+2),length)
```

54 Functions and procedures

By evaluating the function using the equal sign operator

Some functions, both FoxPro internal functions as well as your own, don't calculate a return value (although RETURN by itself implies RETURN .T.) In such cases, you don't have to DO the function or to assign it a value. You simply use the evaluate operator to tell FoxPro to do whatever that function does, then to come back (this is different from the EVALUATE( ) function, which simply calculates the value of an expression):

= *FunctionName*( )

Note that the paired parentheses are required, even in the absence of a formal parameter list, so that FoxPro knows this is a function. This operator can be used to turn printer output on or off, display information, or do anything else that any other function does.

The following function turns the insert mode off, so that data entry will work the way most users expect it to:

= INSMODE (.F.)

The program in LISTING 3-8 is an example of a UDF that can be called from the command line or from within a program, simply by forcing an evaluation. The syntax is:

= BELL( )

If the bell is on, this turns it off. If it's off, it turns the bell on. After toggling the bell, this program displays a brief message telling what it did. If the result left the bell on, it also gives a little beep. In a bit of self-reference that Douglas Hofstadter would be proud of, this program itself calls another routine using the same technique. It's called MaBell because ... well, try it and see.

Listing 3-8

```
* Program-ID....: BELL.PRG - Toggles bell on/off
*
BellSet = IIF ( SET('BELL') = [ON] , [OFF] , [ON] )
SET BELL &BellSet    && Toggle setting.
IF ( SET ([BELL]) = [ON] )
   = MaBell()         && Audible confirmation.
ENDIF
WAIT "BELL " + BellSet WINDOW TIMEOUT 1 && Display result.

RETURN .T.

PROCEDURE MaBell
PRIVATE I
FOR I = 1 TO 3
   SET BELL TO 1400,1
   ?? CHR(7)
   SET BELL TO 1600,1
   ?? CHR(7)
ENDFOR

RETURN
```

The function in LISTING 3-9 checks to see if the printer is on. If it isn't on, the function either redirects output to a user-supplied print file name or cancels the print request. Figure 3-3 shows what the program looks like.

To run a screen or menu program created using the generators, use, for example:

DO MYSCREEN.SPR

or

DO FUNCT2 IN MYMENU.MPR

Listing 3-9

```
* Program-ID....: PRINTFUN.PRG

@ 0, 0, 24, 79 BOX REPL("ý",9)
DO PrintOn

IF NOT PrintStatus()
   RETURN
ELSE
   SET CONSOLE OFF
   SET PRINT ON
   ? ' Print this wherever the report would be sent'
   SET PRINT OFF
   SET CONSOLE ON
   SET DEVICE TO SCREEN
ENDIF

PROCEDURE PrintOn

DEFINE WINDOW PRWINDOW FROM 17, 20 TO 22, 58 DOUBLE SHADOW
ACTIVATE WINDOW PRWINDOW

SET COLOR TO GR+/B,W+/R
CLEAR

@  0, 3 SAY 'Printer is off: Do you want to:'
@  1, 0 TO 1, WCOLS()
@  2,     1 PROMPT [ Try again ]
@  2, COL() PROMPT [ Output to file ]
@  2, COL() PROMPT [ Cancel ]

option = 1
MENU TO option

DO CASE
   CASE option = 1
      RELEASE WINDOW PRWINDOW
      RETRY
   CASE option = 2
      filename = SPACE ( 8 )
      DO WHILE filename = [        ]
         @ 3, 2 SAY [File name]           ;
         GET filename                     ;
         FUNCTION [!]                     ;
         VALID filename <> [        ]    ;
         ERROR [You must enter a file name]
```

56   Functions and procedures

```
        READ
     ENDDO
     RELEASE WINDOW PRWINDOW
     SET PRINTER TO FILE (filename)
     RETURN
  OTHERWISE
    RELEASE WINDOW PRWINDOW
    RETURN
ENDCASE
```

3-3 Screen display from PRINTFUN.PRG.

In VALID, WHEN, ACTIVATE/DEACTIVATE, and SHOW clauses

FoxPro's READ command supports five clauses that can invoke either an expression or a function. Either of them can do other things, but their real mission in life is to return either a logical .T. (true) or .F. (false). In addition, the @ SAY...GET command supports both a WHEN and a VALID clause, which work the same way.

It was always possible to do a certain number of things in VALID clauses, with some frustrating exceptions (notably, the ability to issue another READ). In FoxPro 2.0, not only are you permitted to do more things in the UDFs referenced by VALID and similar clauses, but also, it's actually the only way to accomplish many of the new tricks seen in FoxPro's GOODIES applications. I'll delve into these techniques in great detail in following chapters.

Special procedures

There are two procedures that all programs should have:

ON ERROR

and

>   ON ESCAPE

FoxPro 2.0 makes it particularly easy to design event handlers for situations that might arise at any time the user chooses (for example, stopping a report that's taking longer than the user expected or trapping an error like a loose printer cable). For these types of situations, you define event handlers and attach them to the previous two conditions.

Error trapping

If an error occurs during the debugging process, wouldn't it be nice to know where the program is, what line the error is on, and what the error was? If you provide a good error trapping routine, you can make debugging easier and can release software for beta testing without driving your users nuts.

The error routine in LISTING 3-10 should meet a wide variety of needs. A sample of the screen produced by this program when an error occurs is shown in FIG. 3-4.

Listing 3-10

```
* Program-ID...: ERRTRAP.PRG
*
PROCEDURE ERRTRAP
PARAMETERS ProgName,ProgLine,Errnum,ErrMsg,ProgText

ON ERROR    && avoid recursive call...
RELEASE WINDOWS

SET DEVICE TO SCREEN
SET PRINT OFF

SaveColor = SET ( 'COLOR' )
SaveMsg   = SET ( 'MESSAGE' )

DEFINE   WINDOW ERRWINDO FROM 8, 8 TO 19, 72 DOUBLE SHADOW COLOR GR+/B
ACTIVATE WINDOW ERRWINDO

SET COLOR TO GR+/B,W+/R
CLEAR

@  0, 27 SAY '** ERROR **'
@  1,  0 TO 1, WCOLS()
@  2,  4 say 'Error in program ' + ProgName
@  3,  4 say 'Program was on line ' ;
         + ALLTRIM (STR(ProgLine,4) )+' when the error occurred.'
@  4,  4 say 'Error number '+ALLTRIM(STR(ErrNum,4))+' - message follows:'

SET COLOR TO W+/R
@  5,  4 say ErrMsg
SET COLOR TO GR+/B,W+/R

IF LEN(TRIM(ProgText)) <> 0
   @  6,  4 say 'The program code that caused the error follows:'
```

```
   SET COLOR TO W+/R
   @ 7,  4 say LTRIM(ProgText)
   SET COLOR TO GR+/B,W+/R
ENDIF

@ 8,  0 TO  8, WCOLS()

@ 9,         3 prompt " Debug "  MESSAGE " Suspend program execution"
@ 9, col()+2 prompt " Retry "    MESSAGE " Try the same command again"
@ 9, col()+2 prompt " Ignore "   MESSAGE;
                      " Go on to the next line in the program"
@ 9, col()+2 prompt " Quit "     MESSAGE " Return to DOS"

whatnow = 1
MENU TO whatnow

RELEASE WINDOW ERRWINDO

SET COLOR TO &SaveColor
SET MESSAGE TO &SaveMsg
ON ERROR DO ErrTrap WITH PROGRAM(),LINENO(),ERROR(),MESSAGE(),MESSAGE(1)

DO CASE
  CASE whatnow = 1
    SUSPEND
  CASE whatnow = 2
    RETRY
  CASE whatnow = 3
    && no action....defaults to 'next statement'
  CASE whatnow = 4
    QUIT

ENDCASE

RETURN
```

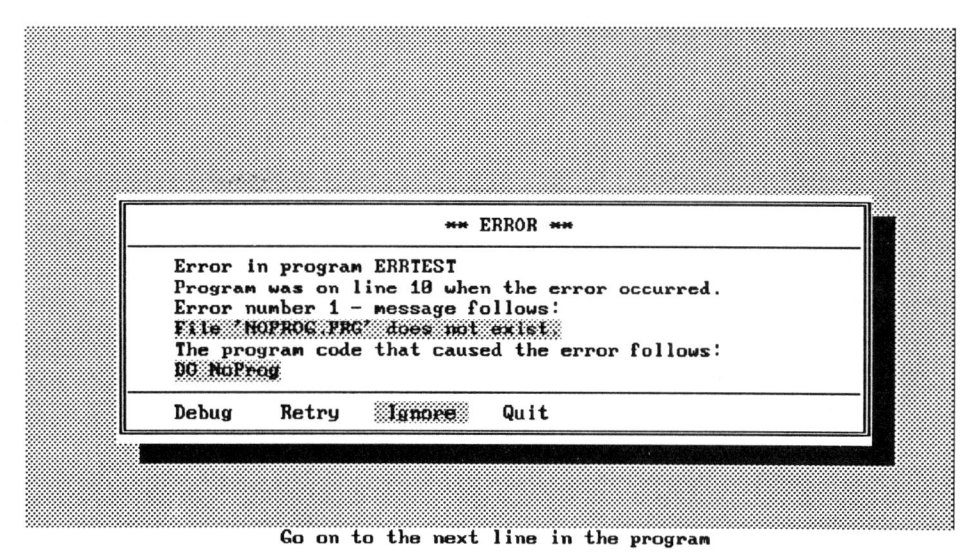

3-4 Screen display from ERRTRAP.PRG.

Special procedures 59

Escape routines

Some types of processing, notably reports, can be candidates for cancellation. Just about all of my clients ask for the ability to pause a report at mid-processing with the option to cancel it. Using the ON ESCAPE command, it's not hard. The routine in LISTING 3-11 is general enough to be used in a wide variety of situations. Figure 3-5 shows a dialog produced by pressing Esc.

Listing 3-11

```
* Program-ID...: EscTest.PRG
* Purpose......: Demonstrates ESCAPE trapping.

ON ESCAPE   DO ESCTRAP
SET ESCAPE ON

USE INVOICES
DEFINE WINDOW COUNTWIN FROM 5, 20 TO 9, 60 DOUBLE SHADOW
ACTIVATE WINDOW COUNTWIN
CLEAR
= center ( 0 , 'Counting nondeleted invoices' )

SET TALK    ON
SET ODOM    TO  1

COUNT TO TOTRECS FOR ID_CODE <> [~]
SET TALK OFF

CLEAR

IF EOF()
   = center ( 1, ALLTRIM(STR(TOTRECS,5)) + [ invoices on file.] )
ELSE
   = center ( 1, [Request canceled] )
ENDIF

USE
READ

RELEASE WINDOW COUNTWIN

RETURN


PROCEDURE EscTrap

ON ESCAPE       && avoid recursive call to ESCAPE TRAPPING ROUTINE
SET ESCAPE OFF

DEFINE   WINDOW ESCWINDO IN SCREEN FROM 17, 25 TO 21, 55 DOUBLE SHADOW
ACTIVATE WINDOW ESCWINDO

SET CONSOLE OFF
STORE SET('TALK') TO SaveTalk
SET TALK OFF
SET CONSOLE ON
STORE SET('COLOR') TO SaveColor
SET COLOR TO W+/B,W+/R
```

```
CLEAR

= center ( 0, 'Processing Interrupted' )
@ 1, 0 TO  1, WCOLS()
@ 2,         2 PROMPT " Cancel "  MESSAGE " Return to previous program"
@ 2, col()+1 PROMPT " Resume "  MESSAGE " Continue processing"
@ 2, col()+1 PROMPT " Quit "    MESSAGE " Exit to DOS"

option = 2
SET CONFIRM OFF
MENU TO option
SET CONFIRM ON

RELEASE WINDOW ESCWINDO

option = IIF ( option = 0 ,[Q] , SUBSTR ( [CRQ] , option , 1 ) )

DO CASE

   CASE option = [C]

      CLOSE DATABASES        && If required...
      RETURN TO MASTER       && See discussion about program flow, above.

   CASE option = [R]

      ON ESCAPE   DO EscTrap  && Turn escape processing back on.
      SET ESCAPE ON
      SET COLOR TO &SaveColor
      SET TALK     &SaveTalk
      RETRY                   && goes back to line where escape was pressed.

   CASE option = [Q]
      QUIT
ENDCASE

RETURN
```

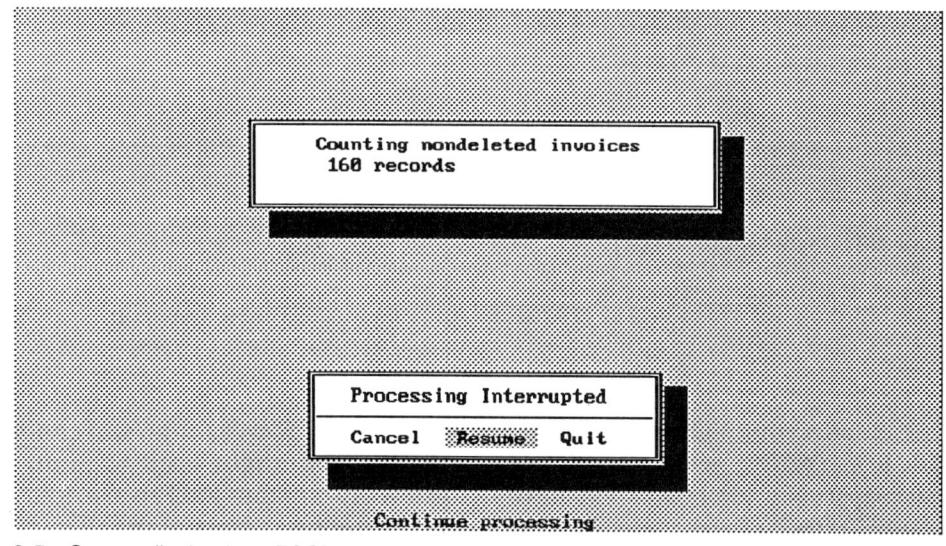

3-5 Screen display from ESCTRAP.PRG.

Notes on escape trapping

What you can do upon selecting Cancel from the Escape dialog box is determined by what you were doing when Esc was pressed. For example, if you were in the middle of reindexing a file, the reindexing operation already has begun to rewrite the .IDX or .CDX file. Stopping the operation at that point will leave an unusable index. That might or might not be permissible in your situation.

An additional concern that escape trapping gives rise to is the current setting of SET variables. For example, if you're counting records, you might choose to SET TALK ON and SET ODOMETER TO 50 to give your users some reassurance that the computer isn't broken. If you trap Esc, the current setting of SET TALK ON will make your escape trap routine look pretty messy unless you SET CONSOLE OFF, then SET TALK OFF and clear the screen, then SET TALK ON again if the user elects to resume.

An additional issue involves returning with the correct file selected. For example, look at the code in LISTING 3-12. If you press Esc while INVOICES is selected, your routine will return you to the SCAN loop with the wrong file selected. You'll get the error message:

```
Variable not found.
ENDSCAN
```

Because ENDSCAN isn't a variable, this is a very disconcerting message. The missing variable is CUSTCODE of CUSTOMER.DBF, which it can't find because INVOICES is the selected database. This is a problem peculiar to escape trapping and one that has to be dealt with. I sometimes SET ESCAPE OFF just before selecting the INVOICES file, then SET ESCAPE ON when I reselect CUSTOMER. The Esc key doesn't do anything for a fraction of a second, but your program doesn't blow up. Thank heaven for small favors. By the way, to turn off Esc completely, use ON KEY LABEL ESCAPE *.

Listing 3-12

```
ON ESCAPE DO EscTrap
SELECT CUSTOMERS
SEEK [A]                                && count invoices for customers AA..AZ
SCAN WHILE CUSTCODE = [A]
   SELECT INVOICES
   SEEK CUSTOMER.CUSTCODE
   COUNT TO NumInvoic WHILE INVOICES.CUSTID = CUSTOMER.CUSTCODE
   SELECT CUSTOMER
ENDSCAN
```

Finally, you might not want to RETURN TO MASTER every time you cancel. If you're five levels deep in your program, you might want to jump back up to, say, level two, then activate the level two menu. FoxPro also lets you RETURN TO *procedurename*. That opens the door to a host of problems, like the one mentioned in the preceding paragraph, but it might give you what you need.

Subsequent chapters deal in more detail with event-driven programming. I want to stress that event-driven procedures require a great deal more care than traditional event loops, because you permit jumping around from one window to another and from one select area to another. If you don't feel comfortable with this new world, take it slowly. The older techniques still work.

Procedure libraries

Once you've written and debugged your application, if you're not using the project manager, you'll want to group most of your functions and procedures into a procedure library. Unless told where to look, FoxPro 2.0 looks for your functions and procedures in three places:

- If you DO a program that calls another program, the active program is searched for additional functions and procedures included within the same file.
- If FoxPro doesn't find the program within the active file and if you've included the statement SET PROCEDURE TO *filename*, FoxPro searches *filename* for the function.
- If the function is not found in either of those locations, the default directory is searched, then the FOX PATH (set either using SET PATH TO *path* or in CONFIG.FP using PATH = *directories*.

DOS gets very slow if it has to search a directory containing more than 128 filenames (including erased entries). Once you're finished developing and debugging, do what you can to package all programs except your main program in procedure files or in a project.

Note that if you're inside a program that's within the file currently opened as the procedure file, you can't CLOSE PROCEDURE or SET PROCEDURE TO *another procedure filename*. If you do, FoxPro can't get back to wherever it came from.

You also can have more than one procedure file, even though you only use one SET PROCEDURE TO *filename* statement. If you package your routines into a small number of files, each of which looks like a procedure file, you can tell FoxPro to:

DO *xyz* IN MYLIB2

FoxPro will search MYLIB2.FXP for procedure *xyz* and run it. So, you can have, in effect, one principal procedure library that stays open all of the time and others whose purpose is simply to keep the number of directory entries under control.

Note that, if you compile all of your source code into .FXP files, copy the .PRG files to a source directory, and erase them from the production directory, you still might have very slow response from DOS. The reason is that all of those deleted filenames still are out there with a high-values byte in the first position of the filename. You need to use Norton's Speed-Disk, PCTOOLS, or VOPT from Golden Bow to squeeze out those deleted filenames. If you have over 128 or so files in your directory at any time, you'll notice immediate improvement after using one of these utilities. If you use the project manager, you won't have any .FXPs cluttering up your directory.

Summary

Functions in FoxPro are available in a variety of formats and can be designed with great flexibility. If the over 200 built-in functions aren't enough for your needs, you can write your own. Some user-defined functions belong in every FoxPro programmer's library. Several of these were presented in this chapter, by way of demonstrations of technique.

4
Control structures and techniques

FoxPro has a full complement of looping and control structures for good program design. Most of these structures work about the same way they do in other languages, but a brief review won't hurt. The newest command, READ with its various clauses, is a bit more subtle but very powerful.

DO WHILE...ENDDO

The most common looping structure used in FoxPro is the DO loop. The syntax is

DO WHILE *condition*
.
.
.
ENDDO

where *condition* evaluates to a logical .T. or .F. If *condition* is false, the program skips directly to the statement following ENDDO. The condition that terminates the loop can be a complex condition linked by OR and AND statements. Within the loop, you can do anything that you want.

A special case is the nonterminating condition DO WHILE .T., which usually is used in menus to control program flow, as shown in LISTING 4-1. This menu loop is the one most commonly used in FoxPro. The menu bar, which will be discussed later, also is useful, especially in an integrated product with an invariant design. However, during the development process, you might want to use the type of menu loop seen in LISTING 4-1. It's easy to change and easy to understand. You then can convert to the menu bar style once the design is finalized. Notice that EXIT is used to get out of the loop.

Listing 4-1

```
* Program-ID.....: MENULOOP.PRG
CLEAR
SET MESSAGE TO 24

@  0,  0, 24, 79 BOX REPL(CHR(178),9)
@ 22,  0 TO 22, 79

@ 10, 20, 14, 60 BOX [èë£¤¥èà¤ ]
@ 11, 32 SAY [ Your Data Base ]
DO WHILE .T.

   @ 23,       0 CLEAR

   @ 23,       0 PROMPT " Add "     MESSAGE " Add a record"
   @ 23, COL() PROMPT " Edit "    MESSAGE " Edit a record"
   @ 23, COL() PROMPT " Print "   MESSAGE " Print a record"
   @ 23, COL() PROMPT " Delete "  MESSAGE " Delete a record"
   @ 23, COL() PROMPT " Find "    MESSAGE " Search for a record"
   @ 23, COL() PROMPT " Quit "    MESSAGE " Search for a record"
   MENU TO choice
   choice = IIF ( choice = 0 , [Q] , SUBSTR ( [AEPDFQ] , choice , 1 ) )
   ... Do whatever you need here...

ENDDO
```

DO WHILE .T. also can be used to set up a loop that checks for every keystroke. The loop in LISTING 4-2 moves a pointer down the center of the screen, cycling back up to the top of the screen when it passes line 20. This code will be used later on in this book to develop tools of extreme precision. For example, I have a timed wait menu routine that acts like the POPUP command or HELP in the sense that it waits for you to type in a key value and assumes that you've entered all of the keystrokes that you want to if more than half a second passes without another keystroke.

Listing 4-2

```
* Program-ID....: InkeyTst.PRG
*
Line = 3
SET CURSOR OFF
@ Line, 45 SAY "--->"
DO WHILE .T.
   KeyPressed = INKEY(0)
   @ Line, 45 SAY "    "
   DO CASE
      CASE KeyPressed = 27      && escape
         @ 24, 0 SAY "ESCAPE key pressed"
         EXIT
      CASE KeyPressed = 13      && ENTER
         @ 24, 0 SAY "ENTER key pressed"
         Line = Line + 1
         IF Line > 20
            Line =  3
```

Listing 4-2 Continued

```
        ENDIF
        @ Line, 45 SAY "--->"
    ENDCASE
ENDDO
```

Using DO WHILE to read through a file

One of the common uses of a DO WHILE loop is to read through a file, performing processing on some or all of the records encountered. The DO WHILE loop doesn't presume that a file is being read, but if a SKIP statement is located within the loop, the buffer will be loaded with the next available record. As the next record is read, the record previously in the buffer is automatically written to disk.

The code in LISTING 4-3 frequently precedes the use of a MENU command. The loop will terminate if either:

- The end of file is reached
- The number of items read exceeds 128

Listing 4-3

```
* Program-ID...: DoLoop1.PRG
*
DIMENSION data ( 128 )
USE CLIENTS
I = 1
DO WHILE .NOT. EOF() .AND. I < 128
  data ( I ) = LEFT ( NAME , 45 )
  I = I + 1
  SKIP
ENDDO
NumItems = I - 1
WindowSize = IIF ( NumItems <= 17, NumItems, 17 )
@ 1, 30 MENU data, NumItems, WindowSize TITLE " Names "
READ MENU TO whichone
Chosen = IIF ( whichone = 0 , SPACE( 45 ) , name ( whichone )
RETURN
```

If the file is empty, no records will be loaded. If over 128 items are in the file, only the first 128 will be loaded.

What if you want to load only those names that begin with A. If the records are sorted, you can use the code in LISTING 4-4. However, what if the data isn't sorted? You still can do it, but you have to add a new construct: the IF...ENDIF pair (LISTING 4-5).

Listing 4-4

```
* Program-ID.....: DoLoop2.PRG
*
DIMENSION data ( 128 )
USE CLIENTS INDEX CLIENTS
```

Listing 4-4 Continued

```
SEEK [A]
I = 1
DO WHILE .NOT. EOF() .AND. I < 128 .AND. NAME = [A]
  data ( I ) = LEFT ( NAME , 45 )
  I = I + 1
  SKIP
ENDDO
NumItems = I - 1
WindowSize = IIF ( NumItems <= 17, NumItems, 17 )
@ 1, 30 MENU data, NumItems, WindowSize TITLE " 'A' list"
READ MENU TO whichone
Chosen = IIF ( whichone = 0 , SPACE( 45 ) , name ( whichone )
RETURN
```

Listing 4-5

```
* Program-ID...: DoLoop3.PRG
*
DIMENSION data ( 128 )
USE CLIENTS
I = 1
DO WHILE .NOT. EOF() .AND. I < 128
  IF NAME = [A]
    data ( I ) = LEFT ( NAME , 45 )
    I = I + 1
  ENDIF
  SKIP
ENDDO
NumItems = I - 1
WindowSize = IIF ( NumItems <= 17, NumItems, 17 )
@ 1, 30 MENU data, NumItems, WindowSize TITLE " 'A' list"
READ MENU TO whichone
```

SCAN...ENDSCAN

If you're reading a file, the SCAN...ENDSCAN pair might save you a few lines of code and will add additional depth to the loop. The scenario described earlier can be dealt with on the first line in LISTING 4-6.

Listing 4-6

```
* Program-ID....: ScanTst1.PRG
*
DIMENSION data ( 128 )
USE CLIENTS
I = 1
SCAN;
  WHILE I < 128 ;
  FOR NAME = 'A'
  data ( I ) = LEFT ( NAME , 45 )
  I = I + 1
ENDSCAN
NumItems = I - 1
WindowSize = IIF ( NumItems <= 17, NumItems, 17 )
@ 1, 30 MENU data, NumItems, WindowSize TITLE " 'A' list"
READ MENU TO whichone
```

WHILE .NOT. EOF( ) is no longer necessary, because SCAN...END-SCAN stops at EOF( ). SKIP is gone, because SCAN skips automatically. Also, the internal IF...ENDIF is not needed, because SCAN will look only at the records that meet the FOR NAME = 'A' part of the SCAN statement.

If your file is indexed, you can change one word and make this code run a lot faster (LISTING 4-7). This is quite an improvement, actually. It permits you to look only at those records that match the selection conditions and to do so in a single statement. The cleaner and simpler code means less debugging.

Listing 4-7

```
* Program-ID....: ScanTst2.PRG
*
DIMENSION data ( 128 )
USE CLIENTS INDEX CLIENTS
I = 1
SEEK [A]
SCAN;
   WHILE I    < 128 AND NAME = 'A'
   data ( I ) = LEFT ( NAME , 45 )
   I = I + 1
ENDSCAN
NumItems = I - 1
WindowSize = IIF ( NumItems <= 17, NumItems, 17 )
@ 1, 30 MENU data, NumItems, WindowSize TITLE " 'A' list"
READ MENU TO whichone
```

FOR...ENDFOR

The next type of looping structure is the FOR...ENDFOR (or FOR...NEXT) pair. A sample of the complete syntax is shown in LISTING 4-8.

This construct also can be used to read a file, but that's not what it was designed to do. If you do use it, you have to be responsible for end-of-file conditions; there is no built-in mechanism to check for records that match selection conditions; and you have to enter the SKIP command and be sure you're not trying to skip past end-of-file. That doesn't sound too hard; however, if you've got complex selection conditions within the loop, it takes only one mistake to get a bug that takes an hour to find.

Listing 4-8

```
* Program-ID...: PRODUCT.PRG
*
Max = 20
PRODUCT = 1
FOR I = 1 TO Max
  PRODUCT = PRODUCT * I
  IF PRODUCT > 100000
    EXIT
  ENDIF
ENDFOR

? 'The sum of the first ' +STR ( I , 3 ) +' is ' +STR ( PRODUCT , 7 )
```

You're more likely to use the FOR...ENDFOR loop to process the contents of arrays that were previously loaded. Also, if you load data into doubly-subscripted arrays, you can use a pair of FOR...ENDFOR loops to perform matrix multiplication (LISTING 4-9), which produces the display shown in TABLE 4-1.

Listing 4-9

```
* Program-ID....: MatMult.prg
* Purpose.......: Demonstrates matrix multiplication using FOR loops
CLEAR

DIMENSION One    ( 2 , 2 )
DIMENSION Two    ( 2 , 3 )
DIMENSION Three  ( 2 , 3 )

One ( 1, 1 ) =  1
One ( 1, 2 ) =  2
One ( 2, 1 ) =  3
One ( 2, 2 ) =  4

Two ( 1, 1 ) =  1
Two ( 1, 2 ) =  2
Two ( 1, 3 ) =  3
Two ( 2, 1 ) =  4
Two ( 2, 2 ) =  5
Two ( 2, 3 ) =  6

DO MatDisp with 'One',2,2
DO MatDisp with 'Two',2,3

FOR I = 1 TO 2
  FOR J = 1 TO 3
    Three ( I , J ) = 0
    FOR K = 1 TO 2
      Three (I,J) = Three (I,J) + One (I,K) * Two (K,J)
    ENDFOR K
  ENDFOR J
ENDFOR I

? 'Product:'
DO MatDisp WITH 'Three', 2, 3

RETURN

PROCEDURE  MatDisp
PARAMETERS Name, rows, cols

? []
? [Matrix ] + Name

FOR    I = 1 TO rows
  ? []
  FOR J = 1 TO cols
    ?? STR ( &Name ( I , J ) , 4 )
```

70   Control structures and techniques

Listing 4-9 Continued
```
  ENDFOR
ENDFOR
RETURN
```

Table 4-1 Output of the matrix manipulation program.

	Matrix One		
	1	2	
	3	4	
	Matrix Two		
	1	2	3
	4	5	6
Product:	Matrix Three		
	9	12	15
	19	26	33

DO CASE...ENDCASE

The DO CASE...ENDCASE pair isn't a looping structure. Rather, it's a replacement for the IF...ENDIF. Back in the bad old days, programmers used to see code like that shown in LISTING 4-10. This sort of code is very hard to read. Also, the way IFs are evaluated internally, the program will run slowly.

The alternative is the DO CASE structure. Listing 4-11 demonstrates its capabilities. This structure is used to produce the often-seen screen in FIG 4-1.

Listing 4-10
```
* Program-ID....: IfNest.PRG
*
IF MAJOR = 1
  IF MINOR = 1
    DO ABC
  ENDIF
  IF MINOR = 2
    DO XYZ
  ENDIF
ENDIF
IF MAJOR = 2
  IF MINOR = 1
    DO WWW
  ENDIF
  IF MINOR = 2
    DO RRR
  ENDIF
ENDIF
```

Listing 4-11

```
* Program-ID...: CaseTest.PRG
*
CLEAR
SET MESSAGE TO 24

@  0,  0, 24, 79 BOX REPL(CHR(178),9)
@ 22,  0 TO 22, 79

@ 10, 20, 14, 60 BOX [èë£¤¥ëà¤ ]
@ 11, 32 SAY [ Your Data Base ]

DO WHILE .T.

   @ 23,      0 CLEAR

   @ 23,      0 PROMPT " Add "    MESSAGE " Add a record"
   @ 23, COL() PROMPT " Edit "   MESSAGE " Edit a record"
   @ 23, COL() PROMPT " Print "  MESSAGE " Print a record"
   @ 23, COL() PROMPT " Delete " MESSAGE " Delete a record"
   @ 23, COL() PROMPT " Find "   MESSAGE " Search for a record"
   @ 23, COL() PROMPT " Quit "   MESSAGE " Search for a record"

   SET CONFIRM OFF
   MENU TO choice

   choice = IIF ( choice = 0 , [Q] , SUBSTR ( [AEPDFQ] , choice , 1 ) )
   DO CASE
     CASE choice = [A]
       DO AddRec
       LOOP
     CASE choice = [E]
       DO EditRec
       LOOP
     CASE choice = [P]
       DO PrintRec
       LOOP
     CASE choice = [D]
       DO DelRec
       LOOP
     CASE choice = [F]
       DO FindRec
       LOOP
     CASE choice = [Q]
       EXIT
   ENDCASE
ENDDO

QUIT
```

This is what is now referred to as an *event loop*. Fox Software doesn't seem to be too fond of these guys, but you can get a lot of mileage out of them before you're forced to respond to the event-driven paradigm. More on that later.

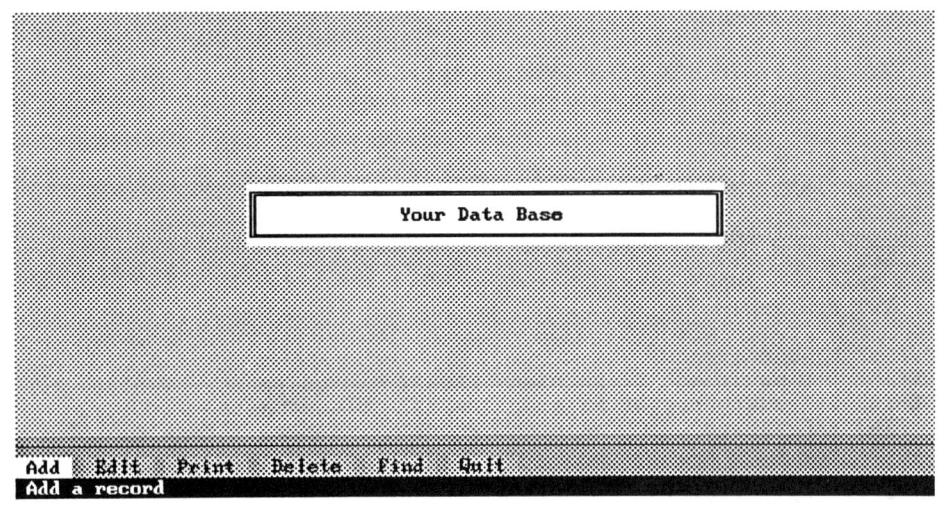

4-1 Screen display from CASETEST.PRG.

Menus

In the example shown previously, the MENU TO *varname* stops the program, waits for the user to select one of a limited range of choices, then takes the appropriate action based on the choice. This is the Lotus-like menu that has become a standard in my library of screen designs. It's easy to do, my users understand it and know how to make it work. Also, I can add or change the selections with a minimum amount of violence to the budget.

There are some drawbacks to this approach. The main one is that the user has to do some fancy footwork to see what else is on the menu. Perhaps a little graphic illustration will help.

Suppose you have a system consisting of two master files, a dozen table files, and a reports menu. If you use the flat-file with Lotus-style menu approach, you can look at only one menu and screen combination at a time. Users unfamiliar with the system have to roam around the screens to find out what else there is to see. If you pick Employees, you go down to the employees screen and menu. If you pick Equipment, the same thing happens.

FoxPro provides an alternative in the form of the *menu bar*. Using this system, you can easily view all of the menu choices without changing the data on the screen. The program in LISTING 4-12, MenuBar, is an example of a way to separate your menus and data screens.

Listing 4-12

```
* Program-ID....: MenuBar.prg

CLEAR
```

Listing 4-12 Continued

```
@  3,  0, 21, 79 BOX REPLICATE ( CHR(177) , 9 )
@ 22,  0 TO   22, 79
@  0,  0 TO    2, 79

SELECT 1
USE EQUIPMNT INDEX EQUIPMNT
SELECT 2
USE CUSTS    INDEX CUSTS
SELECT 3
USE TABLES   INDEX TABLES
SELECT EQUIPMNT

DEFINE MENU mainmenu
DEFINE PAD equipment OF mainmenu PROMPT '\<Equipment' AT 01,01
DEFINE PAD customers OF mainmenu PROMPT '\<Customers' AT 01,12
DEFINE PAD tables    OF mainmenu PROMPT '\<Tables'    AT 01,23
DEFINE PAD reports   OF mainmenu PROMPT '\<Reports'   AT 01,31

* -- If these next 4 lines are used instead of the ON PAD statements,
* -- the sliding bar popups don't pull down unless selected. For
* -- most purposes. use the ON PAD command.

* ON SELECTION PAD equipment OF mainmenu ACTIVATE POPUP EquiPop
* ON SELECTION PAD customers OF mainmenu ACTIVATE POPUP CustPop
* ON SELECTION PAD tables    OF mainmenu ACTIVATE POPUP TabPop
* ON SELECTION PAD reports   OF mainmenu ACTIVATE POPUP ReptPop

ON PAD equipment OF mainmenu ACTIVATE POPUP EquiPop
ON PAD customers OF mainmenu ACTIVATE POPUP CustPop
ON PAD tables    OF mainmenu ACTIVATE POPUP TabPop
ON PAD reports   OF mainmenu ACTIVATE POPUP ReptPop

DEFINE POPUP EquiPop FROM 03,01
DEFINE BAR  1 OF EquiPop PROMPT '\<Add '
DEFINE BAR  2 OF EquiPop PROMPT '\<Edit'
DEFINE BAR  3 OF EquiPop PROMPT '\<Delete'
DEFINE BAR  4 OF EquiPop PROMPT '\<Print'
DEFINE BAR  5 OF EquiPop PROMPT '\<Find'
ON SELECTION POPUP equipop DO emenu WITH POPUP(), PROMPT()

DEFINE POPUP CustPop FROM 03,12
DEFINE BAR  1 OF CustPop PROMPT '\<Add'
DEFINE BAR  2 OF CustPop PROMPT '\<Edit'
DEFINE BAR  3 OF CustPop PROMPT '\<Delete'
DEFINE BAR  4 OF CustPop PROMPT '\<Print'
DEFINE BAR  5 OF CustPop PROMPT '\<Find'
ON SELECTION POPUP CustPop DO cmenu WITH POPUP(), PROMPT()

DEFINE POPUP TabPop FROM 03,23
DEFINE BAR  1 OF TabPop PROMPT '\<States'
DEFINE BAR  2 OF TabPop PROMPT '\<Equipment Types'
DEFINE BAR  3 OF TabPop PROMPT '\<Depreciation Codes'
DEFINE BAR  4 OF TabPop PROMPT '\<Route Codes'
DEFINE BAR  5 OF TabPop PROMPT '\<Job Codes'
DEFINE BAR  6 OF TabPop PROMPT '\<Course Codes'
DEFINE BAR  7 OF TabPop PROMPT 's\<tatus Codes'
DEFINE BAR  8 OF TabPop PROMPT 'sa\<lary Grades'
ON SELECTION POPUP TabPop DO tmenu WITH POPUP(), PROMPT()
```

```
DEFINE POPUP ReptPop FROM 03,31
DEFINE BAR  1 OF ReptPop PROMPT '\<Assignments'
DEFINE BAR  2 OF ReptPop PROMPT '\<Depreciation'
DEFINE BAR  3 OF ReptPop PROMPT '\<Maintenance'
DEFINE BAR  4 OF ReptPop PROMPT '\<Vacation'
DEFINE BAR  5 OF ReptPop PROMPT '\<Training'
ON SELECTION POPUP ReptPop DO rmenu WITH POPUP(), PROMPT()
ACTIVATE MENU mainmenu

RETURN   && QUIT in production

PROCEDURE emenu
PARAMETER mpopup, mprompt
HIDE POPUP ALL

SELECT EQUIPMNT
DO DispEScr
DO DispEDat

DO CASE
   CASE mpopup = 'ADD'
      DO AddEqp
   CASE mpopup = 'EDIT'
      DO EditEqp
   CASE mpopup = 'DELETE'
      DO DelEqp
   CASE mpopup = 'PRINT'
      DO PrntEqp
   CASE mpopup = 'FIND'
      DO FindEqp
ENDCASE
WAIT WINDOW

DEACTIVATE POPUP
RETURN

PROCEDURE cmenu
PARAMETER mpopup, mprompt
HIDE POPUP ALL

SELECT CUSTS
DO DispCScr
DO DispCDat

DO CASE
   CASE mpopup = 'ADD'
      DO AddEmpl
   CASE mpopup = 'EDIT'
      DO EditEmpl
   CASE mpopup = 'DELETE'
      DO DelEmpl
   CASE mpopup = 'PRINT'
      DO PrntEmpl
   CASE mpopup = 'FIND'
      DO FindEmpl
ENDCASE
WAIT WINDOW

DEACTIVATE POPUP
RETURN
```

Listing 4-12 Continued

```
PROCEDURE tmenu
PARAMETER mpopup, mprompt
HIDE POPUP ALL

DO CASE
  CASE mpopup = 'STATES'
  CASE mpopup = 'EQUIPMENT TYPES'
  CASE mpopup = 'DEPRECIATION CODES'
  CASE mpopup = 'ROUTE CODES'
  CASE mpopup = 'JOB CODES'
  CASE mpopup = 'COURSE CODES'
  CASE mpopup = 'STATUS CODES'
  CASE mpopup = 'SALARY GRADES'
ENDCASE
Wait WINDOW

DEACTIVATE POPUP
RETURN

PROCEDURE rmenu
PARAMETER mpopup, mprompt
HIDE POPUP ALL

DO CASE
  CASE mpopup = 'ASSIGNMENTS'     && These stubs
  CASE mpopup = 'DEPRECIATION'    && show where to
  CASE mpopup = 'MAINTENANCE'     && test for menu
  CASE mpopup = 'VACATION'        && selections; follow
  CASE mpopup = 'TRAINING'        && each with proper code.
ENDCASE
WAIT WINDOW

DEACTIVATE POPUP
RETURN

PROC DispCScr

@ 3, 0 CLEAR
@ 3, 0 TO 22, 79 DOUBLE
@ 5, 1 SAY PADC([ Customers ] , 78 )

*   Structure for database: CUSTS.DBF
*   Field   Field Name   Type         Width
*      1    NAME         Character      30
*      2    ADD1         Character      30
*      3    CITY         Character      20
*      4    STATE        Character       2
*      5    ZIP          Character      10
*   ** Total **                         93

@  8, 10 SAY [    Name: ]
@  9, 10 SAY [ Address: ]
@ 10, 10 SAY [    City: ]

PROC DispCDat

@  8, 25 SAY CUSTS->Name
@  9, 25 SAY CUSTS->Add1
@ 10, 25 SAY CUSTS->City
@ 10, 46 SAY CUSTS->State
@ 10, 49 SAY CUSTS->Zip
```

```
RETURN

PROC DispEScr

@ 3, 0 CLEAR
@ 3, 0 TO 22, 79 DOUBLE
@ 5, 1 SAY PADC([ Equipment ] , 78 )
*     Structure for database: EQUIPMNT.DBF
*     Field  Field Name  Type       Width    Dec    Index
*       1    EQUIPMENT   Character    10
*     ** Total **                     11

@ 10, 10 SAY [ Equipment Code: ]

RETURN

PROC DispEDat

@ 10, 35 SAY EQUIPMNT->Equipment

RETURN

PROC DispTScr
@ 15, 35 SAY ' Tables    '
* dummied out...

PROC DispTDat
* dummied out...
```

In FIG. 4-2, the user selects a menu option. In FIG. 4-3, the selected option has taken effect.

As can be seen, the screen changes only after a menu selection has been made. Just looking at the menus doesn't change the active file. This sort of menu reinforces the idea that you need to open all of your data files and keep them open. The resulting system runs faster and is less likely to get you into trouble trying to open files that are open already.

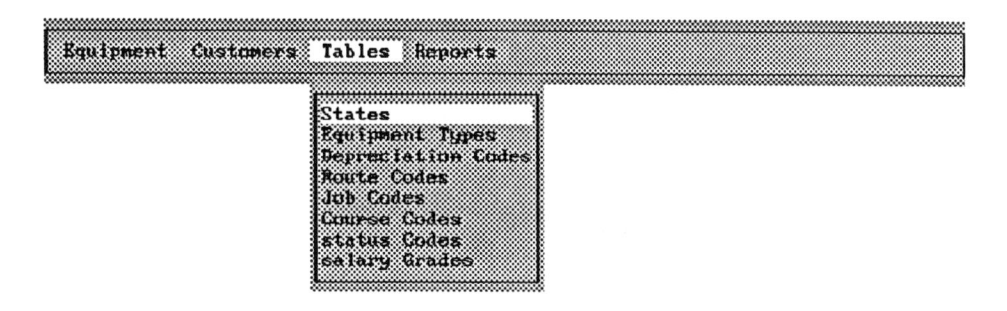

4-2 Screen display from MENUBAR.PRG.

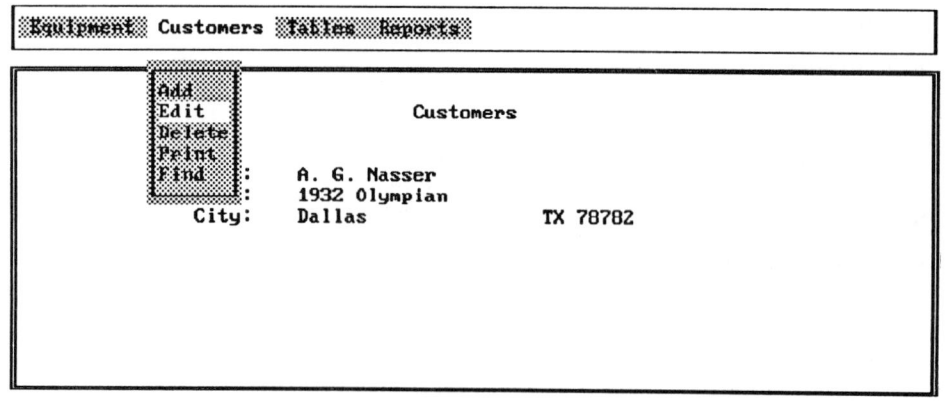

4-3 Second screen display from MENUBAR.PRG.

A hybrid case

I've included an example of a hybrid—an error trapping routine in the form of a pulldown menu (see LISTING 4-13). You might find some interesting use for the technique, which I got from Galen Hall of HALLoGRAM Software in Aurora, Colorado. Figure 4-4 shows the type of error message it produces.

Listing 4-13

```
* Program-ID....: ErrMenu.PRG
* Purpose.......: Demonstrates an error routine using the MENU command.
* Note..........: the technique of preceding nonselectable items with "\".
* How used......: ON ERROR DO ErrMenu WITH ERROR(),PROGRAM()

PARAMETERS Error, Program

SET TALK OFF
SAVE SCREEN
?? CHR ( 7 )

IF LTRIM ( LEFT ( MESSAGE(1) , 1 )) = '&'; .AND. LEN(TRIM ( MESSAGE(1))) > 1
   ErrMsg = SUBS(MESSAGE(1) , 2 )
   ErrMsg = &ErrMsg
ELSE
   ErrMsg = MESSAGE(1)
ENDIF

ERRLEN = LEN ( TRIM ( ErrMsg ) )

RELEASE Err

DO CASE
   CASE ErrLen <= 34
      DIMENSION Err ( 9 )
      Cnt = 9
   CASE ErrLen <= 77
      DIMENSION Err ( 10 )
      Cnt = 10
      Err ( 10 ) = '\' + SUBSTR ( ErrMsg , 35 )
```

```
   OTHERWISE
      DIMENSION Err ( 11 )
      Cnt = 11
      Err(10) = '\' + SUBSTR ( ErrMsg , 35 , 48 )
      Err(11) = '\' + SUBSTR ( ErrMsg , 83 , 48 )
ENDCASE

Err(1) = 'Ignore Error'
Err(2) = 'Retry'
Err(3) = 'Cancel'
Err(4) = 'Display Memory'
Err(5) = '\-'
Err(6) = '\Error Number: ' + LTRIM ( STR ( ERROR, 4 ) )
Err(7) = '\Description-: ' + LEFT ( MESSAGE() , 34 )
Err(8) = '\Called from-: ' + Program
Err(9) = '\code/command: ' + LEFT ( ErrMsg , 34 )
Ch = 0

@ 9,25 MENU Err,Cnt,Cnt TITLE 'Error Message Status'
READ MENU TO Ch

* -- reinstate error trapping
ON ERROR DO ERROR WITH ERROR(),PROGRAM()
RESTORE SCREEN

DO CASE
   CASE Ch = 2
      RETRY
   CASE Ch = 3
      CLEAR
      CANCEL
   CASE Ch = 4
      DISPLAY MEMORY
      WAIT
      CLEAR
   OTHERWISE
      RETURN
ENDCASE
```

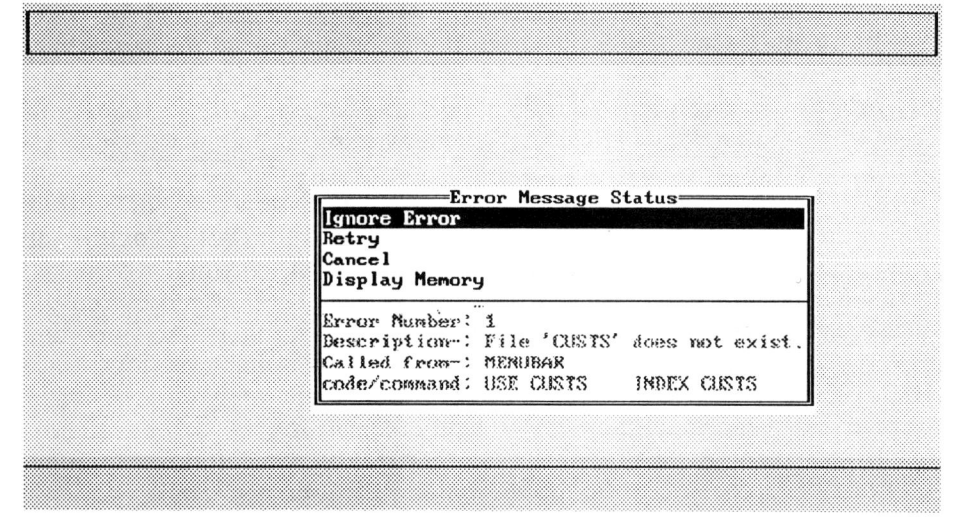

4-4 Screen from the ERRMENU error trapping routine.

A hybrid case

Event handlers

Controlling the flow of programs through an event loop is the traditional way of writing software in X-Base languages. FoxPro 2.0 has added a new set of commands that open up a whole new world of design possibilities. This new set is referred to generally as *event-driven programming*.

The following commands cause your program to stop what it's doing (with a few exceptions) and respond immediately to the interrupt request:

ON ERROR *command*
ON ESCAPE *command*
ON KEY *command*
ON KEY = *specific-INKEY( )-value command*
ON KEY LABEL *key-name-or-key-combination command*
ON PAD *padname command*
ON SELECTION PAD *padname command*
ON SELECTION POPUP *popupname command*

If you start your program with a series of these event handler declarations and inform your users of what the various keys do, they can press the appropriate key at any time and go directly to the desired function.

This technique implies a huge responsibility to ensure that the correct window is activated, that the appropriate files are selected and coordinated, and that local variables are preserved and restored after the event has been processed.

In subsequent chapters, I'll show examples of event handlers that preserve the state of the system and restore things after deactivation. It's not as easy as event loop programming; you might want to ease into it.

READ

The READ clause in FoxPro 1.02 was pretty simple; it activated the GETs that had been issued and not cleared. The good news was that it was very straightforward. The new READ command in FoxPro 2.0 is not simple. You might work with it for a very long time before its full implications become clear. However, a journey of a thousand miles begins with a single step, so let's get to it.

If you ACTIVATE WINDOW ABC NOSHOW, then issue some GETs, then ACTIVATE WINDOW XYZ NOSHOW, then issue some more GETs, FoxPro will show window ABC when you issue a READ. Then, when you leave the last GET field in window ABC, it will activate window XYZ. If you issued the READ CYCLE command, then, when you leave the last field in screen XYZ, window ABC will pop up again. By defining screen sets that have several screens, you can get the screen builder to generate your code ready to run in this way. That's how easy it is to build multi-page screens in FoxPro. However, there are all manner of other things you can do when moving from screen to screen. So, hold on, there's more.

READ has five clauses that can name user-defined functions that are executed at specific times during the READ process. For example, the WHEN clause is evaluated to determine whether or not to read a screenful of GETs. It happens at the beginning of the READ. So, if you want something to happen every time you enter a READ, put it into the READ WHEN function.

That's the basic idea behind using READ clauses to control processing within your program. It can come in handy in virtually every application. In the case of a foundation read, it actually controls the entire show. That's why it's considered a control device.

READ clauses

The syntax of the READ command is:

```
READ ;
    CYCLE                       ;
    ACTIVATE    function        ;
    DEACTIVATE  function        ;
    SHOW        function        ;
    VALID       function        ;
    WHEN        function        ;
    OBJECT      number          ;
    TIMEOUT     number          ;
    SAVE        number          ;
    NOMOUSE                     ;
    COLOR pair (or COLOR SCHEME number)
```

CYCLE CYCLE tells FoxPro to go back to the first GET field upon leaving the last one, unless

- You press Ctrl-Q or ESC
- You press Ctrl-W
- A control that terminates is selected
- The VALID clause returns a logical .T.

Ctrl-Q leaves the record unchanged, while Ctrl-W, or Ctrl-END or a CHR(23), permits the record to be updated (this presumes GETs of fields, which is a practice that I don't generally recommend).

Certain types of @...GET commands include the ability to specify termination of the read. For example:

```
action = [Save]
@ 20, 10 SAY [What next?] GET action PICTURE [@*TH Save;Cancel]
```

produces the following:

What next? <Save> <Cancel>

with the word Save highlighted. The H means horizontal display; the T means *terminate the read if they select one of these options*. If the user tabs or arrows through the field, nothing happens. If Enter is pressed or if one of the options is marked as a hot key and the hot key is pressed, the READ terminates.

ACTIVATE/DEACTIVATE   The ACTIVATE and DEACTIVATE clauses are executed when you enter and leave windows, respectively. They don't operate exactly as you might think, although it actually is completely reasonable. The program in LISTING 4-14 demonstrates how they work.

Listing 4-14

```
* Program-ID.....: ReadAct.PRG
* Purpose........: Demonstrates READ ACTIVATE and DEACTIVATE clauses
DEFINE WINDOW FIRST  FROM  1, 5 TO 12, 75 DOUBLE SHADOW
DEFINE WINDOW SECOND FROM 13, 5 TO 21, 75 DOUBLE SHADOW

Counter = 0

ACTIVATE WINDOW FIRST NOSHOW

name     = SPACE(40)
address1 = SPACE(40)
address2 = SPACE(40)

@ 2, 10 SAY [    Name: ] GET NAME
@ 4, 10 SAY [ Address: ] GET Address1
@ 5, 10 SAY [          ] GET Address2

ACTIVATE WINDOW SECOND NOSHOW

CHILD1 = SPACE(40)
CHILD2 = SPACE(40)
CHILD3 = SPACE(40)
CHILD4 = SPACE(40)

@ 1, 10 SAY [Children: ] GET CHILD1
@ 2, 10 SAY [          ] GET CHILD2
@ 3, 10 SAY [          ] GET CHILD3
@ 4, 10 SAY [          ] GET CHILD4

ACTIVATE WINDOW FIRST

READ CYCLE ;
   COLOR ,W+/R ;
   ACTIVATE START() ;
   DEACTIVATE END()

CLEAR WINDOWS

FUNCTION START
counter = counter + 1

IF counter > 3
   WAIT WINDOW [Only three tries permitted - cancelling] TIMEOUT 1
   KEYBOARD CHR(23)
ENDIF
```

```
FUNCTION END
* Allow leaving screens once adult and at least one child were entered.
IF NAME <> [        ] .AND. CHILD1 <> [       ]
  RETURN .T.
ELSE
  WAIT WINDOW [At least one child's name must be entered] TIMEOUT 1
  RETURN .F.
ENDIF
```

The ACTIVATE function gets executed every time you enter any window, so the counter will reach three sooner than you might have expected. Returning .T. from the DEACTIVATE clause terminates the READ. Notice the use of keyboard stuffing the Ctrl–W, CHR(23), to force exiting the read.

SHOW The GETs are redisplayed every time you SHOW GETS, but you might be skipping through a file and need to show the record number—RECNO( )—which isn't a GET. Doing this is not a problem. Just display it within the SHOW clause and use SHOW GETS to display the data on the screen—usually within a control VALID clause (LISTING 4-15).

Listing 4-15

```
* Program-Id....: ReadShow.PRG
* Purpose.......: Demonstrates READ SHOW and SHOW GETS interaction

*Structure for database: CLIENTS.DBF
*Field   Field Name    Type          Width
*   1    NAME          Character       30
*   2    ADD1          Character       30
*   3    CITY          Character       20
*   4    STATE         Character        2
*   5    ZIP           Character       10

USE CLIENTS

CLEAR

@ 5, 10 SAY [     Name:    ]          GET Name
@ 7, 10 SAY [     Address: ]          GET Add1
@ 8, 10 SAY [              ]          GET City
@ 8,  $ SAY [ ]                       GET STATE
@ 8,  $ SAY [ ]                       GET ZIP

action = [Next]

@ 11, 20 GET action ;
         PICTURE [@*HN Next;Previous;Top;Bottom;Quit] ;
         VALID WhatAction()

READ ;
  CYCLE ;
  SHOW ShowProg()

FUNCTION WhatAction
```

Listing 4-15 Continued

```
DO CASE
  CASE action = [Next]
    SKIP
    IF EOF()
      ?? CHR(7)
      GO BOTTOM
    ENDIF
  CASE action = [Previous]
    SKIP -1
    IF BOF()
      ?? CHR(7)
      GO TOP
    ENDIF
  CASE action = [Top]
    GO TOP
  CASE action = [Bottom]
    GO BOTTOM
  CASE action = [Quit]
    CLEAR READ
ENDCASE

SHOW GETS

RETURN

FUNCTION ShowProg

@ 1, 30 SAY [Record: ] + TRAN(RECNO(),[@L ###])

RETURN .F.
```

This is the simplest way to move some common options off of the menu and onto on-screen controls. However, you might not want your customers to always be in EDIT mode. Still, the SHOW clause can be used to real advantage.

VALID The function referred to in your READ VALID clause tells FoxPro when the read is over. If you don't want users leaving a screen until some condition is satisfied, here's the place to do it. Consider the program in LISTING 4-16.

Listing 4-16

```
* Program-ID....: ReadVal.PRG
* Demonstrates READ VALID clause

STORE 0 TO Amount1, Amount2, Amount3

@ 15, 60 GET Amount1   PICTURE [###.##]
@ 16, 60 GET Amount2   PICTURE [###.##]
@ 17, 60 GET Amount3   PICTURE [###.##]

READ VALID Maximum()
```

```
FUNCTION Maximum
Max = Amount1+Amount2+Amount3
IF Max > 100
  WAIT WINDOW [Can't exceed 100] TIMEOUT 1
  RETURN .F.
ELSE
  RETURN .T.     && Default, so not really necessary.
ENDIF
```

The VALID clause function MAXIMUM is evaluated as the last GET field is exited. In this example, it won't let you out of the screen if the total of the three amounts exceeds $100.

WHEN The WHEN clause is used to do things that need to happen at the beginning of a READ. (For example, examine LISTING 4-17.) WHEN clauses also are used to define a new _MSYSMENU for a particular data entry screen.

Listing 4-17

```
* Program-ID......: ReadWhen.PRG
* Purpose.........: Demonstrates the READ WHEN clause
SET TALK OFF
USE CLIENTS
SCATTER MEMVAR

DO ShowGets

READ ;
  SAVE  ;
  SHOW  ShowGets() ;
  WHEN  SetupScr() ;
  VALID SaveVars()

CLEAR

FUNCTION SetupScr
SET SYSMENU OFF
@  0,  0 SAY PADC( [BATCH ID ] + SYS(3) , 80 )

FUNCTION SaveVars
GATHER MEMVAR
IF LASTKEY() = 18
  SKIP -1
ELSE
  SKIP
ENDIF

SCATTER MEMVAR
SHOW GETS
IF EOF() OR LASTKEY() = 27
  CLEAR READ
  SET SYSMENU TO DEFAULT
  RETURN .T.
```

Listing 4-17 Continued

```
ENDIF
RETURN .F.

FUNCTION ShowGets

@  3,  0 SAY PADC([Data Edit - Clients],80)

@  5, 10 SAY [     Name: ] GET m.Name
@  7, 10 SAY [  Address: ] GET m.Add1
@  8, 10 SAY [           ] GET m.City
@  8,  $ SAY [ ]                        GET m.STATE
@  8,  $ SAY [ ]                        GET m.ZIP
@ 11, 30 SAY [Record No: ] + TRANSFORM(RECNO(), [@L ####])

@ 14,  0 SAY PADC([Edit; Press PgDn for next client or ESCAPE to cancel],80)
```

OBJECT You can select the number of the first GET item on a screen using the READ OBJECT *number* command. Remember that each selectable option of a control has its own number. For example, in the code fragment:

@ 10, 20 GET NAME
@ 12, 20 GET action PICTURE [@* Save;Don't save])

the value of Don't save is object number 3.

TIMEOUT TIMEOUT has one and only one purpose: it can force FoxPro to issue it's own Ctrl–W after the stated number of seconds. Also, the READKEY( ) function, with a numeric argument (e.g., READKEY(1), returns one of the following values:

1. None of the following
2. CLEAR READ issued
3. Terminating control chosen
4. READ window closed
5. DEACTIVATE clause returned .T.
6. READ timed out

So, with the following fragment, you can clean up after users that open a screen and go to lunch:

READ TIMEOUT 60

IF READKEY(1) = 6
    CLOSE DATABASES
    RETURN TO MASTER
ENDIF

SAVE SAVE allows you to reread variables. If you don't use this command, exiting the last GET in a screen is the equivalent of issuing CLEAR GETS. If you're using screen controls that take you from record to record, you'll need this. Ordinarily, when you terminate a READ, FoxPro clears the GETs. This leaves them active. This parameter was more important before READ CYCLE but still might be applicable in cases where you want to control the screen in some unusual way.

NOMOUSE Ordinarily, you can select any GET on the screen with a click of the mouse. NOMOUSE prevents users from doing this.

COLOR One of the nicest things about the READ LOOP technique that I've touted for so long is it's ability to give the current input field a different color than the rest of the GETS on the screen. Try the code in LISTING 4-18 on for size.

Listing 4-18

```
CLEAR
STORE [          ] TO A,B,C,D
SET COLOR TO GR+/B,N/W
@ 2,30 GET A
@ 4,30 GET B
@ 6,30 GET C
@ 8,30 GET D
READ COLOR ,R+/W
```

You might have bought this book just to find out how to do that. I sure would have paid an hour's wages to figure out how to do this a while back, when I spent a week making it happen using other techniques.

Order of processing

FoxPro processes these clauses in a definite order:

1. READ-level WHEN clause
2. First GET's window is activated
3. READ-level ACTIVATE clause
4. READ-level SHOW clause
5. GET-level WHEN clause for the first GET

When a new window is activated, the order is

1. VALID clause for the exiting field
2. READ-level DEACTIVATE clause
3. Window of the exiting field is deactivated
4. The new GET field's window is activated
5. READ-level ACTIVATE clause
6. WHEN clause for new field

READ processes all of the GETs on all of your screens, including any and all controls, in the order that the GETs were issued. If you move your GETs around, just pull down the Edit menu and Select All, then pull down the Screen menu and select Reorder. (The bottom half of the Screen menu is active only if you've got something SELECTed on the screen.) The use of Bring to Front and Move to Back is more arcane, but you might never need it.

Controls are different from ordinary GETs in the fancy features they provide and in the fact that they can be made to terminate READ, generally by including a T right after the @ character in the PICTURE clause. This is the equivalent of having the control variable's valid clause issue a KEYBOARD CHR(23) or KEYBOARD {[Ctrl-W]}.

Summary

These control devices—DO WHILE loops, FOR...NEXT loops, SCAN... ENDSCAN loops, CASE...ENDCASE structures, IF...ENDIF pairs, and menus—are all ways to control what happens within your program. The examples in this chapter showed how to implement these commands. By looking at the more complex cases in subsequent chapters, you'll get a better notion of when to use each one and how to do things you might have thought you couldn't do.

5
Windows

The single most critical aspect of the text window is its small size. In standard text mode, you have 25 lines of 80 characters per line. That's a very tiny space on which to make your statement. Windows are used, among other things, to mitigate that limitation.

A *window* is a rectangle that appears when you want it to appear, then disappears, leaving the screen as before. In this sense, the window is like an extension of the text screen—a sort of off-the-menu menu.

Traditionally, windows were done in three steps:

1. SAVE SCREEN
2. {draw a box and do whatever you need to do}
3. RESTORE SCREEN

Listing 5-1 demonstrates this.

Listing 5-1

```
* Program-ID.....: OldWindo.PRG
* Purpose........: Demonstrates previous windowing technique
SAVE SCREEN
SaveColor = SET ( [COLOR] )
SET COLOR TO N/N
@ 16, 31, 19, 52 BOX [          ]
SET COLOR TO W+/RB
@ 16, 30, 19, 51 BOX [┌─┐│ =└┘ ]
@ 17, 32 SAY     [ Continue printing? ]
@ 18, 34 PROMPT [ Yes ]
@ 18, 42 PROMPT [ No ]
yn = 2
MENU TO yn
RESTORE SCREEN
SET COLOR TO &SaveColor
IF yn <> 1
   RETURN TO MASTER
ENDIF
```

This method isn't bad, but you have to draw your own box, figure out what characters to use, draw your own shadow, calculate coordinates relative to the upper left corner of the screen (not your window), and restore the original colors and screen when done.

Compare this to LISTING 5-2. It's less code and fewer things can go wrong. Also, moving the window to another location on the screen is easier, because the inside coordinate references are window-relative.

Listing 5-2

```
* Program-ID.....: NewWindo.PRG
* Purpose........: Demonstrates FoxPro's DEFINE WINDOW command.
DEFINE   WINDOW PRINTCON FROM 15, 30 TO 18, 51 ;
   DOUBLE SHADOW COLOR SCHEME 5
ACTIVATE WINDOW PRINTCON
@  0,         1 SAY     [Continue Printing?]
@  1,         4 PROMPT [ Yes ]
@  1, COL()+3 PROMPT [ No ]
yn = 2
MENU TO yn
RELEASE WINDOW PRINTCON
IF yn <> 1
   RETURN TO MASTER
ENDIF
```

The DEFINE WINDOW and ACTIVATE WINDOW commands

The DEFINE WINDOW command syntax is as follows:

DEFINE WINDOW *window name* ;
 FROM *row1,col1* TO *row2,col2* ;
 IN WINDOW *windowname* | IN SCREEN ;
 FOOTER *string expression* ;
 TITLE *string expression* ;
 DOUBLE | PANEL | NONE | SYSTEM | *border string* ;
 CLOSE | NOCLOSE ;
 FLOAT | NOFLOAT ;
 GROW | NOGROW ;
 MINIMIZE ;
 SHADOW ;
 ZOOM | NOZOOM ;
 COLOR *color pair list* | COLOR SCHEME *scheme #*

Most of these parameters are self-explanatory. ZOOM, FLOAT, GROW, and MINIMIZE add the functionality that you might associate with Microsoft Windows applications. The DOUBLE/PANEL/NONE/SYSTEM group indicates what kind of border you want. If you want to define your own border, use eight individual characters, each one in quotes (or eight character variables). Run LISTING 5-3 for some examples.

Listing 5-3

```
* Program-ID....: WnBorder.PRG
* Purpose.......: Demonstrates custom window borders.

* First one shows positions:
DEFINE    WINDOW namelist FROM 14,1 TO 22, 72 ;
  [1],[2],[3],[4],[5],[6],[7],[8]
SHOW WINDOW namelist
WAIT WINDOW

* Double top and bottom
DEFINE    WINDOW namelist FROM 14,1 TO 22, 72 ;
  chr(205),chr(205),chr(179),chr(179),chr(213),chr(184),chr(212), chr(190)
SHOW      WINDOW namelist
WAIT window

* Double left and right
DEFINE    WINDOW namelist FROM 14,1 TO 22, 72 ;
  chr(196),chr(196),chr(186),chr(186),chr(214),chr(183),chr(211), chr(189)
SHOW      WINDOW namelist
WAIT window

* Thin panel
DEFINE    WINDOW namelist FROM 14,1 TO 22, 72 ;
  chr(220),chr(223),chr(221),chr(222),chr(220),chr(220),chr(223), chr(223)
SHOW      WINDOW namelist
WAIT window

DEFINE    WINDOW namelist FROM 14,1 TO 22, 72 PANEL   && for comparison
SHOW      WINDOW namelist
WAIT window

CLEAR WINDOW
```

To make the window appear, type:

ACTIVATE WINDOW *NAMELIST*

This command creates a window 7 rows high and 40 characters wide and makes it the active output area. The command:

DEACTIVATE WINDOW *xyz*

returns the previous output area to active status. The command:

RELEASE WINDOW *xyz*

removes all traces of the window's existence. You can create a window, write to it, then activate it for a very crisp appearance using the following sequence:

DEFINE WINDOW *xyz* FROM 5,5 TO 12,45
ACTIVATE WINDOW *xyz* NOSHOW
(@ *SAY...GET commands*)
SHOW WINDOW *xyz*

Window commands and functions

FoxPro 2.0 has a few new window commands and functions and has expanded the role of windows in many, many others. The basic window commands (related pairs of commands are listed together) are shown in TABLE 5-1.

Table 5-1 The basic window commands.

Window commands:
DEFINE WINDOW
ACTIVATE/DEACTIVATE WINDOW
SHOW/HIDE WINDOW
SAVE/RESTORE WINDOW
RELEASE WINDOW
CLEAR WINDOWS
MOVE WINDOW

Window functions:
WBORDER( )
WCHILD( )/WPARENT( )
WEXIST
WLCOL( )/WLROW( )
WCOL( )/WROW( )
WCOLS( )/WROWS( )
WONTOP( )
WOUTPUT( )
WVISIBLE( )

Ordinarily, a window's row and column coordinates are relative to the screen. However, some commands let you open a window inside (and relative to) the location of another window. Table 5-2 lists the commands that permit the use of the optional IN WINDOW clause.

Table 5-2 Commands permitting the IN WINDOW clause.

ACTIVATE WINDOW
BROWSE
CHANGE/EDIT
CREATE LABEL/MENU/PROJECT/REPORT/SCREEN
DEFINE MENU
FILER
HELP
HIDE WINDOW/SHOW WINDOW
MODIFY COMMAND/FILE/LABEL/MEMO/MENU/PROJECT/REPORT/SCREEN
SET TALK ON WINDOW <windowname> (you must ACTIVATE WINDOW also)

Ordering of windows

If you define a few windows, then use Alt – W to pull down the Windows pop-up from the system menu, you'll see the windows listed at the bottom of the menu with numbers before the window names, starting with zero. The last one listed is the current output window. The windows will be selected in the order you see them if you use Ctrl – F1 to cycle from window to window. Listing 5-4 will give you some insight into what happens when you are within windows.

Listing 5-4

```
* Program-ID.....: WINDOWS.PRG
* Purpose........: Demonstrates characterstics of groups of windows

DEFINE WINDOW first  FROM  1, 1 TO  5, 60 TITLE [first]  FLOAT SHADOW
DEFINE WINDOW second FROM  4, 5 TO 12, 52 TITLE [second] FLOAT SHADOW
DEFINE WINDOW third  FROM 10,15 TO 17, 48 TITLE [third]  FLOAT SHADOW

counter = 0
next    = [More]

ACTIVATE WINDOW first
@ 0, 11 GET next DEFAULT 1 PICTURE [@*HT More;No More]
ACTIVATE WINDOW second
@ 0, 11 GET next DEFAULT 1 PICTURE [@*HT More;No More]
ACTIVATE WINDOW third
@ 0, 11 GET next DEFAULT 1 PICTURE [@*HT More;No More]

READ ;
  CYCLE ;
  ACTIVATE   Changer() ;
  DEACTIVATE Leaving() ;
  VALID      Stopper()

CLEAR WINDOWS

RETURN

FUNCTION Changer
counter = counter + 1
? STR(counter,2)
IF NOT MDOWN()
  DO CASE
    CASE WONTOP([First])
      ACTIVATE WINDOW Second
    CASE WONTOP([Second])
      ACTIVATE WINDOW Third
    CASE WONTOP([Third])
      ACTIVATE WINDOW First
  ENDCASE
ENDIF
IF counter > 10
  CLEAR READ
ENDIF
RETURN .F.
```

Listing 5-4 Continued

```
FUNCTION Leaving
? [Leaving...] + WLAST()
RETURN .F.

 FUNCTION Stopper
IF Next = [No More]
   RETURN .T.
ELSE
   RETURN .F.
ENDIF
```

Use of windows in programs

Programs can make use of windows to add texture to the screen. A screen that's too cluttered or busy can confuse users. You don't want your users confused, do you?

Windows also can greatly simplify applications development by encapsulating groups of objects for use together. Browsing or scrolling secondary file records within a smaller window leaves the user with the sense that the secondary records are related to the underlying screen.

Popping up confirming dialogs over active screens similarly conveys a sense of parenthetical comment to the dialog contents. A shadowed box asking whether to SAVE OR DISCARD CHANGES, apparently popping out of an edit screen, wordlessly conveys the impression that the question relates to the entire screen underneath.

In the sections that follow, I'll explore use of windows as screen design tools.

Principles of operation

Windows can be activated and deactivated in several ways. First, if you define several windows in a sequence, with GETs inside of each one, each respective window is activated when your READ gets to the first GET inside a new window. Listing 5-5 illustrates this. As you press Enter to go from field to field, the window that owns each successive field is activated.

Listing 5-5

```
* Program-ID.....: WindSet1.PRG
* Purpose........: Demonstrates a read across several windows

DEFINE WINDOW A FROM  1, 1 TO  4, 45
DEFINE WINDOW B FROM 11,11 TO 14, 55
DEFINE WINDOW C FROM 21,21 TO 24, 65

First   = [This is text]
Second  = [This is more text]
Third   = [This is the last text]
```

```
@ 24, 0 SAY PADC([Press Ctrl-W to exit],80)

ACTIVATE WINDOW A NOSHOW
@ 1,2 GET First
ACTIVATE WINDOW B NOSHOW
@ 1,1 GET Second
ACTIVATE WINDOW C NOSHOW
@ 1, 1 GET Third

READ CYCLE

CLEAR SCREEN
CLEAR
```

This simple example doesn't clean up after itself; the windows stay on the screen after you leave them. Because things can get a bit cluttered, you can use a DEACTIVATE clause to hide all but the active window, as shown in LISTING 5-6.

Listing 5-6

```
* Program-ID.....: WindSet2.PRG
* Purpose........: Demonstrates a read across several windows

DEFINE WINDOW A FROM  1, 1 TO  4, 45
DEFINE WINDOW B FROM  6,11 TO  9, 55
DEFINE WINDOW C FROM 11,21 TO 14, 65

First  = [This is text]
Second = [This is more text]
Third  = [This is the last text]

@ 24, 0 SAY PADC([Press Ctrl-W to exit],80)

ACTIVATE WINDOW A NOSHOW
@ 1,2 GET First
ACTIVATE WINDOW B NOSHOW
@ 1,1 GET Second
ACTIVATE WINDOW C NOSHOW
@ 1, 1 GET Third

READ CYCLE DEACTIVATE Hidem()

CLEAR SCREEN
CLEAR

FUNCTION HIDEM
HIDE WINDOWS ALL
RETURN .F.
```

Using the mouse

If you have several windows on the screen, clicking on the window with the mouse will activate the window, as well as the GETs within it.

When you run LISTING 5-7, you can do several things with the mouse. The resulting screen appears in FIG. 5-1.

Listing 5-7

```
* Program-ID.....: WindSet3.PRG
* Purpose........: Demonstrates a read across several windows

DEFINE WINDOW A FROM  1, 1 TO  4, 45 FLOAT MINIMIZE
DEFINE WINDOW B FROM  6,11 TO  9, 55 FLOAT MINIMIZE
DEFINE WINDOW C FROM 11,21 TO 14, 65 FLOAT MINIMIZE

First  = [This is text]
Second = [This is more text]
Third  = [This is the last text]

@ 24, 0 SAY PADC([Press Ctrl-W to exit],80)

ACTIVATE WINDOW A NOSHOW
@ 1,2 GET First
ACTIVATE WINDOW B NOSHOW
@ 1,1 GET Second
ACTIVATE WINDOW C NOSHOW
@ 1, 1 GET Third

SHOW WINDOWS ALL

READ CYCLE COLOR ,W+/R

CLEAR WINDOWS
CLEAR
```

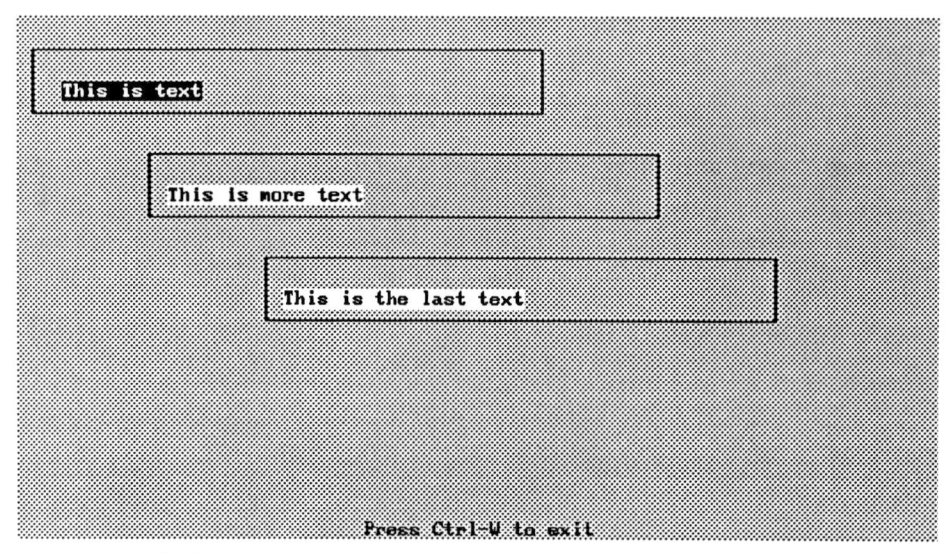

5-1 Screen display from WINDSET3.PRG—a read scanning several windows.

If you click on a window and hold the mouse down, you can move the window anywhere on the screen. Clicking twice on the top of the box makes the window disappear, except for its name. The name can be moved around, then made to reappear in its former location by clicking on the minimized name.

This is the type of window that Microsoft Windows users are accustomed to. These are easy to include in your application, where appropriate. However, I wouldn't run right out and convert all of my windows to FLOAT ZOOM GROW COLORIZE or whatever until I had a better feel for what looks best where.

Sometimes I design screens that have a lot of input fields. Users don't like to be required to press the Enter key a dozen times in order to get to the field they want to work with. Listing 5-8 is a sample of an application that separates inputs into two groups, each of which occupies its own window. The user can click with the mouse to move from the top half to the bottom half of the input screen. This effect is shown in FIG. 5-2.

Listing 5-8

```
* Program-ID.....: WININPUT.PRG
* Author.........: Les F. Pinter
* Purpose........: Demonstrates READ with several windows
SET UDFPARMS TO REFERENCE

DEFINE WINDOW FIRST   FROM  1,  5 TO  9, 75 DOUBLE SHADOW
DEFINE WINDOW SECOND  FROM 12,  5 TO 19, 75 DOUBLE SHADOW
DEFINE WINDOW CONFIRM FROM 21, 25 TO 23, 55 DOUBLE SHADOW

ACTIVATE WINDOW FIRST NOSHOW

name     = SPACE(40)
address1 = SPACE(40)
address2 = SPACE(40)

@ 1, 10 SAY [    Name: ] GET name     VALID Capitalize ( name     )
@ 3, 10 SAY [ Address: ] GET address1 VALID Capitalize ( address1 )
@ 4, 10 SAY [          ] GET address2 VALID Capitalize ( address2 )

ACTIVATE WINDOW SECOND NOSHOW

child1 = SPACE(40)
child2 = SPACE(40)
child3 = SPACE(40)
child4 = SPACE(40)

@ 1, 10 SAY [Children: ] GET child1 VALID Capitalize ( Child1 )
@ 2, 10 SAY [          ] GET child2 VALID Capitalize ( Child2 )
@ 3, 10 SAY [          ] GET child3 VALID Capitalize ( Child3 )
@ 4, 10 SAY [          ] GET child4 VALID Capitalize ( Child4 )

SHOW    WINDOW SECOND

ACTIVATE SCREEN

@ 24, 0 SAY ;
   PADC ( [ Press F10 to SAVE , ESCAPE to cancel without saving] , 80 )
ON KEY LABEL F10 KEYBOARD CHR(23) && Stuff Ctrl-W into the keyboard buffer.

ACTIVATE WINDOW FIRST

READ ;
```

Listing 5-8 Continued

```
CYCLE                    ;
COLOR  ,W+/R             ;
DEACTIVATE ENDWIND()     ;
   VALID      DONE()

CLEAR WINDOWS

RETURN

FUNCTION ENDWIND

IF WLAST([FIRST])
   ACTIVATE WINDOW SECOND
ELSE
   ACTIVATE WINDOW FIRST
ENDIF

RETURN .F.

FUNCTION DONE

ACTIVATE WINDOW CONFIRM

@ 0, 2 SAY [Finished?  ] ;
       GET answer ;
       PICTURE [@*HT Yes;No] ;
       SIZE   1,3,2 ;
       DEFAULT [Yes] ;
       COLOR  ,W+/R

READ       && Nested (level 2) read

DEACTIVATE WINDOW CONFIRM

RETURN IIF ( answer = [Yes] , .T. , .F. )


FUNCTION Capitalize
PARAMETERS variable

variable = PROPER ( variable )
SHOW GET Variable
RETURN .T.
```

Moving among windows

When you permit users to activate windows by clicking on them, you don't always know what window they're in. That's the hardest part of event-driven programming.

Several functions exist that can make the job easier. The WONTOP("*window name*") function can test to determine which window has been brought foremost. The code generated by the screen builder ensures that the window is defined and activated and (if you want it to) that the appropriate files get opened and closed at the right time.

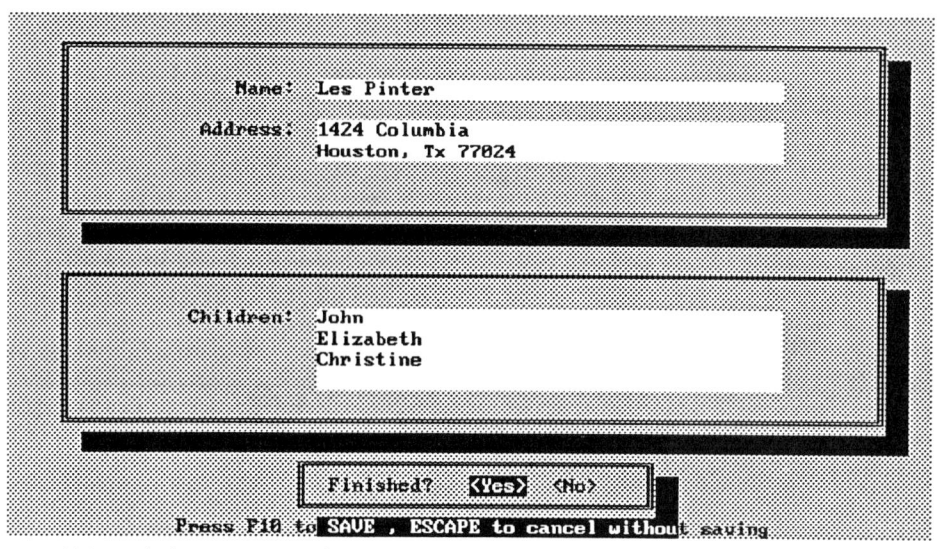

5-2 Using windows to group data entry fields (WININPUT.PRG).

In the sample program EX1.PRG in FoxPro's GOODIES\FNDA-TION\PRGS directory, you'll find an informative example. Here, the READ clause actually is issued without any active GETs. The engine that drives the program is the READ VALID clause, which triggers the program code shown in LISTING 5-9.

Listing 5-9

```
* Program-ID......: EX1.PRG
* Author..........: Fox Software Staff, with modifications.
* Purpose.........: Demonstrates Foundation Read using WONTOP()

PUBLIC dropdead, tobedone
dropdead  = .F.
tobedone  = ""

DO ex1.mpr                      && Run their MENU program

READ VALID myhandler()          &&    <=== Foundation READ!

CLEAR WINDOW ALL
CLOSE DATABASES

POP MENU _MSYSMENU

QUIT



FUNCTION myhandler
PRIVATE m.temp, m.x

IF dropdead
   RETURN .T.                   && Only when 'Exit' is selected
ENDIF                           && from the menu.
```

Moving among windows 99

Listing 5-9 Continued

```
IF LEN(tobedone) > 0          && Launches an SPR which was
   m.temp = tobedone          && specified from the menu
   tobedone = ""
   DO (m.temp)
   RETURN .F.
ENDIF

DO CASE                       && Handles all other cases
CASE WONTOP("cust")           && When 'Customer' screen foremost
   DO excust.spr
CASE WONTOP("parts")          && When 'Parts' screen foremost
   DO exparts.spr
CASE WONTOP("inv")            && When 'Invoices' screen foremost
   DO exinv.spr
CASE WONTOP("sman")           && When 'Salesman' screen foremost
   DO exsman.spr
CASE WONTOP("control3")
   m.temp = ""
   m.x = WCHILD("",0)         && What was active before?
   DO WHILE LEN(m.x) > 0
      DO CASE
      CASE m.x = "CUST"
         m.temp = "excust.spr"
      CASE m.x = "PARTS"
         m.temp = "exparts.spr"
      ENDCASE
      m.x = WCHILD("",1)
   ENDDO
   IF LEN(m.temp) > 0
      DO (m.temp)             && Launch code to handle foremost
   ENDIF                      && application screen
ENDCASE

RETURN .F.
```

The code that follows the WONTOP("CONTROL3") finds the foremost application window, then launches the .SPR that controls that window. It is executed when the control panel is foremost.

The foundation read terminates when this valid routine returns .T.. As long as it returns .F., execution of the foundation read will continue.

This is a complex example and not one that you should try to emulate just yet. I want to give you some insight into where you're going, but you're not there yet. Be patient; it's worth the wait.

Windows in screen design

The ability to re-use areas of the screen permits screen designs that were very difficult in the past. An example is the confirming dialog. A decision point occurs in the program and the user has to make a choice. A pop-up window avoids clutter on the screen and gets the user's attention.

Listing 5-10 is a confirming dialog, asking whether the user wants to print a report or not. Notice how simple the code is. The associated dialog box appears in FIG. 5-3.

Listing 5-10

```
* Program-ID.....: PrintCon.PRG
* Usage..........: ON ESCAPE DO PRINTCON

DEFINE   WINDOW PRINTCON FROM 15, 30 TO 18, 51 DOUBLE SHADOW COLOR SCHEME 2
ACTIVATE WINDOW PRINTCON
@   0,        1 SAY    [Continue Printing?]
@   1,        4 PROMPT [ Yes ]
@   1, COL()+3 PROMPT [ No ]
yn = 2
MENU TO yn

RELEASE WINDOW PRINTCON
```

5-3 A confirming dialog window (PRINTCON.PRG).

Browse windows

You can design some simple yet useful interfaces using a special kind of window, the BROWSE window. BROWSE in FoxPro provides an embarrassment of riches. In conjunction with a window, it becomes a powerful tool for interface design. I'll use BROWSE a dozen times in future models.

BROWSE can split the screen into two windows, a BROWSE window and an EDIT window, using a command like:

BROWSE REDIT LPARTITION PARTITION 40

This mechanism, shown in FIG. 5-4, is very useful for displaying enough key information to identify the record at the left, with a more complete display of information at the right. I've never gotten a chance to use it in my clients' software, but I'm sure that users find it convenient.

```
 System  File  Edit  Database  Record  Program  Window  Browse
```

```
                        INVOICES
   Invoiceno  Date      Descrip            Invoiceno  000001
                                           Date       01/02/90
   000001     01/02/90  Raincoat           Descrip    Raincoat
   000002     01/03/90  Milk Carton Protec Custcode   PEGASUS
   000003     01/04/90  Asafedita Bags     Amount        1234.00
   000004     01/05/90  Sheep Mittens
   000005     01/06/90  Sheep Mittens      Invoiceno  000002
   000006     01/07/90  Raincoat           Date       01/03/90
   000007     01/08/90  Milk Carton Protec Descrip    Milk Carton Protector
   000008     01/09/90  Asafedita Bags     Custcode   DAWN
   000009     01/10/90  Sheep Mittens      Amount         432.00
   000010     01/11/90  Sheep Mittens
```

5-4 A BROWSE and EDIT window using LPARTITION.

An interesting variation is the one-to-many browse produced with the SET SKIP command. Listing 5-11 demonstrates a few techniques using BROWSE and windows, including redefining the BROWSE borders. Figure 5-5 shows how a SET SKIP BROWSE looks.

Listing 5-11

```
* Program-ID......: BrowSkip.PRG
* Purpose.........: Demonstrates BROWSE with 1-to-many relationship

DEFINE WINDOW FIRST  FROM 5,5 TO 21, 70 SHADOW TITLE [F10 - Exit]
DEFINE WINDOW SECOND FROM 5,5 TO 21, 70 NONE

ON KEY LABEL F10 KEYBOARD CHR(23)

USE CUSTS    INDEX CUSTS    IN A
USE INVOICES INDEX INVCUST  IN B

*Structure for database: INVOICES.DBF
*Field  Field Name  Type        Width      Dec     Index
*   1   INVOICENO   Character     10                  2
*   2   DATE        Date           8
*   3   DESCRIP     Character     35
*   4   CUSTCODE    Character     10                  1
*   5   AMOUNT      Numeric       10        2
*** Total **                      74

SELECT CUSTS
SET RELATION TO CUSTS.CUSTOMER INTO INVOICES

SET SKIP TO INVOICES

ACTIVATE WINDOW FIRST

BROWSE       ;
  NOMODIFY ;
  FIELDS     ;
    CUSTS.CUSTOMER    , ;
    INVOICES.INVOICENO, ;
    INVOICES.DATE     , ;
```

102 Windows

```
         INVOICES.DESCRIP  , ;
         INVOICES.AMOUNT     ;
         WINDOW SECOND IN WINDOW FIRST

CLEAR WINDOW
CLOSE DATA
```

5-5 BROWSE with SET SKIP (BROWSKIP.PRG).

I like the built-in features, but I don't often get a chance to use them. I usually have to work with a screen design supplied by my customers. They don't appreciate my stock techniques.

Often, they ask for a design that looks more or less like an invoice—hence the name *invoice model*. There really is no built-in mechanism to do this, so I have to write a program.

This first example (LISTING 5-12) is a very simple program to display basic customer information, together with the dozen oldest invoices for the currently displayed customer. I've embedded the example in a menu loop, so that you can see what happens when you skip to the next customer.

Listing 5-12

```
* Program-ID......: BrowWind.PRG
* Purpose.........: Demonstrates BROWSE window with input screen.

CLEAR
USE Custs IN A
USE Invoices INDEX INVCUST IN B

SELECT Custs
SET RELATION TO CUSTOMER INTO INVOICES  && find first one...

DEFINE WINDOW tophalf FROM 2,4 TO 14, 75 COLOR SCHEME 5

DO WHILE .T.
```

Listing 5-12 Continued

```
SELECT INVOICES
ACTIVATE WINDOW tophalf
BROWSE NOCLEAR NOWAIT IN WINDOW tophalf ;
  FIELDS INVOICENO, Date, DESCRIP, AMOUNT ;
  KEY CUSTS->CUSTOMER,CUSTS->CUSTOMER
ACTIVATE SCREEN
SELECT CUSTS

@ 16,  2 SAY 'Customer'
@ 16, 12 SAY CUSTS->NAME
@ 17, 12 SAY CUSTS->Address1
@ 18, 12 SAY CUSTS->Address2
@ 19, 12 SAY CUSTS->Phone

@ 21, 15 SAY 'Balance: ' + TRAN(balance,'###,###.##')
@ 21, 45 SAY 'Last Payment: ' + DTOC ( LastPaid )

@ 22, 0 CLEAR
@ 22, 0 TO 22, 79
@ 23,         0 PROMPT ' \<Add '       MESSAGE ' Add a record'
@ 23, col()+1 PROMPT ' \<Edit '        MESSAGE ' Edit this record'
@ 23, col()+1 PROMPT ' \<Delete '      MESSAGE ' Delete this record'
@ 23, col()+1 PROMPT ' P\<rint '       MESSAGE ' Print this record'
@ 23, col()+1 PROMPT ' \<Next '        MESSAGE ' Next invoice'
@ 23, col()+1 PROMPT ' \<Previous '    MESSAGE ' Previous invoice'
@ 23, col()+1 PROMPT ' \<Quit '        MESSAGE ' Exit this screen'

z = 1
MENU TO z
DEACTIVATE WINDOW tophalf

choice = IIF ( z = 0 , [ ] , SUBSTR ( [AEDRNP ] , z , 1 ) )
  DO CASE
    CASE choice = [ ]
      EXIT
    CASE choice = [N]
.......... SELECT CUSTS
        SKIP
        IF EOF()
           GO BOTTOM
        ENDIF
    CASE choice = [P]
.......... SELECT CUSTS
        SKIP -1
        IF BOF()
           GO TOP
        ENDIF
    OTHERWISE
        =Chirp()
  ENDCASE

ENDDO



FUNCTION Chirp
FOR I = 1 TO 4
  SET BELL TO 1300,1
  ?? CHR(7)
```

```
      SET BELL TO 1400,1
      ?? CHR(7)
   ENDFOR
   RETURN .T.
```

Figure 5-6 shows the power of the BROWSE command. The parameters NOWAIT and NOCLEAR let the program continue while leaving the BROWSE window displayed on the screen. By constructing clever indexes, you can show the related invoices in a variety of ways (e.g., most recent first).

5-6 Using BROWSE for detail record display (BROWWIND.PRG).

Browses as table lookups

One of the interesting ways to use BROWSE is to use it to add a table lookup feature to your standard menu. In most flat file systems, you have a menu containing the following options:

  ADD EDIT DELETE NEXT PREVIOUS FIND PRINT QUIT

with a form view of a single record displayed on the screen. Often, my users would like to look at their records as a table, or full-screen pulldown menu, to point to the record they want to edit. If spelling errors or unfamiliar keys are a problem, this sort of feature is sure to be asked for. You might want to modify your menu to look like this:

  ADD EDIT DELETE NEXT PREVIOUS FIND TABLE
PRINT QUIT

and add the code in LISTING 5-13 within the DO CASE of your main loop.

Listing 5-13

```
CASE choice = [T]
  WhereWasI = RECNO()
  ON KEY LABEL ENTER KEYBOARD CHR(23)
  BROWSE NOMODIFY
  ON KEY LABEL ENTER
  IF LASTKEY() = 27   && escape was pressed
    GOTO WhereWasI
  ELSE
    DO DispRec
  ENDIF
```

The redefinition of the Enter key lets them point and press Enter to say *I found it*. The NOMODIFY parameter ensures that no data gets trashed during the lookup. The WhereWasI...LASTKEY( ) = 27 tests to see whether Esc was pressed, so that they end up back where they started if they don't find what they're looking for and press Enter.

I was always impressed by Luis Castro's extremely clever generated LIST functions to simulate this operation. However, it was hard to modify unless you went back through the template. The BROWSE approach is so easy to change. For example, you can take the FIRSTNAME and LASTNAME fields and form a single calculated field called NAME = LEFT (TRIM(FirstName)+[ ]+LastName,30) to display a 30-character NAME field that isn't even in your database. How about that, sports fans?

I should point out that Luis' most recent STAGE template generates a set of BROWSE commands that lets you tab right or left a full screen instead of a field at a time. So, there's always a way to use code to get a little faster or more efficient.

Dialog boxes

In chapter 3, I presented an escape trapping routine that popped up a window asking whether you wanted to continue or quit. That sort of dialog can be used to provide extreme flexibility in your software, with little disturbance of your underlying application.

A common use of windows is to facilitate dialog boxes. These little guys pop up and ask you what to do next and return options that control subsequent program flow.

Listing 5-14 produces a window-based dialog box to direct printer output for a subsequent report. The associated screen is shown in FIG. 5-7.

Listing 5-14

```
* Program-ID......: PrinCon2.PRG
* Purpose.........: FoxPro 2.0 "Print to where?" dialog
SET BLINK OFF
AtrBright = [N/GR*,W+/R]
DEFINE   WINDOW PrintCon ;
```

```
    FROM 5, 5 TO 13, 45 DOUBLE SHADOW COLOR &AtrBright FLOAT ZOOM
ACTIVATE WINDOW PrintCon
= center ( 0,[Print to:] )
@  1,  0 TO 1, WCOLS()
whereto = [Printer]
@  2,  7 GET whereto FUNCTION [*R] PICTURE [ Printer;Screen;File  ]
@  5,  0 TO 5, WCOLS()
go_on = [Continue]
@  6,  7 GET go_on FUNCTION [*H] PICTURE [  Continue ; Quit ]
READ CYCLE
DEACTIVATE WINDOW PrintCon
```

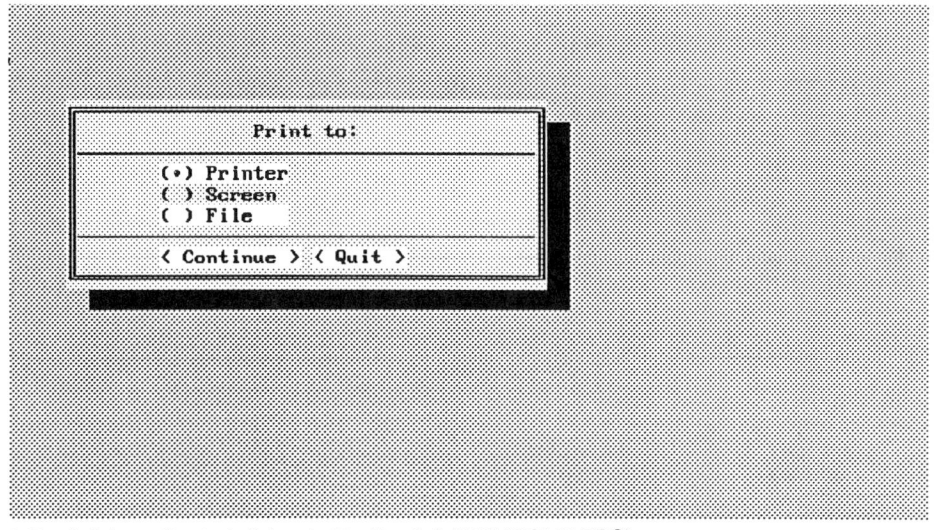

5-7 A Printer Control dialog in FoxPro 2.0 (PRINCON2.PRG).

The 2.0 version is a little different; you have to use it just as it comes out of the box, but just compare the amount of code required. Listing 5-15 is the equivalent program in FoxPro 1.02 code, by way of comparison. The output is shown in FIG. 5-8.

Listing 5-15

```
* Program-ID.....: PrinCon3.PRG
* Purpose........: Printer control using 'radio buttons'
* Notes..........: Can be used with mouse or keyboard
* Language.......: FoxPro 1.02

SET ESCAPE OFF
ON KEY LABEL F1 DO Instruct

Letters    = "PSFCQpsfcq"

Home       = CHR (  1 )
PgDn       = CHR (  3 )
RtArrow    = CHR (  4 )
UpArrow    = CHR (  5 )
End        = CHR (  6 )
```

Dialog boxes   107

Listing 5-15 Continued

```
Tab        = CHR (  9 )
Enter      = CHR ( 13 )
BackTab    = CHR ( 15 )
PgUp       = CHR ( 18 )
LeftArrow  = CHR ( 19 )
DnArrow    = CHR ( 24 )
EscKey     = CHR ( 27 )
HelpKey    = CHR ( 28 )

ValidKeys = Letters ;
 +Home   +PgDn +RtArrow   +UpArrow +End     ;
 +Enter  +PgUp +LeftArrow +DnArrow +EscKey  ;
 +Tab    +BackTab + HelpKey

AtrNormal = IIF ( IsColor() , [W+/RB] , [W/N]  )
AtrActive = IIF ( IsColor() , [W+/GR] , [W/N]  )
AtrNormal = IIF ( IsColor() , [GR+/B] , [W+/N] )

SET COLOR TO &AtrNormal

DEFINE    WINDOW PrintCon FROM 5, 5 TO 14, 45 ;
   DOUBLE SHADOW COLOR &AtrNormal FLOAT ZOOM
ACTIVATE WINDOW PrintCon

OldConf = SET ( [CONFIRM] )
OldCurs = SET ( [CURSOR] )

= center ( 0,[Print to:] )
@  1,  0 TO 1, WCOLS()
@  2,  3 SAY [ ( )   Printer ]
@  2, 20 SAY [ ( )   Screen  ]
@  3,  3 SAY [ ( )   File    ]
@  4,  0 TO 4, WCOLS()

@  5,  5, 7, 18 BOX [íë¡°fëå° ]
@  6,  7 SAY [ Continue ]
@  5, 21, 7, 35 BOX [íë¡°fëå° ]
@  6, 25 SAY [ Quit ]

ToPrint    = .T.
ToScreen   = .F.
ToFile     = .F.

Counter    = 1
mCanceled  = .F.
PrintOpt   = [P]
PrintFile  = [          ]

DO HighLite
DO DispButn

DO GetInput

SET CONFIRM &OldConf
SET CURSOR  &OldCurs

DO CASE
  CASE mCanceled
    WAIT [Print canceled by operator] WINDOW TIMEOUT 2
```

```
      CLOSE DATABASES
      RELEASE WINDOW PRINTCON
      RETURN TO MASTER
   CASE PrintOpt = [ ]
      CLOSE DATABASES        && No option was selected.
      RELEASE WINDOW PRINTCON
      RETURN
   CASE PrintOpt = [P]
      SET DEVICE TO PRINT
      SET PRINT ON
      DO DevTest
      RELEASE WINDOW PRINTCON
      RETURN
   CASE PrintOpt = [S]
      RELEASE WINDOW PRINTCON
      RETURN
   CASE PrintOpt = [F]
      SET CURSOR ON
      @  3, 18 GET PrintFile PICTURE "!!!!!!!!!"
      SET CONFIRM ON
      READ
      SET CURSOR OFF
      @  3, 18 SAY PrintFile
      IF LEN ( ALLTRIM ( PrintFile ) ) = 0
         WAIT [File name required - canceled] WINDOW TIMEOUT 2
         CLOSE DATABASES
         RELEASE WINDOW PRINTCON
         RETURN
      ELSE
         SET PRINTER TO &PrintFile
         SET PRINT ON
         RELEASE WINDOW PRINTCON
         DO DevTest
         RETURN
      ENDIF
ENDCASE


PROCEDURE DispButn

IF Counter = 1
   SET COLOR TO &AtrActive
ELSE
   SET COLOR TO &AtrNormal
ENDIF
@  2,  6 SAY IIF ( ToPrint  , [ª] , [ ] )

IF Counter = 2
   SET COLOR TO &AtrActive
ELSE
   SET COLOR TO &AtrNormal
ENDIF
@  2, 23 SAY IIF ( ToScreen , [ª] , [ ] )

IF Counter = 3
   SET COLOR TO &AtrActive
ELSE
   SET COLOR TO &AtrNormal
ENDIF
@  3,  6 SAY IIF ( ToFile   , [ª] , [ ] )
```

Listing 5-15 Continued

```
SET COLOR TO &AtrNormal

RETURN



FUNCTION CENTER
PARAMETERS line, text
@ line, (WCOLS()/2) - LEN(text)/2 SAY text
RETURN .T.


PROCEDURE DevTest
PRIVATE test

ON ERROR test = 1      && If this is the first use of the printer today,
??? []                 && The SYS(13) function won't return a correct status.

IF SYS(13) = [OFFLINE]
  SET DEVICE TO SCREEN
  WAIT [Printer is offline - check and try again] WINDOW TIMEOUT 3
  CLOSE DATABASES
  RELEASE WINDOW PRINTCON
  RETURN TO MASTER
ENDIF

RETURN


PROCEDURE GetInput

mCanceled = .F.
Finished  = .F.
Counter   = 1
KeyStroke = [ ]

DO WHILE .T.

  DO GetKey

  DO CASE

    CASE KeyStroke = HelpKey

      DO Instruct

    CASE KeyStroke = EscKey

      mCanceled = .T.
      EXIT

    CASE mCanceled

      EXIT

    CASE KeyStroke $ Letters

      Counter = AT ( UPPER ( KeyStroke ) , Letters )
      KeyStroke = enter
      IF Counter > 3
```

```
         KEYBOARD enter
       ENDIF
       DO Action
       LOOP

     CASE val(KeyStroke) > 127    && mouse was clicked

       DO Action                  && Store a letter to PrintOpt

       IF Finished
         EXIT
       ELSE
         LOOP
       ENDIF

     CASE KeyStroke = Enter

       DO Action                  && Store a letter to PrintOpt
       IF Finished .OR. mCanceled
         EXIT
       ELSE
         LOOP
       ENDIF

     CASE KeyStroke = Tab       ;
     .OR. KeyStroke = RtArrow   ;
     .OR. KeyStroke = DnArrow

       Counter = Counter + 1
       IF Counter > 5
         Counter = 1
       ENDIF
       DO Action
       LOOP

     CASE KeyStroke = BackTab    ;
     .OR. KeyStroke = LeftArrow ;
     .OR. KeyStroke = UpArrow

       Counter = Counter - 1
       IF Counter = 0
         Counter = 5
       ENDIF
       DO Action
       LOOP

   ENDCASE

ENDDO

RETURN


PROCEDURE GetKey

DO WHILE .T.

  KeyStroke = INKEY(0,"HM")

  IF KeyStroke >= -9
```

Listing 5-15 Continued

```
     DO CASE

       CASE BETWEEN ( KeyStroke , -9 , -1 )    && Trap function keys...
         KeyStroke = [F] + ALLTRIM ( STR ( ABS ( KeyStroke ) + 1 , 2 ) )
       CASE KeyStroke = 151             && mouse down...
         row = MROW()                && Get mouse pointer position
         col = MCOL()

         DO CASE
           CASE row = 2 .AND. col < 20
             Counter   = 1
           CASE row = 2 .AND. col >=20
             Counter   = 2
           CASE row = 3
             Counter   = 3
           CASE row >=4 .AND. col < 20
             Counter   = 4
             Finished  =.T.
             KeyStroke = Enter
           CASE row >=4 .AND. col >=20
             Counter   = 5
             mCanceled =.T.
             KeyStroke = Enter
         ENDCASE
         KeyStroke = Enter
         EXIT

       OTHERWISE

         KeyStroke = CHR ( KeyStroke )

       ENDCASE

       IF KeyStroke $ ValidKeys
         EXIT
       ELSE
         =Chirp()
       ENDIF

   ENDIF

ENDDO

RETURN

PROCEDURE Action

DO HighLite

DO CASE

  CASE Counter = 1

    IF KeyStroke = enter
      ToPrint    = .NOT. ToPrint
      IF ToPrint
        PrintOpt = [P]
```

112   Windows

```
      ENDIF
    ENDIF
    IF ToPrint
      ToScreen = .F.
      ToFile   = .F.
    ENDIF

  CASE Counter = 2

    IF KeyStroke = enter
      ToScreen = .NOT. ToScreen
      IF ToScreen
        PrintOpt = [S]
      ENDIF
    ENDIF
    IF ToScreen .AND. KeyStroke = enter
      ToPrint = .F.
      ToFile  = .F.
    ENDIF

  CASE Counter = 3

    IF KeyStroke = enter
      ToFile  = .NOT. ToFile
      IF ToPrint
        PrintOpt = [F]
      ENDIF
    ENDIF
    IF ToFile .AND. KeyStroke = enter
      ToPrint  = .F.
      ToScreen = .F.
    ENDIF

  CASE Counter = 4

    IF KeyStroke = enter
      Finished = .T.
    ENDIF

  CASE Counter = 5

    IF KeyStroke = enter
      mCanceled = .T.
    ENDIF

ENDCASE

DO DispButn

RETURN


PROCEDURE HighLite

    @  2, 0 FILL TO 2, WCOLS() COLOR &AtrNormal
    @  3, 0 FILL TO 3, 20      COLOR &AtrNormal
    @  4, 0 FILL TO 4, WCOLS() COLOR &AtrNormal
    @  5, 0 FILL TO 5, WCOLS() COLOR &AtrNormal
    @  6, 0 FILL TO 6, WCOLS() COLOR &AtrNormal
    @  7, 0 FILL TO 7, WCOLS() COLOR &AtrNormal
```

Listing 5-15   Continued
```
DO CASE
   CASE Counter = 1
      @ 2,  4 FILL TO 2, 17 COLOR &AtrActive
   CASE Counter = 2
      @ 2, 21 FILL TO 2, 34 COLOR &AtrActive
   CASE Counter = 3
      @ 3,  4 FILL TO 3, 17 COLOR &AtrActive
   CASE Counter = 4
      @ 5,  5 FILL TO 7, 18 COLOR &AtrActive
   CASE Counter = 5
      @ 5, 21 FILL TO 7, 35 COLOR &AtrActive
ENDCASE

RETURN

PROCEDURE Chirp

FOR I = 1 TO 4
   SET BELL TO 1400,1
   ?? CHR(7)
   SET BELL TO 1600,1
   ?? CHR(7)
ENDFOR

RETURN .T.

PROCEDURE Instruct

DEFINE WINDOW HELPME FROM 4, 6 TO 23, 74 ;
DOUBLE ;
COLOR SCHEME 5 ;
IN SCREEN

ACTIVATE WINDOW HelpME

Text
                        Output Director

   This dialog lets you direct report output to any of three
   destinations:

        ª The current printer
        ª The screen ( note: wide output will look funny)
        ª A file in the current directory

   Use the tab or arrow keys to move to the option that you
   want to choose. If you press ENTER to 'turn on' an option,
   alternate mutually exclusive options will be turned off.

   If you select 'file', you'll be asked to provide a file name.
   A blank file name will cancel the request.

EndText
WAIT WINDOW TIMEOUT 3

RELEASE WINDOW HelpMe

RETURN
```

5-8 Printer Control dialog in 1.02 (PRINCON3.PRG).

Written in FoxPro 1.02, this program also supports mouse input and press-the-first-letter control. It might surprise you to note that I only had to include a small amount of code to add these two additional control methods. However, the @ *row,col* PROMPT *string* command isn't used anywhere. PROMPT appropriates the mouse in ways that preclude some of the other things I wanted to do here.

I hope this technique gave you a little enthusiasm for what can be done with dialog boxes and an appreciation for FoxPro 2.0's new commands.

Validation pop-up windows

Just to clarify the terminology, there's a type of pop-up window that FoxPro simply calls a *pop-up*. This example (LISTING 5-16) is used to validate input into a field. The related pop-up is shown in FIG. 5-9.

Listing 5-16

```
* Program-ID.....: ValWind.PRG
* Purpose........: Demonstrates validation windows.
DIMENSION DeptName  ( 5 )
DIMENSION DeptCodes ( 5 )

DeptCodes ( 1 ) = [ACCT]
DeptCodes ( 2 ) = [MKTG]
DeptCodes ( 3 ) = [PERS]
DeptCodes ( 4 ) = [LEGL]
DeptCodes ( 5 ) = [EXEC]

DeptName ( 1 ) = [ ACCT - Accounting ]
```

Listing 5-16 Continued

```
DeptName ( 2 ) = [ MKTG - Marketing  ]
DeptName ( 3 ) = [ PERS - Personnel ]
DeptName ( 4 ) = [ LEGL - Legal     ]
DeptName ( 5 ) = [ EXEC - Executive ]

M->DeptCode = [    ]

@ 12, 5 SAY 'Department code: ' ;
        GET M->DeptCode ;
        PICTURE "!!!!"  ;
        VALID DeptCode();
        ERROR [You must enter a department code]
READ

FUNCTION DeptCode
IF .NOT. INLIST ( M->DeptCode , DeptCodes )
  @ 5, 25 MENU DeptName , 5 , 5 SHADOW TITLE [Dept Codes]
  DeptNum = 1
  READ MENU TO DeptNum
  IF DeptNum = 0
    RETURN .F.
  ELSE
    M->DeptCode = DeptCodes ( DeptNum )
    RETURN .T.
  ENDIF
ENDIF
```

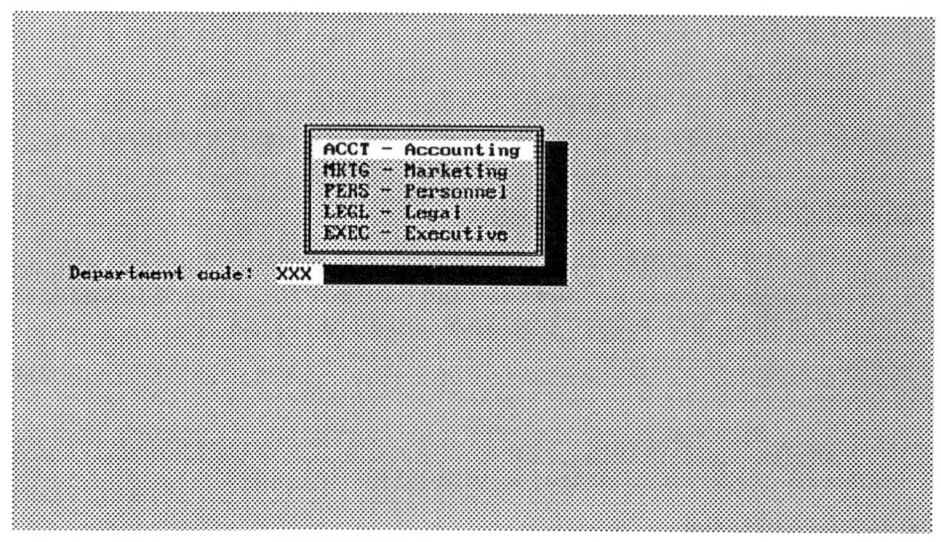

5-9 A validation pop-up (VALWIND.PRG).

Moving and resizing windows

Listing 5-17 is used to demonstrate some of the properties of windows. I don't know how useful the MOVE feature is, but it sure is cute.

Listing 5-17

```
* Program-ID.....: WINDEX.PRG
* Purpose........: Program to demonstrate window features
DEFINE WINDOW a FROM  1,  1 TO 15, 15  ;
       FLOAT GROW ZOOM SHADOW MINIMIZE ;
       TITLE [ Window A ]
ACTIVATE WINDOW a
HIDE     WINDOW a
FOR I = 1 TO 12
  ? REPLICATE(STR(I,2),6)
ENDFOR
DEFINE WINDOW b FROM 16, 16 TO 22, 75  ;
       FLOAT GROW ZOOM SHADOW MINIMIZE ;
       TITLE [ Window B ]
ACTIVATE WINDOW b
FOR I = 1 TO 5
  ? REPLICATE(STR(6-I,2),28)
ENDFOR
ACTIVATE WINDOW a
HIDE     WINDOW b
DO WHILE .T.
  ACTIVATE SCREEN
  @ 24, 0 SAY ;
          PADC([Notice that Ctrl-F7 (or the MOUSE) works during the READ,;
          but not during MENU],80)
  @ 23, 1 Prompt [ Window \<A ] COLOR ,GR+/B,W+/R,,,W+/R
  @ 23, $ Prompt [ Window \<B ] COLOR ,GR+/B,W+/R,,,W+/R
  @ 23, $ Prompt [ \<Move ]     COLOR ,GR+/B,W+/R,,,W+/R
  @ 23, $ Prompt [ E\<xit ]     COLOR ,GR+/B,W+/R,,,W+/R
  MENU TO WHICH
  @ 23, 0 CLEAR TO 23, 79
  DO CASE
    CASE WHICH = 1
      HIDE     WINDOW b
      ACTIVATE WINDOW a
      X = [       ]
      @ WROWS()-1,WCOLS()/2-1 GET X
      READ
    CASE WHICH = 2
      HIDE     WINDOW a
      ACTIVATE WINDOW b
      X = [       ]
      @ WROWS()-1,WCOLS()/2-1 GET X
      READ
    CASE WHICH = 3
      SHOW     WINDOW a
      SHOW     WINDOW b
      FOR I = 1 TO 4
        a = INKEY(.3)
        MOVE     WINDOW a BY 1,4
        MOVE     WINDOW b BY -1,-2
      ENDFOR
.....     WAIT WINDOW
      FOR I = 1 TO 4
        a = inkey(.3)
        MOVE     WINDOW a BY -1,-4
        MOVE     WINDOW b BY  1, 2
      ENDFOR
```

Listing 4-17   Continued

```
.....        WAIT WINDOW
      CASE WHICH = 4
         EXIT
   ENDCASE
ENDDO
CLEAR WINDOWS
CLEAR
RETURN
```

Limiting access to windows

If you define several windows, then use Alt-W to activate the system menu Windows menu, you'll see all of your windows listed and numbered at the bottom of the pulldown. The Ctrl-F1 key cycles from one window to the next. Also, you can highlight one and press Enter (or point and click) to select a particular window. In some applications, your system menu will be defined so as to let users select their window from a pulldown in lieu of using a mouse (see the foundation read example in the FoxPro GOODIES subdirectory).

FoxPro permits you to group a collection of windows that are mutually active during a READ operation. If you have 10 windows but want your users to have access to only four of them within a particular input screen, the command:

READ WITH patient,calendar,dates,scratch

will do the trick. The command:

READ MODAL

restricts the READ to the current window only. You might not see the usefulness of this yet. However, if you try letting your users cycle through a dozen windows, half of which don't relate to the current screen, this new feature will look very appealing.

Summary

This chapter has been an overview of some of the ways that FoxPro windows can make your coding simpler and your screens more interesting. I'm sure that your experimentation will yield even more ways to implement this feature. If you'd like to share your discoveries with the world, please contact my newsletter.

6
The screen builder and @...SAY/GET

The screen builder is one of the most striking differences between 1.02 and 2.0. At first glance, it looks like Luis Castro's ViewGen screen and does many of the things that were done by that venerable product. However, it does a number of new things and does the old ones quite differently.

The new buzzword is snippets. *Snippets* are lines of code that are placed in various windows that can be entered within the screen builder. Each window deposits its stored code at a predictable location within the generated code produced by the screen builder. The result operates exactly as if you had coded the program yourself.

I should point out that there are times when you never look at the generated code. If you work within the project manager, the screen code is generated, compiled, and stored in the project file's memo fields without being saved as source code (unless you specifically request that it be saved).

The question is, how can you make the screen builder do what you used to do by hand? The key is to understand where the screen builder puts your snippets. Once you know that, you can comfortably move to the new environment and do the same things you used to do in your editor.

A simple example

The example I'll use is very simple, but I hope that it illustrates the point as well as a more complicated one would. I like to strip an example down to it's barest essentials; I can always add more complexity later.

If I wanted to write a program to input the radius of a circle, then display the diameter, perimeter, and area, I'd write the code shown in LISTING 6-1. The screen builder's idea of how to do this is only slightly different (LISTING 6-2).

Listing 6-1

```
* Program-ID.....: CIRCLE1.PRG
* Purpose........: A simple demonstration program to calculate area.
DEFINE WINDOW CIRCLE FROM 5,12 TO 11, 68 ;
  TITLE "Enter zero radius to exit" ;
  SHADOW COLOR SCHEME 1

* Initialize memory variables
radius    = 0
diameter  = 0
perimeter = 0

ACTIVATE WINDOW CIRCLE NOSHOW

@ 0,19 SAY "Circle Evaluation"
@ 1,0 TO 3,54

@ 2,21 SAY "Radius:"
@ 4, 1 SAY "Diameter:"
@ 4,21 SAY "Perimeter:"
@ 4,40 SAY "Area:"

ACTIVATE WINDOW CIRCLE

DO WHILE .T.

   @ 2,29 GET m.radius PICTURE "##.##"
   READ

   IF radius = 0
     EXIT
   ENDIF

   DO CircCalc

ENDDO

RELEASE WINDOW CIRCLE

RETURN


FUNCTION CircCalc

Pi        = 3.14159           && initialize constant and
Diameter  = radius    * 2     && calculate results
Perimeter = Diameter  * Pi
Area      = Radius ^ 2 * Pi

@ 4, 12 SAY Diameter  PICTURE [####.##]    && display the results
@ 4, 31 SAY Perimeter PICTURE [####.##]
@ 4, 46 SAY Area      PICTURE [#####.##]

WAIT WINDOW                   && Wait to see results, and

@ 4, 12 SAY [        ]        && clear the three
@ 4, 31 SAY [        ]        && output areas.
@ 4, 46 SAY [         ]
```

```
Radius = 0

RETURN
```

Listing 6-2

```
* Program-ID.....: CIRCLE2.PRG
* Purpose........: Screen Builder's way to do what CIRCLE1.PRG did.
DEFINE WINDOW CIRCLE FROM 5,12 TO 11, 68 ;
   TITLE "Enter zero radius to exit" ;
   SHADOW COLOR SCHEME 1

* Initialize memory variables
radius    = 0
diameter  = 0
perimeter = 0

ACTIVATE WINDOW CIRCLE NOSHOW

@ 0,19 SAY "Circle Evaluation"
@ 1,0 TO 3,54

@ 2,21 SAY "Radius:"
@ 4, 1 SAY "Diameter:"
@ 4,21 SAY "Perimeter:"
@ 4,40 SAY "Area:"

@ 2,29 GET m.radius ;
       PICTURE "##.##" ;
       VALID CircCalc()

ACTIVATE WINDOW CIRCLE

READ CYCLE

RELEASE WINDOW CIRCLE

RETURN



FUNCTION CircCalc       &&  m.radius VALID
* They just exited the READ of field m.Radius; what next?

IF Radius = 0
  CLEAR READ
  RETURN
ENDIF

Pi        = 3.14159              && initialize constant and
Diameter  = radius    * 2        && calculate results
Perimeter = Diameter  * Pi
Area      = Radius ^ 2 * Pi

@ 4, 12 SAY Diameter  PICTURE [####.##]    && display the results
@ 4, 31 SAY Perimeter PICTURE [####.##]
@ 4, 46 SAY Area      PICTURE [#####.##]
WAIT WINDOW                                && Wait to see results, and

@ 4, 12 SAY [          ]                   && clear the three
```

Listing 6-2   Continued

```
@ 4, 31 SAY [       ]                && output areas.
@ 4, 46 SAY [          ]
Radius = 0

RETURN
```

What are the differences? First, the DO loop to repeat the read until a terminating condition occurs is replaced by READ CYCLE and a CLEAR READ statement inside the VALID clause. Second, the VALID clause is executed every time you leave the field being read, so the condition that terminates the DO loop is tested every time you exit a field.

That's it. That's what has stumped you since you first saw the screen builder example. The examples that accompany FoxPro 2.0 are a bit more complex and involve a few more bells and whistles—in particular, the READ WHEN, VALID, and SHOW clauses—but this is the core of this new world.

Actually, my screen builder produces the code shown in LISTING 6-3.

Listing 6-3

```
*       ø£££££££££££££££££££££££££££££££££££££££££££££££££££ñ
*       ¤                                                    ¤
*       ¤ 08/11/91            CIRCLE.SPR             11:30:07 ¤
*       ¤                                                    ¤
*       Ú£££££££££££££££££££££££££££££££££££££££££££££££££££Ñ
*       ¤                                                    ¤
*       ¤ Author's Name                                      ¤
*       ¤                                                    ¤
*       ¤ Copyright (c) 1991 Company Name                    ¤
*       ¤ Address                                            ¤
*       ¤ City,    Zip                                       ¤
*       ¤                                                    ¤
*       ¤ Description:                                       ¤
*       ¤ This program was automatically generated by GENSCRN. ¤
*       ¤                                                    ¤
*       Æ£££££££££££££££££££££££££££££££££££££££££££££££££££§

#REGION 0
REGIONAL m.currarea, m.talkstat, m.compstat

IF SET("TALK") = "ON"
  SET TALK OFF
  m.talkstat = "ON"
ELSE
  m.talkstat = "OFF"
ENDIF
m.compstat = SET("COMPATIBLE")
SET COMPATIBLE FOXPLUS

*       ø£££££££££££££££££££££££££££££££££££££££££££££££££££ñ
*       ¤                                                    ¤
*       ¤                 Window definitions                 ¤
*       ¤                                                    ¤
*       Æ£££££££££££££££££££££££££££££££££££££££££££££££££££§
```

```
*
IF NOT WEXIST("x")
  DEFINE WINDOW x ;
    FROM INT((SROW()-7)/2),INT((SCOL()-56)/2) ;
    TO INT((SROW()-7)/2)+6,INT((SCOL()-56)/2)+55 ;
    TITLE "Enter zero radius to exit" ;
    NOFLOAT ;
    NOCLOSE ;
    SHADOW ;
    COLOR SCHEME 1
ENDIF
```

```
*
*
*          CIRCLE Setup Code - SECTION 2
*
*
```

```
#REGION 1
* Initialize memory variables

radius    = 0
diameter  = 0
perimeter = 0
```

```
*
*
*          CIRCLE Screen Layout
*
*
```

```
#REGION 1
IF WVISIBLE("x")
  ACTIVATE WINDOW x SAME
ELSE
  ACTIVATE WINDOW x NOSHOW
ENDIF
@ 0,19 SAY "Circle Evaluation"
@ 2,21 SAY "Radius:"
@ 4,1  SAY "Diameter:"
@ 4,21 SAY "Perimiter:"
@ 4,40 SAY "Area:"
@ 2,29 GET m.radius ;
  SIZE 1,5 ;
  DEFAULT 0 ;
  PICTURE "##.##" ;
  VALID _pxw0onipl()
@ 1,0 TO 3,53

IF NOT WVISIBLE("x")
  ACTIVATE WINDOW x
ENDIF

READ CYCLE

RELEASE WINDOW x
```

Listing 6-3 Continued

```
#REGION 0
IF m.talkstat = "ON"
  SET TALK ON
ENDIF
IF m.compstat = "ON"
  SET COMPATIBLE ON
ENDIF


*
*
*       ┌─────────────────────────────────────────────────────┐
*       │                                                     │
*       │   _PXW0ONIPL              m.radius VALID            │
*       │                                                     │
*       │   Function Origin:                                  │
*       │                                                     │
*       │   From Screen:        CIRCLE,     Record Number:  7 │
*       │   Variable:           m.radius                      │
*       │   Called By:          VALID Clause                  │
*       │   Object Type:        Field                         │
*       │   Snippet Number:     1                             │
*       │                                                     │
*       └─────────────────────────────────────────────────────┘
*
* They just exited the READ of field m.Radius; what next?

FUNCTION _pxw0onipl      &&  m.radius VALID
#REGION 1
IF Radius = 0
  CLEAR READ
  RETURN
ENDIF
Pi        = 3.14159              && initialize constant and
Diameter  = radius * 2           && calculate results
Perimiter = Diameter * Pi
Area      = Radius ^ 2 * Pi

@ 4, 12 SAY Diameter  PICTURE [####.##] && display the results
@ 4, 31 SAY Perimiter PICTURE [####.##]
@ 4, 46 SAY Area      PICTURE [#####.##]

WAIT WINDOW                      && Wait to see results, and

@ 4, 12 SAY [          ]         && clear the three
@ 4, 31 SAY [          ]         && outout areas.
@ 4, 46 SAY [          ]

Radius = 0
```

I see a few SET statements and some REGION directives, both of which could be dispensed with in this simple case. Also, the WVISIBLE function references aren't important in this context. So, there are a few differences. In our simple example, however, they're not relevant.

The funny-looking function and procedure names are the hallmark of FoxPro 2.0. Every time you generate the source code, they change. These generated names are guaranteed to be unique and thus avoid duplication. I personally vote to let the programmer assign a procedure name and live with the risk.

@...SAY/GET controls

Perhaps the biggest change in FoxPro 2.0 screens is the addition of a formidable array of additions to the @...SAY/GET command. Features that once required pages of coding to implement are now one- or two-line commands. These enhancements, coupled with the screen builder, permit the development of spectacular code in a very short time.

Most of these new @...SAY/GET controls can be defined as terminating, which means that, in a READ CYCLE command, they do the same thing that you would ordinarily do by pressing Ctrl–W. So, if you want a particular screen variable to execute the READ VALID clause (which executes when you exit a READ), make it a terminating control by including the T option in the FUNCTION or FORMAT statement. Any control valid clause that issues the command CLEAR READ also ends the read.

Controls also can be used to move some commands off of their traditional place in the menu. For example, commands to move forward or backward within a database are typically found on a menu. In FoxPro 2.0, you can do the same thing with an on-screen control (usually a push-button control), so that the user only goes to the menu to take more important actions.

New features available as enhancements to the @...SAY/GET command include:

- @...SAY/GET SIZE clause and K PICTURE code
- @...GET check boxes
- @...GET invisible buttons
- @...GET pop-ups
- @...GET radio buttons
- @...GET lists
- @...GET push buttons
- @...EDIT text editing regions

This little list, together with a few structural changes, has huge implications for the way you'll design applications. A brief discussion of each follows.

@...SAY/GET SIZE clause and K PICTURE code

In FoxPro 1.02, the sequence:

```
X = [Hi]
@ 5, 5 GET X
```

would produce an input field two characters in length. In 2.0, the statements:

```
X = [Hi]
@ 5,5 GET X SIZE 1,10 FUNCTION [K]
```

would display a GET field 10 characters long, allowing you to enter up to 9 (not 10) characters, which would be stored in the memory variable X.

@...GET check boxes

The function code *C is used with LOGICAL variables to produce *check boxes*, which are features that can toggle between [ ] and [X], representing .F. and .T. respectively, using the space bar. You also can use the SIZE command together with check boxes to tidy up the display. For example:

```
NewHire = .F.
@ 12, 30 GET NewHire FUNCTION [*C New Hire]
```

will display on the screen as:

[ ] New Hire

and will permit the user to toggle between [X] and [ ].

@...GET invisible buttons

You might want to write a screen in which the highlighted area cycles over a group of text regions, as is shown in LISTING 6-4. The CYCLE command tells READ to go from the last choice back to the first until Enter is pressed or one of the other terminating requirements is met. The H tells FoxPro that the boxes are horizontal.

Listing 6-4

```
* Program-Id...: Seasons.prg
* demonstrates : Invisible buttons

SET TALK OFF
STORE 0 TO season
CLEAR
@ 2, 10 SAY [Winter]    && Display in
@ 2, 25 SAY [Spring]    && James Taylor
@ 2, 40 SAY [Summer]    && order.
@ 2, 55 SAY [ Fall ]    &&
@ 1, 9, 3, 16 BOX       && Draw boxes around text
@ 1,24, 3, 31 BOX
@ 1,39, 3, 46 BOX
@ 1,54, 3, 61 BOX

@ 1, 9 GET season PICTURE [@*IH ;;;] SIZE 3,    8,          7
*                                         height,width,distance between
READ CYCLE
```

@...GET pop-ups

One nice feature of 2.0 is the addition of several easy ways to add pick lists to your data entry screens. Fields can use either an array or simply a picture clause to specify the items to be displayed in the pick list.

The value of a variable that's associated with a pop-up using the [^] function appears within a little box that looks like this:

```
┌─────────┐
│  DOG   ║
└─────────┘
```

When your cursor gets to this field, pressing Enter makes the pop-up list appear. Listing 6-5 gives examples of both the ARRAY and the picture clause forms.

Listing 6-5

```
* Program-Id....: PopNames.PRG
* Purpose.......: Demonstrates 2 types of POPUP GET

SET TALK OFF
CLEAR

@ 1, 0 SAY PADC([ Popups using @..GET],80)
@ 2, 0 SAY PADC([ Type 1 - using a PICTURE clause],80)

@ 4, 10 GET whichone ;
        FUNCTION [^] ;
        DEFAULT  [Second];
        PICTURE  [ First;\Second;Third]
READ

@ 7, 0 SAY PADC([ Type 2 - from an array],80)

RELEASE whichone

DIMENSION Names(3)
Names(1) = [Joe Smith       ]
Names(2) = [Maria Schnell   ]
Names(3) = [Ivan Denisovich]

@ 9, 10 GET whichone FROM Names FUNCTION [^] DEFAULT Names(3)
READ
```

The DEFAULT statement lets you go in without initializing the MEMVAR. The backwards slash in front of the word Second in the first example tells the pop-up to display the word Second but not permit it to be selected.

If you use the FROM *arrayname*, you can't disable any of the selections. However, if you have an array with 10 elements and you want only items 1 through 6 and items 8 and 9 to appear, use the code in LISTING 6-6. Then, the statement:

@ 9, 10 GET whichone FROM Names FUNCTION [^] DEFAULT Names(3)

will display only the eight selected names.

Listing 6-6

```
DIMENSION Names(10),NewNames(8)

Names( 1) = [Joe Smith      ]         && previously defined....
```

Listing 6-6 Continued

```
Names( 2) = [Maria Schnell    ]
Names( 3) = [Ivan Denisovich]
Names( 4) = [Evander Holyfie]
Names( 5) = [Joe Louis       ]
Names( 6) = [Maximillian Sch]
Names( 7) = [Don Knotts      ]
Names( 8) = [Marissa Berenge]
Names( 9) = [Joe Pinter      ]
Names(10) = [Duke of Alba    ]

=ACOPY(Names,Names2,1,6,1)
=ACOPY(Names,Names2,8,2,7)
```

@...GET radio buttons

In a sea of exciting new features, the radio buttons feature is particularly interesting. If you enter the command:

@ 5, 5 GET button FUNCTION [*R] ;
PICTURE [Winter;Spring;Summer;Fall] DEFAULT 1

you'll get the following on the screen:

(•) Winter
( ) Spring
( ) Summer
( ) Fall

The vertical/horizontal option displays the buttons in vertical (the default) or horizontal orientation. The terminate/non-terminate option determines whether or not the READ is terminated if one of the values is chosen, either by a mouse click or by pressing Enter when one of the buttons is highlighted.

In FoxPro 1.02, I generally told users to press Enter to move from one field to the next. Because terminating controls end the READ if you press Enter, tabbing (or arrow-keying) through the fields and controls on the screen is much more commonly used now than in FoxPro 1.02.

I should mention that all of these @...GET functions also support a number of other options, including COLOR, SIZE, VALID, WHEN, MESSAGE, selective disabling of options (by prefixing the disabled options with a double backslash), and probably a few others by the time this book hits the street.

@...GET POPUP or @...GET FROM

If you want to assign a value to a variable based on the contents of a list and you don't want the current contents displayed within the little box produced by FUNCTION [^], you'll want to use the variation shown in LISTING 6-7. Examine the listing for an example. The pop-up looks like this:

```
┌─────────┐
│  Larry  │
│  Moe    │
│  Curly  │
└─────────┘
```

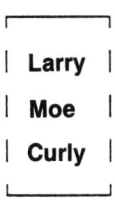

My experiments with the command permit a number to be used as the default choice if FROM POPUP is used, while the array-based variety can default to a defined character string. The pop-up list only appears when reading the field; the selected result is stored into the variable unless Esc was pressed.

Listing 6-7

```
* Program-ID....: PopList.PRG
* Purpose.......: Demonstrate GET LISTS
CLEAR

DEFINE POPUP NAMES FROM 5, 5 COLOR W+/R
DEFINE BAR 1 OF NAMES PROMPT [ Larry ]
DEFINE BAR 2 OF NAMES PROMPT [ Moe ]
DEFINE BAR 3 OF NAMES PROMPT [ Curly ]
choice = 1
@ 5, 5 GET choice POPUP NAMES
READ

* From an array...
DIMENSION NAMES(3)
Names(1) = [ Larry ]
Names(2) = [ Moe   ]
Names(3) = [ Curly ]

choice   = [ Moe   ]
@ 12, 5 GET choice FROM names
READ
```

@...GET push buttons

The <Continue> <Cancel> pair at the bottom of dialog boxes has become a feature that users readily recognize. You can add it to your dialogs with this function, simply by putting the list of options in the associated PICTURE clause.

The function PrtOrNot contained in the following test bed (LISTING 6-8) will return .T. if the user doesn't cancel, as well as a value for WhereTo. The GET WhatNext statement is the one I'm using to demonstrate the [*] function. The H in the function statement means *horizontal display*.

Listing 6-8

```
* Program-Id....: PrtTest
* Purpose.......: Demonstrates push buttons

IF PrtOrNot()
   DO REPORT     && needs to know what to do with <WhereTo>
```

Listing 6-8 Continued

```
ELSE
  WAIT [Cancelled by Operator] WINDOW TIMEOUT 1
ENDIF

PROCEDURE REPORT
* dummy for testing

FUNCTION PrtOrNot
DEFINE    WINDOW WhatNext FROM 15, 20 TO 20, 60 TITLE [ Print where? ]
ACTIVATE  WINDOW WhatNext
RELEASE   WhereTo
PUBLIC    WhereTo
WhatNow = 1
@ 1, 4 GET WhereTo   ;
       FUNCTION [*RH];
       PICTURE   [ Screen;Printer;File]
@ 2, 0 TO 2, WCOLS()      && Draw a horizontal line...
@ 3, 9 GET WhatNext  ;
       FUNCTION [*H] ;
       PICTURE   [ \<Continue;C\<ancel] DEFAULT 1
READ
RELEASE WINDOW WhatNext

RETURN IIF ( WhatNext = 1 , .T. , .F. )
```

Notice that the READ in FUNCTION PrtOrNot activates all of the hot keys for all of the variables in the READ. If you're in the (•) Printer field and you press a (the hot key for Cancel), the function completes the read immediately and returns the logical value .F.

@...EDIT text editing regions

The text editing regions feature gives you a sort of mini-memo field editing ability for string variables. Using this feature, your applications can use small text fields to save a few sentences of word-wrapped information.

A complex example

The fine folks at Fox Software have included a sample screen that demonstrates beautifully the many new GET statements, as well as a few new commands. The LASER database included in the samples that come with FoxPro 2.0 is the basis for this screen. The file structure is shown in LISTING 6-9. The sample screen LASER in the FOXPRO2\GOODIES\LASER\SCREENS directory is shown in FIG. 6-1.

Listing 6-9

```
Structure for database: LASER.DBF
Memo file block size  :      64
Field  Field Name  Type        Width    Dec     Index
    1  CATNO       Character      10            Asc
    2  TITLE       Character      80            Asc
    3  PRICE       Numeric         6     2      Asc
```

```
     4  RATING       Character    5            Asc
     5  XQUALITY     Numeric      2
     6  CRITICS      Numeric      1            Asc
     7  ACQUIRED     Date         8            Asc
     8  SDIGITAL     Logical      1
     9  XDIGITAL     Logical      1
    10  CX           Logical      1
    11  STEREO       Logical      1
    12  SURROUND     Logical      1
    13  LETTERBOX    Logical      1
    14  BLK_WHT      Logical      1
    15  CLOSECAP     Logical      1
    16  CAV          Logical      1
    17  SUBTITLED    Logical      1
    18  DUBBED       Logical      1
    19  SILENT       Logical      1
    20  COMMENTARY   Logical      1
    21  SUPPLEMENT   Logical      1
    22  DURATION     Numeric      3            Asc
    23  SIDES        Numeric      2
    24  YEAR         Numeric      4            Asc
    25  DESCRIPT     Memo        10
    26  STUDIO       Character   20            Asc
    27  KIDS         Logical      1
** Total **                      167
```

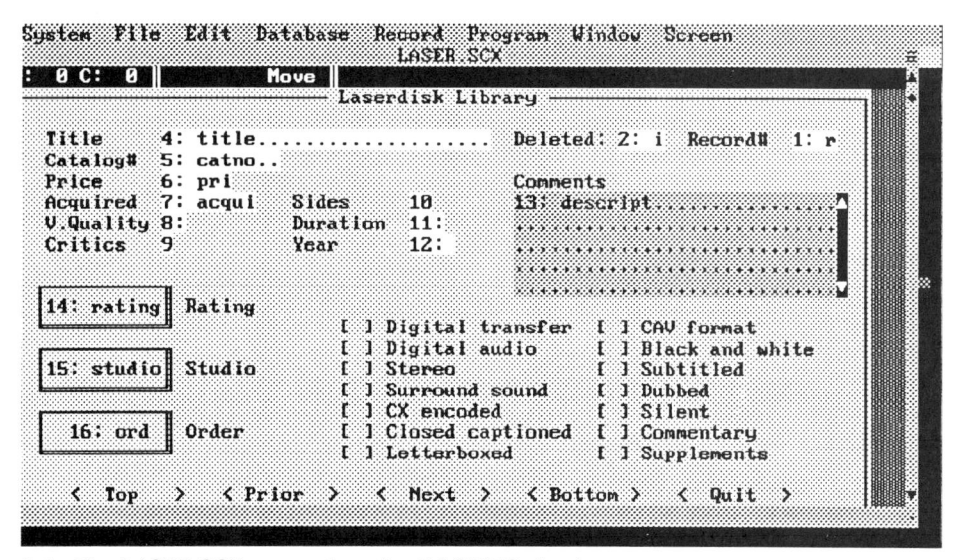

6-1 The LASER.SCX screen from the GOODIES directory.

As you move from field to field using the arrow or tab keys, the cursor appears in the current input field. In the case of screen controls (radio buttons and the like), the current object is highlighted. You can cause the current input field to change color as well with the READ COLOR *ColorPair* command.

Figure 6-2 shows how subsequent cursor movements highlight objects on the screen. Pressing Enter on a pop-up box causes the box to appear for item selection. A list pop-up doesn't show it's true nature until you get into the field and press Enter.

Listing 6-10 contains the code that vitiates this screen. I've changed a few lines to simplify discussion at this point.

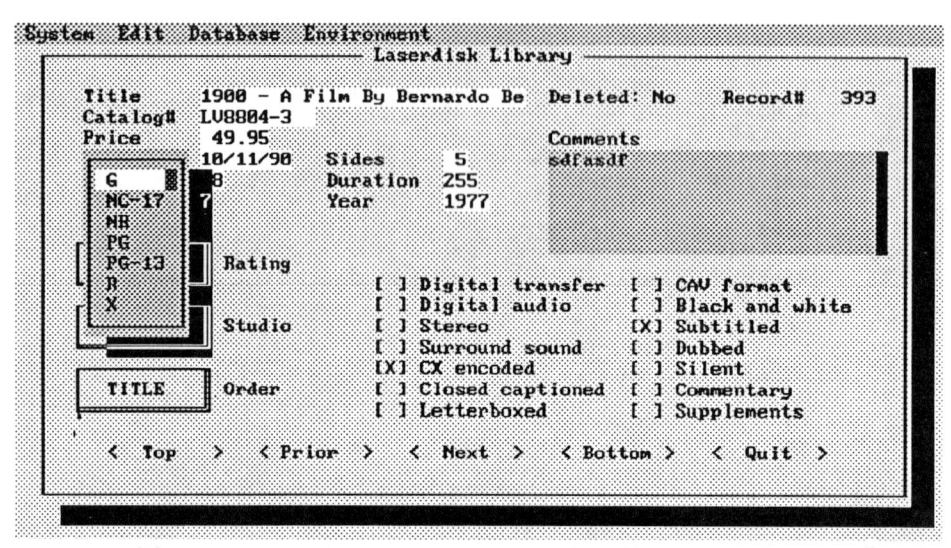

6-2 A List pop-up in action.

Listing 6-10

```
*
*
*       03/27/91              LASER.SPR              08:38:14
*
*
*
*     Author's Name
*
*     Copyright (c) 1991 Company Name
*     Address
*     City,      Zip
*
*     Description:
*     This program was automatically generated by GENSCRN.
*
*
```

```
#REGION 0
REGIONAL m.currarea, m.talkstat, m.compstat

IF SET("TALK") = "ON"
  SET TALK OFF
  m.talkstat = "ON"
ELSE
  m.talkstat = "OFF"
ENDIF
m.compstat = SET("COMPATIBLE")
SET COMPATIBLE OFF
```

```
DEFINE WINDOW laser ;
  FROM INT((SROW()-22)/2),INT((SCOL()-75)/2) ;
  TO INT((SROW()-22)/2)+21,INT((SCOL()-75)/2)+74 ;
  TITLE " Laserdisk Library " ;
  FLOAT ;
  CLOSE ;
  SHADOW ;
  MINIMIZE ;
  COLOR SCHEME 1
```

The REGION statement is used to tell FoxPro to hybridize the local variable names. If a conflict occurs, the suffix _____2 (or whatever current region number is active) is added to distinguish the variable names. The number of underscores is not always the same; it's determined by padding out to the end of the maximum permitted length for a variable name.

The statements in LISTING 6-11 save the current select area number, then either switch to the LASER file, if it already is open, or find and open it if it's not already in use. If it's not found on the FoxPro path, the LOCFILE dialog box appears, with your user-supplied prompt. This code is generated if you check the Open Files option on the main Screen dialog.

Listing 6-11

```
m.curarea = SELECT()

IF USED("laser")
   SELECT laser
ELSE
   SELECT 0
   USE (LOCFILE("laser.dbf","DBF","Where is laser?")) ORDER 0
ENDIF
```

The SETUP code is copied from the snippet that opens up if you check Setup on the main Screen dialog. It doesn't open up until you leave the screen, but you can see it getting itself ready in the background as soon as you check Setup.

In the past, my applications have maintained a master file of all validation fields. For example, if 12 different department codes existed, I'd have a DEPART.DBF with 12 records in it that I could use for validation, pop-ups, and user maintenance.

The Rushmore technology reads the index file so quickly and cleverly that LISTING 6-12, which was used to build an array of unique studio codes on the fly, takes about 1 second on a 450 record file. There are cases where a table file still is desirable, such as when you want to use codes with an occasional display of the meaning of each code. If you don't need descriptions, this command builds an array that supports the validation pop-up and does so without the need for table files. The code in LISTING 6-12 is the screen display code and the associated GETs. Note in particular the new @...SAY/GET statements.

Listing 6-12

```
#REGION 1
*
*    Initialize the arrays
*
regional studs, rats, st, rt, x
select     distinct studio;
      order by studio;
      from laser;
      into arra studs

select     distinct rating;
      order by rating;
      from laser;
      into arra rats

ord = 2
set order to title
go top
* push menu _MSYSMENU     && commented out for this example
* do laserm.mpr           &&     ""
*
*   ┌─────────────────────────────────────────────────────┐
*   │                                                     │
*   │               LASER Screen Layout                   │
*   │                                                     │
*   └─────────────────────────────────────────────────────┘
*
*

#REGION 1
ACTIVATE WINDOW laser NOSHOW
@ 1,3 SAY "Title"
@ 3,3 SAY "Price"
@ 9,15 SAY "Rating"
@ 4,3 SAY "Acquired"
@ 5,24 SAY "Duration"
@ 4,24 SAY "Sides"
@ 6,24 SAY "Year"
@ 3,43 SAY "Comments"
@ 2,3 SAY "Catalog#"
@ 5,3 SAY "V.Quality"
@ 6,3 SAY "Critics"
@ 15,15 SAY "Order"
@ 1,58 SAY "Record#"
@ 12,15 SAY "Studio"
@ 1,43 SAY "Deleted:"
@ 1,67 SAY recno() ;
    SIZE 1,4 ;
    PICTURE "9,999"
@ 1,52 SAY iif(DELETED(),'Yes','No ') ;
    SIZE 1,4
```

This is where the action gets thick. The assortment of GET statements in the listings that follow should be compared with the previous screen to keep your bearings. Notice particularly the GET statement in LISTING 6-13.

This is a radical departure from the way programmers are used to doing screen management. Instead of having the menu under the screen,

Listing 6-13

```
@ 18,5 GET action ;
   PICTURE "@*HN Top;Prior;Next;Bottom;Quit" ;
   SIZE 1,10,3 ;
   DEFAULT 0 ;
   VALID _pu30iihjz()
```

using prompts to let the user select choices, simply make the Next/Previous/Top/Bottom/I'm Done menu a single control. The entire screen is alive during what traditionally was a menu operation. The VALID function __pu30iihjz determines what to do next, based on the value for action selected by the user.

There still are many ways to write applications in FoxPro. This is an important new tool that will allow you to consider designs that weren't possible in the past. In a subsequent chapter, I'll look at the example in LISTING 6-14 in more detail.

Listing 6-14

```
@ 1,13 GET laser.title ;
   SIZE 1,28  ;
   DEFAULT " "
@ 2,13 GET laser.catno ;
   SIZE 1,10  ;
   DEFAULT " "
@ 3,13 GET laser.price ;
   SIZE 1,6  ;
   DEFAULT 0 ;
   PICTURE "999.99"
@ 4,13 GET laser.acquired ;
   SIZE 1,8  ;
   DEFAULT {  /  /  }
@ 5,13 GET laser.xquality ;
   SIZE 1,2  ;
   DEFAULT 0
@ 6,13 GET laser.critics ;
   SIZE 1,1  ;
   DEFAULT 0
@ 4,34 GET laser.sides ;
   SIZE 1,2  ;
   DEFAULT 0
@ 5,34 GET laser.duration ;
   SIZE 1,3  ;
   DEFAULT 0
@ 6,34 GET laser.year ;
   SIZE 1,4  ;
   DEFAULT 0
@ 4,43 EDIT laser.descript ;
   SIZE 5,29 ;
   DEFAULT " " ;
   SCROLL
```

Because I've already built an array of all rating codes and studios currently in the database, I can use them to produce the next two pop-ups (LISTING 6-15). Note the function code [^] in the PICTURE clause, preceded by the required @ sign.

Listing 6-15

```
@ 8,2 GET rating ;
   PICTURE "@^" ;
   FROM rats ;
   SIZE 3,12 ;
   DEFAULT 1

@ 11,2 GET studio ;
   PICTURE "@^" ;
   FROM studs ;
   SIZE 3,12 ;
   DEFAULT 1
```

The next pop-up (LISTING 6-16) is done using the PICTURE clause method, because the categories are fixed. The associated VALID clause redefines the active INDEX TAG according to the selection and repositions the record pointer. Figure 6-3 shows what the pop-up looks like.

Listing 6-16

```
@ 14,2 GET ord ;
   PICTURE "@^ Record#;Title;Catalog#;Year;Quality;Critics" ;
   SIZE 3,12 ;
   DEFAULT "Record#"         ;
   VALID _pu3Oiiiep()
```

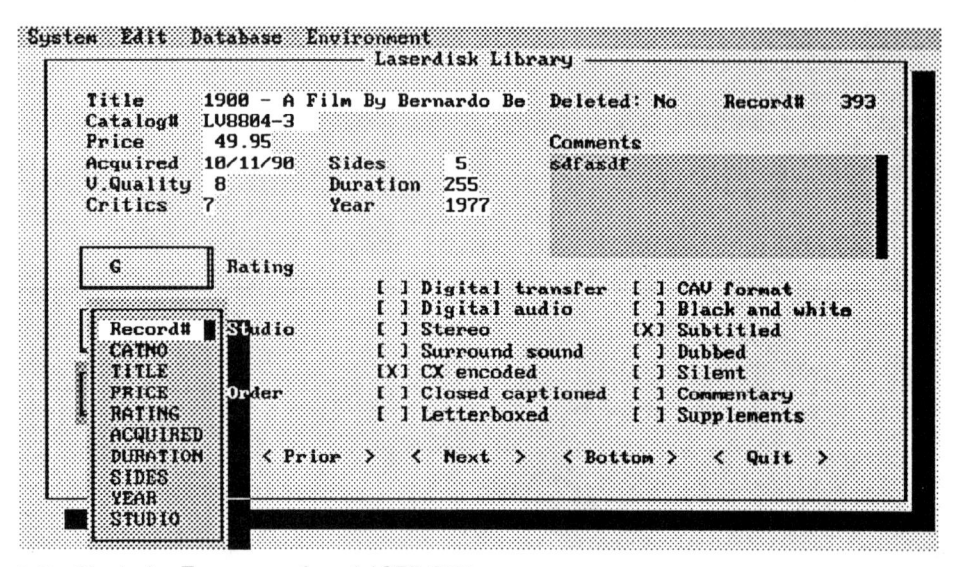

6-3 The Index Tag pop-up from LASER.SPR.

The next group of variables are all of the yes/no (logical) variety. You'll appreciate how easy these check boxes are compared to alternative techniques (LISTING 6-17). These check boxes appear in FIG. 6-4.

Listing 6-17

```
@ 10,28 GET laser.xdigital ;
    PICTURE "@*C Digital transfer" ;
    SIZE 1,20 ;
    DEFAULT 0
@ 11,28 GET laser.sdigital ;
    PICTURE "@*C Digital audio" ;
    SIZE 1,17 ;
    DEFAULT 0
@ 12,28 GET laser.stereo ;
    PICTURE "@*C Stereo" ;
    SIZE 1,10 ;
    DEFAULT 0
@ 13,28 GET laser.surround ;
    PICTURE "@*C Surround sound" ;
    SIZE 1,18 ;
    DEFAULT 0
@ 14,28 GET laser.cx ;
    PICTURE "@*C CX encoded" ;
    SIZE 1,14 ;
    DEFAULT 0
@ 15,28 GET laser.closecap ;
    PICTURE "@*C Closed captioned" ;
    SIZE 1,20 ;
    DEFAULT 0
@ 16,28 GET laser.letterbox ;
    PICTURE "@*C Letterboxed" ;
    SIZE 1,15 ;
    DEFAULT 0
@ 10,50 GET laser.cav ;
    PICTURE "@*C CAV format" ;
    SIZE 1,14 ;
    DEFAULT 0
@ 11,50 GET laser.blk_wht ;
    PICTURE "@*C Black and white" ;
    SIZE 1,19 ;
    DEFAULT 0
@ 12,50 GET laser.subtitled ;
    PICTURE "@*C Subtitled" ;
    SIZE 1,13 ;
    DEFAULT 0
@ 13,50 GET laser.dubbed ;
    PICTURE "@*C Dubbed" ;
    SIZE 1,10 ;
    DEFAULT 0
@ 14,50 GET laser.silent ;
    PICTURE "@*C Silent" ;
    SIZE 1,10 ;
    DEFAULT 0
@ 15,50 GET laser.commentary ;
    PICTURE "@*C Commentary" ;
    SIZE 1,14 ;
    DEFAULT 0
@ 16,50 GET laser.supplement ;
    PICTURE "@*C Supplements" ;
    SIZE 1,15 ;
    DEFAULT 0
```

6-4 Check boxes in LASER.SPR.

The fields are active except when the MENU has been selected. Pressing the Spacebar toggles these logical fields on and off.

Here's where the action starts. The READ CYCLE command loops through the fields, unless you use the Alt key plus an option letter hot key to invoke the system menu (LISTING 6-18).

Listing 6-18

```
ACTIVATE WINDOW laser
READ CYCLE ;
  SHOW _pu3oiij6x()
```

Instead of running this screen as the edit option of a menu, the Forward/Back/Top/Bottom options have been incorporated as valid clauses of a memory variable in an on-screen control. In chapter 11, I'll look more closely at this interesting new way of controlling applications.

Finally, the cleanup code closes files and returns settings to their pre-screen status. The first snippet comes from checking the Close Files selection on the main Screen dialog; the second is the user-supplied snippet in the CLEANUP code window (LISTING 6-19).

Listing 6-19

```
RELEASE WINDOW laser

#REGION 0
IF USED("laser")
  SELECT laser
  USE
ENDIF
SELECT (m.curarea)
```

138 The screen builder and @...SAY/GET

```
IF m.talkstat = "ON"
  SET TALK ON
ENDIF
IF m.compstat = "ON"
  SET COMPATIBLE ON
ENDIF
```

From the CLEANUP window snippet:

```
*
*
*                   ┌─────────────────────────────────────────────┐
*                   │              LASER Cleanup Code             │
*                   │                                             │
*                   └─────────────────────────────────────────────┘
*
*

#REGION 1
*pop menu _MSYSMENU        && commented out for this example
```

The CLEANUP code segment is also where you put all of the routines that you want to be able to find from calls in the main body of your screen. The reason is 'geographical'; this code is physically placed at the bottom of the generated code (LISTING 6-20). This is the code that's executed upon selection of the very first GET on the screen—the Next/Previous/etc. prompt.

Listing 6-20

```
procedure menuhit
do case
case prompt() = ``Find''
  set cursor off
  wait window ``Find executed''
  set cursor on
case prompt() = ``Sailor''
  set cursor off
  wait window ``Hello, Sailor!''
  set cursor on
endcase
```

The rest of the code that appears in LISTING 6-21 comes from the VALID snippets for various screen controls. In each case, while in the screen builder, if you click on the control (or tap the Spacebar a few times in rapid succession), a dialog will appear that offers several options. If you click on the VALID control, a window will open up for your code snippet. Type it in or give it the name of one of your library functions. If you don't have a library of functions, I'll bet that Tom Rettig or Alan Griver have some for sale. I might, too, come to think of it.

The SHOW GETS statement in LISTING 6-21 is very important for control snippets that change the record pointer. If you move to a new record, it won't show on the screen unless you SHOW GETS. The SHOW GETS clause also executes the READ SHOW *function-name* routine, so any additional displays that aren't GETs also can be displayed. Also, if you've skipped to another record, you might want to display the record number

Listing 6-21

```
*
*
*     ┌─────────────────────────────────────────────────────┐
*     │                                                     │
*     │   _PU30IIHJZ             action VALID               │
*     │                                                     │
*     │   Function Origin:                                  │
*     │                                                     │
*     │   From Screen:         LASER,    Record Number:  20 │
*     │   Variable:            action                       │
*     │   Called By:           VALID Clause                 │
*     │   Object Type:         Push Button                  │
*     │                                                     │
*     └─────────────────────────────────────────────────────┘
*
FUNCTION _pu30iihjz
#REGION 1
do case
case action = 1
  go top
case action = 2
  skip -1
  if bof()
    go top
  endif
case action = 3
  skip 1
  if eof()
    go bottom
  endif
case action = 4
  go bottom
case action = 5
  clear read
  pop menu _msysmenu         && Activate the menu!
endcase
show gets    && redisplay the data for the 'current' record...
* If we moved to another record, data will show as changed.

return 0


*
*
*     ┌─────────────────────────────────────────────────────┐
*     │                                                     │
*     │   _PU30IIIEP             ord VALID                  │
*     │                                                     │
*     │   Function Origin:                                  │
*     │                                                     │
*     │   From Screen:         LASER,    Record Number:  33 │
*     │   Variable:            ord                          │
*     │   Called By:           VALID Clause                 │
*     │   Object Type:         Popup                        │
*     │                                                     │
*     └─────────────────────────────────────────────────────┘
*
FUNCTION _pu30iiiep
#REGION 1
do case
case ord = 1
  set order to
case ord = 2
```

```
  set order to title
case ord = 3
  set order to catno
case ord = 4
  set order to year
case ord = 5
  set order to xquality
case ord = 6
  set order to critics
endcase
go top
show gets
```

on the screen. The record number is not a GET, so this is how you show it when it changes.

To get this code into the SHOW GETS routine, check SHOW on the main Screen dialog. A window opens up for you to type in whatever you want.

The main Screen dialog lets you check any or all of five boxes that will open up a snippet window for you to enter code:

- SHOW
- ACTIVATE
- DEACTIVATE
- VALID
- WHEN

Each of these code snippets executes at a specific point in the course of your program's execution, as discussed previously. Listing 6-22 contains the READ SHOW clause in LASER.SPR.

Listing 6-22

```
*
*
*      _PU30IIJ6X              Read Level Show
*
*      Function Origin:
*
*      From Screen:            LASER
*      Called By:              READ Statement
*
*
*
FUNCTION _pu30iij6x
PRIVATE currwind
  STORE WOUTPUT() TO currwind
  *
  * Show Code from screen: LASER
  *
  #REGION 1
  x = recno()
  IF SYS(2016) = "laser" OR SYS(2016) = "*"
    ACTIVATE WINDOW laser SAME
    @ 1,67 SAY recno() ;
```

Listing 6-22 Continued

```
        SIZE 1,4 ;
        PICTURE "9,999"
    @ 1,52 SAY iif(DELETED(),'Yes','No ') ;
        SIZE 1,4
ENDIF
IF NOT EMPTY(currwind)
    ACTIVATE WINDOW (currwind) SAME
ENDIF
RETURN .T.               && _pu3Oiij6x
```

The references to currwind are there in the event another screen is popped up over this one. The IF NOT EMPTY(currwind) will prevent lots of error messages until you get the hang of screens, because ACTIVATE WINDOW <empty variable> blows up big time.

Are code generators dead?

Code generators are not dead, absolutely not. Code generators like STAGE, UI2 (particularly, the SMART TEMPLATES from Management Factware in San Francisco), and GENIFER have data dictionaries that maintain the relationships among coordinated files transparently. I've got software packages with 80 data files and who knows how many index tags. Keeping everything straight is no small task. Also, these products enforce a particular design methodology, so that there's less design time—you just fill in the blanks and go. Many users never modify the templates that come with the products. Finally, in the off chance that you do something fabulous in FoxPro and a new customer wants the same thing in Clipper, you might wish you'd written in some format other than screen builder snippets. I personally would migrate to archaeology before I'd leave FoxPro, but everyone's different.

Summary

The new GET features in FoxPro 2.0 are a tantalizing peek into a world of innovative software design. The screen builder, although similar to traditional code generators, permits greater flexibility than anything programmers have ever had.

In a subsequent chapter, you'll see the screen builder used on a more complex example that illustrates additional techniques. I think you'll be convinced that there actually is little that you can't do with the screen builder.

7
Menus

Most FoxPro applications are run under the control of a menu system. Menu systems allow the user to choose from among available functions in a structured way that minimizes confusion and facilitates learning the system.

Menus are built using the DEFINE MENU and DEFINE POPUP commands. When activated, they enable trapping routines that know when the menu was exited and how. From there, trapping routines defined by the ON SELECTION POPUP *popupname* and ON SELECTION BAR *barname* commands do the real work.

Menus can be preceded by setup code that opens files, displays sign-on screens, and checks for necessary conditions—for example, availability of resources. Upon exiting the menu, you can include clean-up code that closes files and updates summary information.

Theory of menus

Menus are a good way for organizing what your program does. They also provide your users with a memory gym for navigating around the application. Sometimes, the mere ability to see what the program can do without actually doing it does a lot to avoid frustration.

FoxPro has automated that process, plus a lot more, in the menu builder. Not only will it write the code for you, it lets you do things you couldn't do before. You can:

- Assign hot keys to specific menu options
- Insert functions from the FoxPro system menu into your menus
- Use your menus as you would the system menu

New ways to use menus

In traditional X-base languages, Programmers designed their applications as event loops consisting of a DO WHILE...ENDDO control loop, with a menu at the top of the loop. They'd display the menu bar, make a selection, execute the selection, and redisplay the menu again.

The traditional menu consists of several steps:

1. SETUP code: open files, set colors, and check resources
2. MAIN MENU LOOP:

   Present Main Options Menu
   (Select an option or EXIT the main menu loop)
   IF SubMenu 1 selected,
       SubMenu 1 LOOP
           SubMenu 1 option 1
           SubMenu 1 option 2
           SubMenu 1 option 3
   ENDIF (SubMenu 1 was chosen)
   IF SubMenu 2 selected,
       SubMenu 2 LOOP
           SubMenu 2 option 1
           SubMenu 2 option 2
           SubMenu 2 option 3
   ENDIF (SubMenu 2 was chosen)

3. CLEANUP code: close files and reset switches

FoxPro 2.0 has a better idea. The menu is no longer what controls the application. It can be, but it isn't required. The menu bar appears at the top of the screen, waiting to be activated with an Alt–key combination (Alt plus the first letter of one of the menu bar choices). If hidden, the menu can be popped up using the F10 key—the same way you can pop up the FoxPro system menu—at any time. That's because your menu *is* the FoxPro system menu, temporarily appropriated for your application. When your program's finished, you SET SYSMENU TO DEFAULT to give it back to FoxPro. In the meantime, you can pop up your menu any time you want, make a selection, then let the menu lapse back into the ether until you pop it up again.

In the examples that accompany FoxPro 2.0, primarily the FOXPRO2\GOODIES\LASER subdirectory contents, the screen is generally in edit mode. That is, at any time, users can make changes to the data on the screen. If they want the menu, they press Alt plus the first letter of their choice. I have a fair number of applications that allow most users read-only access to screens, so I won't adhere strictly to the LASER example in my practice, but the message is the same. The menu doesn't control the program; it just helps out.

Traditional menus

Listing 7-1 shows a sample menu using the old event loop technique. Figure 7-1 shows what this menu looks like when you run it.

Listing 7-1

```
* Program-ID.....: SampMenu.PRG
* Purpose........: Demonstrates sample menu
CLEAR

DEFINE MENU MAIN BAR AT LINE 0
SET COLOR OF SCHEME 4 TO ,GR+/B,,,,N/W,W+/R
SET COLOR OF MESSAGE TO GR+/B       && line 24 of menu popups

DEFINE PAD one    OF MAIN PROMPT " \<Files "
DEFINE PAD two    OF MAIN PROMPT " \<Data "
DEFINE PAD three  OF MAIN PROMPT " \<Reports "
DEFINE PAD four   OF MAIN PROMPT " \<Other "
DEFINE PAD five   OF MAIN PROMPT " \<Quit "

DEFINE POPUP     Menu1 FROM 1, 1
DEFINE BAR 1 OF Menu1 PROMPT [ \<Open ]  MESSAGE [ Open files ]
DEFINE BAR 2 OF Menu1 PROMPT [ \<Find ]  MESSAGE [ Find files ]
DEFINE BAR 3 OF Menu1 PROMPT [ \<Close ] MESSAGE [ Close files ]

DEFINE POPUP     Menu2 FROM 8, 1
DEFINE BAR 1 OF Menu2 PROMPT [ \<List ]
DEFINE BAR 2 OF Menu2 PROMPT [ \<Delete ]
DEFINE BAR 3 OF Menu2 PROMPT [ \<Edit ]

DEFINE POPUP     Menu3 FROM 14, 1
DEFINE BAR 1 OF Menu3 PROMPT [ \<First ]
DEFINE BAR 2 OF Menu3 PROMPT [ \<Second ]
DEFINE BAR 3 OF Menu3 PROMPT [ \<Third ]

DEFINE POPUP     Menu4 FROM 22, 1    && Other
DEFINE BAR _MST_ASCII OF Menu4 PROMPT [ \<Ascii Chart ]
DEFINE BAR _MST_PUZZL OF Menu4 PROMPT [ \<Puzzle ]
DEFINE BAR _MST_DIARY OF Menu4 PROMPT [ \<Diary ]

ON PAD one   OF MAIN Activate POPUP Menu1
ON PAD two   OF MAIN Activate POPUP Menu2
ON PAD three OF MAIN Activate POPUP Menu3
ON PAD four  OF MAIN Activate POPUP Menu4

PadName = "one"

DO WHILE .T.

   ON SELECTION PAD one   OF MAIN DO Files   WITH MENU(), PAD()
   ON SELECTION PAD two   OF MAIN DO Data    WITH MENU(), PAD()
   ON SELECTION PAD three OF MAIN DO Reports WITH MENU(), PAD()
   ON SELECTION PAD four  OF MAIN DO Other   WITH MENU(), PAD()
   ON SELECTION PAD five  OF MAIN CANCEL   && QUIT

   ACTIVATE MENU MAIN PAD &PadName
ENDDO
```

Listing 7-1   Continued

```
PROCEDURE Files
PARAMETERS menuname,pad,bar
PadName = [one]
DO CASE
  CASE
ENDCASE

PROCEDURE Data
PARAMETERS menuname,pad
PadName = [two]

PROCEDURE Reports
PARAMETERS menuname,pad
PadName = [three]

PROCEDURE Other
PARAMETERS menuname,pad
PadName = [four]
```

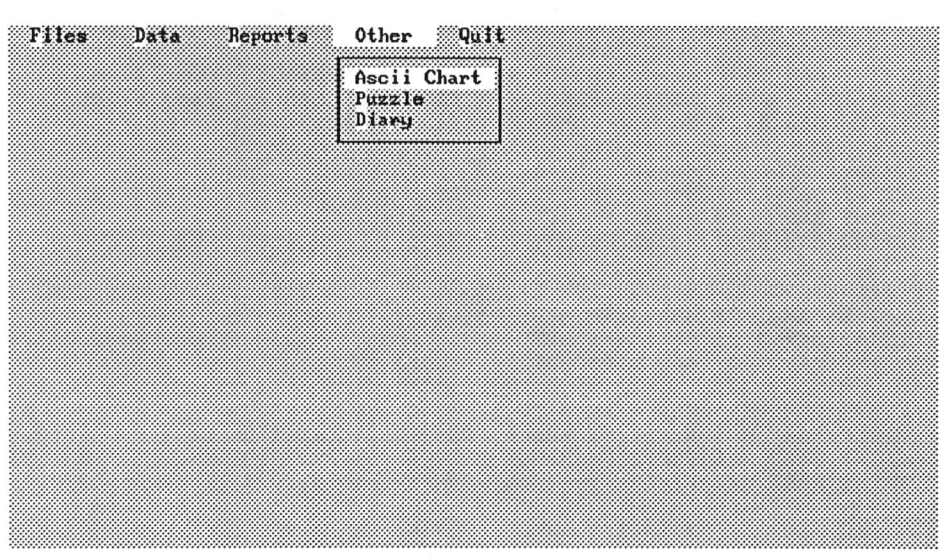

7-1   Sample menu screen (SAMPMENU.PRG).

Another approach to menus

Fox Software recommends that you instead write your application as follows:

```
PUSH _MSYSMENU          && save the system menu
DO MYMENU.MPR           && define the new menu
SET SYSMENU AUTOMATIC
DO screen program
```

and upon CLEAR READ or exit from application:

```
SET SYSMENU TO DEFAULT
```

As you can see, the menu doesn't loop; it just sits there like ugly on Aggies, waiting to be activated with an Alt-key combination.

What can you do with the menu once you pop it up? Whatever you want. If you change to another SELECT area, you'll need to get back where you were before you SELECTED, so you need to plan to handle that little problem. In the age of windows, another little concern arises: where were you, window-wise?

When you generate an APP file from the screen builder, you'll notice that the code in LISTING 7-2 generally is present at the top of the program. The PUSH MENU command saves the system menu that was defined before coming into this screen. This might have been the standard FoxPro menu or might have been the previous application's menu. Either way, it's pushed on the stack and can be retrieved later.

The variable m.currarea contains the number of the SELECT area that was open at the time this program started. Why does it need that? Because you could have picked this program from a menu, you might have been in some other select area. This remembers where you were, so that you can go back when you're done. The code in LISTING 7-2 says *if the file you need isn't open already, open it; otherwise, select the area you need.*

Listing 7-2

```
PUSH MENU _MSYSMENU
DO LASER.MPR

m.currarea = SELECT()

IF USED("laser")
  SELECT laser
  SET ORDER TO 0
ELSE
  SELECT 0
  USE (LOCFILE("dbfs\laser.dbf","DBF","Where is laser?"));
  AGAIN ALIAS laser ;
  ORDER 0
ENDIF


#REGION 1
IF WVISIBLE("_pxn1c7i55")
  ACTIVATE WINDOW _pxn1c7i55 SAME
ELSE
  ACTIVATE WINDOW _pxn1c7i55 NOSHOW
ENDIF
```

Finally, if the window you need already exists, just open it; otherwise, activate it with the NOSHOW option, which allows you to draw the window, then pop it up with the following:

```
IF NOT WVISIBLE("_pxn1c7i55")
  ACTIVATE WINDOW _pxn1c7i55
ENDIF
```

The @...SAY/GET statements that define the screen follow, then the READ activates the screen. Notice the SHOW clause:

```
READ CYCLE;
  SHOW _pxn1c7ky1()
```

After your user leaves the screen, presumably by selecting a control variable with a TERMINATING option, you can:

```
RELEASE WINDOW _pxn1c7i55
```

The file can be closed if you want to, as follows:

```
IF USED("laser")
  SELECT laser
  USE
ENDIF
```

Finally, don't forget to go back where you came from:

```
SELECT (m.currarea)
```

A final bit of menu-related magic occurs here. FoxPro recommends that you PUSH MENU _MSYSMENU before defining a new menu. Then, at the end of each application, you can include this code:

```
#REGION 1
POP MENU _MSYSMENU
```

This restores the menu that was in effect before you entered this screen. The SHOW function, aptly named _pxn1c7ky1, does the following:

```
FUNCTION _pxn1c7ky1      && Read Level Show

PRIVATE currwind
STORE WOUTPUT() TO currwind

#REGION 1

ord = IIF(LEN(ORDER())=0,"Record#",ORDER())

IF SYS(2016) = "_PXN1C7I55" OR SYS(2016) = "*"
  ACTIVATE WINDOW _pxn1c7i55 SAME
  @ 1,65 SAY recno() ;
    SIZE 1,4 ;
    PICTURE "9,999"
  @ 1,51 SAY iif(DELETED(),'Yes','No ') ;
    SIZE 1,4
ENDIF

IF NOT EMPTY(currwind)
  ACTIVATE WINDOW (currwind) SAME
ENDIF
```

The STORE WOUTPUT() TO m.currwind saves the window that was open before you opened the window for this application. Afterwards, the previous window (if there was one) is restored.

You saved the previous menu, select area, and output window. After the program ran, you restored the previous window, selected the previous select area, and restored the previous menu (POP __MSYSMENU). I think I see a pattern here.

So, in the new world, you need to preserve the current window, database, and select area, then restore them when you're done. Will that keep you out of trouble? Most of the time, it will. If you do a lookup in the file that you're already in in another screen, you'll lose your place, but there's even something to deal with that: the USE AGAIN command, which lets you go into a file that's already open without losing your place. These Fox Software guys think of everything.

A sample menu builder session

The following is a small sample menu builder session. Once you've built a library of procedures, code snippets, and techniques, you can write much of your applications from within this utility.

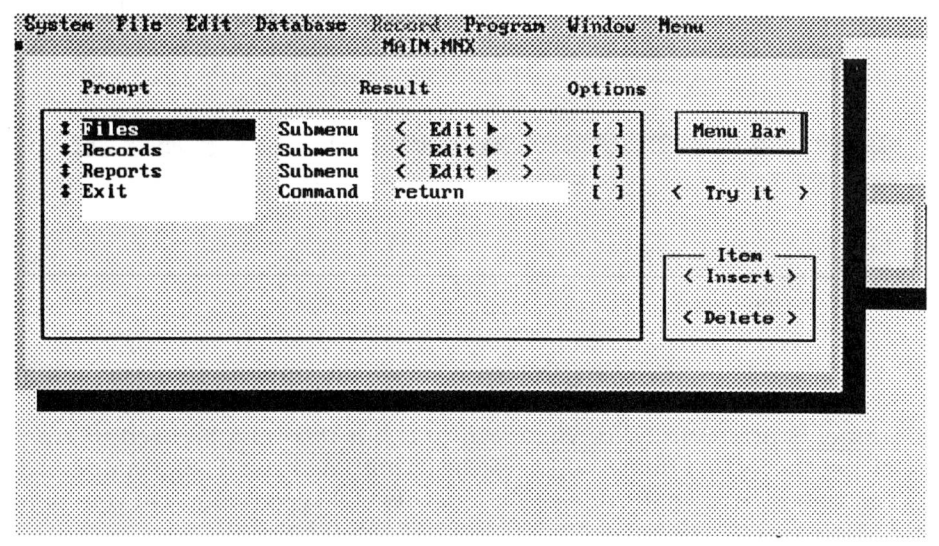

7-2 The Menu Bar level of the menu builder.

Figure 7-2 shows a first-level menu. FoxPro lets you select one of four options when a main menu bar is selected:

- Command—you can do a command file or a FoxPro Command.
- SubMenu—FoxPro builds and saves your next level pulldown menu, which also can have any of the four choices named here attached to each selection.

- Bar Number—you can select a predefined menu pop-up or one of the FoxPro system menu pop-up names, which are listed in TABLE 7-1 later in this chapter.
- Procedure—You can write a code snippet to be executed in conjunction with this selection. FoxPro will generate a funny-looking function name for you, so don't enter a PROCEDURE statement.

In FIG. 7-3, I've gone down a level and begun to define the Reports Sub-Menu. Item 3 is going to have a hot key that users can press to run the third report without having to arrow down to this menu option and press Enter.

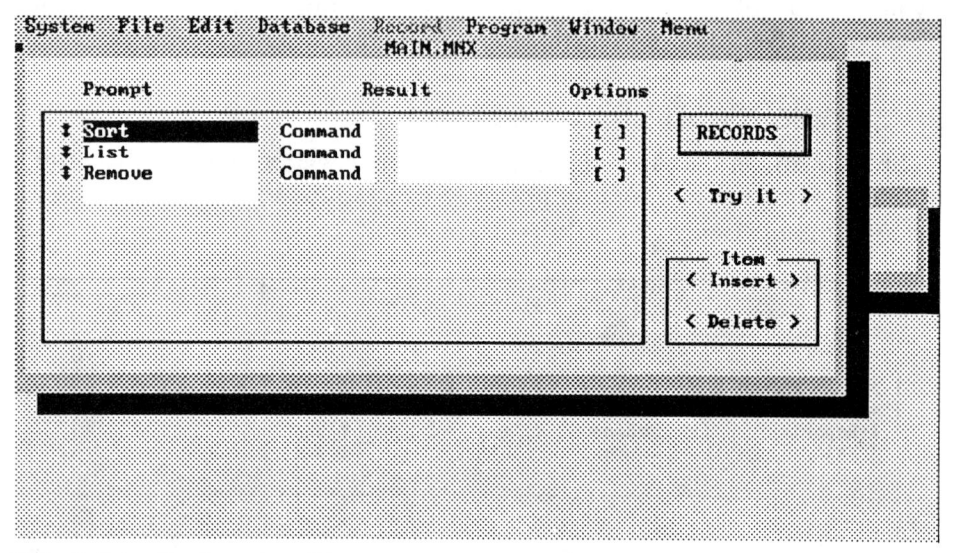

7-3 Defining the Reports pulldown.

In FIG. 7-4, I've selected Options. One of the options that you might make a habit of is entering a comment that explains what the item is. Comments are entirely for your own use, but they can be used to enter user's remarks that might otherwise be forgotten. If you design your prototypes with your user sitting beside you, this will keep them, and you, honest. Also, you can define a hot key for this menu option.

Figure 7-5 looks a lot like the Define Macro dialog. That actually is what it's doing. This is where you assign hot keys to individual menu options.

Once you return to the menu builder main screen, you can press Alt-M to pull down the Menu menu. One of the options, General Options, is of particular interest. This is where you define setup and cleanup code, among other things. It's shown in FIG. 7-6.

If you toggle either of these two options on, a subsequent dialog window will let you type in setup code of any type. One of the common uses of

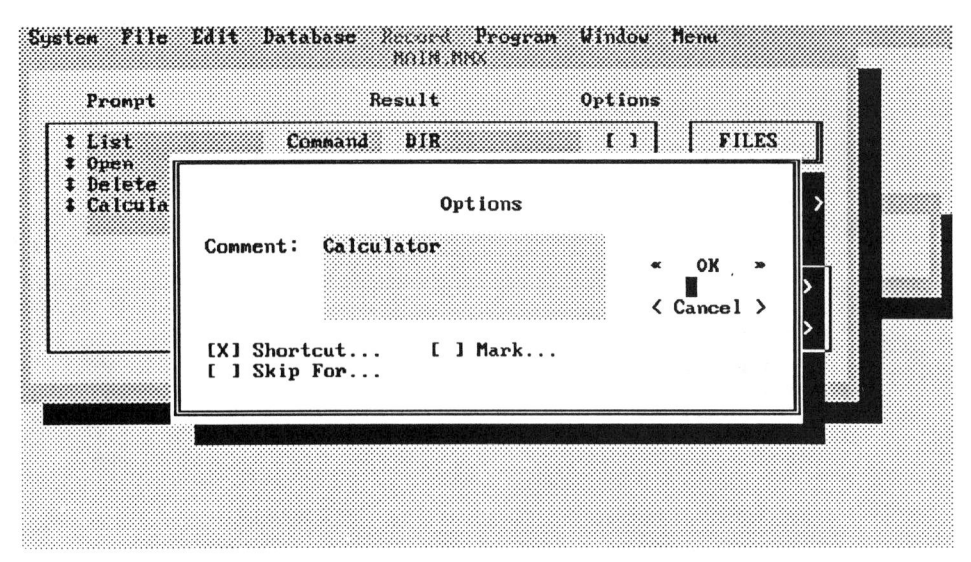

7-4 The Options dialog of menu item definition.

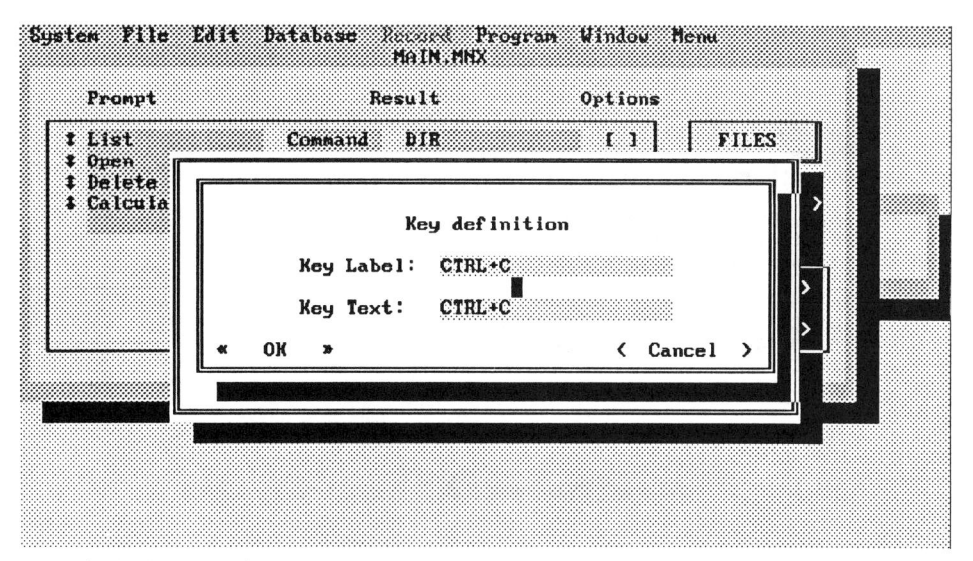

7-5 Assigning a hot key to a menu item.

setup code is to open and relate files, while cleanup code closes files and indexes. Figure 7-7 demonstrates the process of entering setup code.

Generating the code

Once your menu looks about right, use Alt–P to pull down the Program menu, then select Generate. FoxPro will generate source code for your

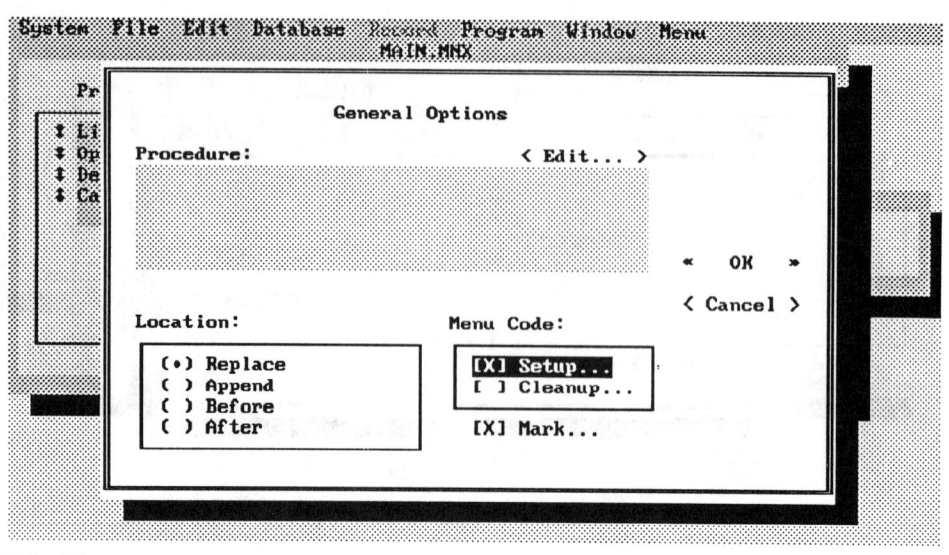

7-6 The menu builder General Options dialog.

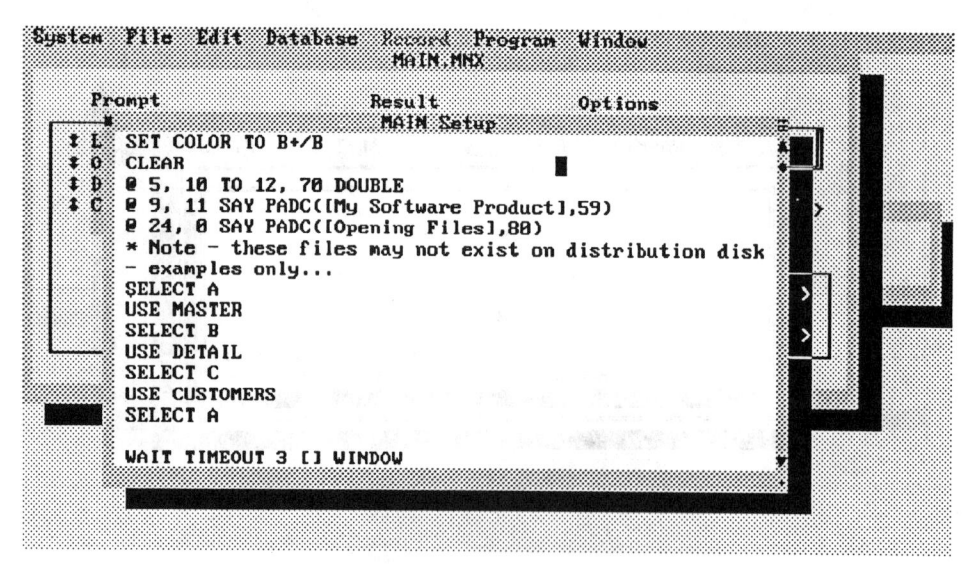

7-7 Entering setup and cleanup code for a menu.

menu, creating a file with an extension of .MPR (for *menu program*). The screen shown in FIG. 7-8 shows the process in which a menu program is created. You can use the command DO MAIN.MPR to run the program.

It might take a fair amount of practice to get to the point where you're better at this than you are at writing the code directly. Once you can navigate without thinking about it, you should be producing applications about twice as fast as you ever did without this tool.

However, that doesn't give you the full flavor of this feature. The menu

7-8 Generating the .MPR menu program.

builder allows you to quickly and easily change the way an application looks and feels. It lets your user see what his/her ideas would look like. It makes changing an application that's been written already relatively easy. That's the biggest pain in the neck in my practice and probably in yours as well.

Using parts of the FoxPro system menu

You can use options from FoxPro's system menu in your own menu pop-ups. The pads on the system menu bar, system menu pop-up, and each option in the system menu pop-ups have unique names, which can be used to change the FoxPro interface and create menu pop-ups.

Table 7-1 provides the names of system menu items. You also can use the SYS(2013) to display a listing of system menu names.

Table 7-1 System menu pads and names.

The system menu bar name is __MSYSMENU.

System menu pads and their names:

System	__MSM__SYSTM
File	__MSM__FILE
Edit	__MSM__EDIT
Database	__MSM__DATA
Record	__MSM__RECRD
Program	__MSM__PROG
Window	__MSM__WINDO

Table 7-1 Contiunued.

System menu pop-up and its options:

System pop-up	_MSYSTEM
About FoxPro...	_MST_ABOUT
Help...	_MST_HELP
Macros...	_MST_MACRO
1st Separator	_MST_SP100
Filer	_MST_FILER
Calculator	_MST_CALCU
Calendar/Diary	_MST_DIARY
Special Characters	_MST_SPECL
ASCII Chart	_MST_ASCII
Capture	_MST_CAPTR
Puzzle	_MST_PUZZL

File menu pop-up and its options:

File pop-up	_MFILE
New...	_MFI_NEW
Open...	_MFI_OPEN
Close	_MFI_CLOSE
Close All	_MFI_CLALL
1st Separator	_MFI_SP100
Save	_MFI_SAVE
Save as...	_MFI_SAVAS
Revert	_MFI_REVRT
2nd Separator	_MFI_SP200
Printer Setup...	_MFI_SETUP
Print...	_MFI_PRINT
3rd Separator	_MFI_SP300
Quit	_MFI_QUIT

Edit menu pop-up and its options:

Edit pop-up	_MEDIT
Undo	_MED_UNDO
Redo	_MED_REDO
1st Separator	_MED_SP100
Cut	_MED_CUT
Copy	_MED_COPY
Paste	_MED_PASTE
Clear	_MED_CLEAR
2nd Separator	_MED_SP200
Select All	_MED_SLCTA
3rd Separator	_MED_SP300
Goto Line...	_MED_GOTO
Find...	_MED_FIND
Find Again	_MED_FINDA
Replace and Find Again	_MED_REPL
Replace All	_MED_REPLA
4th Separator	_MED_SP400
Preferences...	_MED_PREF

Database menu pop-up and its options:

Database pop-up	_MDATA
Setup...	_MDA_SETUP
Browse	_MDA_BROW
1st Separator	_MDA_SP100
Append From...	_MDA_APPND
Copy To...	_MDA_COPY
Sort...	_MDA_SORT
Total...	_MDA_TOTAL
2nd Separator	_MDA_SP200
Average...	_MDA_AVG
Count...	_MDA_COUNT
Sum...	_MDA_SUM
Calculate...	_MDA_CALC
Report...	_MDA_REPRT
Label...	_MDA_LABEL
3rd Separator	_MDA_SP300
Pack	_MDA_PACK
Reindex	_MDA_RINDX

Record menu pop-up and its options:

Record pop-up	_MRECORD
Append	_MRC_APPND
Change	_MRC_CHNGE
1st Separator	_MRC_SP100
Goto...	_MRC_GOTO
Locate...	_MRC_LOCAT
Continue	_MRC_CONT
Seek...	_MRC_SEEK
2nd Separator	_MRC_SP200
Replace...	_MRC_REPL
Delete...	_MRC_DELET
Recall...	_MRC_RECAL

Program menu pop-up and its options:

Program pop-up	_MPROG
Do...	_MPR_DO
1st Separator	_MPR_SP100
Cancel	_MPR_CANCL
Resume	_MPR_RESUM
2nd Separator	_MPR_SP200
Compile...	_MPR_COMPL
Generate...	_MPR_GENER
FoxDoc	_MPR_DOCUM
FoxGraph...	_MPR_GRAPH

Window menu pop-up and its options:

Window pop-up	_MWINDOW
Hide	_MWI_HIDE
Hide All	_MWI_HIDEA
Show All	_MWI_SHOWA

Table 7-1 Contiunued.

Clear	_MWI_CLEAR
1st Separator	_MWI_SP100
Move	_MWI_MOVE
Size	_MWI_SIZE
Zoom	_MWI_ZOOM
Cycle	_MWI_ROTAT
Color...	_MWI_COLOR
2nd Separator	_MWI_SP200
Command	_MWI_CMD
Debug	_MWI_DEBUG
Trace	_MWI_TRACE
View	_MWI_VIEW

You can add, change, or delete anything in the system menu bar and the system menu pop-ups. You can delete items from or create and place items in the system menu bar and system menu pop-ups.

Using the two special names, _MFIRST and _MLAST, you can refer to the first and last items in a menu bar or menu pop-up. _MFIRST and _MLAST can be used in the BEFORE and AFTER clauses of the DEFINE PAD and DEFINE POPUP commands as well.

The set of commands in LISTING 7-3 places an exclamation point next to each pad in the system menu bar except for the File pad, which is marked with an asterisk.

Listing 7-3

```
* Examples:
DEFINE PAD beforesys OF _MSYSMENU BEFORE _MFIRST PROMPT "\<Me first!"
SET MARK OF MENU _MSYSMENU TO "!"
SET MARK OF MENU _MSYSMENU TO .T.
SET MARK OF PAD  _MSM_EDIT OF _MSYSMENU TO "*"
SET MARK OF PAD  _MSM_EDIT OF _MSYSMENU TO .T.
```

To remove pads from the system menu bar, use the following commands:

    RELEASE PAD _MSM_SYSTM OF _MSYSMENU
    RELEASE PAD _MSM_WINDO OF _MSYSMENU

These commands remove the System and Window pads from the system menu bar respectively.

To restore all pads to the system menu bar, use the following command:

    SET SYSMENU TO DEFAULT

To place a selected subset of pads in the system menu bar, use this command:

    SET SYSMENU TO _MSYSTEM, _MFILE, _MWINDOW

The following program example (LISTING 7-4), named SYSTIME.PRG, places a Time & Date pad in the system menu bar. The clock, date, and day of the week can be toggled on and off from within the time pop-up. Listing 7-4 is a typical example of a menu system except that the menu pad is placed in the system menu bar. Note the use of the SET MARK command and MRKBAR( ) function to place or remove a check mark character to the left of each option and to determine if an option has a check mark.

Listing 7-4

```
SET PROCEDURE TO SYSTIME      && Set procedure to itself
SET TALK OFF

DEFINE PAD time OF _MSYSMENU PROMPT "\<Time & Date" ;
    AFTER _MSM_SYSTM KEY ALT+T

DEFINE POPUP timepop MARGIN && Menu popup for System menu pad

DEFINE BAR 1 OF timepop PROMPT "\<Clock "    KEY SHIFT+F2, "8F2"
DEFINE BAR 2 OF timepop PROMPT "\<Date "     KEY SHIFT+F3, "8F3"
DEFINE BAR 3 OF timepop PROMPT "Da\<y "      KEY SHIFT+F4, "8F4"
DEFINE BAR 4 OF timepop PROMPT "\-"                   && Draw a separator
DEFINE BAR 5 OF timepop PROMPT "\<Show All " KEY SHIFT+F5, "8F5"
DEFINE BAR 6 OF timepop PROMPT "Clear \<All " KEY SHIFT+F6, "8F6"

IF SET("CLOCK") = "ON"
  SET MARK OF BAR 1 OF timepop TO .T.
ELSE
  SET MARK OF BAR 1 OF timepop TO .F.
ENDIF

ON PAD time OF _MSYSMENU ACTIVATE POPUP timepop

ON SELECTION POPUP timepop DO toggle WITH BAR()

PROCEDURE toggle
PARAMETER barnumber

DO CASE      -- CASE for each option

  CASE barnumber = 1

    *** Set clock on or off, toggle mark character ***

    SET MARK OF BAR 1 OF timepop TO NOT MRKBAR("timepop",1)
    IF MRKBAR("timepop", 1) = .T.
      SET CLOCK ON
    ELSE
      SET CLOCK OFF
    ENDIF

  CASE barnumber = 2

    *** Show or clear date, toggle mark character ***

    SET MARK OF BAR 2 OF timepop TO NOT MRKBAR("timepop",2)
    IF MRKBAR("timepop", 2) = .T.
      STORE SCHEME(1,7) TO clockcolor
      @ 1,69 SAY DATE() COLOR (clockcolor)
```

Listing 7-4 Continued

```
      ELSE
         @ 1,68 CLEAR TO 1,79
      ENDIF
   CASE barnumber = 3

      *** Show or clear day, toggle mark character ***

      SET MARK OF BAR 3 OF timepop TO NOT MRKBAR("timepop",3)
      IF MRKBAR("timepop", 3) = .T.
         STORE SCHEME(1,7) TO clockcolor
         @ 2,69 SAY CDOW(DATE()) COLOR (clockcolor)
      ELSE
         @ 2,69 CLEAR TO 2,79
      ENDIF

   CASE barnumber = 5

      *** Set all marks to .T., turn on clock, show date and day ***

      STORE SCHEME(1,7) TO clockcolor
      SET MARK OF BAR 1 OF timepop TO .T.
      SET MARK OF BAR 2 OF timepop TO .T.
      SET MARK OF BAR 3 OF timepop TO .T.
      SET CLOCK ON
      @ 1,69 SAY DATE() COLOR (clockcolor)
      @ 2,69 SAY CDOW(DATE()) COLOR (clockcolor)

   CASE barnumber = 6

      *** Set all marks to .F., turn off clock, clear date and day ***

      SET MARK OF BAR 1 OF timepop TO .F.
      SET MARK OF BAR 2 OF timepop TO .F.
      SET MARK OF BAR 3 OF timepop TO .F.
      SET CLOCK OFF
      @ 1,69 CLEAR TO 2,79

   ENDCASE
RETURN
```

Options appearing on system menu pop-ups also can be created or deleted. Listing 7-5 is a program example named MYAPPLIC.PRG, which demonstrates the addition of an option on the system pop-up.

Listing 7-5

```
SET PROCEDURE TO MYAPPLIC.PRG          && Set procedure to itself
DEFINE BAR 1 OF _MSYSTEM PROMPT "A\<bout My Application..." ;
   AFTER _MST_ABOUT
ON SELECTION BAR 1 OF _MSYSTEM DO myabout

PROCEDURE myabout

DEFINE WINDOW mywind FROM 6,15 TO 16,64 ;
   DOUBLE SHADOW COLOR SCHEME 5
ACTIVATE WINDOW mywind
@1,17 SAY "My Application"
```

```
@3,18 SAY "Version 1.0"
@5,14 SAY "Serial Number 123456"
@7,12 SAY "Press any key to continue"
=INKEY(8, "HM")       && Wait 8 secs or for a key press or a mouse click
DEACTIVATE WINDOW mywind
RETURN
```

The following command will remove the About My Application option from the system menu pop-up:

RELEASE BAR 1 OF _msystem

The default options of system pop-ups can be removed in a similar manner:

RELEASE BAR _MED_UNDO OF _MEDIT

This command removes the Undo option from the Edit pop-up.

Summary

The menu builder is a powerful application design tool. You can modify the system menu to add many of the built-in FoxPro features to your applications merely by including their menu pad names. In addition, the menu builder helps you design and manage the flow of your application with relatively little effort. Finally, using redefinition of the system menu allows you to incorporate the power of event-driven programming into your software.

8
More on the screen builder

FoxPro 2.0 is a backward-compatible language; everything you wrote in FoxPro 1.02 still will run. Notwithstanding that fact, you might want to start all over again after you read this chapter.

Before FoxPro 2.0, screen design hadn't changed much since the ability to address specific row and column positions on the screen came along. Programmers drew boxes, lined things up as best they could, and tried to balance the screen's various parts.

Screen design programs, or application generators with screen designers included, have helped programmers do the work of designing screens. UI2, Genifer, ViewGen/FoxView, Stage, and Scrimage are among the better-known of these products. Unlike some types of tools, which might or might not be worth the money depending on how you use them, every single one of these tools will pay for itself, literally, the first day you use it. They generally work with the way you write code.

Now for something completely different. FoxPro's screen designer not only generates code; it is meant to be the only place you design your screens. You never touch the generated code. Not that you can't; the screen builder produces a file with an extension of .SPR, which you can edit with your favorite program editor. However, the code that the screen builder generates can do anything you would want to do with edited code, and more.

A simple screen

I recently finished a bookstore software package called Anthology. The screens and menus were designed by the owner, Pei-shan Van Zoeren (a lovely Chinese-Dutch name) under the dBASE III/IV paradigm. It looked pretty nice. Just as we finished up the product, I got FoxPro 2.0. It got me thinking. How long would it take to do one of our screens in FoxPro 2.0?

I decided to start with the Book Inventory screen, the heart of a bookstore management program. The basic file structure of a book inventory starts with the fields shown in TABLE 8-1.

Table 8-1 File structure for BOOKS.DBF.

Field	Field Name	Type	Width	Dec	Index
1	ISBN	Character	10		Asc
2	TITLE	Character	60		Asc
3	AUTHOR	Character	40		Asc
4	PUBLISHER	Character	8		Asc
5	VENDOR	Character	8		Asc
6	CATEGORY	Character	10		Asc
7	TYPE	Character	10		Asc
8	COVERPRICE	Numeric	7	2	
9	RETAILPRIC	Numeric	7	2	
10	DISCOUNT	Numeric	5	2	
11	DATERECVD	Date	8		
12	SOLDTODATE	Numeric	4		
13	ONHAND	Numeric	4		
14	ONORDER	Numeric	4		
15	STATUS	Character	8		
16	ORDERDATE	Date	8		
** Total **			202		

The TAG fields for the structural CDX file were created by typing, for example:

INDEX ON UPPER(TITLE) TAG TITLE

I always use uppercase indexes so that I can match on whatever the user types in a search-for-what field, which is converted to uppercase upon input. I next typed:

USE BOOKS

to attach the file, then typed the command:

CREATE SCREEN BOOKS

I got a blank screen. However, the Alt–C menu had a QuickScreen option at the bottom, so I selected it. The dialog that followed had a memory variables option, as shown in FIG. 8-1.

Using the QuickScreen (Alt–S, Q) command, I built a row-major screen, then rearranged the prompts and fields. The results are shown in FIG. 8-2, which is a particularly handsome screen. I think you'll agree.

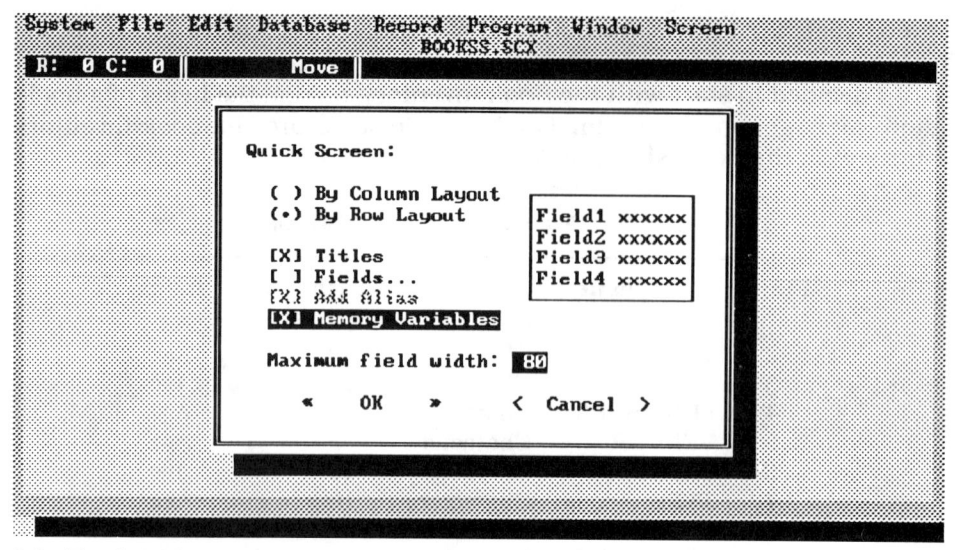

8-1 The QuickScreen dialog in screen builder.

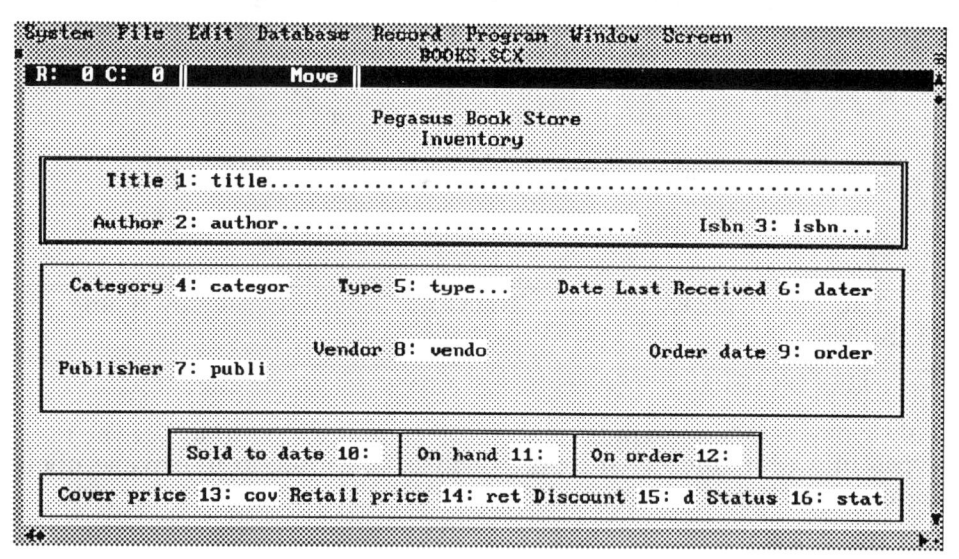

8-2 A screen design within the screen builder.

Rearranging fields

In the process of defining fields, I moved things around and got them out of order. The first time I generated and ran the program, the cursor moved from field to field in what appeared to be completely random order. Actually, it was the order of the fields in the database, but it takes only a few of these guys out of order to get you dizzy. So I needed to get my GETs in order.

It turns out that you can use Alt–Edit/Ctrl–A to SELECT ALL FIELDS, then Alt–C, R to rearrange fields. That renumbers them to conform to your new screen display. If the left-to-right, top-to-bottom arrangement that results isn't right, use your mouse to click on the fields in the order in which you want READ to process them, then select Alt–C, Reorder.

How screens are stored

If you enter the command:

```
USE BOOKS.SCX
LIST OFF
```

part of what follows will look like TABLE 8-2. So your screen is a database, with fields to hold the information that the screen builder needs to do its magic. Will wonders never cease?

Table 8-2 Partial contents of BOOKS.SCX.

Rec #	VPOS	HPOS	NAME	EXPR
1	0	0		
2	0	0	BOOKS.DBF	
3	6	58		"Isbn"
4	4	7		"Title"
5	6	6		"Author"
6	12	3		"Publisher"
7	12	25		"Vendor"
8	9	4		"Category"
9	9	27		"Type"
10	19	44		"Discount"
11	19	59		"Status"
12	19	3		"Cover price"
13	19	23		"Retail price"
14	17	14		"Sold to date"
15	17	34		"On hand"
16	17	49		"On order"
17	12	54		"Order date"
18	3	1		
19	10	1		" "
20	18	1		
21	9	46		"Date Last Received"
22	17	32		"│"
23	17	47		"│"
24	18	47		"┴"
25	18	32		"┴"
26	18	12		"┴"
27	17	12		"│"
28	16	12		"┌"
29	16	63		"┐"
30	17	63		"│"
31	18	63		"┘"

A simple screen 163

Table 8-2 Continued.

Rec #	VPOS	HPOS	NAME	EXPR
32	16	13		
33	16	32		"〒"
34	16	47		"〒"
35	1	30		"Pegasus Book Store"
36	2	34		"Inventory"
37	4	13	m.title	
38	6	13	m.author	
39	6	63	m.isbn	
40	9	13	m.category	
41	9	32	m.type	
42	9	65	m.daterecvd	
43	12	13	m.publisher	
44	12	32	m.vendor	
45	12	65	m.orderdate	
46	17	27	m.soldtodate	
47	17	42	m.onhand	
48	17	58	m.onorder	
49	19	15	m.coverprice	
50	19	36	m.retailpric	
51	19	53	m.discount	
52	19	66	m.status	
53	8	1		

Adding a menu

I also defined a menu, which appears in FIG. 8-3. The menu definition is a traditional menu bar. The Order and Find menu options needed some custom code, which I entered after selecting Procedure as the action to take when those two menu options were selected. These can be seen in FIGS. 8-4 and 8-5.

So far I've got about 20 minutes sunk into this screen. Now, I pressed the Alt–P, N and holy cow! What I got is shown in FIG. 8-6. The Edit screen uses the READ...COLOR N/W,W+/R command to highlight the current input field. The pop-ups took one line of typing each (FIG. 8-7).

I have a confirmed dialog that precludes inadvertent deletes. Also, because I defined this data file with seven index tags, all I have to do to change indexes is select the proper tag from a pop-up and the find command knows what to ask for.

How it works

This program is started by the command DO BOOKS.SPR. The generated screen program runs the menu program BOOKS.MPR, which sets up _MSYSMENU with my menu. I can pull down my menu at any time, because the actions to be taken are commands within the menu program.

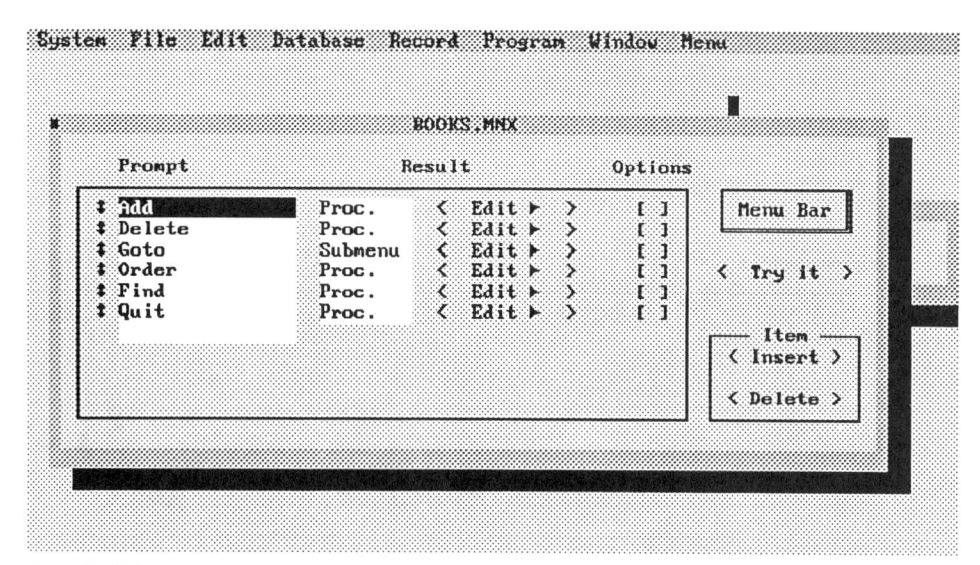

8-3 Defining a menu.

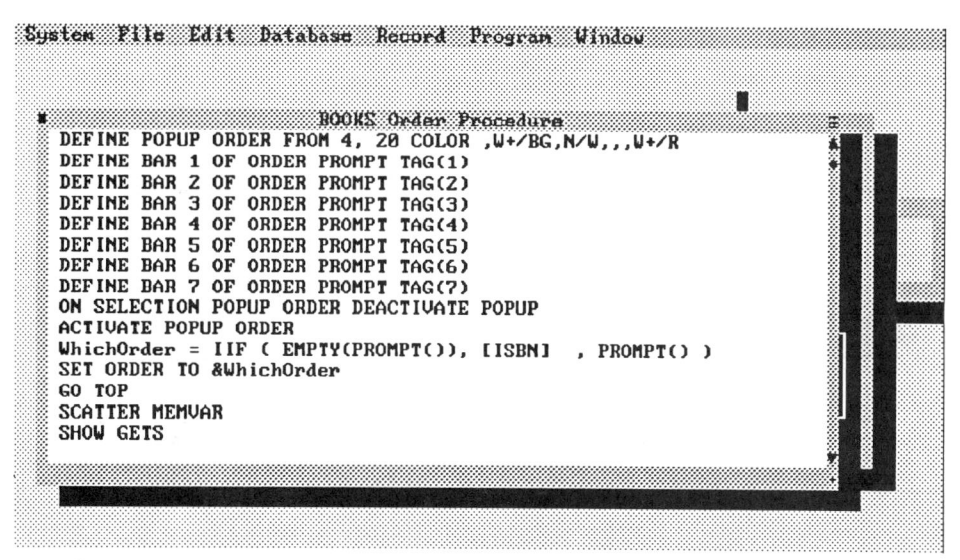

```
DEFINE POPUP ORDER FROM 4, 20 COLOR ,W+/BG,N/W,,,W+/R
DEFINE BAR 1 OF ORDER PROMPT TAG(1)
DEFINE BAR 2 OF ORDER PROMPT TAG(2)
DEFINE BAR 3 OF ORDER PROMPT TAG(3)
DEFINE BAR 4 OF ORDER PROMPT TAG(4)
DEFINE BAR 5 OF ORDER PROMPT TAG(5)
DEFINE BAR 6 OF ORDER PROMPT TAG(6)
DEFINE BAR 7 OF ORDER PROMPT TAG(7)
ON SELECTION POPUP ORDER DEACTIVATE POPUP
ACTIVATE POPUP ORDER
WhichOrder = IIF ( EMPTY(PROMPT()), [ISBN]  , PROMPT() )
SET ORDER TO &WhichOrder
GO TOP
SCATTER MEMVAR
SHOW GETS
```

8-4 Custom menu code.

The input screen is always live. If users type anything, it goes into the current screen.

In LISTING 8-1, I load the menu, open the data files, and set the initial order (it defaults to NO ORDER, or record number order). I also initialize the memory variables corresponding to the fields in the DBF, effectively making them public to this application. I also initialize a flag called adding that I'll use to determine whether or not I need an empty record when it's time to save data.

How it works   165

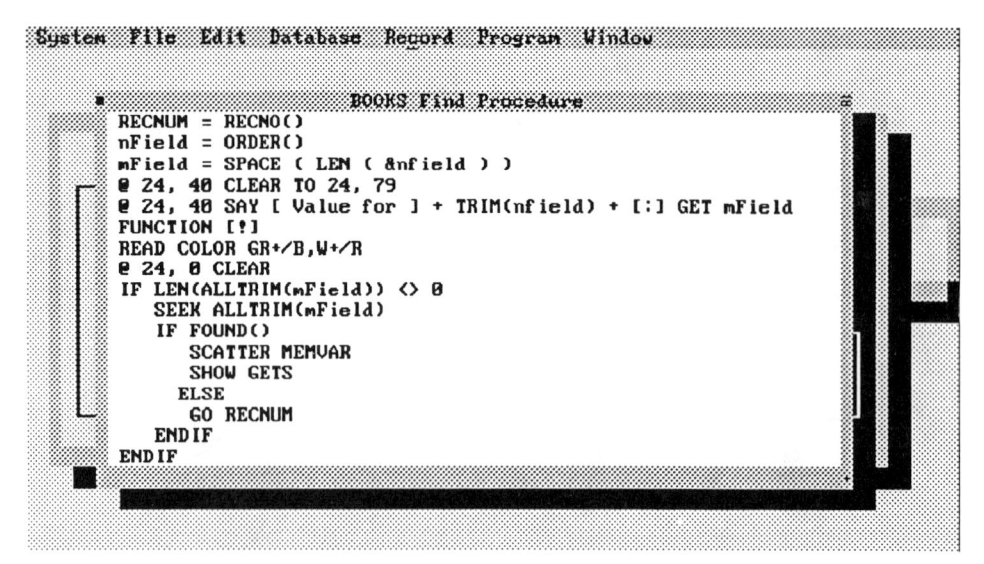

```
                      BOOKS Find Procedure
RECNUM = RECNO()
nField = ORDER()
mField = SPACE ( LEN ( &nfield ) )
@ 24, 40 CLEAR TO 24, 79
@ 24, 40 SAY [ Value for ] + TRIM(nfield) + [:] GET mField
FUNCTION [?]
READ COLOR GR+/B,W+/R
@ 24, 0 CLEAR
IF LEN(ALLTRIM(mField)) <> 0
   SEEK ALLTRIM(mField)
   IF FOUND()
      SCATTER MEMVAR
      SHOW GETS
   ELSE
      GO RECNUM
   ENDIF
ENDIF
```

8-5 More custom menu code.

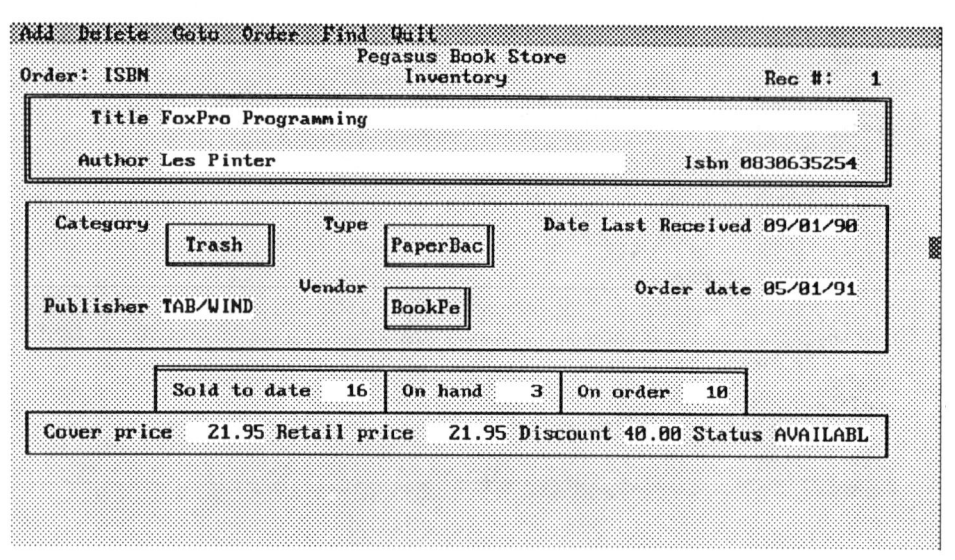

8-6 My generated application in action.

In LISTING 8-2 on page 168, I have a few pop-up fields to force users to select correct values. Attempts to enter category, type, and vendor are all forced to pick from a list (LISTING 8-3 on page 169).

The READ command drives this entire application. The SHOW clause is the very last function defined in the screen program; it displays record number, as well as the current index tag. See LISTING 8-4 on page 170.

That's the body of the program. The called functions follow. The annotation is courtesy of the screen builder's code generator.

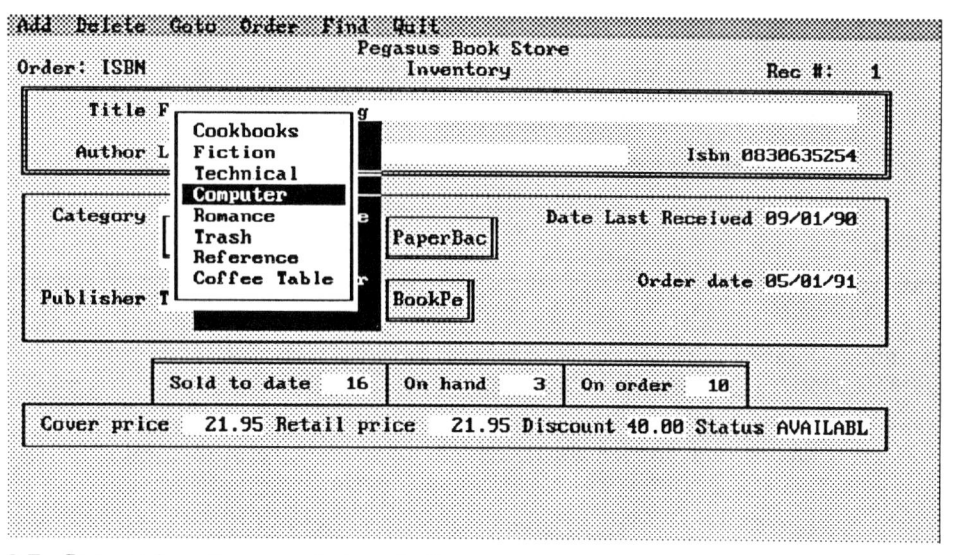

8-7 Pop-ups from the generated application.

Listing 8-1

```
* Program-ID.....: BOOKS.SPR
* Generated code...

#REGION 0
REGIONAL m.currarea, m.talkstat, m.compstat

IF SET("TALK") = "ON"
  SET TALK OFF
  m.talkstat = "ON"
ELSE
  m.talkstat = "OFF"
ENDIF
m.compstat = SET("COMPATIBLE")
SET COMPATIBLE FOXPLUS

*
*
*            S7757273 Databases, Indexes, Relations
*
*
*

IF USED("books")
  SELECT books
  SET ORDER TO 0
ELSE
  SELECT 0
  USE (LOCFILE("books.dbf","DBF","Where is books?"));
    AGAIN ALIAS books ;
    ORDER 0
ENDIF
```

How it works

Listing 8-1 Continued

```
*
*
*  ┌─────────────────────────────────────────────────────┐
*  │              BOOKS Setup Code - SECTION 2           │
*  └─────────────────────────────────────────────────────┘
*
```

Listing 8-2

```
#REGION 1
SET COLOR TO GR+/B
CLEAR
DO BOOKS.MPR
SELECT BOOKS
SCATTER MEMVAR
Adding = .F.
* Here's where the screen is drawn and memory variable GETS displayed:
*
*  ┌─────────────────────────────────────────────────────┐
*  │                  BOOKS Screen Layout                │
*  └─────────────────────────────────────────────────────┘
*
*

#REGION 1
@ 6,58 SAY "Isbn" ;
    COLOR SCHEME 1
@ 4,7 SAY "Title" ;
    COLOR SCHEME 1
@ 6,6 SAY "Author" ;
    COLOR SCHEME 1
@ 13,3 SAY "Publisher" ;
    COLOR SCHEME 1
@ 12,25 SAY "Vendor" ;
    COLOR SCHEME 1
@ 9,4 SAY "Category" ;
    COLOR SCHEME 1
@ 9,27 SAY "Type" ;
    COLOR SCHEME 1
@ 19,44 SAY "Discount" ;
    COLOR SCHEME 1
@ 19,59 SAY "Status" ;
    COLOR SCHEME 1
@ 19,3 SAY "Cover price" ;
    COLOR SCHEME 1
@ 19,23 SAY "Retail price" ;
    COLOR SCHEME 1
@ 17,14 SAY "Sold to date" ;
    COLOR SCHEME 1
@ 17,34 SAY "On hand" ;
    COLOR SCHEME 1
@ 17,49 SAY "On order" ;
    COLOR SCHEME 1
@ 12,54 SAY "Order date" ;
    COLOR SCHEME 1
@ 3,1 TO 7,75 DOUBLE ;
    COLOR SCHEME 1
@ 10,1 SAY " " ;
    COLOR SCHEME 1
```

```
@ 18,1 TO 20,75 ;
    COLOR SCHEME 1
@ 9,46 SAY "Date Last Received" ;
    COLOR SCHEME 1
@ 17,32 SAY "o" ;
    COLOR SCHEME 1
@ 17,47 SAY "o" ;
    COLOR SCHEME 1
@ 18,47 SAY "ê" ;
    COLOR SCHEME 1
@ 18,32 SAY "ê" ;
    COLOR SCHEME 1
@ 18,12 SAY "ê" ;
    COLOR SCHEME 1
@ 17,12 SAY "o" ;
    COLOR SCHEME 1
@ 16,12 SAY "î" ;
    COLOR SCHEME 1
@ 16,63 SAY "¡" ;
    COLOR SCHEME 1
@ 17,63 SAY "o" ;
    COLOR SCHEME 1
@ 18,63 SAY "ê" ;
    COLOR SCHEME 1
@ 16,13 TO 16,62 DOUBLE ;
    COLOR SCHEME 1
@ 16,32 SAY "î" ;
    COLOR SCHEME 1
@ 16,47 SAY "î" ;
    COLOR SCHEME 1
@ 1,30 SAY "Pegasus Book Store" ;
    COLOR SCHEME 1
@ 2,34 SAY "Inventory" ;
    COLOR SCHEME 1
@ 4,13 GET m.title ;
    SIZE 1,60 ;
    COLOR SCHEME 1
@ 6,13 GET m.author ;
    SIZE 1,40 ;
    COLOR SCHEME 1
@ 6,63 GET m.isbn ;
    SIZE 1,10 ;
    PICTURE "!!!!!!!!!!" ;
    COLOR SCHEME 1
```

Listing 8-3

```
@ 9,13 GET m.category ;
    SIZE 1,10 ;
    PICTURE "@^
Cookbooks;Fiction;Technical;Computer;Romance;Trash;Reference;Coff ee Table" ;
    COLOR SCHEME 1
@ 9,32 GET m.type ;
    SIZE 1,10 ;
    PICTURE "@^ HardCover;SoftCover;PaperBack;Novelty;Other" ;
    COLOR SCHEME 1
@ 9,65 GET m.daterecvd ;
    SIZE 1,8 ;
    COLOR SCHEME 1
@ 13,13 GET m.publisher ;
```

Listing 8-3   Continued

```
    SIZE 1,8 ;
    COLOR SCHEME 1
@ 12,32 GET m.vendor ;
    SIZE 1,8 ;
    PICTURE "@^ Ingram;B&T;BookPeople;Publisher" ;
    COLOR SCHEME 1
@ 12,65 GET m.orderdate ;
    SIZE 1,8 ;
    COLOR SCHEME 1
@ 17,27 GET m.soldtodate ;
    SIZE 1,4 ;
    COLOR SCHEME 1
@ 17,42 GET m.onhand ;
    SIZE 1,4 ;
    COLOR SCHEME 1
@ 17,58 GET m.onorder ;
    SIZE 1,4 ;
    COLOR SCHEME 1
@ 19,15 GET m.coverprice ;
    SIZE 1,7 ;
    COLOR SCHEME 1
@ 19,36 GET m.retailpric ;
    SIZE 1,7 ;
    COLOR SCHEME 1
@ 19,53 GET m.discount ;
    SIZE 1,5 ;
    COLOR SCHEME 1
@ 19,66 GET m.status ;
    SIZE 1,8 ;
    PICTURE "!!!!!!!!!!" ;
    COLOR SCHEME 1
@ 8,1 TO 15,75 ;
    COLOR SCHEME 1
```

Listing 8-4

```
READ CYCLE ;
  SHOW _pxx0ymg1v()
#REGION 0
IF m.talkstat = "ON"
  SET TALK ON
ENDIF
IF m.compstat = "ON"
  SET COMPATIBLE ON
ENDIF
*
*
*                    BOOKS Cleanup Code
*
*
*

#REGION 1
CLEAR
CLEAR WINDOW
CLOSE DATABASES
SET SYSMENU TO DEFAULT
```

Listing 8-5 contains all of the code for the screen program. The work of skipping around the database, changing the order in which the database is read, and searching for specific information is handled by the menu program. It also was generated from the menu builder. The generated code is shown in LISTING 8-6. That defines the menu code. Next, close the file and leave.

Listing 8-5

```
*
*
*       _PXX0YMG1V              Read Level Show
*
*       Function Origin:
*
*       From Screen:            BOOKS
*       Called By:              READ Statement
*       Snippet Number:         1
*
*
*
FUNCTION _pxx0ymg1v      && Read Level Show
PRIVATE currwind

STORE WOUTPUT() TO currwind

* Show Code from screen: BOOKS
*

#REGION 1
x=recno()
@ 2, 1 say [Order: ] + ORDER()
@ 2, 65 SAY [Rec #: ] + STR(x,3)

IF NOT EMPTY(currwind)
   ACTIVATE WINDOW (currwind) SAME
ENDIF
```

Listing 8-6

```
* Program-Id....: BOOKS.MPR
* Generated code

SET SYSMENU TO

SET SYSMENU AUTOMATIC
*
* This tells FoxPro to allow the menu to be popped up
* like the FoxPro menu is.
*
DEFINE PAD _pxx0yob01 OF _MSYSMENU PROMPT "Add"      COLOR SCHEME 3
DEFINE PAD _pxx0yob1m OF _MSYSMENU PROMPT "Delete"   COLOR SCHEME 3
DEFINE PAD _pxx0yob2f OF _MSYSMENU PROMPT "Goto"     COLOR SCHEME 3
DEFINE PAD _pxx0yob3q OF _MSYSMENU PROMPT "Order"    COLOR SCHEME 3
DEFINE PAD _pxx0yob4k OF _MSYSMENU PROMPT "Find"     COLOR SCHEME 3
DEFINE PAD _pxx0yob5f OF _MSYSMENU PROMPT "Quit"     COLOR SCHEME 3

ON SELECTION PAD _pxx0yob01 OF _MSYSMENU DO _pxx0yob7x
ON SELECTION PAD _pxx0yob1m OF _MSYSMENU DO _pxx0yoba1
```

Listing 8-6 Continued

```
ON PAD _pxx0yob2f OF _MSYSMENU ACTIVATE POPUP goto

ON SELECTION PAD _pxx0yob3q OF _MSYSMENU DO _pxx0yobcm
ON SELECTION PAD _pxx0yob4k OF _MSYSMENU DO _pxx0yobep
ON SELECTION PAD _pxx0yob5f OF _MSYSMENU DO _pxx0yobgt

DEFINE POPUP goto MARGIN RELATIVE SHADOW COLOR SCHEME 4
DEFINE BAR 1 OF goto PROMPT "Next"
DEFINE BAR 2 OF goto PROMPT "Previous"
DEFINE BAR 3 OF goto PROMPT "Top"
DEFINE BAR 4 OF goto PROMPT "Bottom"

ON SELECTION BAR 1 OF goto DO _pxx0yobol
ON SELECTION BAR 2 OF goto DO _pxx0yobqo
ON SELECTION BAR 3 OF goto DO _pxx0yobsq
ON SELECTION BAR 4 OF goto DO _pxx0yobut

ON SELECTION MENU _MSYSMENU
ON SELECTION POPUP ALL
```

One of the problems with a live data entry screen is that changes might have been made to the data prior to moving from record to record. So, any time you move forward or backward, including responding to a search, you have to save the current screen's information.

In addition, you might have been in the process of adding a record. In the world of event-driven processes, you never know. I've added a flag called adding, which is true (.T.) if the ADD procedure was selected and is false otherwise. I also created a set of empty memory variables to display on the screen and used SHOW GETS to display them. However, the data isn't saved until I move to another record. That means that the repositioning routines have to take care of it. Also, I want them to be able to press Esc if they don't want to save the changes to the add screen. See LISTING 8-7.

Listing 8-7

```
*
*   ┌─────────────────────────────────────────────┐
*   │          Cleanup Code & Procedures           │
*   │                                              │
*   └─────────────────────────────────────────────┘
*
PROCEDURE Adder

* Code to save the current screen information and move to next record.
* First, determine whether the current screen was an add. If so, it
* needs a blank record.

IF ( Adding .and. LastKey() <> 27 )
  OldOrder = ORDER()
  SET ORDER TO ISBN
  GO BOTTOM
  IF ISBN <> [~]
    APPEND BLANK
  ENDIF
  SET ORDER TO &OldOrder
```

```
ENDIF
GATHER MEMVAR
SHOW GETS
```

Listing 8-8 is where the program sets the adding flag to .T. and creates blank memory variables. My delete routine forces them to confirm before continuing (LISTING 8-9).

Listing 8-8

```
*
*
*   ┌─────────────────────────────────────────────────┐
*   │                                                 │
*   │   _PXX0YOB7X   ON SELECTION PAD                 │
*   │                                                 │
*   │   Procedure Origin:                             │
*   │                                                 │
*   │   From Menu:   BOOKS.MPR,        Record:    3   │
*   │   Called By:   ON SELECTION PAD                 │
*   │   Prompt:      Add                              │
*   │   Snippet:     1                                │
*   │                                                 │
*   └─────────────────────────────────────────────────┘
*
PROCEDURE _pxx0yob7x
SCATTER MEMVAR BLANK
Adding = .T.
SHOW GETS
```

Listing 8-9

```
*
*
*   ┌─────────────────────────────────────────────────┐
*   │                                                 │
*   │   _PXX0YOBA1   ON SELECTION PAD                 │
*   │                                                 │
*   │   Procedure Origin:                             │
*   │                                                 │
*   │   From Menu:   BOOKS.MPR,        Record:    4   │
*   │   Called By:   ON SELECTION PAD                 │
*   │   Prompt:      Delete                           │
*   │   Snippet:     2                                │
*   │                                                 │
*   └─────────────────────────────────────────────────┘
*
PROCEDURE _pxx0yoba1
DEFINE WINDOW CONFIRM FROM 20,30 TO 22, 50;
      DOUBLE SHADOW TITLE [ Are you sure? ]
ACTIVATE WINDOW CONFIRM
CLEAR
@ 0, 3 PROMPT [ Yes ]
@ 0,$ PROMPT [ No ]
yn = 2
MENU TO yn
RELEASE WINDOW CONFIRM
IF yn <> 1
   RETURN
ENDIF
SCATTER MEMVAR BLANK
GATHER MEMVAR
SET ORDER TO ISBN
```

Listing 8-9 Continued
```
SaveIsbn = BOOKS->ISBN
FOR I = 1 TO 26
  IF .NOT. EMPTY(TAG(I))
    Field = TAG(I)
    REPLACE NEXT 1 &Field WITH [~]
  ENDIF
ENDFOR
SET  NEAR ON
SEEK SaveIsbn
SET  NEAR OFF
IF ISBN = [~]
  SKIP -1
ENDIF
RETURN
```

The ORDER routine displays all available index tags and lets the user choose one. If the user presses Esc, it goes back to the primary index tag (LISTING 8-10). The FIND routine knows what the current index order is, so it precedes its prompt with the correct label (LISTING 8-11).

To exit a READ CYCLE, just issue a CLEAR READ. I also close the database at this time and reset the system menu. If the system menu isn't reset, you can't pull down the Trace and Debug windows with Alt–W–T and Alt–W–D,

Listing 8-10

```
*
*
*     _PXX0YOBCM   ON SELECTION PAD
*
*     Procedure Origin:
*
*     From Menu:   BOOKS.MPR,              Record:    11
*     Called By:   ON SELECTION PAD
*     Prompt:      Order
*     Snippet:     3
*
*
*
PROCEDURE _pxx0yobcm
DEFINE POPUP ORDER FROM 4, 20 COLOR ,W+/BG,N/W,,,W+/R
DEFINE BAR 1 OF ORDER PROMPT TAG(1)
DEFINE BAR 2 OF ORDER PROMPT TAG(2)
DEFINE BAR 3 OF ORDER PROMPT TAG(3)
DEFINE BAR 4 OF ORDER PROMPT TAG(4)
DEFINE BAR 5 OF ORDER PROMPT TAG(5)
DEFINE BAR 6 OF ORDER PROMPT TAG(6)
DEFINE BAR 7 OF ORDER PROMPT TAG(7)
ON SELECTION POPUP ORDER DEACTIVATE POPUP
ACTIVATE POPUP ORDER
WhichOrder = IIF ( EMPTY(PROMPT()), [ISBN]  , PROMPT() )
SET ORDER TO &WhichOrder
GO TOP
SCATTER MEMVAR
SHOW GETS
```

Listing 8-11

```
*
*       ┌─────────────────────────────────────────────────────┐
*       │                                                     │
*       │   _PXX0YOBEP   ON SELECTION PAD                     │
*       │                                                     │
*       │   Procedure Origin:                                 │
*       │                                                     │
*       │   From Menu:   BOOKS.MPR,          Record:    12    │
*       │   Called By:   ON SELECTION PAD                     │
*       │   Prompt:      Find                                 │
*       │   Snippet:     4                                    │
*       │                                                     │
*       └─────────────────────────────────────────────────────┘
*
PROCEDURE _pxx0yobep
RECNUM = RECNO()
nField = ORDER()
mField = SPACE ( LEN ( &nfield ) )
@ 24, 40 CLEAR TO 24, 79
@ 24, 40 SAY [ Value for ] + TRIM(nfield) + [:] GET mField FUNCTION [!]
READ COLOR GR+/B,W+/R
@ 24, 0 CLEAR
IF LEN(ALLTRIM(mField)) <> 0
  SEEK ALLTRIM(mField)
  IF FOUND()
    SCATTER MEMVAR
    SHOW GETS
  ELSE
    GO RECNUM
  ENDIF
ENDIF
```

so be sure to do this in your ON ERROR routines as well—at least during debugging (LISTING 8-12). Skipping to the next or previous record or to top or bottom of file is pretty straightforward, except for that business about storing the current memory variables to the file (LISTING 8-13).

Listing 8-12

```
*
*       ┌─────────────────────────────────────────────────────┐
*       │                                                     │
*       │   _PXX0YOBGT   ON SELECTION PAD                     │
*       │                                                     │
*       │   Procedure Origin:                                 │
*       │                                                     │
*       │   From Menu:   BOOKS.MPR,          Record:    13    │
*       │   Called By:   ON SELECTION PAD                     │
*       │   Prompt:      Quit                                 │
*       │   Snippet:     5                                    │
*       │                                                     │
*       └─────────────────────────────────────────────────────┘
*
PROCEDURE _pxx0yobgt
CLEAR READ
CLEAR
SET SYSMENU TO DEFAULT
```

How it works

Listing 8-13

```
*
*
*     _PXX0YOBOL   ON SELECTION BAR 1 OF POPUP goto
*
*     Procedure Origin:
*
*     From Menu:   BOOKS.MPR,            Record:    7
*     Called By:   ON SELECTION BAR 1 OF POPUP goto
*     Prompt:      Next
*     Snippet:     6
*
*
*

PROCEDURE _pxx0yobol
DO Adder
Adding = .F.
IF EOF() .OR. ISBN = [~]
  WAIT WINDOW [End of data] TIMEOUT 1
ELSE
  SKIP
  IF EOF() .OR. ISBN = [~]
    WAIT WINDOW [End of data] TIMEOUT 1
    IF ISBN = [~]
      SKIP -1
    ELSE
      GO BOTTOM
    ENDIF
  ENDIF
  SCATTER MEMVAR
  SHOW GETS
ENDIF


*
*
*     _PXX0YOBQO   ON SELECTION BAR 2 OF POPUP goto
*
*     Procedure Origin:
*
*     From Menu:   BOOKS.MPR,            Record:    8
*     Called By:   ON SELECTION BAR 2 OF POPUP goto
*     Prompt:      Previous
*     Snippet:     7
*
*
*
PROCEDURE _pxx0yobqo
DO Adder
Adding = .F.
IF BOF()
  WAIT WINDOW [Top of file] TIMEOUT 1
ELSE
  SKIP -1
  IF BOF()
```

```
      WAIT WINDOW [Top of file] TIMEOUT 1
      GO TOP
   ENDIF
   SCATTER MEMVAR
   SHOW GETS
ENDIF
```

```
*
*
*    _PXX0YOBSQ   ON SELECTION BAR 3 OF POPUP goto
*
*    Procedure Origin:
*
*    From Menu:    BOOKS.MPR,             Record:      9
*    Called By:    ON SELECTION BAR 3 OF POPUP goto
*    Prompt:       Top
*    Snippet:      8
*
*
```

```
PROCEDURE _pxx0yobsq
DO Adder
Adding = .F.
GO TOP
SCATTER MEMVAR
SHOW GETS
```

```
*
*
*    _PXX0YOBUT   ON SELECTION BAR 4 OF POPUP goto
*
*    Procedure Origin:
*
*    From Menu:    BOOKS.MPR,             Record:     10
*    Called By:    ON SELECTION BAR 4 OF POPUP goto
*    Prompt:       Bottom
*    Snippet:      9
*
*
*
```

```
PROCEDURE _pxx0yobut
DO Adder
Adding = .F.
GO BOTTOM
IF ISBN = [~]
   SEEK [~]
   SKIP -1
ENDIF
SCATTER MEMVAR
SHOW GETS
```

That, friends, is how I redesigned my little screen and added a menu. There actually are quite a few more things I can do at this point, but I have to leave something for another chapter, don't I?

Summary

FoxPro 2.0 screen design is powerful and easy. You have to take a slightly different approach, but the rewards are well worth it. In the next chapter, I'll look at a different approach to the screen-with-menu problem.

9
Pop-ups and pulldowns

There are many different ways to pop up a list of items. The POPUP and LIST functions within @...GET are two very powerful features, but they aren't the only way that you might want to pop up lists or options.

Pop-ups are used for menus, data entry validation, help systems, and screen management. They're used both when the list of elements to be displayed in the pop-up is known in advance and when the list is read from a file and, therefore, might be of variable length. You can force users to select an element to stuff an input field. They also can be used when what you want to pop up is not the same as what you want entered into the input field being validated (e.g., show state names, but enter state codes).

Given the addition of the function codes to produce lists and pop-ups with the GET statement, my main focus here is on pop-ups for menuing or informational purposes. I get a lot of clients who want to have it their way, and the variety is endless. You can either construct your own windows and pop-ups or use the MENU or DEFINE POPUP commands to do them. Happily, FoxPro is flexible enough to do anything I need.

Fixed length versus variable length pop-ups

In some cases, you might know in advance exactly what elements are involved. There might be options or elements that should be displayed as non-selectable. However, some menus or lists vary from time to time, so loading some or all of the contents of a file means that the precise size of the menu isn't known until it's loaded for display.

Fixed length lists

Commands used to display fixed-length lists of pop-up data include PROMPT, MENU, and DEFINE POPUP. Example of fixed-length lists are the days of the week, the seasons, and the options available in a program. It's typical of these pop-ups that you know how much space they'll occupy, so aesthetic considerations are uppermost. You want the pop-up to look right.

Commands used to display variable lists of data include DEFINE POP UP...PROMPT FIELD *field_name* and @ *row,col* MENU *menu_name*. You also can roll your own.

The MENU command

The MENU command was demonstrated at the end of chapter 5. Listing 9-1 contains a pop-up dialog to redirect output to printer, screen, or file, using the MENU command. The dialog appears in FIG. 9-1.

Listing 9-1

```
* Program-ID.....: WhereTo.PRG
* Purpose........: Demonstrates menu window using MENU with array.

SAVE SCREEN

OldCursor = SET ( [ CURSOR] )

SET COLOR OF SCHEME 12 TO SCHEME 2     && save scheme
SET COLOR OF SCHEME  2 TO ;
    W+/B, R+/B, GR+/B, N/W, N/W, GR+/R, N/W, N/W, N/W, N/W

Dimension MenuList ( 5 )

MenuList ( 1 ) = [\      Report Output    ]
MenuList ( 2 ) = [\-                      ]
MenuList ( 3 ) = [       Printer          ]
MenuList ( 4 ) = [       Screen           ]
MenuList ( 5 ) = [       File             ]
Option = 1
@ 5, 25 MENU MenuList , 5, 5 SHADOW
READ MENU TO Option

* -- The following is necessary to display the menu again.

= ShowMenu()

Option = IIF ( Option = 0 , [ ] , SUBSTR ( MenuList ( Option ) , 5 , 1 ) )

* -- This returns the letter P, S or F...

@ IIF ( Option = [P] , 8 , IIf ( Option = [S] , 9 , 10 )), 28 SAY [*]
```

```
   IF Option = [F]
     mFileName = [          ]
     @ 10, 36 GET mFileName PICTURE "!!!!!!!!!"
     READ
     IF .NOT. EMPTY ( mFileName )
       SET PRINTER TO &mFileName
     ENDIF
   ENDIF
   SET CURSOR OFF
   IF Option <> [S]
     IF Option = [P] .AND. .NOT. PrintStatus()
       WAIT [Please turn on the printer and press any key] WINDOW
     ENDIF
     SET PRINT ON
   ENDIF

   WAIT WINDOW [ Printing report ] TIMEOUT 5   && Simulate report printing.
   SET CURSOR &OldCursor
   RESTORE SCREEN

   SET COLOR OF SCHEME 2 TO SCHEME 12              && restore scheme

   RETURN

   FUNCTION ShowMenu
   @ 5, 25 TO 11, 48 DOUBLE
   @ 6, 26 SAY SUBSTR ( MenuList ( 1 ) , 2 , LEN ( MenuList ( 1 ) ) - 1 )
   @ 7, 26 TO 7, 47
   FOR I = 3 TO 5
     @ 5+I, 26 SAY MenuList ( I )
   ENDFOR
   RETURN
```

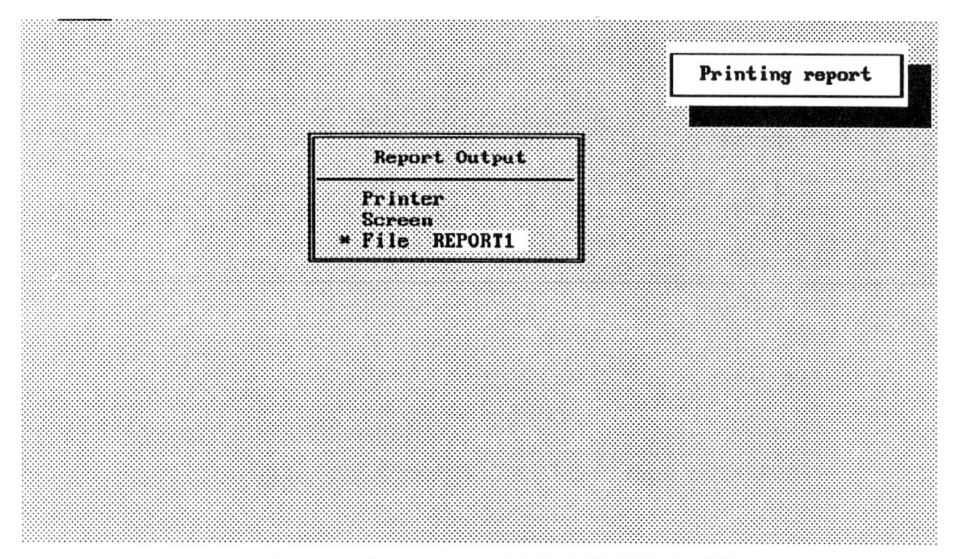

9-1 A printer output redirection dialog using MENU (WHERETO.PRG).

Notice that the UDF ShowMenu is required to redisplay the menu after the READ MENU TO *varname* command is executed. The DEFINE POPUP command has a companion, SHOW POPUP, which has no counterpart here (The SHOW MENU command is used with the MENU BAR, not the array used in @ *coordinates* MENU...).

In some ways, I prefer the MENU command, because it requires a little less planning. If you already have an array loaded, MENU can use it. For long lists, it is much faster. Other than that, you'll find that they both have advantages and disadvantages.

The DEFINE POPUP command

A related command is the DEFINE POPUP and DEFINE BAR *n* OF *pop-up*. For fixed length lists, it's really very similar to using MENU. See LISTING 9-2. Figure 9-2 contains the related screen.

Listing 9-2

```
* Program-ID.....: GetaCode.PRG
* Purpose........: Demonstrates validation windows using DEFINE POPUP.
DIMENSION DeptCodes ( 5 )
SET BLINK OFF           && enables high-intensity colors
SET COLOR OF SCHEME 12 TO SCHEME 2
SET COLOR OF SCHEME  2 TO B+/B, GR+/B,,,, N/GR*

DeptCodes ( 1 ) = [ACCT]
DeptCodes ( 2 ) = [MKTG]
DeptCodes ( 3 ) = [PERS]
DeptCodes ( 4 ) = [LEGL]
DeptCodes ( 5 ) = [EXEC]

DEFINE POPUP DeptPop FROM 3, 35 MARGIN SHADOW
ON SELECTION POPUP DeptPop DEACTIVATE POPUP DeptPop

DEFINE BAR 1 OF DeptPop PROMPT [\ACCT - Accounting]
DEFINE BAR 2 OF DeptPop PROMPT [MKTG - Marketing]
DEFINE BAR 3 OF DeptPop PROMPT [\PERS - Personnel]
DEFINE BAR 4 OF DeptPop PROMPT [LEGL - Legal]
DEFINE BAR 5 OF DeptPop PROMPT [EXEC - Executive]

M->DeptCode = [    ]

@ 12, 5 SAY 'Department code: ' ;
        GET M->DeptCode ;
        PICTURE "!!!!"  ;
        VALID DeptCode();
        ERROR [You must select a department code]
READ

WAIT WINDOW

SET COLOR OF SCHEME  2 TO SCHEME 12    && restore colors

RETURN
```

182 Pop-ups and pulldowns

```
* Note: Pressing ESC in a blank field will bypass the VALID clause...
FUNCTION DeptCode
IF .NOT. INLIST ( M->DeptCode , DeptCodes )
  ACTIVATE POPUP DeptPop
  m.DeptCode = IIf ( BAR() = 0 , [     ], DeptCodes ( BAR() ) )
  IF M->DeptCode = [    ]
    RETURN .F.
  ELSE
    RETURN .T.
  ENDIF
ENDIF
```

9-2 Using DEFINE POPUP to select a value (GETACODE.PRG).

This example includes the backslash prefix to suppress the ability to select certain of the elements in the pop-up. Note that you can include such suppression conditionally. For example, if you insert the following lines:

```
IF ctod(date( )) = 'Sunday'
  DEFINE BAR 2 OF DeptPop PROMPT [ \ MKTG - Marketing ]
ENDIF
```

before the @...SAY/GET, then menu bar 2 will be non-selectable on Sundays. The slash must be the first character, with no space before it. If you need a space to line things up, put it after the backslash.

Prompts

You can build a two-column fixed-list prompt pop-up using the PROMPT command (LISTING 9-3). Figure 9-3 shows such an animal.

Listing 9-3

```
* Program-ID....: Seasonal.PRG
* Purpose.......: Two-column menu using PROMPT

ColrSwitch = []    && For Mono Colors, use [.NOT.]
MenuColor = IIF ( &ColrSwitch IsColor() , [GR+/B,W+/R] , [W+/N,N/W] )
SET COLOR TO &MenuColor
@ 20, 0 CLEAR
@ 20, 6 TO 24, 30 DOUBLE
@ 21, 10 PROMPT [ Winter ]
@ 21, 20 PROMPT [ Spring ]
@ 23, 10 PROMPT [ Summer ]
@ 23, 20 PROMPT [  Fall  ]
@ 20,  7 SAY [ *** Pick a season *** ]
MENU TO Season
@ 20, 0 CLEAR
@ 21, 0 SAY ;
   IIF ( Season = 1 , [ Winter ] , ;
     IIF ( Season = 2 , [ Spring ] , ;
       IIF ( Season = 3 , [ Summer ] , ;
         IIF ( Season = 4 , [  Fall  ] , [ None ] )))) + [selected]
WAIT WINDOW
```

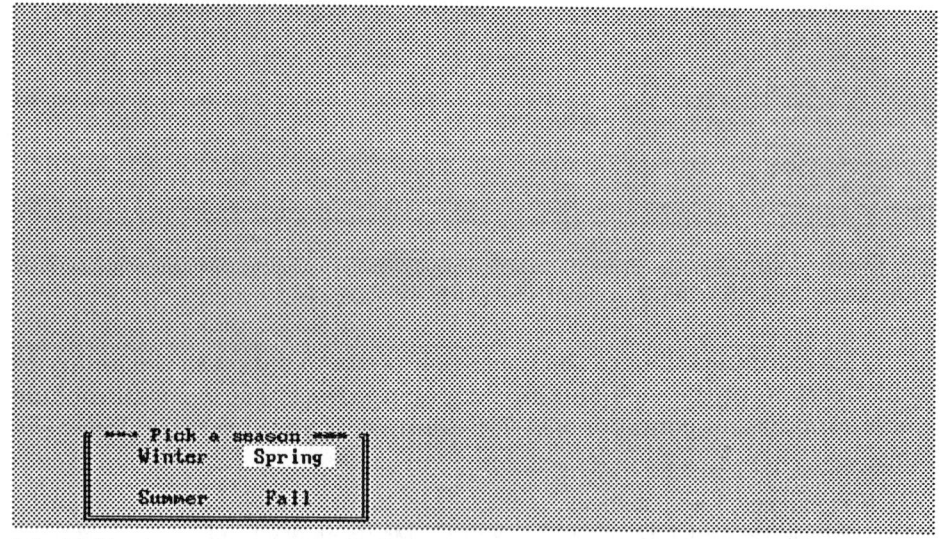

9-3 Multi-column pop-ups using PROMPT (SEASONAL.PRG).

Color control in pop-ups

Color scheme 2 is assigned to pop-up colors, as follows:

1. Disabled Options
2. Enabled Options (normal)
3. Border
4. Titles
5. Messages (line 24)
6. Selected Options

7. Hot Keys
8. Shadow

(Colors 9 and 10 are not used.) So, you could use:

DEFINE BAR n OF Pop-upName COLOR 1,2,3,4,5,6,7,8

where the numbers represent the color assignments listed previously. Generally, it's easier to use:

SET COLOR OF SCHEME 2 TO
W+/N,W+/R,GR+/BR,N/W,GR+/B,N/
GR*,BG+/W,N+/N

Finally, you can use any of the unassigned color schemes 13 through 24 and assign them your own set of colors, leaving scheme 2 alone:

SET COLOR OF SCHEME 13 TO W+/N,N/R,GR+/BG,,N/W
DEFINE POPUP Zippy FROM 3,3
DEFINE BAR 1 OF Zippy PROMPT [Hi] COLOR SCHEME 13

and so on.

Specialty pop-ups

The DEFINE POPUP command also can be used to create confirming windows, as shown in LISTING 9-4. Figure 9-4 is the screen it produces.

Listing 9-4

```
* Program-ID.....: Confirm1.PRG
* Purpose........: Demonstrates menu window using DEFINE POPUP.

OldCursor = SET ( [ CURSOR] )

DEFINE      POPUP MenuPop FROM 10, 29 MARGIN SHADOW
ON SELECTION POPUP MenuPop DEACTIVATE POPUP MenuPop

DEFINE BAR 1 OF MenuPop PROMPT [\] + PADC ( [Report Output] , 20 )
DEFINE BAR 2 OF MenuPop PROMPT [\-]
DEFINE BAR 3 OF MenuPop PROMPT PADC ( [Printer] , 20 )
DEFINE BAR 4 OF MenuPop PROMPT PADC ( [Screen]  , 20 )
DEFINE BAR 5 OF MenuPop PROMPT PADC ( [File]    , 20 )

ACTIVATE POPUP MenuPop
SHOW     POPUP MenuPop  && Redisplay with choice indicated.

Option = IIF ( LEN(PROMPT()) = 0 , [ ], PROMPT() )
RELEASE POPUP MENUPOP

@ IIF ( [Print]  $ option , 13    , ;
   IIF ( [Screen] $ option , 14    , ;
                             15 )) , 25 SAY [-->]

IF [File] $ option
  mFileName = [         ]
  @ 10, 40 GET mFileName PICTURE "!!!!!!!!"
  READ
```

Specialty pop-ups 185

Listing 9-4 Continued

```
    IF .NOT. EMPTY   ( mFileName )
      SET PRINTER TO &mFileName
    ENDIF
ENDIF

SET CURSOR OFF

* If they asked for printer but one isn't available, store output.

IF NOT [Screen] $ Option

* On my computer, the first time you check print status, it's always ok.
* If it's a bug in DOS, you might have it, too. Try this....
  ON ERROR a=1
  ??? [ ]
  ON ERROR

    IF [Print] $ Option .AND. .NOT. PrintStatus()
      WAIT WINDOW [Printing to file "HOLD.PRN" ] NOWAIT
      SET PRINTER TO HOLD.PRN
    ENDIF
    SET PRINT ON
ENDIF

WAIT WINDOW [ Printing report ] TIMEOUT 5   && Simulate report printing.

SET CURSOR &OldCursor

CLEAR

RETURN
```

```
┌─────────────────┐
│  Report Output  │
├─────────────────┤
│     Printer     │
│     Screen      │
│     File        │
└─────────────────┘
```

9-4 A confirming dialog using DEFINE POPUP (CONFIRM1.PRG).

Often, when your users might not want to take a particular action, a simple *yes* or *no* will do. A confirming pop-up is an excellent way to get your answer and provide a clean and readable flow of control.

In LISTING 9-5, the title is passed as a parameter, and the pop-up resizes itself to handle the title. The related screen is shown in FIG. 9-5.

Listing 9-5

```
* Program-ID.....: Confirm2.PRG
* Purpose........: Yes/No process control routine.

IF Confirm ( [ Proceed? ] )
  DO Posting
ELSE
  WAIT WINDOW [Posting cancelled]
ENDIF


PROCEDURE Posting
* simulates posting delay
WAIT [Posting invoices - do not mess with] WINDOW TIMEOUT 3

RETURN


FUNCTION CONFIRM
PARAMETERS m.title

length = LEN ( m.title )

OldCursor = SET ( [ CURSOR] )
SET CURSOR OFF

TestColor = IsColor()
*TestColor = .NOT. IsColor()   && for simulating mono on color screens

IF TestColor
  SET COLOR OF SCHEME 2 TO N/W,N/W,N/W,N/W,N/W,W+/R
ELSE
  SET COLOR OF SCHEME 2 TO W+/N,W/N,W/N,W/N,W/N,N/W
ENDIF

SET BORDER TO DOUBLE

DEFINE        POPUP YesNo FROM 11, 40-length MARGIN SHADOW
ON SELECTION POPUP YesNo DEACTIVATE POPUP YesNo

DEFINE BAR 1 OF    YesNo PROMPT [\] + m.title
DEFINE BAR 2 OF    YesNo PROMPT [\-]
DEFINE BAR 3 OF    YesNo PROMPT PADC ( [Yes] , length )
DEFINE BAR 4 OF    YesNo PROMPT PADC ( [No]  , length )

ACTIVATE POPUP YesNo  && At 'DEAC POPUP', control returns to next line.

Option = IIF ( [Yes] $ PROMPT() , .T. , .F. )
```

Listing 9-5 Continued

```
RELEASE POPUP YesNo
SET CURSOR &OldCursor
RETURN Option
```

9-5 *A general-purpose confirming dialog (CONFIRM2.PRG).*

Scrolling information displays

Sometimes, the amount of data you need to present is just too large to fit in the space available. There are several ways you can deal with this, but a single scrolling window might be the easiest way to do it (LISTING 9-6). Figure 9-6 shows the result.

Listing 9-6

```
* Program-ID....: ScrlText.PRG
* Purpose.......: Example of a popup HELP window using MENU

SET COLOR TO W+/N
CLEAR

PRIVATE info,key

DIMENSION Info(10)

Info (  1 ) = [   The monthly closing  ]
Info (  2 ) = [ schedule depends on    ]
Info (  3 ) = [ verifying that all of  ]
Info (  4 ) = [ the month's transac-   ]
Info (  5 ) = [ tions have been put    ]
Info (  6 ) = [ into the database and  ]
Info (  7 ) = [ control reports have   ]
Info (  8 ) = [ been printed. Check    ]
```

```
Info (  9 ) = [ with the closing sched-]
Info ( 10 ) = [ use before continuing. ]

@ 5,30 MENU Info, 10, 5 TITLE [ Closing Notes ] SHADOW
Key = 1
SET  CONFIRM ON
READ MENU TO Key
SET  CONFIRM OFF

RETURN
```

```
╔══ Closing Notes ══╗
║ The monthly closing║
║ schedule depends on║
║ verifying that all of║
║ the month's transac-║
║ tions have been put ║
╚═════════▼═════════╝
```

9-6 A scrolling help window using MENU (SCRLTEXT.PRG).

Variable length pop-ups

When the amount of data is variable, as in using the contents of a file, the easiest technique is the DEFINE POPUP PROMPT FIELD.

The example in LISTING 9-7 demonstrates the simple case where the user just wants to pick a code from a list. If you want to display a more descriptive phrase, then return the associated code, use the code in LISTING 9-8. Figure 9-7 is the simple case. In FIG. 9-8, however, you'll notice that the displayed values are not the ones stuffed into the field being validated.

Listing 9-7
```
* Program-Id....: StateVal.PRG
* Purpose.......: Demonstrates State Validation.

USE STATES
DEFINE       POPUP StateVal FROM 3, 16 TO 12, 21;
  MARGIN SHADOW PROMPT FIELD CODE
ON SELECTION POPUP StateVal DO StatePop WITH PROMPT()

M->StateCode = [ ]
@ 5, 5 SAY [State: ] GET M->StateCode PICTURE [!!] VALID GetState()
READ
```

Listing 9-7 Continued

```
SET CONFIRM OFF        && turned on by GetState if popup was activated...
@ 5,13 SAY M->StateCode
WAIT WINDOW

RETURN


FUNCTION GetState

SELECT STATES
LOCATE FOR CODE = M->StateCode
IF FOUND()
   RETURN .T.
ENDIF
SET CONFIRM ON
ACTIVATE POPUP StateVal
RETURN .T.


FUNCTION StatePop
PARAMETERS mPrompt

HIDE POPUP StateVal
M->StateCode = mPrompt
DEACTIVATE POPUP StateVal

RETURN
```

9-7 Using **DEFINE POPUP PROMPT FIELD** field (STATEVAL.PRG).

So why not use the DEFINE POPUP/PROMPT FIELD command every time? The main reason is that I don't always want to see every value in the file. Narrowing down the search to the most likely candidates can make the pop-up a lot more useful. Another reason is that loading a 400-element

Listing 9-8

```
* Program-Id....: StatVal2.PRG
* Purpose.......: Demonstrates State Validation.

USE STATES
DEFINE POPUP StateVal    ;
  FROM   2, 17 TO 14, 34 ;
  MARGIN ;
  SHADOW ;
  PROMPT FIELD State

ON SELECTION POPUP StateVal DO StatePop WITH PROMPT()

M->StateCode = [  ]
@ 5, 5 SAY [State: ] GET M->StateCode PICTURE [!!] VALID GetState()
READ
SET CONFIRM OFF
@ 5,13 SAY M->StateCode
WAIT WINDOW

RETURN


FUNCTION GetState

SELECT STATES
LOCATE FOR CODE = M->StateCode
IF FOUND()
  RETURN .T.
ENDIF
M->StateName = [ ]
SET CONFIRM ON
ACTIVATE POPUP StateVal
LOCATE FOR State = M->StateName
M->StateCode = Code

RETURN .T.

FUNCTION StatePop
PARAMETERS mPrompt

HIDE POPUP StateVal
M->StateName = mPrompt
DEACTIVATE POPUP StateVal

RETURN
```

array for a MENU pop-up is a lot faster than loading a 400-element DEFINE POPUP. Try it.

Finding and popping up only the near misses

Sometimes, when users type a code in, they transpose a couple of letters. I haven't done a scientific study, but what I seem to see is that they generally get the first letter right, after which the probability of a mistake goes up with each additional letter typed.

The routine in LISTING 9-9 drops trailing letters until it finds a match,

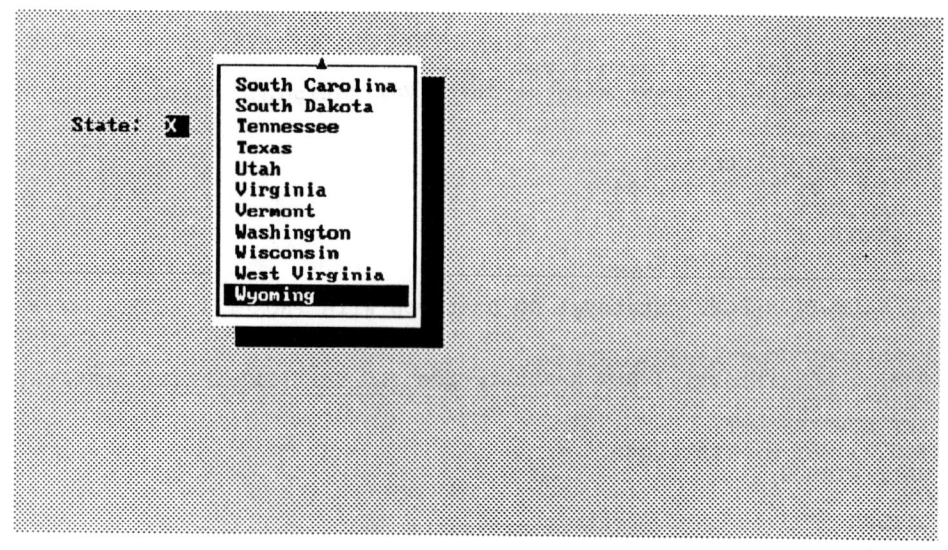

```
                  ┌─────────────────┐
                  │ South Carolina  │
                  │ South Dakota    │
     State: X     │ Tennessee       │
                  │ Texas           │
                  │ Utah            │
                  │ Virginia        │
                  │ Vermont         │
                  │ Washington      │
                  │ Wisconsin       │
                  │ West Virginia   │
                  │ Wyoming         │
                  └─────────────────┘
```

9-8 Using the pop-ups element number to return something else (STATVAL.PRG).

Listing 9-9

```
* Program-ID...: NearMiss.PRG
* Purpose......: Demonstrates 'near miss' popup validation.

CLEAR
SET BELL OFF

USE STATES INDEX STATES   && Must be indexed.

M->StateCode = [  ]
DO WHILE M->StateCode = [  ]
  @ 5, 5 SAY [State: ] GET M->StateCode PICTURE [!!] VALID GetState()
  READ
  IF M->StateCode = [  ]
    ?? CHR(7)
    WAIT WINDOW [ You must pick a state ] TIMEOUT 1
  ENDIF
ENDDO
@ 5,13 SAY M->StateCode

RETURN


FUNCTION GetState

SELECT STATES
SEEK TRIM ( M->StateCode )
IF CODE == M->StateCode
  RETURN .T.
ENDIF

* -- Didn't match.
DIMENSION Table ( 128 )

M->StateCode = TRIM ( M->StateCode )
```

```
SEEK M->StateCode
DO WHILE .NOT. FOUND() .AND. LEN ( M->StateCode ) > 0
  SEEK TRIM ( M->StateCode )
  IF FOUND()
    EXIT
  ENDIF
  IF LEN ( M->StateCode ) > 0
    M->StateCode = LEFT ( M->StateCode , LEN ( M->StateCode ) - 1 )
  ENDIF
ENDDO

IF LEN(M->StateCode) = 0
  GO TOP
ENDIF

I = 0
DO WHILE    I <= 128         ;
  .AND.  CODE = M->StateCode ;
  .AND.  .NOT. EOF()
  I = I + 1
  Table ( I ) = [ ] + CODE + [ | ] + State + [ ]
  SKIP
ENDDO

TotStates = I
OnScreen  = IIF ( TotStates <= 17 , TotStates , 17 )

@ 1, 25 MENU Table, TotStates, OnScreen TITLE [ Similar States ]
Selected =  1
READ MENU TO Selected

M->StateCode = ;
IIF ( Selected = 0 , [ ] , ;
                    SUBSTR ( Table ( Selected ) , 2 , 2 ) )

RETURN
```

then displays a window of everything that matches what's left. My users love this approach. The abbreviated list it produces is demonstrated in FIG. 9-9.

Special effects

The following sections contain several examples of special effects that you can do using FoxPro 2.0. These examples include multi-column menus, airline seating selection using PROMPTs, and custom pop-ups.

Multi-column menus

You can use the PROMPT command to build your own pop-ups, in multi-column format, if you wish. The example in LISTING 9-10 displays a pop-up of states. Figure 9-10 shows the resulting screen. You can use the first letter of a state to get near it, then use the arrow keys to find it. Notice that cursor movement is limited to the order of the @ *coordinates* PROMPT statements in your code.

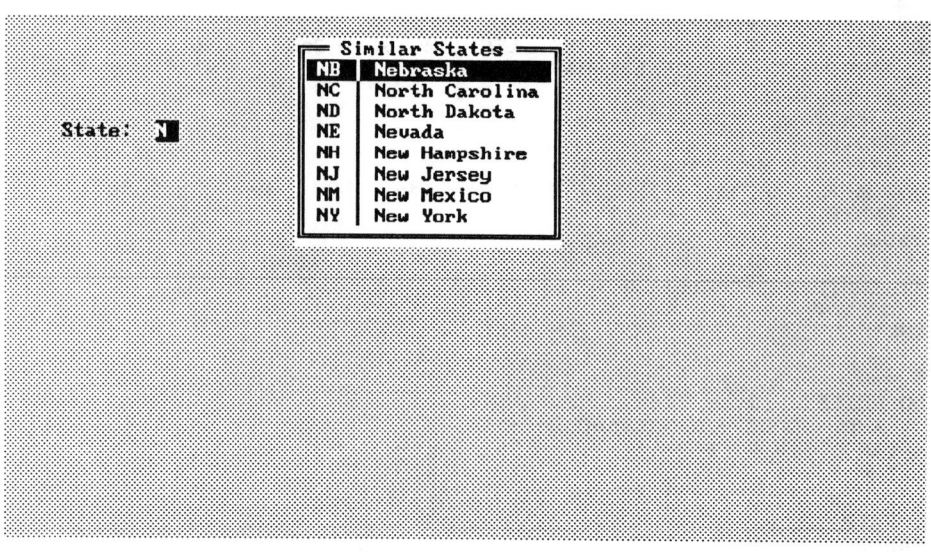

```
                 ┌─ Similar States ─┐
                 │ NB │ Nebraska      │
                 │ NC │ North Carolina│
                 │ ND │ North Dakota  │
   State: N      │ NE │ Nevada        │
                 │ NH │ New Hampshire │
                 │ NJ │ New Jersey    │
                 │ NM │ New Mexico    │
                 │ NY │ New York      │
                 └───────────────────┘
```

9-9   My favorite near-miss search routine (NEARMISS.PRG).

Listing 9-10

```
* Program-ID...: MultProm.PRG

SET COLOR TO GR+/B
CLEAR
DIMENSION state ( 50 )

state (  1 ) = [AK]
state (  2 ) = [AL]
state (  3 ) = [AZ]
state (  4 ) = [CA]
state (  5 ) = [CO]
state (  6 ) = [DE]
state (  7 ) = [FL]
state (  8 ) = [GA]
state (  9 ) = [HI]
state ( 10 ) = [IA]
state ( 11 ) = [ID]
state ( 12 ) = [IL]
state ( 13 ) = [IN]
state ( 14 ) = [KS]
state ( 15 ) = [KY]
state ( 16 ) = [LA]
state ( 17 ) = [MA]
state ( 18 ) = [MD]
state ( 19 ) = [ME]
state ( 20 ) = [MI]
state ( 21 ) = [MN]
state ( 22 ) = [MO]
state ( 23 ) = [MS]
state ( 24 ) = [MT]
state ( 25 ) = [NB]
state ( 26 ) = [NC]
state ( 27 ) = [ND]
state ( 28 ) = [NE]
```

```
state ( 29 ) = [NH]
state ( 30 ) = [NJ]
state ( 31 ) = [NM]
state ( 32 ) = [NY]
state ( 33 ) = [OH]
state ( 34 ) = [OK]
state ( 35 ) = [OR]
state ( 36 ) = [PA]
state ( 37 ) = [RI]
state ( 38 ) = [SC]
state ( 39 ) = [SD]
state ( 40 ) = [TN]
state ( 41 ) = [TX]
state ( 42 ) = [UT]
state ( 43 ) = [VA]
state ( 44 ) = [VT]
state ( 45 ) = [WA]
state ( 46 ) = [WI]
state ( 47 ) = [WV]
state ( 48 ) = [WY]

SET COLOR TO N/W,W+/R
DO Prompts
SET COLOR TO N/W,W+/R

SET CONFIRM ON
MENU TO z

DO WHILE z = 0
  WAIT WINDOW [You must select a state] TIMEOUT 2
  DO Prompts
  MENU TO z
ENDDO

SET COLOR TO GR+/B
@ 15, 3 SAY 'Selected ' + STATE ( z )

WAIT WINDOW

RETURN STATE ( z )


PROCEDURE Prompts

@ 0, 2 CLEAR TO 13, 78
@ 0, 2       TO 13, 78

@  1, 3 PROMPT [AK   Arkansas      ]
@  2, 3 PROMPT [AL   Alabama       ]
@  3, 3 PROMPT [AZ   Arizona       ]
@  4, 3 PROMPT [CA   California    ]
@  5, 3 PROMPT [CO   Colorado      ]
@  6, 3 PROMPT [DE   Delaware      ]
@  7, 3 PROMPT [FL   Florida       ]
@  8, 3 PROMPT [GA   Georgia       ]
@  9, 3 PROMPT [HI   Hawaii        ]
@ 10, 3 PROMPT [IA   Iowa          ]
@ 11, 3 PROMPT [ID   Idaho         ]
@ 12, 3 PROMPT [IL   Illinois      ]

@  1,22 PROMPT [IN   Indiana       ]
```

Listing 9-10 Continued

```
@  2,22 PROMPT [KS  Kansas        ]
@  3,22 PROMPT [KY  Kentucky      ]
@  4,22 PROMPT [LA  Louisiana     ]
@  5,22 PROMPT [MA  Massachusetts ]
@  6,22 PROMPT [MD  Maryland      ]
@  7,22 PROMPT [ME  Maine         ]
@  8,22 PROMPT [MI  Michigan      ]
@  9,22 PROMPT [MN  Minnesota     ]
@ 10,22 PROMPT [MO  Missouri      ]
@ 11,22 PROMPT [MS  Mississippi   ]
@ 12,22 PROMPT [MT  Montana       ]

@  1,41 PROMPT [NB  Nebraska      ]
@  2,41 PROMPT [NC  North Carolina]
@  3,41 PROMPT [ND  North Dakota  ]
@  4,41 PROMPT [NE  Nevada        ]
@  5,41 PROMPT [NH  New Hampshire ]
@  6,41 PROMPT [NJ  New Jersey    ]
@  7,41 PROMPT [NM  New Mexico    ]
@  8,41 PROMPT [NY  New York      ]
@  9,41 PROMPT [OH  Ohio          ]
@ 10,41 PROMPT [OK  Oklahoma      ]
@ 11,41 PROMPT [OR  Oregon        ]
@ 12,41 PROMPT [PA  Pennsylvania  ]

@  1,60 PROMPT [RI  Rhode Island  ]
@  2,60 PROMPT [SC  South Carolina]
@  3,60 PROMPT [SD  South Dakota  ]
@  4,60 PROMPT [TN  Tennessee     ]
@  5,60 PROMPT [TX  Texas         ]
@  6,60 PROMPT [UT  Utah          ]
@  7,60 PROMPT [VA  Virginia      ]
@  8,60 PROMPT [VT  Vermont       ]
@  9,60 PROMPT [WA  Washington    ]
@ 10,60 PROMPT [WI  Wisconsin     ]
@ 11,60 PROMPT [WV  West Virginia ]
@ 12,60 PROMPT [WY  Wyoming       ]

RETURN
```

Airline seating using PROMPTs

A very interesting variation of this is the visual scheduling menu. Using the same technique seen in the last example, you can perform seating scheduling on a flight on Pinter Airlines (LISTING 9-11). The interior of the First Class cabin is shown in FIG. 9-11.

Custom pop-ups

Sometimes, the interface design requires something that can't be handled satisfactorily using any of the previous techniques. If that's the case, write your own!

One interesting use of pop-up browse windows is to validate a code from a file. As simple as point-and-shoot seems, at least one of my clients wanted his clerks to be able to simply press a single letter corresponding

```
AK  Arkansas       IN  Indiana         NB  Nebraska        RI  Rhode Island
AL  Alabama        KS  Kansas          NC  North Carolina  SC  South Carolina
AZ  Arizona        KY  Kentucky        ND  North Dakota    SD  South Dakota
CA  California     LA  Louisiana       NE  Nevada          TN  Tennessee
CO  Colorado       MA  Massachusetts   NH  New Hampshire   TX  Texas
DE  Delaware       MD  Maryland        NJ  New Jersey      UT  Utah
FL  Florida        ME  Maine           NM  New Mexico      VA  Virginia
GA  Georgia        MI  Michigan        NY  New York        VT  Vermont
HI  Hawaii         MN  Minnesota       OH  Ohio            WA  Washington
IA  Iowa           MO  Missouri        OK  Oklahoma        WI  Wisconsin
ID  Idaho          MS  Mississippi     OR  Oregon          WV  West Virginia
IL  Illinois       MT  Montana         PA  Pennsylvania    WY  Wyoming
```

9-10 A multi-column PROMPT menu (MULTPROM.PRG).

Listing 9-11

```
* Program-ID.....: Seating.PRG
* Purpose........: Demonstrates a multi-column menu to allocate plane seats.
* -- Another file would contain the equipment type, since aircraft type
* -- determines seating arrangement and hence which display routine to call.

SAVE SCREEN

ColrSwitch = []    && For Mono Colors, use [.NOT.], otherwise []

Interior  = IIF ( &ColrSwitch IsColor() , [W+/B]       , [N/W]      )
Ocupado   = IIF ( &ColrSwitch IsColor() , [B+/B]       , [N/W]      )
Libre     = IIF ( &ColrSwitch IsColor() , [GR+/B,W+/R] , [W+/N,N*/W])

USE FLIGHTS INDEX FLIGHTS

*       Structure for database: FLIGHTS.DBF
*       Field  Field Name  Type         Width    Key Seq   -------Notes-------
*         1    FLITENUM    Character      4        1
*         2    DATE        Date           8        2       Key is DTOC(date,1)
*         3    SECTION     Character      1        3
*         4    SEATNUM     Character      2                Row(letter)+seat#
*       ** Total **                      16

* -- This information would be selected by the operator.

Flight  = [1441]
Today   = {02/10/91}  && Ordinarily we'd use DATE(), but test data is 02/10/91
FltDate = DTOC ( Today , 1 )
SectNum = [1]

PUBLIC row, col
DIMENSION SEATS ( 200 )    && Array of available seats.
seat = 1
```

Special effects 197

Listing 9-11 Continued

```
DO WHILE .T.

  * -- Display the seating area of the airplane, blocking out reserved seats.
  DO Seating

  * -- Prompt for seating assignment.
  SET  CONFIRM ON
  MENU TO seat
  SET  CONFIRM OFF

  IF seat = 0
    EXIT
  ENDIF

  WAIT [Get payment for ticket here] WINDOW TIMEOUT 3

* if paid,
  DO Reserve
* endif

ENDDO

RESTORE SCREEN

RETURN


PROCEDURE Seating

SET COLOR TO &Interior

CLEAR

NumSeats = 12    && deHavilland Otter
Width    =  4

@ 1, 17      SAY [Pinter Airlines]
@ 2, 4       SAY  [Flight ] + FliteNum
@ 2, COL()+3 SAY     [Date ] + DTOC ( Today )
@ 2, COL()+3 SAY [Section ] + Section

@ 3, 3 TO NumSeats + 4, Width * 10 + 3 DOUBLE

SeatNo = 0
FOR I = 1 TO NumSeats
  FOR J = 1 TO Width
    SeatNumber = CHR ( 64 + I ) + STR ( J , 1 )
    Key = Flight + FltDate + SectNum + SeatNumber
    SEEK key
    IF FOUND()
      SET COLOR TO &Ocupado
      @ I + 3 , ((J-1)*10) + 5 SAY     "[ " + SeatNumber + " ]"
    ELSE
      SeatNo = SeatNo + 1
      SEATS ( SeatNo ) = SeatNumber
      SET COLOR TO &Libre
      @ I + 3 , ((J-1)*10) + 5 SAY     "[ " + SeatNumber + " ]"
      @ I + 3 , ((J-1)*10) + 6 PROMPT  " " + SeatNumber + " "
    ENDIF
```

```
      ENDFOR J
   ENDFOR I

   SET COLOR TO &Ocupado
   @ NumSeats+6, 4 SAY PADC ( [ Booked ]    , Width*10 )
   SET COLOR TO &Libre
   @ NumSeats+5, 4 SAY PADC ( [ Available ] , Width*10 )
   SET COLOR TO &Interior
   @ 24,  0 SAY PADC ( 'Press ESCAPE to exit without scheduling' , 80 )

RETURN

PROCEDURE Reserve

   GO BOTTOM
   IF FliteNum <> [~]
      APPEND BLANK
   ENDIF

   REPLACE NEXT 1 ;
    FLITENUM WITH Flight   , ;
    DATE     WITH Today    , ;
    Section  WITH SectNum  , ;
    SeatNum  WITH SEATS ( Seat)

RETURN
```

9-11 Geographically correct prompts—Airline reservations (SEATING.PRG).

to the position of an item in the browse window. A sample of what he wanted appears in the FIG. 9-12.

In order to do this specific browse exactly the way the doctor ordered (he's a doctor in Puerto Rico), I had to write the code myself. My client actually provided the starting point and is acknowledged in the program header.

```
                CODE        State

            A   AK          Arkansas
            B   AL          Alabama
            C   AZ          Arizona
            D   CA          California
            E   CO          Colorado
            F   DE          Delaware
            G   FL          Florida
            H   GA          Georgia
            I   HI          Hawaii
            J   IA          Iowa
            K   ID          Idaho
            L   IL          Illinois
            M   IN          Indiana
            N   KS          Kansas
            O   KY          Kentucky

        To exit this table, press the ESCAPE key.
        USE ↑, ↓, PgUp o PgDn - ENTER to select
```

9-12 A Custom pop-up (MYLOOKUP.PRG).

The routine in LISTING 9-12 is generic and can be used by any of your data entry routines, simply by supplying the calling parameters:

- Filename
- Index filename
- Key field name
- Description field name

This program can be used with a mouse, as well. Note that the mouse doesn't do anything except announce its row and column location. So, you have to calculate what menu element that row number corresponds to and stuff the keyboard buffer with the code that says what to do next. I rather generously allowed the user to click the mouse anywhere on the screen; only the row number is looked at.

Listing 9-12

```
* Program-ID...: MyLookup.PRG ( TestBed is DrLookup.PRG )
* Credits......: Based on an idea by Dr. Jose Rodriguez-Santana, Caguas, P.R.
* Purpose......: Does a lookup of an indexed validation file, allowing the
*              : user to select a table entry using either a single letter,
*              : the ENTER key, or a mouse click.
* Usage:.......:
* xvar = MyLookup("DataFileName","IndexFileName","KeyField","DescripField" )
* -- The next 5 lines are required by this routine, and by a subsequent
* -- data entry screen technique. Bear with us for two chapters and you'll
* -- see what this is all about. If you want to use the routine without
* -- the 'read loop' technilogy, remove these lines and those marked XXXXX,
* -- below.
```

```
DIMENSION var(1,1)
page          = 1
it            = 1
var ( 1 , 1 ) = [StateCode]
StateCode     = '12'     && Initial value - usually from data entry field

* -- END of read loop patch.

xvar = MyLookup ( [States],[States],[CODE],[State] )
WAIT WINDOW


PROCEDURE MyLookup
PARAMETERS _file, _index, _key, _descrip

Selected = ALLTRIM(STR(SELECT(),2))

IF USED    ( _file )
   SELECT ( _file )
ELSE
   SELECT 10
   USE &_file INDEX &_Index
ENDIF

* -- Remove this next line if not using read loops    XXXXXX
    x = var ( page , it )
* -- REPLACE WITH THE FOLLOWING:
* -- x = 'Name of variable containing the data to search for'
* -- END OF PATCH AREA.

SEEK &x

IF &_key == &x
   SELECT &Selected
   RETURN .T.
ENDIF
GO TOP

SAVE SCREEN TO LOOKUP
SET COLOR TO GR+/B,N/W

v1 = " "
GenTitle  = " Key Field Name        Description     "
LinMacro  = " " + _key + "+ [              ] +"+ _descrip + " "
TitleStrg =    LinMacro    && was v3
EmptyLin2 = " " + _key + SPACE ( LEN ( &_key ) + 5 + 1 ) + _descrip + " "
ShiftVar  = " " + _key
mkey      =    PWINDOW ( GenTitle, LinMacro, ShiftVar, TitleStrg )

RESTORE SCREEN FROM LOOKUP

SELECT &Selected

* -- Remove this next line if not using read loops    XXXXXX
x = var ( page , it )
* -- End of patch.

&x = mkey

RETURN .T.
```

Special effects

Listing 9-12 Continued

```
PROCEDURE PWINDOW
PARAMETERS GenHead, LineMacro, RetVal, TitlString

PRIVATE RetVal,Pointer,LineKount,ScrnLine,KeyPressed,EmptyLine,Selected
PRIVATE I

Letters    = "ABCDEFGHIJKLMNOabcdefghijklmno"

Home       = CHR (  1 )
PgDn       = CHR (  3 )
UpArrow    = CHR (  5 )
End        = CHR (  6 )
Enter      = CHR ( 13 )
PgUp       = CHR ( 18 )
DnArrow    = CHR ( 24 )
EscKey     = CHR ( 27 )

ValidKeys = Letters +Home +PgDn +UpArrow +End +Enter +PgUp +DnArrow +EscKey

TestLen = MAX ( LEN ( GenHead ), ;
                MAX ( LEN ( &LineMacro ) , LEN ( TitlString ) ) )

IF TestLen + 2 >= 73
   WAIT "Window too wide - resize" WINDOW TIMEOUT 1
   RETURN "ESC"
ENDIF

DIMENSION Where2Go ( 16 )    && can this be 15?

SET COLOR TO GR+/B,N/W
EmptyLine  = [°] + SPACE ( 2 + TestLen ) + [°]
LeftCol = ( ( 80 - LEN ( EmptyLine ) ) / 2 )

@  1, LeftCol    SAY [Í] + REPL ( [ë] , TestLen + 2 ) + [¡]
@  2, LeftCol    SAY EmptyLine
@  2, LeftCol+1  SAY EmptyLin2
@  3, LeftCol    SAY [û] + REPL ( [-] , TestLen + 2 ) + [Ç]
@  4, LeftCol    SAY [°] + SPACE ( 2 + TestLen )      + [°]

FOR I = 1 TO 15
   @ 4+I, LeftCol - 2 SAY CHR(64+I) + [ ] + EmptyLine
ENDFOR

@ 20, LeftCol SAY [å] + REPL ( [ë] , TestLen + 2 ) + [ƒ]

@ 23,  0 CLEAR
@ 23, 15 SAY [    To exit this table, press the ESCAPE key.   ]
@ 24, 15 SAY [    USE 8, 9, PgUp o PgDn - ENTER to select     ]

SET COLOR TO N/W
@ 24, 24 SAY [8]
@ 24, 27 SAY [9]
@ 24, 30 SAY [PgUp]
@ 24, 37 SAY [PgDn]

SET COLOR TO GR+/B,N/W

SAVE SCREEN TO ScrnSave
```

Pop-ups and pulldowns

```
DO WHILE .T.

   SET COLOR TO GR+/B,W+/R

* -- Load data to array

   Pointer = RECNO()
   LineKount = 1
   DO WHILE LineKount <= 15 .AND. .NOT. EOF()
     @ LineKount + 4 , LeftCol + 2 SAY &LineMacro
     Where2Go ( LineKount ) = RECNO()
     LineKount = LineKount + 1
     IF EOF()
       EXIT
     ELSE
       SKIP
     ENDIF
   ENDDO

   NumOnPage = LineKount - 2
   SAVE SCREEN TO SaveScrn

   GO Pointer
   ScrnLine = 5

* -- input loop...

   DO WHILE ScrnLine >= 5 .and. ScrnLine <= 19 .AND. .NOT. EOF()

      SET COLOR TO N/W
      @ ScrnLine,LeftCol+2 SAY &LineMacro
      SET COLOR TO W+/R
      @ ScrnLine,LeftCol    SAY "7"

      SET COLOR TO GR+/B,N/W

      KeyPressed = KeyPress ( ValidKeys )

      DO CASE

         CASE KeyPressed = DnArrow

           SKIP
           IF EOF() .OR. ScrnLine >= 19
             IF EOF()
               GO TOP
             ENDIF
             RESTORE SCREEN FROM ScrnSave
             EXIT
           ELSE
             ScrnLine = ScrnLine + 1
             RESTORE SCREEN FROM SaveScrn
             LOOP
           ENDIF

         CASE KeyPressed = UpArrow

           IF ScrnLine <= 5
             SKIP -(ScrnLine - 4)
```

Special effects

Listing 9-12 Continued

```
      RESTORE SCREEN FROM ScrnSave
      EXIT
    ELSE
      ScrnLine = ScrnLine - 1
      SKIP -1
      RESTORE SCREEN FROM SaveScrn
    ENDIF

CASE KeyPressed = EscKey

    Selected = SPACE ( LEN ( &_key ) )
    RETURN Selected

CASE KeyPressed = Enter

    Selected = &RetVal
    RETURN Selected

CASE KeyPressed = PgDn

    SKIP 15
    IF EOF()
    SKIP -15
    ENDIF
    RESTORE SCREEN FROM ScrnSave
    EXIT

CASE KeyPressed = PgUp

    SKIP -15
    RESTORE SCREEN FROM ScrnSave
    EXIT

CASE KeyPressed = Home

    GO TOP
    RESTORE SCREEN FROM ScrnSave
    EXIT

CASE KeyPressed = End

    GO BOTTOM
    SKIP -14
    RESTORE SCREEN FROM ScrnSave
    EXIT

OTHERWISE

    savLetterNum = ScrnLine
    LetterNum = AT ( UPPER ( KeyPressed ) , Letters )
    IF LetterNum > NumOnPage
      = MaBell()
      LetterNum  = savLetterNum
      LOOP
    ENDIF

    IF TYPE ( "Where2Go ( AT ( UPPER ( KeyPressed ) , Letters ) )" );
         = [N]
```

204   Pop-ups and pulldowns

```
            savLetterNum = ScrnLine
            LetterNum = AT(UPPER(KeyPressed),[ABCDEFGHIJKLMNO])
            where = STR ( Where2Go ( LetterNum ) , 2 , 0 )
            IF LetterNum > NumOnPage
              = MaBell()
              LetterNum  = savLetterNum
              LOOP
            ENDIF
            GO &where
            RESTORE SCREEN FROM SaveScrn
            SET COLOR TO R/W
            @ LetterNum+4,LeftCol+2 SAY &LineMacro
            SET COLOR TO GR+/B,N/W
            @ LetterNum+4,LeftCol    SAY [7]
            Selected = &RetVal
                RETURN Selected

           ENDIF

         ENDCASE

      ENDDO

   ENDDO


   PROCEDURE KeyPress
   PARAMETERS GoodKeys
   PRIVATE KeyStroke

   KeyStroke = 0

   DO WHILE .T.

     KeyStroke = INKEY(0,"HM")

     IF KeyStroke >= -9

       DO CASE

         CASE BETWEEN ( KeyStroke , -9 , -1 )
           KeyStroke = [F] + ALLTRIM(STR(ABS(KeyStroke)+1,2))
*                                    âáááêáááêááááááááááêááááêì*

         CASE KeyStroke = 151          && mouse down...

           row = MROW()                && Get mouse pointer position
           IF row > 5 .AND. row < 21   && clicked inside box...
             KeyStroke = CHR(60+row)   && e.g., row 1 (line 5) is "A", etc.
           ELSE
             KeyStroke = CHR(27)       && escape
           ENDIF

         OTHERWISE

           KeyStroke = CHR(KeyStroke)

       ENDCASE

       IF KeyStroke $ GoodKeys
         EXIT
```

Listing 9-12 Continued
```
    ENDIF

  ENDIF

ENDDO

RETURN KeyStroke

PROCEDURE InCenter
PARAMETERS text,row

@ row, ROUND((79-LEN(text))/2, 0) SAY text

RETURN


PROCEDURE MaBell

FOR I = 1 TO 3
  SET BELL TO 1300,1
  ?? CHR(7)
  SET BELL TO 1400,1
  ?? CHR(7)
ENDFOR

RETURN .T.
```

Pop-ups that display several fields

FoxPro 2.0 now supports many more pop-up commands and features than did FoxPro 1.02. The DEFINE MENU, DEFINE POPUP, and DEFINE PAD commands contain additional options to permit construction of very sophisticated option menus. For example, you can use the code in LISTING 9-13 to display all customer codes on file in a pop-up.

Listing 9-13
```
SELECT CUSTOMER
mcust = [            ]
DEFINE POPUP CUST FROM 1, 1 MARGIN SHADOW ;
   PROMPT FIELDS CUSTCODE + [|] + CUSTNAME
ON SELECTION CUST DO GotACust WITH PROMPT()
ACTIVATE POPUP CUST
LOCATE FOR CUSTCODE = mcust
...

PROCEDURE GotACust
PARAMETERS mprompt
mcust = mprompt
DEACTIVATE POPUP CUST
```

Selecting multiple values from a pop-up

To permit selection of several entries, add the keyword MULTI to the DEFINE POPUP line. Use Ctrl–Spacebar to mark entries. Then, the following code:

```
SCAN
  IF MRKBAR([CUST],RECNO( ))
    ? [Selected ] + Customer
  ENDIF
ENDSCAN
```

will list all selected entries. Having coded more than a few multi-element selection procedures in my time, I'm mighty glad to have one straight out of the box from Fox.

Summary

This chapter contained examples of how to do various types of pop-up menus and demonstrations of some of the things you can do with them. If you don't see exactly the pop-up you need, write your own. One of the examples seen here should give you a healthy head start.

10
Advanced screen building

The previous chapter showed off some of the sensational features of Fox-Pro 2.0's screen builder. However, there's yet another way to use screens and menus to drive applications. FoxPro 2.0 contains two new ideas that together permit a new departure in software design:

- READ CYCLE ACTIVATE/SHOW
- POP/PUSH _MSYSMENU

If you carefully study the design of this application and imitate its component parts, your software can work the same way.

The LaserDisk library example

The example I'll use for this case study is the Laser Video Disk application that comes with FoxPro 2.0. This is one of the nicest demonstration programs I've ever seen. It certainly showcases FoxPro's finer points. The structure of the database is shown in TABLE 10-1.

The sample application is called LASER1.APP. To compile it, go to the command window and type:

BUILD APP LASER1 FROM LASER1

Then type:

DO LASER1

The screen that appears is shown in FIG. 10-1 on page 210.

There's one striking difference from traditional FoxPro applications: you *already are* in EDIT mode. As you move from field to field, you can change the data. Notice the pop-up validation in the Rating field (FIG. 10-2 shown on page 210).

Table 10-1 Structure for the LASER.DBF database.

Memo file block size: 64

Field	Field Name	Type	Width	Dec	Index
1	CATNO	Character	10		Asc
2	TITLE	Character	80		Asc
3	PRICE	Numeric	6	2	Asc
4	RATING	Character	5		Asc
5	XQUALITY	Numeric	2		
6	CRITICS	Numeric	1		Asc
7	ACQUIRED	Date	8		Asc
8	SDIGITAL	Logical	1		
9	XDIGITAL	Logical	1		
10	CX	Logical	1		
11	STEREO	Logical	1		
12	SURROUND	Logical	1		
13	LETTERBOX	Logical	1		
14	BLK_WHT	Logical	1		
15	CLOSECAP	Logical	1		
16	CAV	Logical	1		
17	SUBTITLED	Logical	1		
18	DUBBED	Logical	1		
19	SILENT	Logical	1		
20	COMMENTARY	Logical	1		
21	SUPPLEMENT	Logical	1		
22	DURATION	Numeric	3		Asc
23	SIDES	Numeric	2		
24	YEAR	Numeric	4		Asc
25	DESCRIPT	Memo	10		
26	STUDIO	Character	20		Asc
27	KIDS	Logical	1		
** Total **			167		

If you pop up the menu, you'll see the screen shown in FIG. 10-3. If you select Go To, you'll see the screen shown in FIG. 10-4. If you select Report from the menu, the screen in FIG. 10-5 appears.

They are nice screens; however, so far, it all looks like the sort of programs you're used to. Go to the buttons along the bottom and either highlight Next or click on it with the mouse. Holy Toledo, it skipped to the next record. Is this a menu? If you hold down the Alt key and press D, E, O, or N, you'll get a pulldown menu with more choices on it. So, this must be the menu. If so, what was that thing you clicked on at the bottom of the screen?

For most programmers, the techniques used in these screens are new concepts. To understand them, I'll look at the components first, then see

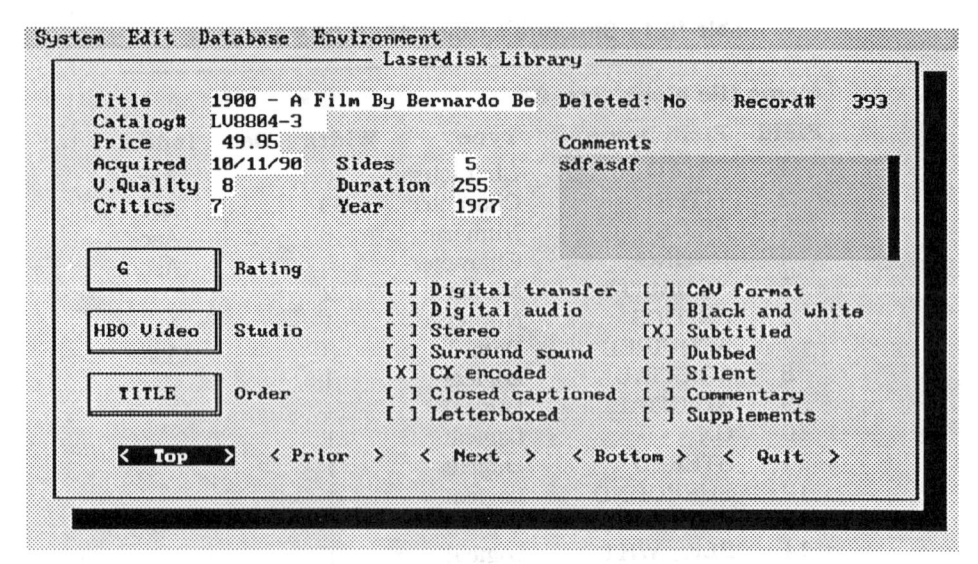

10-1 The LASER1 input screen.

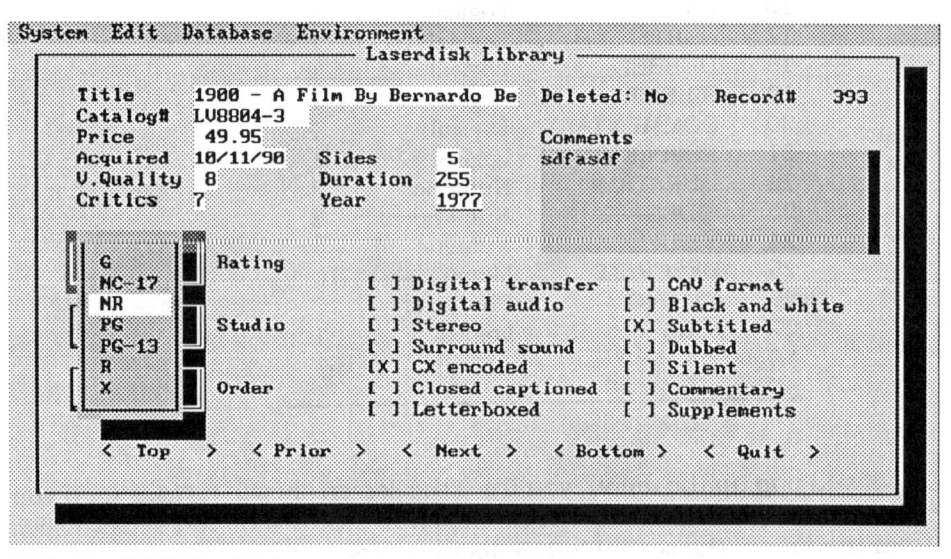

10-2 The RATING validation pop-up.

how the project builder brings them together. Finally, I'll look at the generated code's logic.

The screen builder

The screen definition is found in LASER.SCX. To look at it, go to the FOXPRO2\GOODIES\LASER directory and fire up FoxPro, then type:

    MODIFY PROJECT LASER1

210 Advanced screen building

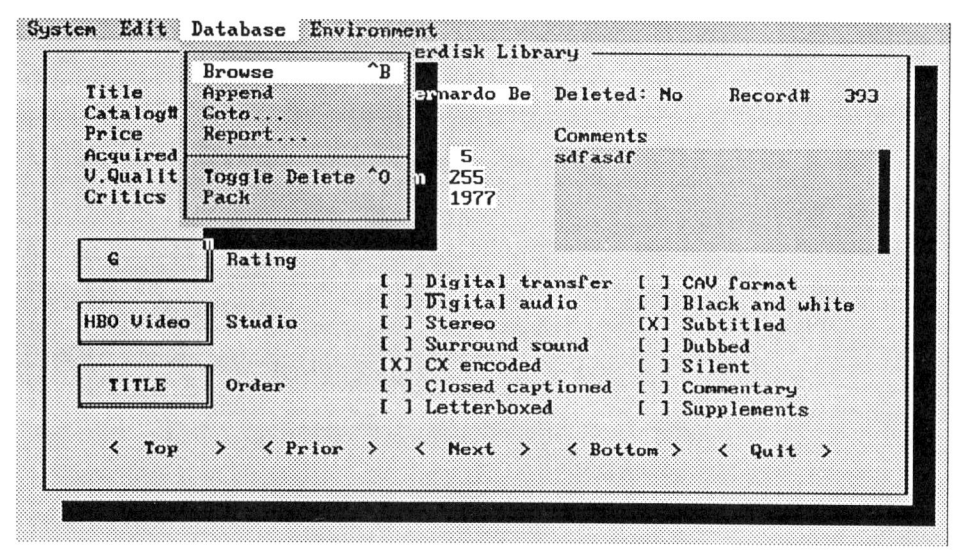

10-3 Pulling down the FoxPro menu over the input screen.

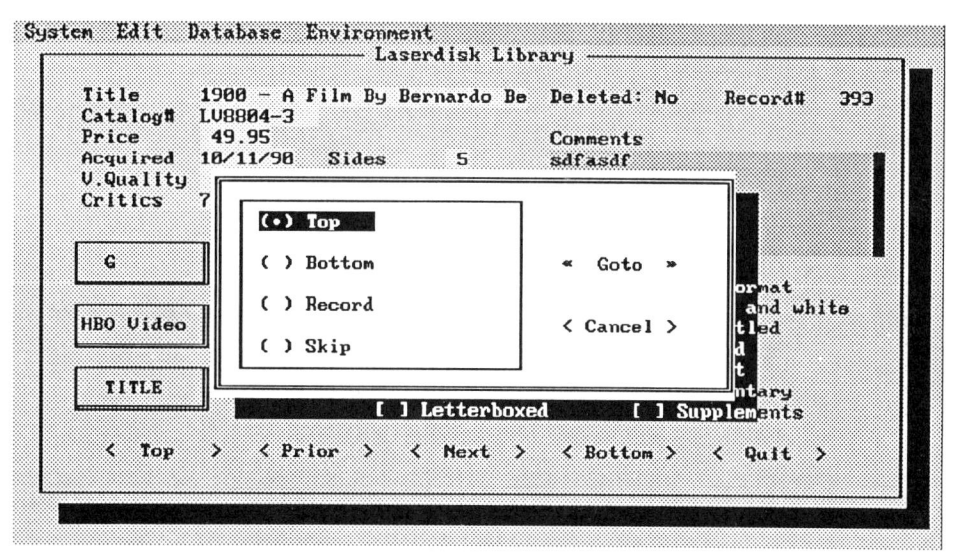

10-4 The Go To dialog from the FoxPro menu.

The components of the project appear in the project manager window. If the window is too small, Ctrl-F10 opens the window up to full-screen height (FIG. 10-6).

To look at the screen, select the LASER screen set and press Enter. If several screens make up the screen set, you have to select one by highlighting or clicking on it. Then, click on Edit and Ok and the screen will appear (FIG. 10-7).

If you select options, FoxPro opens up editing windows to let you store

The screen builder   211

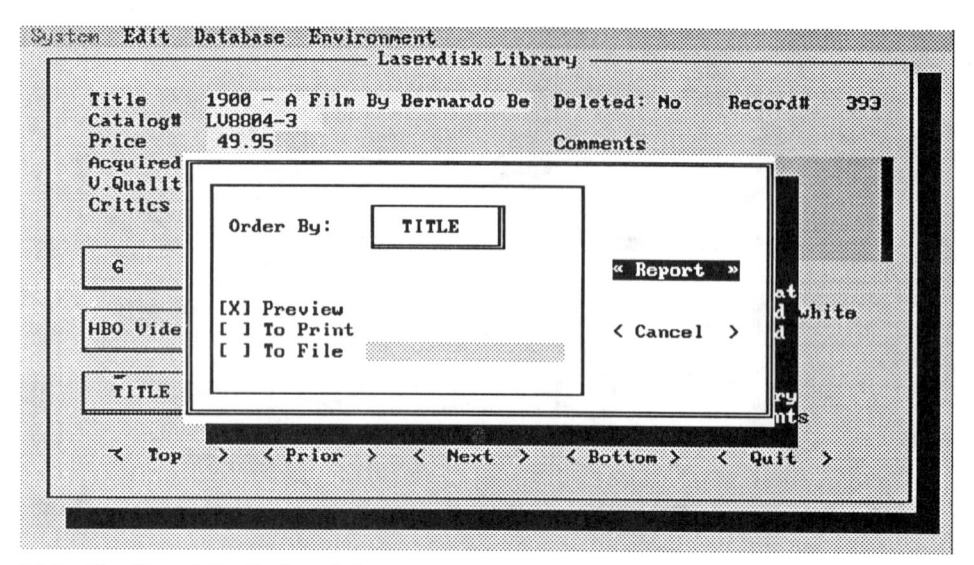

10-5 The Report Destination dialog.

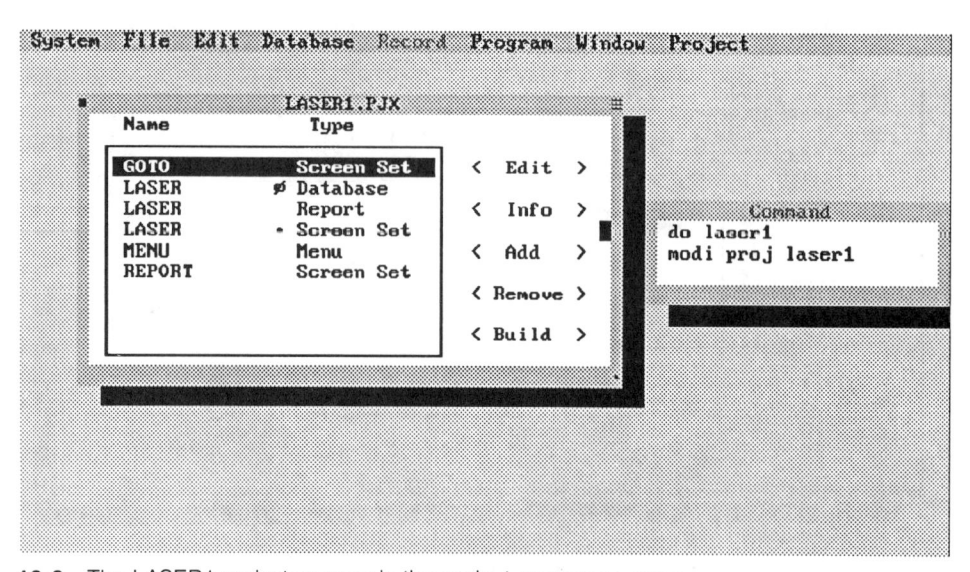

10-6 The LASER1 project as seen in the project manager screen.

code snippets in memo fields within the screen set. Thereafter, it generates those little functions with the unpronounceable names. That's why you're reminded not to use the FUNCTION or PROCEDURE statement in your code; FoxPro generates its own.

The screen code for this application is its starting point. Notice where it runs the menu program. This is analogous to running SideKick's startup program SK.COM, which loads the TSR (Terminate and Stay Resident

212 Advanced screen building

10-7 Editing a screen file within a project.

program) and sets up the activation hot key. Thereafter, the touch of a hot key—one of four, in our case—activates the menu.

It's not necessary to generate the source code for this screen in order to run it; if you ask the project manager to BUILD PROJECT, it will generate the code to a work area, compile it, and store the compiled code in the project file in a memo field. The source code will be saved only in the directory where the screen file lives if you checked the save generated code check box in the dialog window. Once you're confident that it's working, you probably will never look at the generated code again.

The screen builder code

The code in LISTING 10-1 was generated from a sample screen built by none other than Dr. Dave Fulton, President of Fox Software. Note that screen programs have the extension .SPR, not .PRG. (You actually can have a program called LASER.PRG, a screen called LASER.SCX, a report called LASER.FRX, and a project called LASER.PJX, which produce an application called LASER.APP.)

This is all standard generated code, to ensure that the state of the system is returned to the way it was before this program started up. I've not felt the need to set FoxPro's compatibility to anything other than the defaults, but the Fox Software guys are very considerate.

The REGIONAL declaration ensures that the variables currarea, talkstat, and compstat don't conflict with similarly named variables in other generated applications, which use the same variable names. You also can define your own regional variables, and they'll be similarly protected. This is

Listing 10-1

```
*
*
*        ┌─────────────────────────────────────────────────────────┐
*        │                                                         │
*        │    04/11/91              LASER.SPR            12:47:51  │
*        │                                                         │
*        ├─────────────────────────────────────────────────────────┤
*        │                                                         │
*        │    Systems Group                                        │
*        │                                                         │
*        │    Copyright (c) 1991 Fox Software                      │
*        │    134 West South Boundary                              │
*        │    Perrsyburg, OH   43551                               │
*        │                                                         │
*        │    Description:                                         │
*        │    This program was automatically generated by GENSCRN. │
*        │                                                         │
*        └─────────────────────────────────────────────────────────┘
*

#REGION 0
REGIONAL m.currarea, m.talkstat, m.compstat

IF SET("TALK") = "ON"
   SET TALK OFF
   m.talkstat = "ON"
ELSE
   m.talkstat = "OFF"
ENDIF
m.compstat = SET("COMPATIBLE")
SET COMPATIBLE OFF
```

necessitated by the fact that, in the event-driven world, you never know where your program's been.

Next, the LASER window is defined (LISTING 10-2). Saving the prior SELECT area and opening the file needed by this window are standard practices in the new order.

Listing 10-2

```
DEFINE WINDOW laser ;
   FROM INT((SROW()-22)/2),INT((SCOL()-75)/2) ;
   TO INT((SROW()-22)/2)+21,INT((SCOL()-75)/2)+74 ;
   TITLE " Laserdisk Library " ;
   FLOAT ;
   CLOSE ;
   SHADOW ;
   MINIMIZE ;
   COLOR SCHEME 1

m.currarea = SELECT()

IF USED("laser")
   SELECT laser
ELSE
   SELECT 0
   USE (LOCFILE("laser.dbf","DBF","Where is laser?")) ORDER 0
ENDIF
```

214   Advanced screen building

Setup code is declared in the window's SETUP snippet. To get to it, press Alt–C, then click on the Setup check box. You'll see a window open up behind your screen, but it doesn't go there until you click on the Ok control. At that time, you can type in whatever code you want executed before your user gets to type anything in this screen.

The most exciting element in LASER.SPR is the new SQL SELECT commands, which are shown in LISTING 10-3.

Listing 10-3

```
*
*
*                    ┌─────────────────────────────────────────────┐
*                    │                                             │
*                    │              LASER Setup Code               │
*                    │                                             │
*                    └─────────────────────────────────────────────┘
*
*
#REGION 1
*
*    Initialize the arrays
*
regional studs, rats, st, rt, x

select   distinct studio;
         order by studio;
         from laser;
         into arra studs

select   distinct rating;
         order by rating;
         from laser;
         into arra rats

ord = 2
set order to title
go top
```

Next, the previous application's menu (or FoxPro's system menu, if that's where you came from) is pushed onto the menu stack and the new menu is defined:

PUSH MENU _MSYSMENU
DO LASERM.MPR

More about that in the following section on the menu builder.

Next, the screen is painted and the GETs initialized (LISTING 10-4). Note that the window is activated with the NOSHOW option, then is filled in and activated again. This causes a crisp, speedy display. As fast as Fox-Pro is, you still can see the fields displaying on the screen one at a time on most machines.

The next field is a mini-memo. It uses a character field, but the EDIT command performs wordwrapping. The SCROLL command allows you to type as much as will fit in the field, yet scroll within a 5-by-29 rectangle.

The screen builder code   215

Listing 10-4 Continued

```
*
*
*           ┌─────────────────────────────────────────────┐
*           │             LASER Screen Layout             │
*           │                                             │
*           └─────────────────────────────────────────────┘
*
#REGION 1
ACTIVATE WINDOW laser NOSHOW
@ 1,3 SAY "Title"
@ 3,3 SAY "Price"
@ 9,15 SAY "Rating"
@ 4,3 SAY "Acquired"
@ 5,24 SAY "Duration"
@ 4,24 SAY "Sides"
@ 6,24 SAY "Year"
@ 3,43 SAY "Comments"
@ 2,3 SAY "Catalog#"
@ 5,3 SAY "V.Quality"
@ 6,3 SAY "Critics"
@ 15,15 SAY "Order"
@ 1,58 SAY "Record#"
@ 12,15 SAY "Studio"
@ 1,43 SAY "Deleted:"
@ 1,67 SAY recno() ;
    SIZE 1,4 ;
    PICTURE "9,999"
@ 1,52 SAY iif(DELETED(),'Yes','No ') ;
    SIZE 1,4
@ 18,5 GET action ;
    PICTURE "@*HN Top;Prior;Next;Bottom;Quit" ;
    SIZE 1,10,3 ;
    DEFAULT 0 ;
    VALID _pui0rfhvh()
@ 1,13 GET laser.title ;
    SIZE 1,28 ;
    DEFAULT " "
@ 2,13 GET laser.catno ;
    SIZE 1,10 ;
    DEFAULT " "
@ 3,13 GET laser.price ;
    SIZE 1,6 ;
    DEFAULT 0 ;
    PICTURE "999.99"
@ 4,13 GET laser.acquired ;
    SIZE 1,8 ;
    DEFAULT {  /  / }
@ 5,13 GET laser.xquality ;
    SIZE 1,2 ;
    DEFAULT 0
@ 6,13 GET laser.critics ;
    SIZE 1,1 ;
    DEFAULT 0
@ 4,34 GET laser.sides ;
    SIZE 1,2 ;
    DEFAULT 0
@ 5,34 GET laser.duration ;
    SIZE 1,3 ;
    DEFAULT 0
```

```
@ 6,34 GET laser.year ;
   SIZE 1,4 ;
   DEFAULT 0
```

The next two fields are pop-ups from the arrays created by the SQL SELECT commands in the setup code (LISTING 10-5). This code doesn't permit adding new codes, so that's a topic for future investigation. However, it does dispense with collateral table files for validation.

Listing 10-5

```
@ 4,43 EDIT laser.descript ;
   SIZE 5,29 ;
   DEFAULT " " ;
   SCROLL
@ 8,2 GET rating ;
   PICTURE "@^" ;
   FROM rats ;
   SIZE 3,12 ;
   DEFAULT 1
@ 11,2 GET studio ;
   PICTURE "@^" ;
   FROM studs ;
   SIZE 3,12 ;
   DEFAULT 1
```

The next field determines the order in which the database is indexed. See the VALID clause, named _pui0rfioq by the screen generator (LISTING 10-6), to see what the program does when this control is selected. The VALID clause is a code snippet entered by the programmer in response to the window that opens up if you select the variable action on the LASER.SCX screen, then check the Valid box on the dialog that appears. This valid clause will be discussed later.

Listing 10-6

```
@ 14,2 GET ord ;
   PICTURE "@^ Record#;Title;Catalog#;Year;Quality;Critics" ;
   SIZE 3,12 ;
   DEFAULT "Record#" ;
   VALID _pui0rfioq()
```

The fields shown in LISTING 10-7 are check boxes and provide a very neat way of dealing with a lot of yes/no information.

Listing 10-7

```
@ 10,28 GET laser.xdigital ;
   PICTURE "@*C Digital transfer" ;
   SIZE 1,20 ;
   DEFAULT 0
@ 11,28 GET laser.sdigital ;
   PICTURE "@*C Digital audio" ;
   SIZE 1,17 ;
```

Listing 10-7 Continued

```
       DEFAULT 0
@ 12,28 GET laser.stereo ;
     PICTURE "@*C Stereo" ;
     SIZE 1,10 ;
     DEFAULT 0
@ 13,28 GET laser.surround ;
     PICTURE "@*C Surround sound" ;
     SIZE 1,18 ;
     DEFAULT 0
@ 14,28 GET laser.cx ;
     PICTURE "@*C CX encoded" ;
     SIZE 1,14 ;
     DEFAULT 0
@ 15,28 GET laser.closecap ;
     PICTURE "@*C Closed captioned" ;
     SIZE 1,20 ;
     DEFAULT 0
@ 16,28 GET laser.letterbox ;
     PICTURE "@*C Letterboxed" ;
     SIZE 1,15 ;
     DEFAULT 0
@ 10,50 GET laser.cav ;
     PICTURE "@*C CAV format" ;
     SIZE 1,14 ;
     DEFAULT 0
@ 11,50 GET laser.blk_wht ;
     PICTURE "@*C Black and white" ;
     SIZE 1,19 ;
     DEFAULT 0
@ 12,50 GET laser.subtitled ;
     PICTURE "@*C Subtitled" ;
     SIZE 1,13 ;
     DEFAULT 0
@ 13,50 GET laser.dubbed ;
     PICTURE "@*C Dubbed" ;
     SIZE 1,10 ;
     DEFAULT 0
@ 14,50 GET laser.silent ;
     PICTURE "@*C Silent" ;
     SIZE 1,10 ;
     DEFAULT 0
@ 15,50 GET laser.commentary ;
     PICTURE "@*C Commentary" ;
     SIZE 1,14 ;
     DEFAULT 0
@ 16,50 GET laser.supplement ;
       PICTURE "@*C Supplements" ;
     SIZE 1,15 ;
     DEFAULT 0
ACTIVATE WINDOW laser
```

Now, you're ready to activate the screen. All it takes is a READ statement:

```
READ CYCLE ;
   SHOW __pui0rfjh7( )
```

Because the screen is going to display record number and deleted/not

218   Advanced screen building

deleted status, those @...SAYs go in the SHOW clause. This is the function that gets executed whenever the command SHOW GETS is encountered in any of the functions in your program. You also can do other things in addition to displaying data in the SHOW clause.

Once the read is exited, you're done with this screen. Because the Close databases and Release windows check boxes were checked, the program closes the LASER database and releases the window LASER. Also, the SELECT area that was open before you got into this screen is selected again. TALK and COMPATIBLE are returned to their former settings. See LISTING 10-8.

Listing 10-8

```
RELEASE WINDOW laser

#REGION 0
IF USED("laser")
  SELECT laser
  USE
ENDIF

SELECT (m.curarea)

IF m.talkstat = "ON"
  SET TALK ON
ENDIF

IF m.compstat = "ON"
  SET COMPATIBLE ON
ENDIF
```

Finally, the cleanup code is executed:

```
#REGION 1
POP MENU _MSYSMENU
```

This was entered in the screen that appears when you press Alt-C in the screen builder and check the CLEANUP check box.

Placement of your functions and procedures

In FoxPro, you include any functions and procedure that your program will call at the end of the main program. It's like using SET PROCEDURE TO *program_name*, except that it's not required, because the program that's currently running is always its own procedure file. Because the screen clean-up code (LISTING 10-9) is placed at the end, this is the place where you stuff all of your own programs. It might seem a little strange at first, but it works as advertised.

Next is the VALID clause for the ACTION control variable (LISTING 10-10), which was discussed previously. Whenever your user clicks on this control or selects one if its options and presses Enter, the VALID clause is activated. If they just Tab or arrow-key through it, nothing happens.

Listing 10-9

```
*
*
*                  LASER Cleanup Code
*
*
procedure menuhit
do case
case prompt() = "Find"
  set cursor off
  wait window "Find executed"
  set cursor on
endcase
```

Listing 10-10

```
*
*
*     _PUI0RFHVH            action VALID
*
*     Function Origin:
*
*     From Screen:          LASER,   Record Number:   20
*     Variable:             action
*     Called By:            VALID Clause
*     Object Type:          Push Button
*
*
*
FUNCTION _pui0rfhvh
#REGION 1
do case
case action = 1
  go top
case action = 2
  skip -1
  if bof()
    go top
  endif
case action = 3
  skip 1
  if eof()
    go bottom
  endif
case action = 4
  go bottom
case action = 5
  clear read
  pop menu _msysmenu
endcase
show gets
return 0



*
*
*     _PUI0RFIOQ            ord VALID
*
*     Function Origin:
```

220 Advanced screen building

```
*
*         From Screen:       LASER,     Record Number:    33
*         Variable:          ord
*         Called By:         VALID Clause
*         Object Type:       Popup
*
*
*
FUNCTION _pui0rfioq
#REGION 1
do case
case ord = 1
  set order to
case ord = 2
  set order to title
case ord = 3
  set order to catno
case ord = 4
  set order to year
case ord = 5
  set order to xquality
case ord = 6
  set order to critics
endcase
go top
show gets
```

This last SHOW GETS is what causes the program to redisplay the data in the current record. Note that the programmer decided to move the record pointer to the top of the file after changing the index tag. I don't necessarily do that. As near as I can tell, it's not required.

The READ SHOW function is where you display fields that aren't GETs (LISTING 10-11). As a precaution involving the use of associated windows that also can issue a SHOW GETS, the function saves the prior window, activates window LASER, and shows its information, then returns to the window that called this routine. In this code, there is only one window. Look at LASER2, however, where the control variable action is moved to another window. You can see that it flows very nicely. If you click Next in LASER2, this code would show the next record, then continue to display the action variable in its own window, because that's where you were when you initiated the action.

Listing 10-11

```
*
*
*        _PUI0RFJH7              Read Level Show
*
*        Function Origin:
*
*        From Screen:            LASER
*        Called By:              READ Statement
*
*
```

Listing 10-11 Continued

```
FUNCTION _pui0rfjh7
PRIVATE currwind
  STORE WOUTPUT() TO currwind
  *
  * Show Code from screen: LASER
  *
  #REGION 1
  x = recno()
  IF SYS(2016) = "laser" OR SYS(2016) = "*"
    ACTIVATE WINDOW laser SAME
    @ 1,67 SAY recno() ;
      SIZE 1,4 ;
      PICTURE "9,999"
    @ 1,52 SAY iif(DELETED(),'Yes','No ') ;
      SIZE 1,4
  ENDIF
  IF NOT EMPTY(currwind)
    ACTIVATE WINDOW (currwind) SAME
  ENDIF
RETURN .T.              && _pui0rfjh7
```

Other screens

Two other screen files make up the LASER application. The first, GOTO, is called by the menu. The second, REPORT, determines where to send the report out. Both of these screens can be included in your own applications and will pretty much work with your programs as they do with LASER-.SPR, provided you follow the same conventions. Each is executed as a menu selection in LASER.MPR (FIG. 10-8).

The GOTO screen

The code in LISTING 10-12 will look pretty familiar to you by now; this is FoxPro's screen builder ensuring that the state of everything is preserved, so that it can get back to wherever it came from.

In LISTING 10-13, the key definitions and insistence that some file must be open are needed by the GOTO object, even though you know that LASER.DBF is open when you call this routine.

Listing 10-12

```
*
*
*          07/23/91            GOTO.SPR              09:54:40
*
*
*
*          Author's Name
*
*          Copyright (c) 1991 Company Name
*          Address
*          City,    Zip
```

222 Advanced screen building

```
*
*         Description:
*         This program was automatically generated by GENSCRN.
*
*

#REGION 0
REGIONAL m.currarea, m.talkstat, m.compstat

IF SET("TALK") = "ON"
   SET TALK OFF
   m.talkstat = "ON"
ELSE
   m.talkstat = "OFF"
ENDIF
m.compstat = SET("COMPATIBLE")
SET COMPATIBLE FOXPLUS

m.currarea = SELECT()

*
*
*                         Window definitions
*
*
*
IF NOT WEXIST("gotodialog")
   DEFINE WINDOW gotodialog ;
       FROM INT((SROW()-11)/2),INT((SCOL()-45)/2) ;
       TO INT((SROW()-11)/2)+10,INT((SCOL()-45)/2)+44 ;
       FLOAT ;
       NOCLOSE ;
       SHADOW ;
       DOUBLE ;
       COLOR SCHEME 5
ENDIF
```

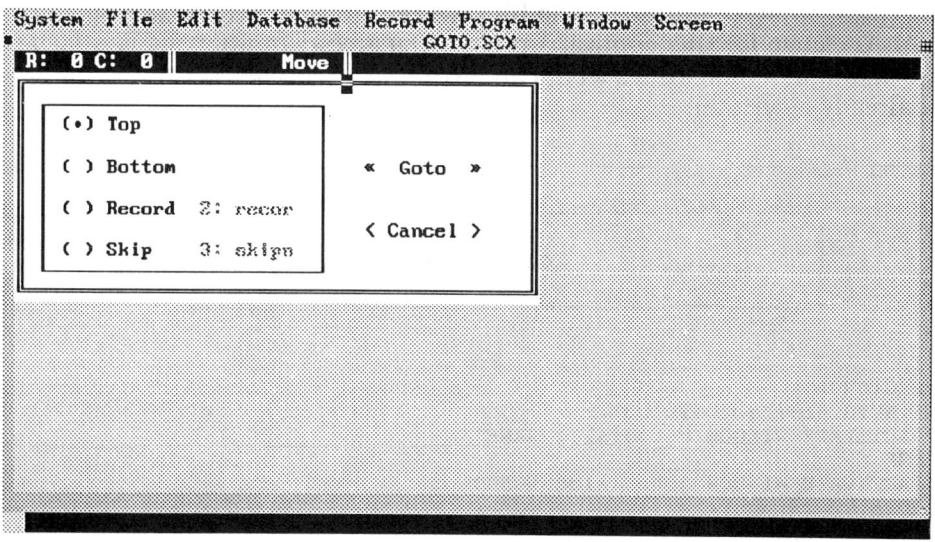

10-8 Editing the Go To screen.

The GOTO screen 223

Listing 10-13

```
*
*
*                    GOTO Setup Code - SECTION 2
*
*
*
```

```
#REGION 1
private file,lastobject,enterkey, tabkey, ;
    shifttabkey, upkey, downkey, leftkey, rightkey
enterkey     = 13
tabkey       = 9
shifttabkey  = 15
upkey        = 5
downkey      = 24
rightkey     = 4
leftkey      = 19
lastobject   = 1

IF empty(dbf())
   file = getfile("DBF","Pick a database")
   IF empty(file)
     wait window "Cancelled" nowait
     return
   ENDIF
   use (file)
ENDIF
```

The next control (LISTING 10-14) is the one that you would think you would use to terminate the screen. To do that, you give it a picture of @*VT... and do whatever you need to in the READ VALID clause. However, that would break the flow of control. So, instead of being a few lines of code that the user might not understand too well, the programmer has decided to take complete control and do his own termination processing. See the VALID clause for this control, _pxd0l8u7o (LISTING 10-15). This is a lot of work, but it demonstrates what can be done if you take the time. Happily, it already is written.

Listing 10-14

```
*
*
*                     GOTO Screen Layout
*
*
*
```

```
#REGION 1
IF WVISIBLE("gotodialog")
   ACTIVATE WINDOW gotodialog SAME
ELSE
   ACTIVATE WINDOW gotodialog NOSHOW
ENDIF
@ 0,1 TO 8,25
@ 1,3 GET radio ;
```

224 Advanced screen building

```
        PICTURE "@*RVN \<Top;\<Bottom;\<Record;\<Skip" ;
        SIZE 1,10,1 ;
        DEFAULT 1 ;
        WHEN _pxd018s2z() ;
        VALID _pxd018slk()
@ 5,15 GET recordnum ;
        SIZE 1,8 ;
        DEFAULT 0 ;
        PICTURE "@Z" ;
        WHEN _pxd018t0h() ;
        VALID _pxd018tha() ;
        DISABLE
@ 7,15 GET skipnum ;
        SIZE 1,8 ;
        DEFAULT 0 ;
        PICTURE "@Z" ;
        WHEN _pxd018tt3() ;
        DISABLE
```

Listing 10-15

```
@ 3,29 GET okcancel ;
    PICTURE "@*VN \!\<Goto;\?\<Cancel" ;
    SIZE 1,10,2 ;
    DEFAULT 1 ;
    WHEN _pxd018u0u() ;
    VALID _pxd018u7o()
* Now, display the window:
IF NOT WVISIBLE("gotodialog")
  ACTIVATE WINDOW gotodialog
ENDIF
```

This screen tells the user what it needs, then waits for a response. The vast amount of code that follows is typical of what it takes to write really idiot-proof software:

```
READ CYCLE ;
  DEACTIVATE _pxd0l8um8( )
```

Note that a DEACTIVATE clause is needed here, because you simply are changing windows (from LASER to GOTODIALOG). Deactivate clauses are executed when exiting a window, as opposed to a READ. Now, clean up and go back where you came from (LISTING 10-16).

Listing 10-16

```
RELEASE WINDOW gotodialog
SELECT (m.currarea)


#REGION 0
IF m.talkstat = "ON"
  SET TALK ON
ENDIF
IF m.compstat = "ON"
  SET COMPATIBLE ON
ENDIF
```

The code in LISTING 10-17 is pretty detailed. If you don't follow all of it, don't worry about it. The same thing could be accomplished with a few lines of code, if you didn't want the screen to look perfect. The precise control is available because during a READ, the current object is number _curobj, so you can control where you go next by assigning it a value.

Listing 10-17

```
*
*
*      ┌─────────────────────────────────────────────────────────┐
*      │                                                         │
*      │   _PXD0L8S2Z                   radio WHEN               │
*      │                                                         │
*      │   Function Origin:                                      │
*      │                                                         │
*      │   From Screen:          GOTO,     Record Number:    3   │
*      │   Variable:             radio                           │
*      │   Called By:            WHEN Clause                     │
*      │   Object Type:          Radio Button                    │
*      │   Snippet Number:       1                               │
*      │                                                         │
*      └─────────────────────────────────────────────────────────┘
*
*
*
*      Place cursor in recordnum field if it is enabled
*      and the last object selected was the radio button
*      record.  Do this only if enter, tab, down arrow or
*      right arrow are pressed to exit the record radio button.
*
FUNCTION _pxd0l8s2z        &&   radio WHEN
#REGION 1
IF _curobj = objnum(radio)+3 ;
       AND radio = objnum(radio)+2 ;
       AND lastobject = objnum(radio)+2 ;
       AND (lastkey() = enterkey ;
           OR lastkey() = tabkey ;
           OR lastkey() = downkey ;
           OR lastkey() = rightkey)
   _curobj = objnum(recordnum)
   lastobject = objnum(recordnum)
   return
ENDIF
*
*      Place cursor in recordnum field if it is enabled
*      and the last object selected was the radio button
*      skip.  Do this only if shift+tab, up arrow or
*      left arrow are pressed to exit the skip radio button.
*
IF _curobj = objnum(radio)+2 ;
       AND radio = objnum(radio)+2 ;
       AND lastobject = objnum(radio)+3 ;
         AND (lastkey() = shifttabkey ;
           OR lastkey() = leftkey ;
           OR lastkey() = upkey)
   lastobject = _curobj
   _curobj = objnum(recordnum)
   return
ENDIF
lastobject = _curobj
```

```
*
*
*   ┌─────────────────────────────────────────────────────────┐
*   │                                                         │
*   │   _PXD0L8SLK                    radio VALID             │
*   │                                                         │
*   │   Function Origin:                                      │
*   │                                                         │
*   │   From Screen:           GOTO,      Record Number:   3  │
*   │   Variable:              radio                          │
*   │   Called By:             VALID Clause                   │
*   │   Object Type:           Radio Button                   │
*   │   Snippet Number:        2                              │
*   │                                                         │
*   └─────────────────────────────────────────────────────────┘
*
*   Enable and disable appropriate get fields when
*   a radio button is punched.
```

The code in LISTING 10-18 ensures that the user can't select options that don't make sense based on his or her prior action. Disabled controls appear in a different color. The user can't highlight them by moving around with Tab or arrow keys. Also, clicking on them with a mouse produces no result. This is what you do if you want a really spiffy interface and if your customer doesn't care how much it costs.

Listing 10-18

```
FUNCTION _pxd0l8slk      && radio VALID
#REGION 1
DO CASE
CASE radio = 1
  store 0 to recordnum,skipnum
  show get recordnum disabled
  show get skipnum disabled
CASE radio = 2
  store 0 to recordnum,skipnum
  show get recordnum disabled
  show get skipnum disabled
CASE radio = 3
  store 0 to skipnum
  show get recordnum enabled
  show get skipnum disabled
  _curobj = objnum(recordnum)
CASE radio = 4
  store 0 to recordnum
  show get recordnum disabled
  show get skipnum enabled
  _curobj = objnum(skipnum)
ENDCASE
```

```
*
*   ┌─────────────────────────────────────────────────────────┐
*   │                                                         │
*   │   _PXD0L8T0H                    recordnum WHEN          │
*   │                                                         │
*   │   Function Origin:                                      │
*   │                                                         │
*   │   From Screen:           GOTO,      Record Number:   4  │
```

The GOTO screen

Listing 10-18 Continued

```
*          ┌─────────────────────────────────────────────┐
*          │   Variable:             recordnum           │
*          │   Called By:            WHEN Clause         │
*          │   Object Type:          Field               │
*          │   Snippet Number:       3                   │
*          │                                             │
*          └─────────────────────────────────────────────┘
*
*
*
*     Routine to bypass the recno field and move to the goto button.
*     Place cursor on goto push button if the last object selected
*     was the radio button skip.  Do this only if tab, down arrow or
*     right arrow are pressed to exit the skip radio button.
*
FUNCTION _pxd0l8t0h        &&   recordnum WHEN
#REGION 1
IF lastobject = objnum(radio)+3 ;
   AND (lastkey() = tabkey ;
   OR lastkey() = downkey ;
   OR lastkey() = rightkey)
   _curobj = objnum(okcancel)
   return
ENDIF
*
*     Routine to bypass the recno field and move to the skip button.
*     Place cursor on skip radio button if the last object selected
*     was the goto push button.  Do this only if shift+tab, up arrow or
*     left arrow are pressed to exit the goto push button.
*
IF lastobject = objnum(okcancel) ;
    AND (lastkey() = shifttabkey ;
    OR lastkey() = upkey ;
    OR lastkey() = leftkey)
   _curobj = objnum(radio)+3
   return
ENDIF
lastobject = _curobj

*
*
*          ┌─────────────────────────────────────────────┐
*          │   _PXD0L8THA            recordnum VALID     │
*          │                                             │
*          │   Function Origin:                          │
*          │                                             │
*          │   From Screen:          GOTO,  Record Number:  4 │
*          │   Variable:             recordnum           │
*          │   Called By:            VALID Clause        │
*          │   Object Type:          Field               │
*          │   Snippet Number:       4                   │
*          │                                             │
*          └─────────────────────────────────────────────┘
*
*
FUNCTION _pxd0l8tha        &&   recordnum VALID
#REGION 1
IF  mdown() ;
        AND (lastkey() = enterkey ;
            OR lastkey() = tabkey ;
            OR lastkey() = downkey ;
            OR lastkey() = rightkey)
   _curobj = objnum(radio)+3
```

```
      return
ENDIF

IF !mdown() ;
   AND (lastkey()= shifttabkey ;
   OR lastkey() = upkey ;
   OR lastkey() = leftkey )
   _curobj = objnum(radio)+2
ENDIF
```

The controls in LISTING 10-19 are the equivalent of next/previous controls in record selection, but at the screen object level.

Listing 10-19

```
*
*
*     _PXD0L8TT3              skipnum WHEN
*
*     Function Origin:
*
*     From Screen:         GOTO,    Record Number:    5
*     Variable:            skipnum
*     Called By:           WHEN Clause
*     Object Type:         Field
*     Snippet Number:      5
*
*
*
FUNCTION _pxd0l8tt3      &&  skipnum WHEN
#REGION 1
lastobject = _curobj
```

```
*
*
*     _PXD0L8U0U              okcancel WHEN
*
*     Function Origin:
*
*     From Screen:         GOTO,    Record Number:    6
*     Variable:            okcancel
*     Called By:           WHEN Clause
*     Object Type:         Push Button
*     Snippet Number:      6
*
*
*
FUNCTION _pxd0l8u0u      &&  okcancel WHEN
#REGION 1
lastobject = _curobj
```

```
*
*
*     _PXD0L8U7O              okcancel VALID
*
*     Function Origin:
*
*     From Screen:         GOTO,    Record Number:    6
*     Variable:            okcancel
```

Listing 10-19 Continued

```
*          Called By:          VALID Clause
*          Object Type:        Push Button
*          Snippet Number:     7
*
*
```

Here, the terminating control on this window was chosen, so you have to figure out what to do next. Note that all of this was required because the "terminating control" couldn't be a real terminating control.

The code in LISTING 10-20 is an object. It works independently of the application that calls it. It doesn't refer to specific files or fields, it pops up and releases its own windows, and it doesn't need to know where it was called from.

Listing 10-20

```
*
FUNCTION _pxd018u7o        && okcancel VALID
#REGION 1
IF okcancel = 1
DO CASE
CASE radio = 1
  go top
CASE radio = 2
  go bottom
CASE radio = 3
  IF recordnum > reccount() OR recordnum < 1
    wait window 'Record out of range' nowait
  ELSE
    go recordnum
  ENDIF
CASE radio = 4
  IF skipnum+recno() > reccount() OR skipnum+recno() < 1
    wait window 'Record out of range' nowait
  ELSE
    skip skipnum
  ENDIF
ENDCASE
ENDIF
clear read
show gets level 1
*
*
*          _PXD0L8UM8              Read Level Deactivate
*
*          Function Origin:
*
*          From Screen:            GOTO
*          Called By:              READ Statement
*          Snippet Number:         8
*
*
*
FUNCTION _pxd018um8        && Read Level Deactivate
*
```

```
* Deactivate Code from screen: GOTO
*
#REGION 1
?? chr(7)
return .f.
```

The REPORT screen

The other screen that comes with the Laser application is a generic output redirection object. I've included a few simple cases of this type of routine in earlier chapters, but this is the granddaddy of them all. Among other things, this routine will let your user select the index order of the report at report time. I usually have to write one version of my report forms for each index order if subtotals are involved. So, if I used a routine like this, it also would have to know which report form to do based on the index order selected. But that's not too hard to add. Figure 10-9 shows the Report Destination dialog.

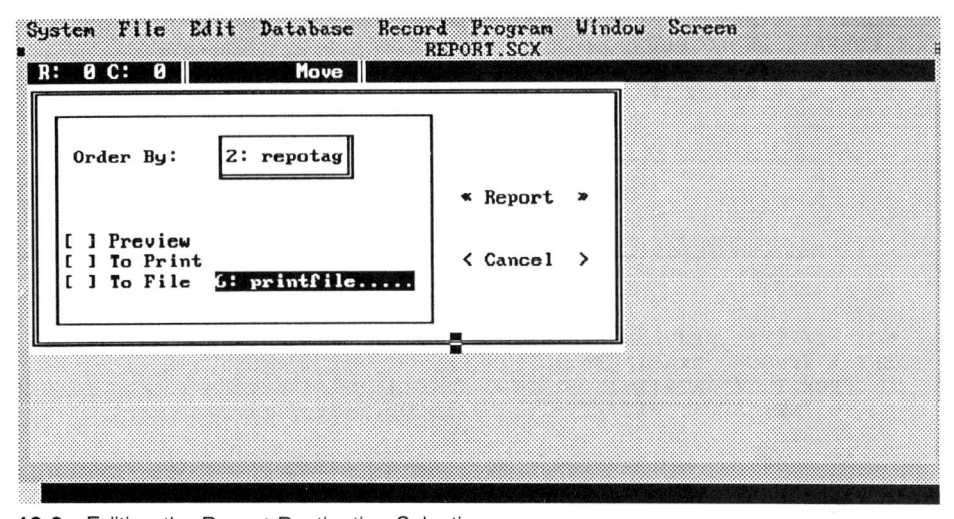

10-9 Editing the Report Destination Selection screen.

Listing 10-21 defines the window for the Report Destination dialog saving the current select area and TALK setting. Listing 10-22 is generic code for displaying all of your index tags from any .CDX file. Don't lose this code!

Listing 10-21

```
*
*
*       07/23/91            REPORT.SPR          09:56:00
*
*
*
*       Author's Name
```

Listing 10-21 Continued

```
*       ╔══════════════════════════════════════════╗
*       ║     Copyright (c) 1991 Company Name      ║
*       ║     Address                              ║
*       ║     City,     Zip                        ║
*       ║                                          ║
*       ║     Description:                         ║
*       ║     This program was automatically generated by GENSCRN. ║
*       ║                                          ║
*       ╚══════════════════════════════════════════╝


#REGION 0
REGIONAL m.currarea, m.talkstat, m.compstat

IF SET("TALK") = "ON"
  SET TALK OFF
  m.talkstat = "ON"
ELSE
  m.talkstat = "OFF"
ENDIF
m.compstat = SET("COMPATIBLE")
SET COMPATIBLE FOXPLUS

m.currarea = SELECT()


*       ╔══════════════════════════════════════════╗
*       ║                                          ║
*       ║              Window definitions          ║
*       ║                                          ║
*       ╚══════════════════════════════════════════╝
*

IF NOT WEXIST("_pxd0lah2s")
  DEFINE WINDOW _pxd0lah2s ;
      FROM INT((SROW()-13)/2),INT((SCOL()-51)/2) ;
      TO INT((SROW()-13)/2)+12,INT((SCOL()-51)/2)+50 ;
      FLOAT ;
      NOCLOSE ;
      SHADOW ;
      DOUBLE ;
      COLOR SCHEME 5
ENDIF


*       ╔══════════════════════════════════════════╗
*       ║                                          ║
*       ║         REPORT Setup Code - SECTION 2    ║
*       ║                                          ║
*       ╚══════════════════════════════════════════╝
*
```

Listing 10-22

```
#REGION 1
private x,repotag
dime rtags(100)
rtags(1) = "Record#"
for i = 2 to 256
```

```
    if len(tag(i-1)) = 0
      i = i - 1
      dimension rtags(i)
      exit
    else
      rtags(i) = tag(i-1)
    endif
endfor
repotag = iif(len(order())=0,"Record#",order())
```

```
*
*
*                 ┌─────────────────────────────────────────────┐
*                 │            REPORT Screen Layout             │
*                 │                                             │
*                 └─────────────────────────────────────────────┘
*
*
#REGION 1
IF WVISIBLE("_pxd01ah2s")
  ACTIVATE WINDOW _pxd01ah2s SAME
ELSE
  ACTIVATE WINDOW _pxd01ah2s NOSHOW
ENDIF
@ 2,3 SAY "Order By:"
```

The reportok control is terminating, as seen by the *VT format codes. The index order pop-up is shown in LISTING 10-23. The check boxes in LISTING 10-24 offer three destinations. Each one has a valid clause that, upon execution, disables the other destinations.

Listing 10-23

```
@ 4,36 GET reportok ;
    PICTURE "@*VT \!\<Report;\?\<Cancel" ;
    SIZE 1,11,2 ;
    DEFAULT 1
@ 1,15 GET repotag ;
    PICTURE "@^" ;
    FROM rtags ;
    SIZE 3,12 ;
    DEFAULT 1 ;
    COLOR SCHEME 5, 6

@ 0,1 TO 10,33
```

Listing 10-24

```
@ 7,2 GET toprint ;
    PICTURE "@*C To Print" ;
    SIZE 1,12 ;
    DEFAULT 0 ;
    VALID _pxd01ahul()
@ 8,2 GET tofile ;
    PICTURE "@*C To File" ;
    SIZE 1,11 ;
    DEFAULT 0 ;
    VALID _pxd01ai46()
```

Listing 10-24 Continued

```
@ 6,2 GET Preview ;
    PICTURE "@*C Preview" ;
    SIZE 1,11 ;
    DEFAULT 0 ;
    VALID _pxd0laigz()
@ 8,15 GET printfile ;
    SIZE 1,17 ;
    DEFAULT " " ;
    VALID _pxd0laigg()
IF NOT WVISIBLE("_pxd0lah2s")
  ACTIVATE WINDOW _pxd0lah2s
ENDIF

READ CYCLE ;
  DEACTIVATE _pxd0laj03()

RELEASE WINDOW _pxd0lah2s
SELECT (m.currarea)


#REGION 0
IF m.talkstat = "ON"
  SET TALK ON
ENDIF
IF m.compstat = "ON"
  SET COMPATIBLE ON
ENDIF
```

The clean-up code (LISTING 10-25) is executed upon exiting this window. If another index tag was selected, it's used here. The VALID clauses generated from the code snippets are shown in LISTING 10-26.

Listing 10-25

```
*
*
*                    REPORT Cleanup Code
*
*
*

#REGION 1
if reportok = 1
  x = alltrim(repotag)
  if x = "Record#"
    set order to
  else
    set order to (x)
  endif
endif
```

Listing 10-26

```
*
*
*      _PXD0LAHUL          toprint VALID
```

234 Advanced screen building

```
*
*             Function Origin:
*
*             From Screen:          REPORT,      Record Number:    6
*             Variable:             toprint
*             Called By:            VALID Clause
*             Object Type:          Check Box
*             Snippet Number:       1
*
*
*
FUNCTION _pxd0lahul      &&   toprint VALID
#REGION 1
if toprint = 1
  show get preview disabled
  show get tofile disabled
  show get printfile disabled
else
  show gets enabled
endif


*
*
*         _PXD0LAI46           tofile VALID
*
*         Function Origin:
*
*         From Screen:          REPORT,      Record Number:    7
*         Variable:             tofile
*         Called By:            VALID Clause
*         Object Type:          Check Box
*         Snippet Number:       2
*
*
*
FUNCTION _pxd0lai46      &&   tofile VALID
#REGION 1
if tofile = 1
  printfile = putfile('Print File:',alltrim(printfile),'TXT')
  if empty(printfile)
    tofile = 0
    show gets enabled
  else
    show get toprint disabled
    show get preview disabled
  endif
  show get printfile
else
  printfile = putfile('Print File:',alltrim(printfile),'TXT')
  if empty(printfile)
    tofile = 0
    show get tofile
  endif
  show gets enabled
endif


*
*
*         _PXD0LAIGZ           Preview VALID
```

The REPORT screen

Listing 10-26 Continued

```
*
*     ┌─────────────────────────────────────────────────────┐
*     │   Function Origin:                                  │
*     │                                                     │
*     │   From Screen:        REPORT,    Record Number:  8  │
*     │   Variable:           Preview                       │
*     │   Called By:          VALID Clause                  │
*     │   Object Type:        Check Box                     │
*     │   Snippet Number:     3                             │
*     │                                                     │
*     └─────────────────────────────────────────────────────┘
*
FUNCTION _pxd0laigz      && Preview VALID
#REGION 1
if preview = 1
  show get toprint disabled
  show get tofile disabled
  show get printfile disabled
else
  show gets enabled
endif


*
*     ┌─────────────────────────────────────────────────────┐
*     │   _PXD0LAIQG              printfile VALID           │
*     │                                                     │
*     │   Function Origin:                                  │
*     │                                                     │
*     │   From Screen:        REPORT,    Record Number:  9  │
*     │   Variable:           printfile                     │
*     │   Called By:          VALID Clause                  │
*     │   Object Type:        Field                         │
*     │   Snippet Number:     4                             │
*     │                                                     │
*     └─────────────────────────────────────────────────────┘
*
FUNCTION _pxd0laiqg      && printfile VALID
#REGION 1
if empty(printfile)
  tofile = 0
  show gets enabled
else
  show get toprint disabled
  show get preview disabled
  tofile = 1
  show get tofile
endif
```

The READ LEVEL deactivate clause simply beeps, because the window should be closed after selecting a control. RETURN .F. means that it can't deactivate this window. You can deactivate it, but only by the means the program permits. Simply attempting to close the window using the mouse or the Ctrl-W-Hide option won't do it.

The code in LISTING 10-27 can be used in almost any program that prints reports. It's another object, of which I hope that many such examples will be available in the near future.

Listing 10-27

```
*
*
*       ┌─────────────────────────────────────────────────────────┐
*       │                                                         │
*       │   _PXD0LAJ03               Read Level Deactivate        │
*       │                                                         │
*       │   Function Origin:                                      │
*       │                                                         │
*       │   From Screen:             REPORT                       │
*       │   Called By:               READ Statement               │
*       │   Snippet Number:          5                            │
*       │                                                         │
*       └─────────────────────────────────────────────────────────┘
*
FUNCTION _pxd0laj03     && Read Level Deactivate
*
* Deactivate Code from screen: REPORT
*
#REGION 1
?? chr(7)
return .f.
```

The LASER screen code is an excellent didactic example of FoxPro's new features in action. Next, I'll look at the menu code and see how it interacts with the screen code.

The menu builder

The menu for this application relies heavily on menu items from the FoxPro system menu. During activation, this menu is the system menu. It takes on the _MSYSMENU name and only goes away when you issue the command:

SET SYSMENU TO DEFAULT

Notice the large number of references to system variables. In your menus, if you choose Pad Name for a menu option, you can refer to any of the system menu selection names, including the calculator, diary, cut, paste, or others.

For your purposes, the main point is that the menu is activated from within the application using the Alt plus the first letter combination familiar to FoxPro users.

The menu program sets up the menu system and knows what to do when selections are made. Many of the routines are useful for almost any application, so you'll want to keep them where you can use the snippets in your own applications.

The liberal use of hot keys ensures that users can perform many of the functions on the menu without actually having to pull the menu down. In that way, the menu becomes a sort of road map to the system. Once you've learned the hot keys, you scarcely need the menu. The code is shown in LISTING 10-28.

Listing 10-28

```
*
*
*       ┌─────────────────────────────────────────────────────────┐
*       │                                                         │
*       │   04/11/91              LASERM.MPR           12:48:02   │
*       │                                                         │
*       ├─────────────────────────────────────────────────────────┤
*       │                                                         │
*       │   Systems Group                                         │
*       │                                                         │
*       │   Copyright (c) 1991 Fox Software                       │
*       │   134 West South Boundary                               │
*       │   Perrysburg, OH  43551                                 │
*       │                                                         │
*       │   Description:                                          │
*       │   This program was automatically generated by GENMENU.  │
*       │                                                         │
*       └─────────────────────────────────────────────────────────┘


*
*       ┌─────────────────────────────────────────────────────────┐
*       │                                                         │
*       │                       Setup Code                        │
*       │                                                         │
*       └─────────────────────────────────────────────────────────┘
*
```

This saves the previous (current) menu and defines menu operations to be automatic, which makes them work like the FoxPro system menu does. The variable skipvar is defined here to make the code easier to read; you could substitute .F. in all cases in the code in LISTING 10-29.

Listing 10-29

```
push menu _msysmenu
set sysmenu automatic
public skipvar
skipvar = .f.


*
*       ┌─────────────────────────────────────────────────────────┐
*       │                                                         │
*       │                    Menu Definition                      │
*       │                                                         │
*       └─────────────────────────────────────────────────────────┘
*

SET SYSMENU TO

DEFINE PAD _pui0rfppj OF _MSYSMENU PROMPT "\<System";
        KEY ALT+S, "ALT+S";
        SKIP FOR skipvar
DEFINE PAD _pui0rfprz OF _MSYSMENU PROMPT "\<Edit";
        KEY ALT+E, ""
DEFINE PAD _pui0rfpsl OF _MSYSMENU PROMPT "\<Database";
        KEY ALT+D, ""
DEFINE PAD _pui0rfpt7 OF _MSYSMENU PROMPT "E\<nvironment";
        MARK "";
        KEY ALT+N, "ALT+N"
ON PAD _pui0rfppj OF _MSYSMENU ACTIVATE POPUP system
```

238   Advanced screen building

```
ON PAD _pui0rfprz OF _MSYSMENU ACTIVATE POPUP edit
ON PAD _pui0rfpsl OF _MSYSMENU ACTIVATE POPUP database
ON PAD _pui0rfpt7 OF _MSYSMENU ACTIVATE POPUP enviro

DEFINE POPUP system MARGIN RELATIVE SHADOW COLOR SCHEME 4
DEFINE BAR _MST_HELP OF system PROMPT "\<Help...";
       KEY F1, "F1";
       SKIP FOR skipvar
DEFINE BAR _MST_FILER OF system PROMPT "\<Filer";
       SKIP FOR skipvar
DEFINE BAR 3 OF system PROMPT "\-";
       SKIP FOR skipvar
DEFINE BAR _MST_CALCU OF system PROMPT "\<Calculator";
       SKIP FOR skipvar
DEFINE BAR _MST_DIARY OF system PROMPT "Calendar/\<Diary";
       SKIP FOR skipvar
DEFINE BAR _MST_ASCII OF system PROMPT "ASC\<II Chart";
       SKIP FOR skipvar
DEFINE BAR _MST_PUZZL OF system PROMPT "Pu\<zzle";
       SKIP FOR skipvar
DEFINE BAR 8 OF system PROMPT "\-";
       SKIP FOR skipvar
DEFINE BAR 9 OF system PROMPT "\<Quit";
       KEY CTRL+Q, "^Q";
       SKIP FOR skipvar
ON SELECTION BAR 9 OF system;
       DO _pui0rfq2u IN LASERM.MPR

DEFINE POPUP edit MARGIN RELATIVE SHADOW COLOR SCHEME 4
DEFINE BAR _MED_UNDO OF edit PROMPT "\<Undo";
       KEY CTRL+U, "^U"
DEFINE BAR _MED_REDO OF edit PROMPT "\<Redo";
       KEY CTRL+R, "^R"
DEFINE BAR _MED_SP100 OF edit PROMPT "\-"
DEFINE BAR _MED_CUT OF edit PROMPT "Cu\<t";
       KEY CTRL+X, "^X"
DEFINE BAR _MED_COPY OF edit PROMPT "\<Copy";
       KEY CTRL+C, "^C"
DEFINE BAR _MED_PASTE OF edit PROMPT "\<Paste";
       KEY CTRL+V, "^V"
DEFINE BAR _MED_SP200 OF edit PROMPT "\-"
DEFINE BAR _MED_SLCTA OF edit PROMPT "Select \<All";
       KEY CTRL+A, "^A"

DEFINE POPUP database MARGIN RELATIVE SHADOW COLOR SCHEME 4
DEFINE BAR 1 OF database PROMPT "\<Browse";
       KEY CTRL+B, "^B";
       SKIP FOR skipvar
DEFINE BAR 2 OF database PROMPT "\<Append";
       SKIP FOR skipvar
DEFINE BAR 3 OF database PROMPT "\<Goto...";
       SKIP FOR skipvar
DEFINE BAR 4 OF database PROMPT "\<Report...";
       SKIP FOR skipvar
DEFINE BAR 5 OF database PROMPT "\-";
       SKIP FOR skipvar
DEFINE BAR 6 OF database PROMPT "T\<oggle Delete";
       KEY CTRL+O, "^O";
       SKIP FOR skipvar
DEFINE BAR 7 OF database PROMPT "\<Pack";
       SKIP FOR skipvar
```

Listing 10-29 Continued

```
ON SELECTION BAR 1 OF database;
        DO _pui0rfqex IN LASERM.MPR
ON SELECTION BAR 2 OF database;
        DO _pui0rfqfq IN LASERM.MPR
ON SELECTION BAR 3 OF database;
        DO _pui0rfqgj IN LASERM.MPR
ON SELECTION BAR 4 OF database;
        DO _pui0rfqhd IN LASERM.MPR
ON SELECTION BAR 6 OF database;
        DO _pui0rfqia IN LASERM.MPR
ON SELECTION BAR 7 OF database;
        DO _pui0rfqj3 IN LASERM.MPR

DEFINE POPUP enviro MARGIN RELATIVE SHADOW COLOR SCHEME 4
DEFINE BAR 1 OF enviro PROMPT "\<Status Bar";
        SKIP FOR skipvar
DEFINE BAR 2 OF enviro PROMPT "\<Clock";
        SKIP FOR skipvar
DEFINE BAR 3 OF enviro PROMPT "\<Extended Video";
        SKIP FOR skipvar

DEFINE BAR 4 OF enviro PROMPT "St\<icky";
        SKIP FOR skipvar
ON SELECTION BAR 1 OF enviro;
        DO _pui0rfqnn IN LASERM.MPR
ON SELECTION BAR 2 OF enviro;
        DO _pui0rfqog IN LASERM.MPR
ON SELECTION BAR 3 OF enviro;
        DO _pui0rfqp9 IN LASERM.MPR
ON SELECTION BAR 4 OF enviro;
        DO _pui0rfqq3 IN LASERM.MPR


*
*
*           ┌─────────────────────────────────────────────┐
*           │         Cleanup Code & Procedures           │
*           └─────────────────────────────────────────────┘
*
*

for i = 1 to cntbar('enviro')
  do case
  case prmbar('enviro',i) = 'Status Bar'
    set mark of bar i of enviro to  set('status') = 'ON'
  case prmbar('enviro',i) = 'Clock'
    set mark of bar i of enviro to  set('clock') = 'ON'
  case prmbar('enviro',i) = 'Extended Video'
    set mark of bar i of enviro to  srow() > 25
  case prmbar('enviro',i) = 'Sticky'
    set mark of bar i of enviro to  set('sticky') = 'ON'
  endcase
endfor


*
*
*      ┌──────────────────────────────────────────────────┐
*      │    _PUI0RFQ2U   ON SELECTION BAR 9 OF POPUP system │
*      │                                                  │
*      │    Procedure Origin:                             │
*
```

240   Advanced screen building

```
*       ║  From Menu:   LASERM.MPR,            Record:    13    ║
*       ║  Called By:   ON SELECTION BAR 9 OF POPUP system      ║
*       ║  Prompt:      Quit                                    ║
*       ║                                                       ║
*
*
PROCEDURE _pui0rfq2u
clear read
pop menu _msysmenu
```

```
*
*
*       ║  _PUI0RFQEX   ON SELECTION BAR 1 OF POPUP database    ║
*       ║                                                       ║
*       ║  Procedure Origin:                                    ║
*       ║                                                       ║
*       ║  From Menu:   LASERM.MPR,            Record:    26    ║
*       ║  Called By:   ON SELECTION BAR 1 OF POPUP database    ║
*       ║  Prompt:      Browse                                  ║
*       ║                                                       ║
*
```

The use of WIDTH 7 in a BROWSE (LISTING 10-30) limits any character field to no more than seven characters. This ensures that as many fields as possible get displayed.

Listing 10-30

```
PROCEDURE _pui0rfqex
define window temp from 1,1 to 13,50 ;
    float grow zoom close system minimize ;
    title "Browse Database" ;
    color scheme 10
browse width 7 window temp
scatter memvar
show gets
release window temp
```

```
*
*
*       ║  _PUI0RFQFQ   ON SELECTION BAR 2 OF POPUP database    ║
*       ║                                                       ║
*       ║  Procedure Origin:                                    ║
*       ║                                                       ║
*       ║  From Menu:   LASERM.MPR,            Record:    27    ║
*       ║  Called By:   ON SELECTION BAR 2 OF POPUP database    ║
*       ║  Prompt:      Append                                  ║
*       ║                                                       ║
*
```

I prefer to use record recycling and only append blanks after determining that no recyclable records exist and that the stuff on the screen actually needed to be saved. However, this is an example program and appends are always treated casually in demonstration software for languages. In actual applications, they're a can of worms (LISTING 10-31).

Listing 10-31

```
PROCEDURE _pui0rfqfq
append blank
scatter memvar
show gets
```

```
*
*
*      _PUI0RFQGJ   ON SELECTION BAR 3 OF POPUP database
*
*      Procedure Origin:
*
*      From Menu:   LASERM.MPR,              Record:    28
*      Called By:   ON SELECTION BAR 3 OF POPUP database
*      Prompt:      Goto...
*
*
*
PROCEDURE _pui0rfqgj
do goto.spr
```

```
*
*
*      _PUI0RFQHD   ON SELECTION BAR 4 OF POPUP database
*
*      Procedure Origin:
*
*      From Menu:   LASERM.MPR,              Record:    29
*      Called By:   ON SELECTION BAR 4 OF POPUP database
*      Prompt:      Report...
*
*
*
PROCEDURE _pui0rfqhd
private reportok, toprint, tofile, preview, ;
        printfile,repoclause
reportok = 'TITLE'
printfile = ''
repoclause = ''
store 0 to reportok,toprint,tofile
store 1 to preview
skipvar = .t.
store recno() TO saverec
store order() to saveorder
```

Listing 10-32

```
do report.spr

if reportok = 2
  skipvar = .f.
  return
endif
do case
case toprint = 1
  if sys(13) = 'READY'
```

```
      repoclause = 'TO PRINT OFF'
      wait window 'Running Report' nowait
    else
      wait window 'Printer not ready, sending report to the screen.' nowait
      repoclause = 'PREVIEW'
    endif
  case tofile = 1
    repoclause = 'TO ' + printfile+' OFF'
    wait window 'Running Report' nowait
  otherwise
    repoclause = 'PREVIEW'
    wait window 'Running Report' nowait
endcase
```

Listing 10-32 is where the REPORT.SPR program is executed. The program displays the Report Output dialog and cancels if requested by the user. Notice the code following the execution of the screen program.

Listing 10-33 is where the REPORT FORM is run.

Listing 10-33

```
report form laser &repoclause

go saverec
if !empty(saveorder)
   set order to (saveorder)
endif
skipvar = .f.
wait window 'Report Complete' nowait
```

```
*
*
*       _PUI0RFQIA   ON SELECTION BAR 6 OF POPUP database
*
*       Procedure Origin:
*
*       From Menu:    LASERM.MPR,              Record:    31
*       Called By:    ON SELECTION BAR 6 OF POPUP database
*       Prompt:       Toggle Delete
*
*
*
PROCEDURE _pui0rfqia
if deleted()
  recall
else
  delete
endif
show gets
```

```
*
*
*       _PUI0RFQJ3   ON SELECTION BAR 7 OF POPUP database
*
*       Procedure Origin:
*
```

The menu builder   243

Listing 10-33 Continued

```
*              From Menu:    LASERM.MPR,              Record:   32
*              Called By:    ON SELECTION BAR 7 OF POPUP database
*              Prompt:       Pack
*
*
*
PROCEDURE _pui0rfqj3
wait window 'Removing Old Records' nowait
pack
go top
scatter memvar
show gets
wait window 'Pack Complete' nowait


*
*
*              _PUI0RFQNN   ON SELECTION BAR 1 OF POPUP enviro
*
*              Procedure Origin:
*
*              From Menu:    LASERM.MPR,              Record:   35
*              Called By:    ON SELECTION BAR 1 OF POPUP enviro
*              Prompt:       Status Bar
*
*
*
PROCEDURE _pui0rfqnn
if mrkbar("enviro",bar())
  set status off
  set mark of bar bar() of enviro       to .f.
else
  set status on
  set mark of bar bar() of enviro       to .t.
endif
return



*
*
*              _PUI0RFQOG   ON SELECTION BAR 2 OF POPUP enviro
*
*              Procedure Origin:
*
*              From Menu:    LASERM.MPR,              Record:   36
*              Called By:    ON SELECTION BAR 2 OF POPUP enviro
*              Prompt:       Clock
*
*
*
PROCEDURE _pui0rfqog
store mrkbar("enviro",bar()) to markset
if markset
  set clock off
  set mark of bar bar() of enviro       to .f.
else
  set clock on
```

244 Advanced screen building

```
       set mark of bar bar() of enviro       to .t.
endif
return
```

```
*
*
*        ┌─────────────────────────────────────────────────────┐
*        │                                                     │
*        │   _PUI0RFQP9   ON SELECTION BAR 3 OF POPUP enviro   │
*        │                                                     │
*        │   Procedure Origin:                                  │
*        │                                                     │
*        │   From Menu:   LASERM.MPR,          Record:    37   │
*        │   Called By:   ON SELECTION BAR 3 OF POPUP enviro   │
*        │   Prompt:      Extended Video                       │
*        │                                                     │
*        └─────────────────────────────────────────────────────┘
*
PROCEDURE _pui0rfqp9
store mrkbar("enviro",bar()) to markset
if markset
  set display to vga25
  set mark of bar bar() of enviro       to .f.
else
  set display to vga50
  set mark of bar bar() of enviro       to .t.
endif
return
```

```
*
*
*        ┌─────────────────────────────────────────────────────┐
*        │                                                     │
*        │   _PUI0RFQQ3   ON SELECTION BAR 4 OF POPUP enviro   │
*        │                                                     │
*        │   Procedure Origin:                                  │
*        │                                                     │
*        │   From Menu:   LASERM.MPR,          Record:    38   │
*        │   Called By:   ON SELECTION BAR 4 OF POPUP enviro   │
*        │   Prompt:      Sticky                               │
*        │                                                     │
*        └─────────────────────────────────────────────────────┘
*
PROCEDURE _pui0rfqq3
store mrkbar("enviro",bar()) to markset
if markset
  set sticky off
  set mark of bar bar() of enviro to .f.
else
  set sticky on
  set mark of bar bar() of enviro to .t.
endif
return
```

The menu builder program can build an elegant and powerful system with considerable flexibility when the inevitable changes are requested. If you need extremely precise control, it can be arranged, but it takes a lot of programming, just as it would in any other environment. If you can take advantage of objects like REPORT and GOTO in your code, do so.

Report forms

This application uses a report form, as described in FIG. 10-10. Report forms now can contain their own initialization logic for local variables. Report forms compile into a format that gets bundled with the .APP (or .EXE) file, so you no longer have to include these little guys on your distribution disks.

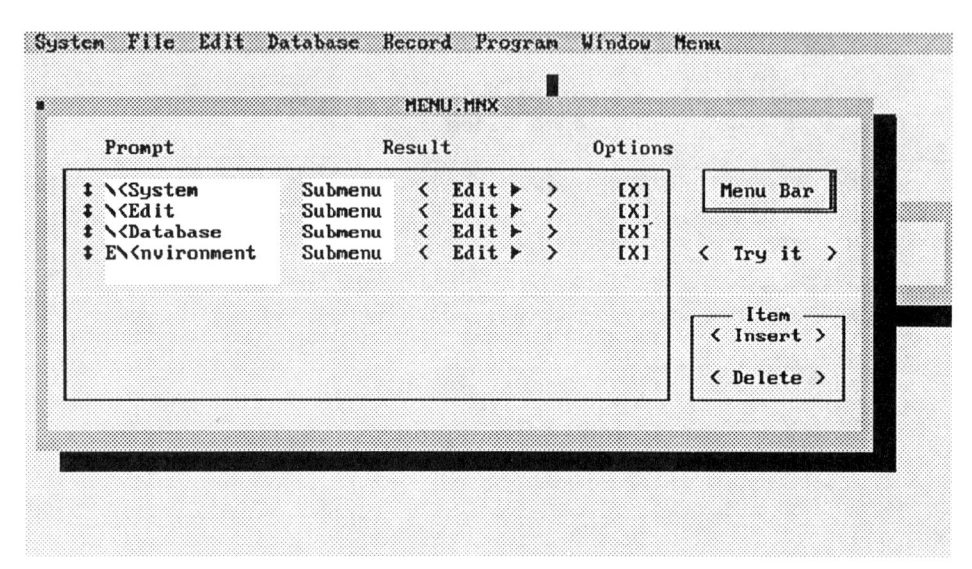

10-10 Editing a Report Form.

The project builder

In the project manager screen shown back in FIG. 10-6, I listed the components of the system. When you select Build from the list of options, it builds your .APP file. The compiled code from all programs, screens, and reports goes into memo fields in the project file and is used to build the .APP (or .EXE) file that is used to run the application. Thereafter, the statement:

    DO LASER1

executes the application from within FoxPro. You also can run this with the runtime module by typing:

    FOXR -T LASER1

from the DOS prompt. If you compiled to .EXE format, the program can be run by typing its name from the DOS prompt.

The project manager bundles all of the elements of your application into a single file. FXPs are stored in memo fields in the project file's associated memo file, so the directory is not cluttered up.

If you select Compile to EXE, you will have to choose between compact format and standalone format. Compact format requires that the FOX-PRO.ESO and FOXPRO.ESL modules be on the path or in the application's directory. If you use FOXR, the runtime module, to run your program, your .APP file also will require these two modules. They're about 1.1 Mb together. If you compile to standalone .EXE format, a "Hello, world" program will be about 700 K. On the other hand, I did a really nice little data entry application in about 820 K that is really simple to distribute, because it's just one program file.

Summary

The LASER program is an excellent example of event-driven programming in FoxPro 2.0. The combination of the screen and the menu builders, coupled with a knowledge of what commands are available within FoxPro, will allow you to write spectacular applications in a fraction of the time it once took. You might soon be writing programs you didn't even know were possible.

11
Reports

FoxPro contains an excellent report writer. If you design your file structures carefully, you can use the report writer to produce most or all of your printed requirements in no time.

If you have an HP LaserJet II or III or compatible, you're in for a treat. I've been fortunate to develop a large number of laser printer report formats for clients and have developed an excellent library of functions for designing beautiful reports.

FoxPro's report form

To many users, reports are your system. It's a well-respected adage that you do systems analysis by getting your users' desired report formats and working backwards. That's because reports can tell you things about hidden requirements that even the users don't know. You simply have to infer data structure requirements that will be essential to produce the requested reporting capabilities.

I'll start with a simple report from a flat file. Then, I'll go to a one-to-many relationship and demonstrate the two requirements that, although not immediately obvious to novices, are essential to using the report writer for reports containing related files. Finally, I'll present the LaserJet Library and demonstrate a few sample reports.

A simple example

I'll start with a customer database with the structure shown in TABLE 11-1. To begin designing the report, type:

```
CREATE REPORT CUSTOMER
```

Table 11-1 Structure for the CUSTOMER.DBF database.

Field	Field Name	Type	Width	Dec	Index
1	NAME	Character	30		
2	CUSTCODE	Character	4		
3	ADDRESS1	Character	30		
4	ADDRESS2	Character	30		
5	CITY	Character	14		
6	STATE	Character	3		
7	ZIP	Character	10		
8	COUNTRY	Character	12		
9	PHONE	Character	12		
10	CONTACT	Character	30		
11	LAST_SALE	Date	8		
12	LASTSALAMT	Numeric	8	2	
13	LAST_PMT	Date	8		
14	LASTPMTAMT	Numeric	8	2	
15	BALANCE	Numeric	8	2	
** Total **			216		

An additional system menu option, Report, appears at the right of the system menu bar. It's activated with Alt–O.

The report screen consists of bands. Each band appears at a different point in your final report and for a different reason:

- The Title band is the first page.
- The Header band appears at the top of each page.
- The Group (n) band appears at the top of each group of records that have the same key value for your first sort/break group key. Groups are defined using the Alt–O/Group selection.
- The Detail band is where you design the line that forms the heart of your report. One of these lines (or groups of lines) prints for each record in the currently selected database. Although it only appears as a single line on your report definition screen, it might produce 99% of the lines in your report.
- The Summary band appears at the end of the report.

I've begun the definition of the CUSTOMER report as shown in FIG. 11-1. I've defined a title, with a page heading, a date on the left, and a page number on the right. To enter the text entries— Date:, Customer File Report, and Page:—just type each word or group of words and press Enter. Note that the Enter key is required to finish each bit of text.

To enter the DATE( ) and _pageno variables, go to the appropriate spot and press Ctrl–F, or use Alt–O and select Field from the Report menu. You can type in these system variable names directly.

To enter field variables, go to the list at left center, highlight your choice, and press Enter. If you need to create a complex expression, as in

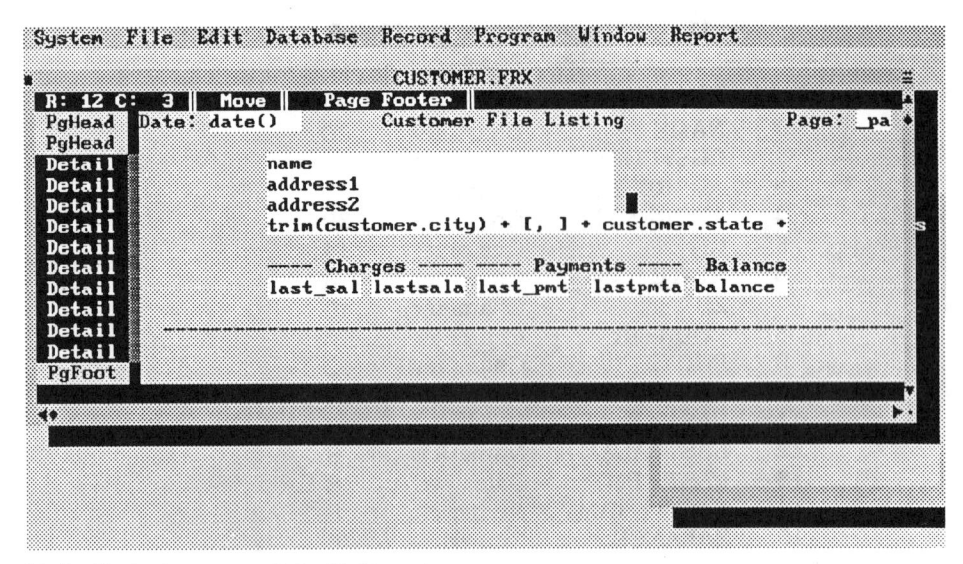

11-1 Designing a report Modify Report.

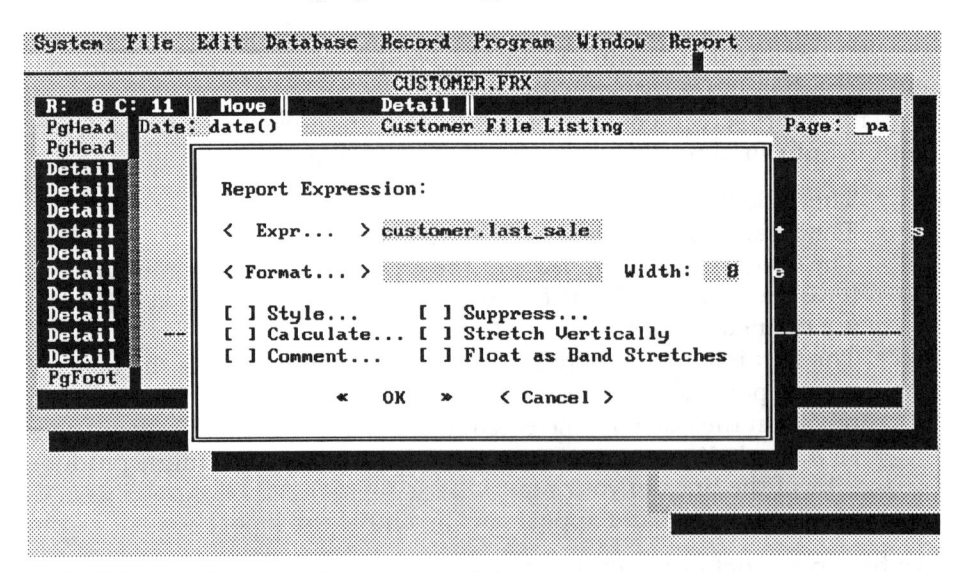

11-2 Using a string expression as a report field.

FIG. 11-2, type it in. This is a city, state, and zip with excess blanks squeezed out.

If you want to move something around, put the cursor anywhere within it and press the Spacebar or click the mouse. It then can be moved around at will. If you want to grab and move several items at once, hold down the Shift key as you move from one object to the next. When you press the Spacebar, the object will be highlighted. Afterwards, all of the highlighted objects can be moved as one. This also is useful to center groups of items on the page. Once one or more objects have been selected, the Reports pop-up produced by pressing Alt–O will show an additional set of options that can be used only with selected objects.

If you want to insert a line into the header, press Ctrl–N. The new line will be inserted above the current line. If you wanted it below the current line, just grab all of the objects on the bottom line (boxing them with the mouse is the easiest way) and move everything up one line.

I've designed this report with some spacing at the bottom to make it easier to read. The final design appears in FIG. 11-3. This report, printed using the command:

REPORT FORM CUSTOMER TO PRINT NOCONSOLE

can be printed from within your programs or from the command line. It also can be listed in the PROJECT BUILD list. The report itself looks like TABLE 11-2.

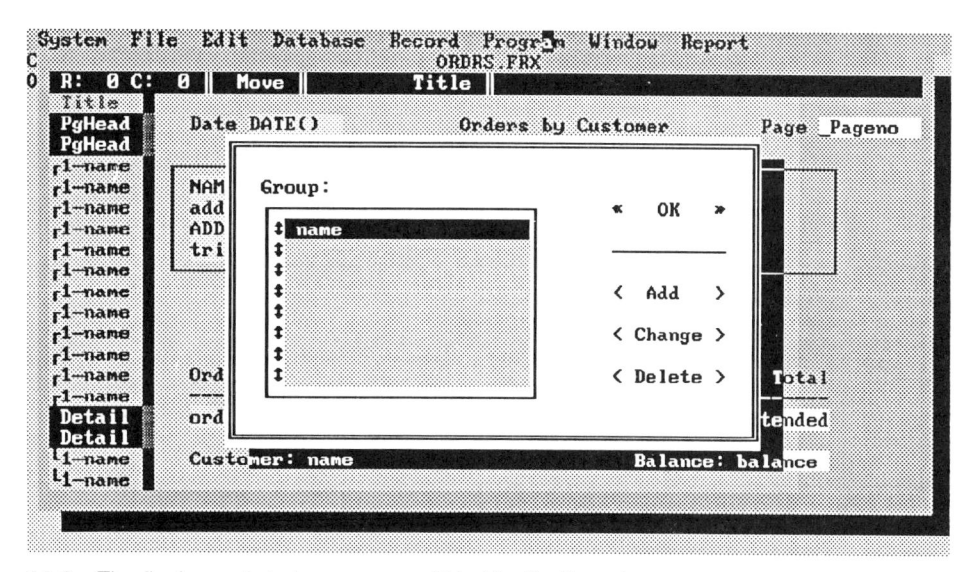

11-3 The final report design as seen within Modify Report.

You also can use boxes, selectable from the reports pulldown menu or using the hot key combination Ctrl–B, to visually group data.

Reports for one-to-many relationships

Where several files are used to produce a single report, you'll need a mechanism for coordinating the various files. Manually, to print the customer's name to the right of each order, you might do something like shown in LISTING 11-1.

Table 11-2 Customer file report format.

Date: 04/13/91   Customer File Listing   Page: 1

Harry Smith
2014 Annabelle
Suite 22
Menlo Park, CA 94025

    – – – – Charges – – – –   – – – – Payments – – – –   Balance
    03/12/91   250.00   02/15/90   35.00   815.25

Les Pinter
1149 Chestnut
Suite 10
Menlo Park, CA 94025

    – – – – Charges – – – –   – – – – Payments – – – –   Balance
    04/12/91   259.00   03/27/91   304.50   259.50

Wyatt Industries
1014 Hempstead Hwy
Houston, TX 77045

    – – – – Charges – – – –   – – – – Payments – – – –   Balance
    01/01/77   142.00   01/03/71   1.00   1,234.00

Listing 11-1

```
* Report logic
SELECT B
USE CUSTOMER INDEX CUSTCODE   && both index name and key field name.
SELECT A
USE ORDERS INDEX ORDERNUM ALIAS ORDERS
SCAN
  ? < detail data from ORDERS file>
  SELECT CUSTOMER
  SEEK ORDERS->CUSTCODE
  ?? CustName
  SELECT ORDERS
ENDSCAN     && go to the next record in ORDERS....
```

When reports contain data from more than one file, things might not always be as they seem. For example, a common requirement is a report of transactions by customer. For this purpose, the average non-programmer would presume that you could use the following commands:

```
USE CUSTOMER INDEX CUSTOMER IN A
USE ORDERS   INDEX ORDERS   IN B
SELECT CUSTOMER
REPORT FORM ORDERS.....
```

However, you have to make ORDERS the primary database, because you want one line of detail for each order. That's what the manual logic earlier did and that's what your SET RELATION has to do. You use the SET RELATION command to coordinate files. Use the following commands:

```
USE ORDERS INDEX ORDERNUM ALIAS ORDERS IN A
USE CUSTOMER INDEX CUSTCODE ALIAS CUSTOMER IN B
SELECT ORDERS
SET RELATION TO CUSTCODE INTO CUSTOMER
```

At this point, you can use the command:

```
CREATE VIEW ORDERRPT
```

to save the file, index, and relation information. Subsequently, you can simply say:

```
SET VIEW TO ORDERRPT
```

before printing the report. Alternatively, if you can check the Save environment box on the Save report dialog, the report will store all current file settings in an .FRV file and restore them when the report runs. SET VIEW actually remembers current record numbers, which might be more than you wanted to remember, so you might prefer the .FRV route.

Alternately, you can use the new SET SKIP command to do the same thing. First, set the relation between the field in the header and the corresponding key field in the detail file. Following that, use:

```
SET SKIP TO detail_filename
```

This new feature of version 2.0 is more intuitive and just as easy.

Having set up your files and relations, you can define the report. Figure 11-4 shows how the process starts. Here, I've defined the field NAME as the sort/break group for this report. Note the resulting GROUP 1 bands on the report definition screen.

I've used the Alt–O/Group keys to define a SORT/BREAK GROUP. You can use the Report menu from the system menu bar to bring down the menu. This also is how the Box option was selected. You also can use the hot key.

The final report screen appears in TABLE 11-3, followed by the report itself. This whole process takes just minutes; however, to your users, it often is all they care about in your entire system.

Printer drivers

FoxPro 2.0 supports printer drivers that integrate seamlessly with the report writer (and, selectively, with the DISPLAY, LIST, and TYPE commands when directed to the printer). A printer driver is a program that knows what to do with printer control codes. FoxPro supplies one called

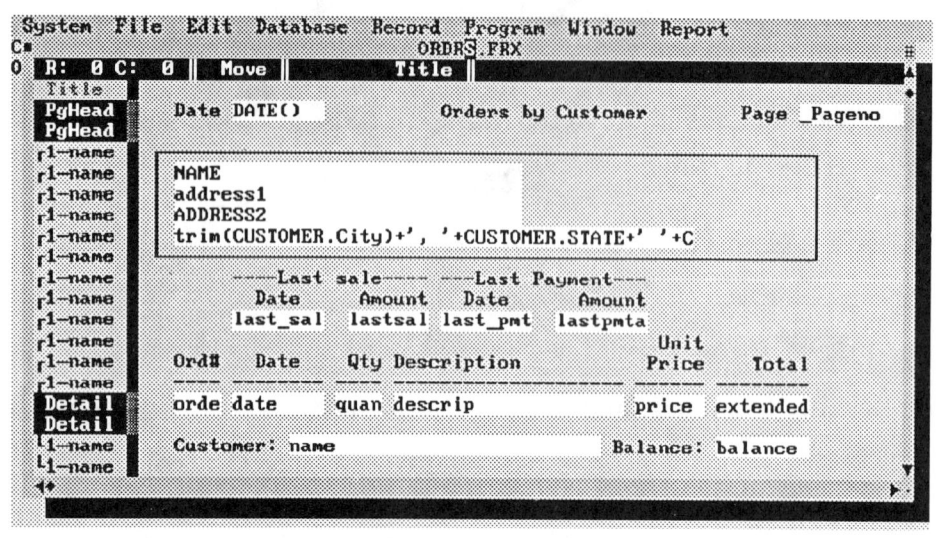

```
System  File  Edit  Database  Record  Program  Window  Report
C:                               ORDRS.FRX
 R:   0 C:   0 ║ Move  ║         Title       ║
  Title
  PgHead   │ Date DATE()            Orders by Customer           Page _Pageno
  PgHead   │
  ┌1-name  │ ┌─────────────────────────────────────────────────────────────┐
  ┌1-name  │ │ NAME                                                        │
  ┌1-name  │ │ address1                                                    │
  ┌1-name  │ │ ADDRESS2                                                    │
  ┌1-name  │ │ trim(CUSTOMER.City)+', '+CUSTOMER.STATE+' '+C                │
  ┌1-name  │ └─────────────────────────────────────────────────────────────┘
  ┌1-name  │        ────Last sale────   ────Last Payment────
  ┌1-name  │          Date     Amount     Date     Amount
  ┌1-name  │        last_sal  lastsal  last_pmt  lastpmta
  ┌1-name  │                                                  Unit
  ┌1-name  │        Ord#   Date    Qty Description            Price      Total
  ┌1-name
  Detail   │ orde  date    quan descrip                       price   extended
  Detail
  ┌1-name  │ Customer: name                            Balance: balance
  ┌1-name
```

11-4 Providing for level breaks in a Report Form.

Table 11-3 Report output.

Date 04/13/91   Orders by Customer   Page   1

Harry Smith
2014 Annabelle
Suite 22
Menlo Park, CA 94025
         – – –Last sale– – –   – –Last Payment– –
          Date   Amount   Date   Amount
         03/12/91   250.00   02/15/90   35.00

| | | | | Unit | |
Ord#	Date	Qty	Description	Price	Total
0002	03/01/91	3	Widget	47.85	47.85
0003	03/01/91	12	Deluxe Frammis	191.40	191.40

Customer: Harry Smith   Balance: 815.25

Wyatt Industries
1014 Hempstead Hwy
Houston, TX 77045
         – – –Last sale– – –   – –Last Payment– –
          Date   Amount   Date   Amount
         01/01/77   142.00   01/03/71   1.00

| | | | | Unit | |
Ord#	Date	Qty	Description	Price	Total
0001	02/09/91	3	Frammis	15.95	47.85

Customer: Wyatt Industries   Balance: 1234.00

GENPD.APP for printers in general, as well as an API general printer driver (DRIVER2) and a pair of PostScript drivers (PS and PSAPI). Also, they supply instructions for writing your own. Try to use theirs first.

When you define an object in the report writer, you're asked to indicate STYLE (FIG. 11-5). If you select one of the on-screen categories, the CODE field is filled in with one or more of the following (except that L and R are mutually exclusive):

Style	Code
Bold	B
Italic	I
Underline	U
Superscript	R
Subscript	L

Actually, you can enter your own codes in the CODE field. The FoxPro printer driver only knows how to handle these five. However, you can write your own printer driver to deal with any additional codes that you need—selection of previously downloaded soft fonts, for example.

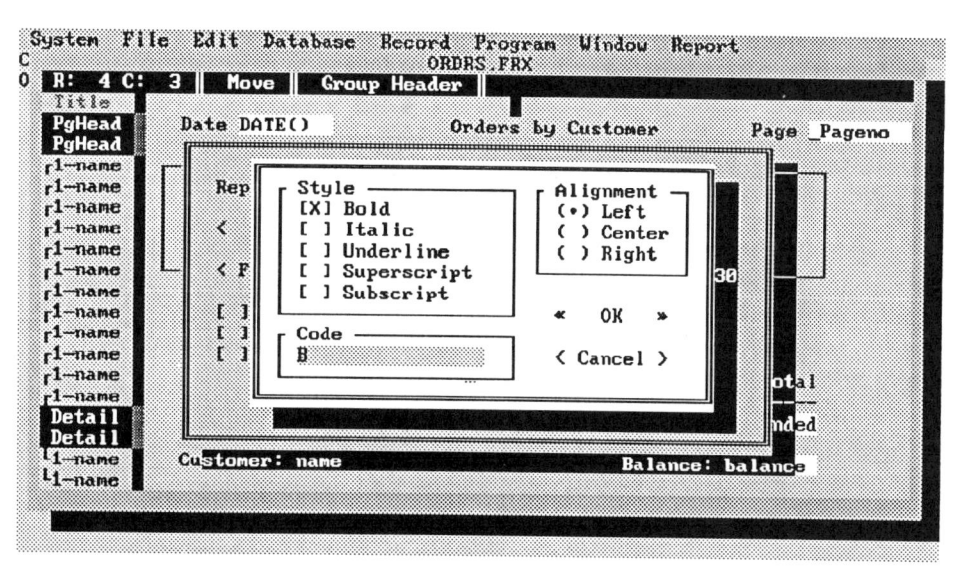

11-5 Using a style code with a report object.

The P_CODES.DBF database contains the names and common function print codes for about 100 printers. It's easy to add more, provided you know the printer control codes.

A printer driver setup is the set of these codes that works with your printer, plus a few other options. The printer driver setup program loads an array to memory that remains there during your session. Using it, the printer driver knows that, if it's printing on an HP LaserJet, for example, to print a bold object, it needs to print the <bold on> code, the object, and the <bold off> code.

Internally, the codes that FoxPro loads from your selected printer driver setup are stored in an array called _PDPARMS.

You can initialize _PDSETUP by entering the command SET PDSETUP TO "HP LASERJET II" or the name of your printer.

If you LIST MEMORY TO PRINT, you'll get a listing of the printer driver codes, as well as other values in memory variables that are involved in printing. You can use these variables as your own, provided you're prepared for the consequences.

If you peek ahead at the LaserPro library code further down in this chapter, you'll see some LaserJet codes assigned to variable names. By matching those up with the values of the array _PDPARMS, you can see what goes where.

Creating a printer driver file

To create a printer driver setup, select File, Printer Drivers↓ from the system menu. This screen is shown in FIG. 11-6.

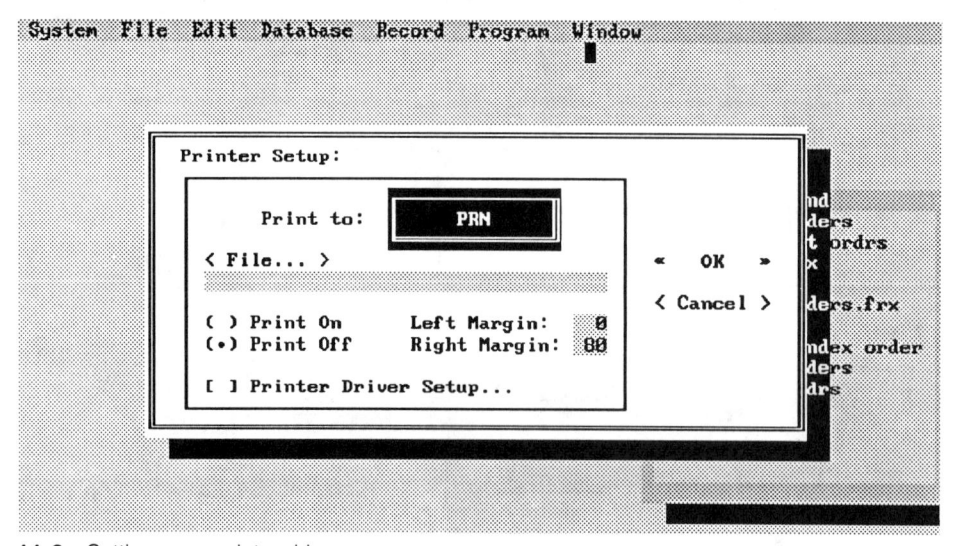

11-6 Setting up a printer driver.

First, select your printer. If you can use one that's on the list, just highlight it and press Enter. Next, select the orientation (portrait or landscape), stroke and style, fonts, lines and characters per inch, and margins (FIG. 11-7).

The list that FoxPro comes with is pretty complete. Because it's a database, if your printer is not on the list and you want to copy a printer name to a similar model and change a few codes, you can use the code in LISTING 11-2.

Listing 11-2

```
USE P_CODES
BROWSE                    && to find the printer you want to copy, then
COPY NEXT 1 TO X
APPEND FROM X
BROWSE                    && you'll be looking at the record just added;
                          && make the desired changes and press Ctrl-W.
```

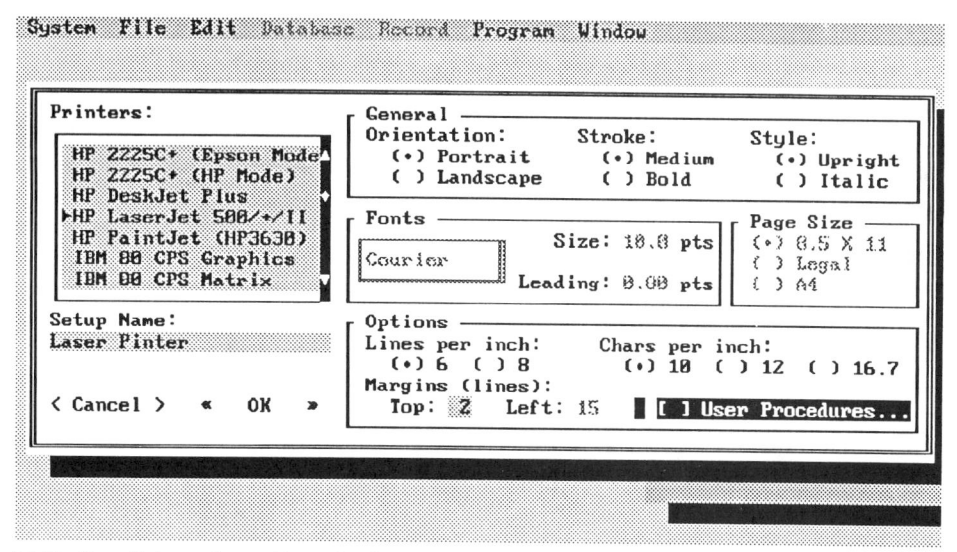

11-7 Specifying printer driver details.

Overriding the printer driver routines

A FoxPro printer driver has to have a set of 12 functions, named as shown in TABLE 11-4. If you have routines that you want to execute in place of the built-in functions, enter them in the boxes provided in the User Procedures dialog that comes up if you check the User Procedures box on the printer driver setup screen. This is where I entered Init_Pri.PRG and FormHead.PRG as my PDDOCST and PDPAGEST routines, respectively. The User Procedures screen is shown in FIG. 11-8.

Table 11-4 Printer driver program procedures.

PDONLOAD	When FoxPro starts up
PDONUNLOAD	When FoxPro shuts down
PDDOCST	Start of document
PDDOCEND	End of document
PDPAGEST	Start of page
PDPAGEEND	End of page
PDLINEST	Start of line
PDLINEEND	End of line
PDOBJST	Start of object

Table 11-4 Continued.

PDOBJECT	Object style code string
PDOBJEND	End of object
PDADVPRT	Prior object ending column, beginning column, or next object.

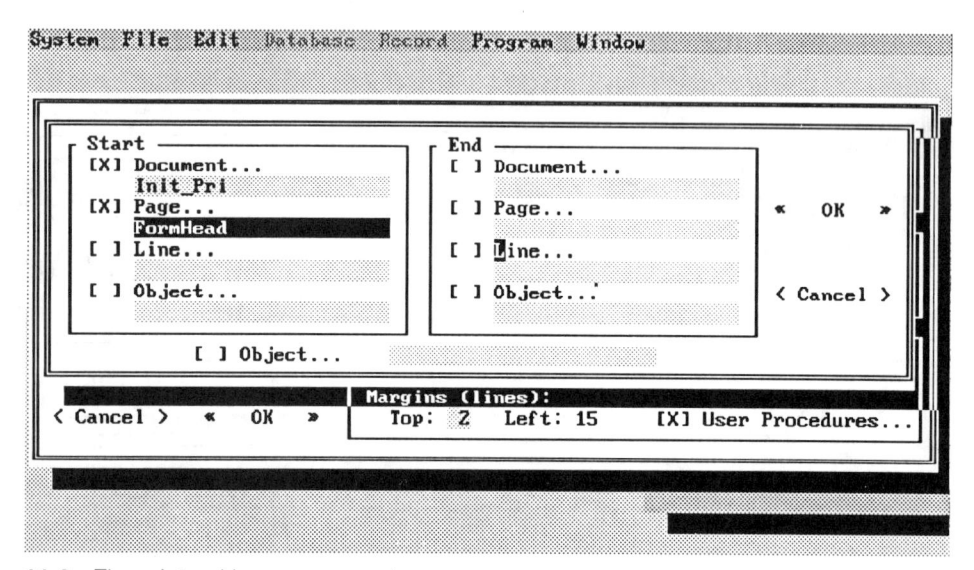

11-8 The printer driver user procedure names screen.

Using your saved printer driver setup

The results of your driver setup session are saved in the FOXUSER resource file. Subsequently, you can set up the printer as defined in your printer driver setup by typing:

_PDSETUP = [Printer setup name]

or

SET PDSETUP TO [Printer setup name]

Assigning _PDPARMS codes directly

You also can stuff values into the array _PDPARMS directly using the command:

SET PDSETUP WITH item1, item2,...

Finally, you can simply assign elements of the _PDSETUP array values. For example, the START PAGE routine for GENPD can be overridden by assigning a program name to _PDPARMS(31).

Tricks of the trade

I have a special fondness for LaserJet reports. The printer driver for the LaserJet does a lot of things, but it gets clumsier as I get fancier. For example, I like to do elegant report formats, including boxing and shading. To do report formats like those shown later in this chapter, you first need to design the report in ordinary code, using the LaserPro library. Then, rename the program and assign it to _PDPARMS(31) as the START PAGE routine for the current report. Nothing else about the driver needs to be changed. Note that, in my forms programs, I use my own codes, rather than the printer driver's codes. There aren't any fields in P_CODES for line drawing, shading, boxing, and some of the other intricacies of LaserJet Forms design.

RQBE and the report writer

The report writer can be designated as the destination for the output of a Relational Query By Example (RQBE) session, so that data goes directly from a query to the report.

From within RQBE Options screen (FIG. 11-9), you can select as the destination for output either Cursor (which means a temporary BROWSE file and window that disappear when you're done), File, Screen, or Report. If you select Report, you can designate a report form that will display the data upon completion of the query. The result often makes more sense than trying to look at raw data.

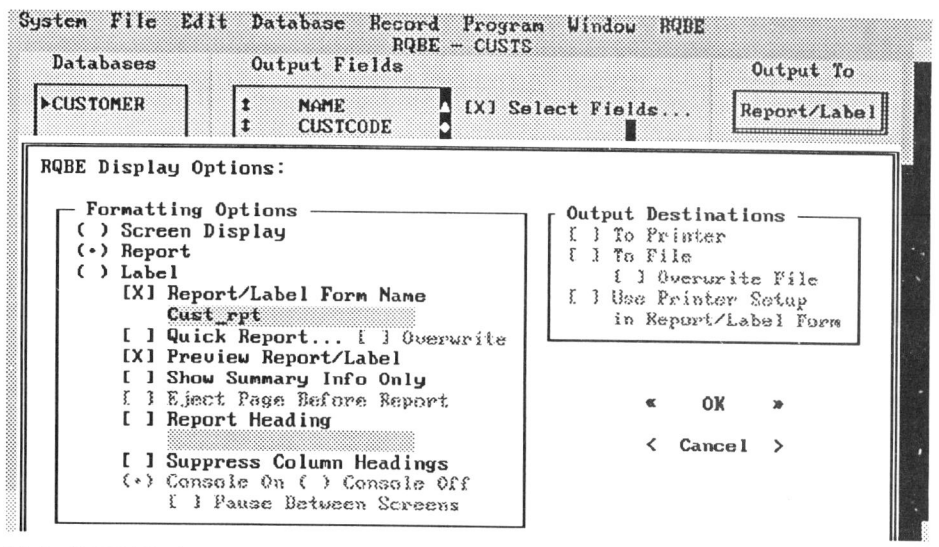

11-9 RQBE Options screen.

A complete treatment of RQBE will have to wait for another book and probably another writer. Report forms, however, are an excellent way to deal with RQBE output.

Reports for laser printers

If you need to exactly reproduce government forms or if you want to design your own forms for laser printers, you'll enjoy using the library that I've developed.

Listing 11-3 contains the source code for the LaserPro library. This code, which originally appeared in my Newsletter and in a previous book, was substantially enhanced by Rich Elliott of Ferret Software.

Listing 11-3

```
* Program-id.....: LaserPro.PRG
* Author.........: Pinter Consulting Staff (Originally LASERLIB.PRG)
* Revised........: 2/28/91 by Richard Elliott, Ferret Software
* Purpose........: HP LaserJet II Procedure Library for Foxpro
* Usage..........: SET PROCEDURE TO LaserPro

* -----------------------------------------------------------

PROCEDURE Init_Print

* PRINTER CONTROL VARIABLES
* Usage: ??? variable_name
* DO Init_Print first to set global variables

    PUBLIC ESC, reset, clearfonts, portrait, landscape, uline_on, uline_off,
pop, push
    PUBLIC bold_on, bold_off, ital_on, ital_off, courier, lineprint
    PUBLIC sym_pc8, sym_pc8dn, sym_pc850, sym_rm8, sym_ecma
    PUBLIC pitch_10, pitch_12, pitch_17, tmargin, lmargin, printport

    ESC         = CHR(27)
    reset       = ESC + 'E'             && Reset printer
    clearfonts  = ESC + '*c0F'          && Clear ALL fonts
    portrait    = ESC + "&l0O"          && Portrait page orientation
    landscape   = ESC + "&l1O"          && Landscape page orientation
    uline_on    = ESC + "&d1D"          && Underline, fixed, on
    uline_off   = ESC + "&d@"           && Underline off
    pop         = ESC + "&f1S"
    push        = ESC + "&f0S"
    bold_on     = ESC + "(s3B"          && Bold type
    bold_off    = ESC + "(s0B"          && Normal type
    ital_on     = ESC + "(s1S"          && Italics on
    ital_off    = ESC + "(s0S"          && Normal upright font
    courier     = ESC + "(s3T"          && Courier typeface
    lineprint   = ESC + "(s0T"          && Lineprinter typeface
    sym_pc8     = ESC + "(10U"          && PC-8 symbol set
    sym_pc8dn   = ESC + "(11U"          && PC-8DN symbol set
    sym_pc850   = ESC + "(12U"          && PC-850 symbol set
    sym_rm8     = ESC + "(8U"           && ROMAN-8 symbol set
    sym_ecma    = ESC + "(0N"           && ECMA symbol set
    pitch_10    = ESC + "(s10h12V"      && Includes 12 point height
```

```
    pitch_12    = ESC + "(s12h10V"          && Includes 10 point height
    pitch_17    = ESC + "(s16.66h8.5V"      && Includes 8.5 point height

 ** SYSTEM PRINTING VARIABLES

    tmargin     = 0                         && In inches, change as needed
    lmargin     = 0                         && In inches, change as needed
    printport   = "LPT1"                    && Assign default printer port

RETURN

* --------------------------------------------------------------

FUNCTION Box
PARAMETERS top_row , bottom_row, left_col, right_col , _thick

  ** Use as: ??? BOX(top_row, botom_row, left_col, right_col, thickness)
  ** First four parameters are in inches from top or left of page.
  ** The last parameter is thickness in decipoints (720 decipoints = 1 inch!)

  _height = (bottom_row - top_row )                && determine line lengths
  _width  = (right_col  - left_col) + (_thick/720) && Adjustment for corner

  top_    = HLINE( top_row    , left_col  , _width  , _thick )
  left_   = VLINE( top_row    , left_col  , _height , _thick )
  bottom_ = HLINE( bottom_row , left_col  , _width  , _thick )
  right_  = VLINE( top_row    , right_col , _height , _thick )

RETURN top_ + left_ + bottom_ + right_

* --------------------------------------------------------------

FUNCTION Copies
PARAMETERS num_copies

  ** Use as: ??? COPIES(number_of_copies)

RETURN ESC+"&l"+ALLTRIM(STR(num_copies))+"X"

* --------------------------------------------------------------

FUNCTION Internal
PARAMETERS _font

  ** Use as: ??? INTERNAL(font_number)
  ** Modify to add any other internal font available

  DO CASE
     CASE _font = 1   && PORTRAIT  COURIER
        string_= portrait+ESC+"(10U"+ESC+"(s0p10h12v0s0b3T"
     CASE _font = 2   && PORTRAIT  COMPRESSED
        string_= portrait+ESC+"(10U"+ESC+"(s0p16.66h8.5v0s0b0T"
     CASE _font = 3   && PORTRAIT  BOLD
        string_= portrait+ESC+"(10U"+ESC+"(s0p10h12v0s3b3T"
     CASE _font = 4   && LANDSCAPE COURIER
        string_= landscape+ESC+"(10U"+ESC+"(s0p10h12v0s0b3T"
     CASE _font = 5   && LANDSCAPE COMPRESSED
        string_= landscape+ESC+"(10U"+ESC+"(s0p16.66h8.5v0s0b0T"
     CASE _font = 6   && LANDSCAPE BOLD
        string_= landscape+ESC+"(10U"+ESC+"(s0p10h12v0s3b3T"
  ENDCASE
```

Listing 11-3 Continued

```
RETURN string_

* ------------------------------------------------------------

FUNCTION Lpi
PARAMETERS lpi_num

   ** Use as: ??? LPI(lpi_number)

RETURN ESC + '&l' + ALLTRIM(STR(lpi_num)) + 'D'

* ------------------------------------------------------------

FUNCTION VLine
PARAMETERS _line , _col , _len , _thick

   ** Use as: ??? VLINE(start_line_number, start_column_number, length,
thickness)
   ** Line, column and length number are in inches
   ** Top line is 0, to column is 0

   line_   = STR(( 720 * (_line + tmargin )) , 4 );
           && Les has a 75 dot adjustment
   col_    = STR(( 720 * (_col  + lmargin )) , 4 );
           && I removed and use margin vars.
   len_    = STR(( 720 * _len ) , 4 );
           && Pesonal preference, I prefer
   thick_  = STR( _thick         , 4 );
           && absolute measures where possible

   curs_   = ESC + '&a' + line_ + "v" + col_  + "H"
   spec_   = ESC + "*c" + len_  + "v" + thick_ + "H"
   prin_   = ESC + "*c" + "0P"

RETURN curs_ + spec_ + prin_

* ------------------------------------------------------------

FUNCTION HLine
PARAMETERS _line , _col , _len , _thick

   ** Use as: ??? HLINE(start_line_number, start_column_number, length,
thickness)

   line_   = STR(( 720 * _line ) , 4 )          && Convert inches to decipoints
   col_    = STR(( 720 * _col  ) , 4 )          && etc.
   len_    = STR(( 720 * _len  ) , 4 )          && etc.
   thick_  = STR( _thick         , 4 )

   curs_   = ESC + "&a" + line_  + "v" + col_ + "H"
   spec_   = ESC + "*c" + thick_ + "v" + len_ + "H"
   prin_   = ESC + "*c" + "0P"

RETURN  curs_ + spec_ + prin_

* ------------------------------------------------------------

FUNCTION Grid
PARAMETERS top_row , bottom_row, left_col, right_col , _grid
```

```
   ** Use as: ??? GRID(top_row_start, bottom_row_start, left_column, ;
   **                 right_column, type_of_grid)
   **
   ** Avilable grid types:   1 = Horizontal lines
   **                        2 = Vertical lines
   **                        3 = Diagonal lines 1
   **                        4 = Diagonal lines 2
   **                        5 = Square grid
   **                        6 = Diagonal grid
   ** See BOX() explanation for more info

   _height = (bottom_row - top_row )
   _width  = (right_col  - left_col)

   _row_   = LTRIM(STR((( top_row + tmargin ) * 720 ) , 4 ))
   _col_   = LTRIM(STR((( left_col + lmargin ) * 720 ) , 4 ))
   _high_  = LTRIM(STR(( _height * 720 ) , 4 ))
   _len_   = LTRIM(STR(( _width * 720 ) , 4 ))

   loc_    = ESC   + "&a"   + _row_  + "v" + _col_ + "H"
   info_   = ESC   + "*c"   + _high_ + "v" + _len_ + "H"
   grid_   = ESC   + "*c"   + STR(_grid,2) + "G"
   last_   = ESC   + "*c"   + "3P"

RETURN loc_  + info_ + grid_ + last_


* ------------------------------------------------------------

FUNCTION Shading
PARAMETERS top_row , bottom_row, left_col, right_col , _shading

   ** Use as: ??? SHADING(top_row_start, bottom_row_start, left_column, ;
   **                 right_column, %_shading)

   _height = (bottom_row - top_row )
   _width  = (right_col  - left_col)

   _row_   = LTRIM(STR((( top_row + tmargin ) * 720 ) , 4 ))
   _col_   = LTRIM(STR((( left_col + lmargin ) * 720 ) , 4 ))
   _high_  = LTRIM(STR(( _height * 720 ) , 4 ))
   _len_   = LTRIM(STR(( _width * 720 ) , 4 ))

   loc_    = ESC   + "&a"   + _row_  + "v" + _col_ + "H"
   info_   = ESC   + "*c"   + _high_ + "v" + _len_ + "H"
   shad_   = ESC   + "*c"   + STR(_shading,2) + "G"
   last_   = ESC   + "*c"   + "2P"

RETURN loc_  + info_ + shad_ + last_

* ------------------------------------------------------------

FUNCTION SoftFont
PARAMETERS _font_

   ** Use as: ??? SOFTFONT(font_id_number)
   ** Fonts must be preloaded with FontLoad() or external program

RETURN ESC + "(" + RIGHT(STR(100000+_font_,6),5) + "X"


* ------------------------------------------------------------
```

Listing 11-3 Continued

```
FUNCTION FontLoad
PARAMETERS font_name,_font_,print_port

  ** Use as: ??? FONTLOAD(font_file,font_id_number,printer_port)

  ??? ESC + "*c" + RIGHT(STR(100000+_font_,6),5) + "D"   &&
  !COPY &font_name /B &print_port /B > nul;
       && font_name may include path
  ??? ESC + "*c5F"                                  && Make font "permanent"

RETURN "

* -----------------------------------------------------------

PROCEDURE SayIt
PARAMETERS _down , _over , _ctext, _pict

  ** Use as: ??? SayIt(inches_down, inches_over, text_to_print,
picture_clause)

  _type = TYPE("_ctext")
  DO CASE
    CASE _type = "C" .OR. _type = "D" .OR. _type = "L"
      DO CASE
        CASE _type = "D"
          text_ = DTOC(_ctext)
        CASE _type = "L"
          IF _ctext
            text_ = "Y"
          ELSE
            text_ = "N"
          ENDIF
        OTHERWISE
          text_ = _ctext
      ENDCASE
    CASE _type = "N"
      text_ = LTRIM(TRANSFORM(_ctext,_pict))
    OTHERWISE
      text_ = 'TYPE ERROR'
  ENDCASE

  _row    = STR(( 720 * ( _down + tmargin )) , 4 )
  _col    = STR(( 720 * ( _over + lmargin )) , 4 )

RETURN ESC + "&a" + _row + "v" + _col + "H" + text_


* -----------------------------------------------------------

FUNCTION MacroID
PARAMETERS id_

  ** Use as: ??? MACROID(macro_id_number)

RETURN  ESC + "&f" + LTRIM(STR(id_,10)) + CHR(89)

* -----------------------------------------------------------
```

```
FUNCTION MacroCtl
PARAMETERS func_

   *0 Start macro definition
   *1 Stop macro definition
   *2 Execute macro
   *3 Call macro
   *4 Enable auto overlay
   *5 Disable auto overlay
   *6 Delete all macros
   *7 Delete all temp macros
   *8 Delete macro
   *9
   *10 Make macro perm

RETURN ESC + "&f" + LTRIM(STR(func_,10)) + CHR(88)

* ----------------------------------------------------------

PROCEDURE LineLoop
PARAMETERS LineMax, StartLine, StartCol, LineWidth, _Lpi

   ** Use as: DO LineLoop WITH max_lines, start_line, start_column,
   **                          line_width, lines_per_inch

   i = 1
   height_ = ROUND(1/_lpi,3)
   DO WHILE (i*height_) <= LineMax
     ??? HLINE ( ( (i*height_) + StartLine) , StartCol , LineWidth, 1 )
     i = i + 1
   ENDDO

RETURN

* ----------------------------------------------------------
```

The sample is a simple, one-page-per-record report. This is an excellent example of a very simple program that looks very elegant. Listing 11-4 contains the code that produced it.

Listing 11-4

```
* Program-ID......: OnePage.PRG
* Author..........: Pinter Consulting Staff
* Purpose.........: Prints a one-page-per-record report on the HP LJII/III
SET PROCEDURE TO LASERPRO
DO Init_Print

USE STUDENTS IN A
* Structure for STUDENTS.DBF

*    1    FIRSTNAME      Character    15
*    2    LASTNAME       Character    15
*    3    ADDRESS1       Character    35
*    4    ADDRESS2       Character    35
*    5    HOMEPHONE      Character    12
*    6    CLASS          Character     4
```

Listing 11-4 Continued

```
*    7    MAJOR           Character    16
*    8    DEGREEOBJ       Character     4
SCAN
  DO Info
ENDSCAN


PROCEDURE Info

??? Landscape
??? Internal ( 6 )

??? Box (  .16 ,  .50 ,   .30 , 10.30 , 5 )
??? Box (  .19 ,  .47 ,   .33 ,  2.30 , 5 )
??? Box (  .19 ,  .47 ,  2.33 ,  8.27 , 5 )
??? Box (  .19 ,  .47 ,  8.30 , 10.27 , 5 )

??? Shading ( .19 ,  .47 ,   .33 ,  2.30 , 25 )
??? Shading ( .19 ,  .47 ,  2.33 ,  8.27 , 25 )
??? Shading ( .19 ,  .47 ,  8.30 , 10.27 , 25 )

??? SayIt ( .40 ,  .43 , "Foothill College"        )
??? SayIt ( .40 , 4.75 , "Student Roster"          )
??? SayIt ( .40 , 8.73 , "Date: " + DTOC(DATE())   )

??? Box (  .50 , 7.03 ,   .30 , 10.30 , 2 )
??? Box (  .53 ,  .83 ,   .33 , 10.27 , 2 )
??? Box (  .86 , 6.66 ,   .33 , 10.27 , 2 )
??? Box ( 6.69 , 7.00 ,   .33 , 10.27 , 2 )

??? Shading ( .53 ,  .83 ,   .33 , 10.27 , 10 )

??? SayIt ( .73 ,  .43 , "Current Information" )
??? SayIt ( .73 , 8.73 , "Time: " + TIME()     )
??? Shading ( .86 , 6.66 ,   .33 ,  3.00 , 10 )
??? Shading ( .86 , 6.66 ,  8.00 , 10.27 , 10 )
??? Shading ( .86 , 1.86 ,  3.00 ,  8.00 , 10 )
??? Shading ( .60 , 6.66 ,  3.00 ,  8.00 , 10 )

??? Box ( 1.86 , 5.60 ,  3.00 ,  8.00 , 2 )
??? Box ( 1.89 , 2.05 ,  3.03 ,  7.97 , 2 )
??? Box ( 2.08 , 5.57 ,  3.03 ,  7.97 , 2 )

??? SayIt ( 2.03 , 5.00 , " Please Verify"  )

DO LineLoop WITH ( 5.57 - 2.08 ) , 2.08 , 3.03 , ( 7.97 - 3.03 ) , 6

??? Internal ( 6 )

??? SayIt ( 2.90 , 3.00 , "          Last Name: " )
??? Sayit ( 3.06 , 3.00 , "         First Name: " )
??? SayIt ( 3.23 , 3.00 , "            Address: " )
??? SayIt ( 3.39 , 3.00 , "                     " )
??? SayIt ( 4.23 , 3.00 , "     Home Telephone: " )
```

```
??? SayIt ( 4.39 , 3.00 , "       Classification: " )
??? SayIt ( 4.55 , 3.00 , "                Major: " )
??? SayIt ( 4.88 , 3.00 , "     Degree Objective: " )

??? Internal ( 5 )

??? SayIt ( 2.90 , 5.40 , LastName  )
??? SayIt ( 3.06 , 5.40 , FirstName )
??? SayIt ( 3.23 , 5.40 , Address1  )
??? SayIt ( 3.39 , 5.40 , Address2  )
??? SayIt ( 4.23 , 5.40 , HomePhone )
??? SayIt ( 4.39 , 5.40 , Class )
??? SayIt ( 4.55 , 5.40 , Major )
??? SayIt ( 4.88 , 5.40 , DegreeObj )

??? Internal ( 5 )

??? SayIt ( 6.90 , 3.50 ,;
    "If any information is not current, please correct and return " )
??? Shading ( .69 , 7.00 ,   .33 , 10.27 , 10 )

EJECT
RETURN
```

Printing data "two up"

If you have small amounts of data, you might want to get two columns on a page (FIG. 11-10) on page 272. The LaserJet is happy to print anywhere on the page at any time. Listing 11-5 contains the code to do it (the report follows the program).

Listing 11-5

```
* Program-Id......: TwoCol.PRG
* Author..........: Pinter Consulting Staff
* Purpose.........: Prints a landscape, two-column general-purpose form
* Calls...........: LaserPro.PRG

SET PROCEDURE TO LASERPRO
CLEAR

@ 11, 27 TO 13, 52 DOUBLE
@ 12, 29 SAY 'Printing Report Layout' + sys(2002)

LinesPerInch = 6

Do Init_Print

??? Landscape

FirstTime = .T.
LineCount = 99
PageCount =  0
```

Listing 11-5 Continued

```
USE Names

* Structure:
*
* FirstName    Character   15
* LastName     Character   15
* CallDate     Date         8
* Phone        Character   12

Do while .not. eof()

  IF LineCount > 72
    IF .NOT. FirstTime
      ? chr(12)
    ENDIF
    FirstTime = .F.
    LineCount = 1
    PageCount = PageCount + 1
    DO ReptForm                    && <-- This puts the form on paper!
    ??? SayIt ( .28 , 9.00 , dtoc(date()) )
    ??? SayIt ( .44 , 9.00 , str(PageCount,8) )
  ENDIF

* -- The following lines put the data onto the report. The graphics were
* -- set up above, and will actually print simultaneously with the data.
  ??? SayIt ( ;
    1.17 + ;
    iif(LineCount>36,LineCount-36,LineCount)*.166 , ;
    iif(LineCount>36, 5 , 0 ) + .43 , ;
    DtoC( CallDate ) )

  ??? SayIt ( ;
    1.17 + ;
    iif(LineCount>36,LineCount-36,LineCount)*.166 , ;
    iif(LineCount>36, 5 , 0 ) + 1.20 , ;
    trim( FirstName ) + ' ' + LastName )

  ??? SayIt ( ;
    1.17 + ;
    iif(LineCount>36,LineCount-36,LineCount)*.166 , ;
    iif(LineCount>36, 5 , 0 ) + 3.20 , ;
    Phone )

  LineCount = LineCount + 1

  SKIP

ENDDO

SET PRINT ON      && This is preferable to EJECT, because on a network
? chr(12)         && printer, EJECT is immediate, even though the report
SET PRINT OFF     && may not print for some time.

??? Reset
```

```
QUIT

PROCEDURE ReptForm
* Purpose.........: Prints a landscape, two-column general-purpose form

* ----------------------------------------------------------------
* Left side title box:
* ----------------------------------------------------------------

??? Box       (  .12 ,   .53 ,   .25,  2.00 ,   1 )
??? Shading   (  .12 ,   .53 ,   .25,  2.00 ,  10 )
??? Internal  (     6 )
??? SayIt     (  .28 ,   .35 , 'KQED Fund Drive' )
??? Internal  (     5 )
??? SayIt     (  .44 ,   .35 , 'Contributor List' )

* ----------------------------------------------------------------
* Center title box:
* ----------------------------------------------------------------

??? Box       (  .12 ,   .53 ,  8.37, 10.12 ,   1 )
??? Shading   (  .12 ,   .53 ,  8.37, 10.12 ,   2 )
??? Internal  (     5 )
??? SayIt     (  .28 ,  8.40 , ' Date ' )
??? SayIt     (  .44 ,  8.40 , ' Page ' )

* -- Left side of form

LMarg1 =   .22
Lmarg2 =   LMarg1 + .03

RMarg2 = 5.00
Rmarg1 = RMarg2 + .03

BoxTop = .73

* -- Do left side title box...
??? Box       (  .70 , 1.03 ,LMarg1,RMarg1 ,   1 )
??? Box       ( BoxTop,1.00 ,LMarg2,RMarg2 ,   1 )

* -- shading inside box

??? Shading   (  .73 , 1.00 ,LMarg2,RMarg2 ,  10 )

* -- Dropshadow under box

??? Shading   (  .75 , 1.08, RMarg1,RMarg1+.05, 45 )
??? Shading   ( 1.03 , 1.03+.05, LMarg1+.05,RMarg1+.05, 45 )

ColA = 1.10
ColB = 3.10
ColC = 4.10

line_len1  =     1.00 -  .73
```

Listing 11-5 Continued

```
??? Vline      ( BoxTop,ColA , line_len1   , 1 )
??? Vline      ( Boxtop,ColB , line_len1   , 1 )
??? Vline      ( Boxtop,ColC , line_len1   , 1 )

??? Internal (    5 )
??? SayIt ( BoxTop + .2 , LMarg2 + .3 , 'Date' )
??? SayIt ( BoxTop + .2 , ColA    +.07 , 'Name' )
??? SayIt ( BoxTop + .2 , ColB    +.07 , 'Phone' )
??? SayIt ( BoxTop + .2 , ColC    +.07 , 'Result' )

* -- Do left side detail box...

BoxTop       =     1.20
??? Box        ( 1.17 , 7.22 ,LMarg1,RMarg1,  1 )
??? Box        ( BoxTop,7.19 ,LMarg2,RMarg2,  1 )

* -- Fill in boxes

??? Shading  ( BoxTop,7.19 ,LMarg2,RMarg2,   2 )

* -- Dropshadow under boxes...

??? Shading  ( 1.25 , 7.27, RMarg1,RMarg1+.05, 45 )
??? Shading  ( 7.22 , 7.27, LMarg1+.05,RMarg1+.05, 45 )

line_len1    =    7.19 - BoxTop
??? Vline      ( BoxTop,ColA , line_len1   , 1 )
??? Vline      ( BoxTop,ColB , line_len1   , 1 )
??? Vline      ( BoxTop,ColC , line_len1   , 1 )

line_len1    = RMarg2 - LMarg2
DO LineLoop with     6 ,BoxTop,    LMarg2    , line_len1 , LinesPerInch

* -- Right side of form

LMarg1 =   LMarg1 + 5.1
Lmarg2 =   LMarg2 + 5.1

RMarg2 =   RMarg2 + 5.1
Rmarg1 =   RMarg1 + 5.1

BoxTop = .73

* -- Do right side title box...
??? Box        (  .70 , 1.03 ,LMarg1,RMarg1 ,  1 )
??? Box        ( BoxTop,1.00 ,LMarg2,RMarg2 ,  1 )

* -- shading inside box

??? Shading  (  .73 , 1.00 ,LMarg2,RMarg2 ,  10 )

* -- Dropshadow under box

??? Shading  (  .75 , 1.08, RMarg1,RMarg1+.05, 45 )
??? Shading  ( 1.03 , 1.03+.05, LMarg1+.05,RMarg1+.05, 45 )
```

```
           ColA = ColA + 5.0
           ColB = ColB + 5.0
           ColC = ColC + 5.0

           line_len1   =    1.00 - .73
           ??? Vline      ( BoxTop,ColA , line_len1   ,   1 )
           ??? Vline      ( Boxtop,ColB , line_len1   ,   1 )
           ??? Vline      ( Boxtop,ColC , line_len1   ,   1 )

           ??? Internal (    5 )
           ??? SayIt ( BoxTop + .2 , LMarg2 + .3 , 'Date'  )
           ??? SayIt ( BoxTop + .2 , ColA   +.07 , 'Name'  )
           ??? SayIt ( BoxTop + .2 , ColB   +.07 , 'Phone' )
           ??? SayIt ( BoxTop + .2 , ColC   +.07 , 'Result' )

           * -- Do right side detail box...

           BoxTop      =    1.20
           ??? Box       ( 1.17 , 7.22 ,LMarg1,RMarg1,  1 )
           ??? Box       ( BoxTop,7.19 ,LMarg2,RMarg2,  1 )

           * -- Fill in boxes

           ??? Shading   ( BoxTop,7.19 ,LMarg2,RMarg2,   2 )

           * -- Dropshadow under boxes...

           ??? Shading   ( 1.25 , 7.27, RMarg1,RMarg1+.05, 45 )
           ??? Shading   ( 7.22 , 7.27, LMarg1+.05,RMarg1+.05, 45 )
           line_len1   =    7.19 - BoxTop
           ??? Vline      ( BoxTop,ColA , line_len1  ,   1 )
           ??? Vline      ( BoxTop,ColB , line_len1  ,   1 )
           ??? Vline      ( BoxTop,ColC , line_len1  ,   1 )

           line_len1   = RMarg2 - LMarg2
           DO LineLoop with    6 ,BoxTop,   LMarg2    , line_len1 , LinesPerInch

           RETURN
```

A LaserJet invoice

If you'd like to dispense with computer forms altogether, you might want to take a look at the next form (FIG. 11-11). This is a very nice invoice, designed and coded by Rich Elliott, that shows off some of the LaserJet II's abilities. The sample (LISTING 11-6) includes soft fonts and a graphics file for a logo. You can use internal fonts instead or get some soft fonts.

In addition to the excellent libraries of fonts available from SofCraft, Bitstream, and SWFTE, there are some good public domain fonts available at your neighborhood computer swap meet. The disk to accompany this book (see the order form at the end of the book) contains the public domain soft fonts used to print this invoice, as well as the logo.

KQED Fund Drive
Contributor List

Date	Name	Phone	Result
01/15/90	Les Pinter	201-1531	
01/15/90	Fred Smith	202-1532	
01/15/90	Joe Jones	203-1533	
01/15/90	Bob Goddard	204-1534	
01/15/90	Dave Howard	205-1535	
01/15/90	Edwin Marcos	206-1536	
01/15/90	Mark Evans	207-1537	
01/15/90	Janice Singleton	208-1538	
01/15/90	Sylvia Stone	209-1539	
01/15/90	Juan Vasconcelos	210-1540	
01/15/90	Egon Brindisi	211-1541	
01/15/90	Ahmed AlBassam	212-1542	
01/15/90	Dale Werner	213-1543	
01/15/90	Evan Scott	214-1544	
01/15/90	Josie Rockefeller	215-1545	
01/15/90	Waylon Erndale	216-1546	
01/15/90	Dolly Carrick	217-1547	
01/15/90	Dean Workman	218-1548	
01/15/90	Lance Prentiss	219-1549	
01/15/90	Bert Allen	220-1550	
01/15/90	Paul Deuts	221-1551	
01/15/90	Scott Thumb	222-1552	
01/15/90	Brent Johnson	223-1553	
01/15/90	Bill Rollins	224-1554	
01/15/90	Alice Winkleman	225-1555	
01/15/90	Jeannine Starr	226-1556	
01/15/90	Sherrie Tambourine	227-1557	
01/15/90	Linda Singer	228-1558	
01/15/90	Paula Spitzenbergr	229-1559	
01/15/90	Edmond Wayne	230-1560	
01/15/90	Ray Needham	231-1561	
01/15/90	Howard Chandler	232-1562	
01/15/90	Donald Maniscalco	233-1563	
01/15/90	Eusebio Buendia	234-1564	
01/15/90	Imelda Matsui	235-1565	
01/15/90	Dottie Wertner	236-1566	

Date 02/11/92
Page 1

Date	Name	Phone	Result
01/15/90	Ron Paul	237-1567	
01/15/90	Howard ElPato	238-1568	
01/15/90	George Lucchesi	239-1569	
01/15/90	Fred Gomez	240-1570	

11-10 A LaserJet report with style—The KQED Fund Drive Form.

FERRET SOFTWARE
1102 Burwick Drive
Herndon, VA 22070
(703) 742-8266

INVOICE

INVOICE NO.

SOLD TO

SHIP TO

INV DATE	SALES REP	ORDER NO.	ORDER DATE	SHIP VIA	TERMS

QTY ORDER	QTY SHIP	ITEM NUMBER/DESCRIPTION	UNIT	UNIT PRICE	AMOUNT
				SALES	
				SALES TAX	
				FREIGHT	
				TOTAL	

11-11 A LaserJet Invoice Form.

Listing 11-6

```
* Program-id...: INVOICE.PRG
* Author.......: Richard H. Elliott, Ferret Software
* Purpose......: Uses LaserPro procedure file routines to
*              : print a report.
*              : Uses soft fonts.
SET TALK off

SET PROCEDURE TO LaserPro                         && Use LaserPro procedure
```

A LaserJet invoice   273

Listing 11-6 Continued

```
DO init_print                                   && Initialize
??? reset                                       && Clean up stuff left behind

** LOAD FONTS, ASSIGN ID NUMBERS
??? FONTLOAD("HELV24ST.SFP", 101,printport)     && Loads fonts and assigns
??? FONTLOAD("HELV6.SFP",    102,printport)     && ID numbers
??? FONTLOAD("ROMN10.SFP",   103,printport)
??? FONTLOAD("ROMN18CB.SFP", 104,printport)
helv24   = 101                                  && Assign font IDs
helv6    = 102                                  && to variables (makes
roman10  = 103                                  && program more readable
roman18  = 104

** DRAW INVOICE
??? BOX( 0.60 , 1.20 , 6.00 , 7.50 , 5 )        && Draws upper right
??? HLINE( 0.80 , 6.00, 1.50, 5 )               && invoice number box
??? SHADING( 0.60 , 0.80 , 6.00 , 7.50 , 20 )

??? BOX( 4.00 , 9.50, 0.50 , 7.50 , 7 )         && Big box for invoice
??? HLINE( 4.20 , 0.50, 7.00, 5 )
??? HLINE( 4.60 , 0.50, 7.00, 5 )
??? HLINE( 4.80 , 0.50, 7.00, 5 )
??? HLINE( 8.40 , 0.50, 7.00, 5 )
??? SHADING( 4.00 , 4.20 , 0.50 , 7.50 , 20 )   && Medium shading for column
??? SHADING( 4.60 , 4.80 , 0.50 , 7.50 , 20 )   && headings
??? VLINE( 4.00 , 1.50, 0.60, 5 )
??? VLINE( 4.00 , 2.50, 0.60, 5 )
??? VLINE( 4.00 , 4.00, 0.60, 5 )
??? VLINE( 4.00 , 5.00, 0.60, 5 )
??? VLINE( 4.00 , 6.50, 0.60, 5 )
??? VLINE( 4.60 , 1.50, 0.20, 5 )
??? VLINE( 4.60 , 2.50, 0.20, 5 )
??? VLINE( 4.60 , 5.00, 0.20, 5 )
??? VLINE( 4.60 , 5.50, 0.20, 5 )
??? VLINE( 4.60 , 6.50, 0.20, 5 )
??? VLINE( 4.80 , 1.50, 3.60, 2 )
??? VLINE( 4.80 , 2.50, 3.60, 2 )
??? VLINE( 4.80 , 5.00, 3.60, 2 )
??? VLINE( 4.80 , 5.50, 3.60, 2 )
??? VLINE( 4.80 , 6.50, 3.60, 2 )
??? VLINE( 8.40 , 5.50, 1.10, 5 )
??? VLINE( 8.40 , 6.50, 1.10, 5 )
??? SHADING( 4.80 , 5.00 , 0.50 , 7.50 , 5 )    && Light shading for invoice
??? SHADING( 5.20 , 5.40 , 0.50 , 7.50 , 5 )    && text bars
??? SHADING( 5.60 , 5.80 , 0.50 , 7.50 , 5 )
??? SHADING( 6.00 , 6.20 , 0.50 , 7.50 , 5 )
??? SHADING( 6.40 , 6.60 , 0.50 , 7.50 , 5 )
??? SHADING( 6.80 , 7.00 , 0.50 , 7.50 , 5 )
??? SHADING( 7.20 , 7.40 , 0.50 , 7.50 , 5 )
??? SHADING( 7.60 , 7.80 , 0.50 , 7.50 , 5 )
??? SHADING( 8.00 , 8.20 , 0.50 , 7.50 , 5 )

** FILL OUT TEXT PORTION OF INVOICE

??? SOFTFONT(roman18)                           && Select 18 point Times-Roman
??? SAYIT( 0.60, 0.50, 'FERRET SOFTWARE',")
??? SOFTFONT(roman10)                           && Select 10 point Times-Roman
```

```
???  SAYIT( 0.80, 0.50, '1102 Burwick Drive')
???  SAYIT( 1.00, 0.50, 'Herndon, VA 22070')
???  SAYIT( 1.20, 0.50, '(703) 742-8266')
???  SOFTFONT(helv24)                            && Select 24 point Helvetica
???  SAYIT( 0.35, 5.90, 'INVOICE',")
???  SOFTFONT(roman10)                           && Select 10 point Times-Roman
???  SAYIT( 0.76, 6.30, 'INVOICE NO.',")
???  SOFTFONT(helv6)                             && Select 6 point Helvetica
???  SAYIT( 2.30, 0.50, 'S',")
???  SAYIT( 2.40, 0.50, 'O',")
???  SAYIT( 2.50, 0.50, 'L',")
???  SAYIT( 2.60, 0.50, 'D',")
???  SAYIT( 2.80, 0.50, 'T',")
???  SAYIT( 2.90, 0.50, 'O',")
???  SAYIT( 2.30, 4.50, 'S',")
???  SAYIT( 2.40, 4.50, 'H',")
???  SAYIT( 2.50, 4.50, 'I',")
???  SAYIT( 2.60, 4.50, 'P',")
???  SAYIT( 2.80, 4.50, 'T',")
???  SAYIT( 2.90, 4.50, 'O',")
???  VLINE( 1.90 , 0.50, 0.30, 1 )
???  VLINE( 2.95 , 0.50, 0.30, 1 )
???  HLINE( 1.90 , 0.50, 0.30, 1 )
???  HLINE( 3.25 , 0.50, 0.30, 1 )
???  VLINE( 1.90 , 4.50, 0.30, 1 )
???  VLINE( 2.95 , 4.50, 0.30, 1 )
???  HLINE( 1.90 , 4.50, 0.30, 1 )
???  HLINE( 3.25 , 4.50, 0.30, 1 )
???  SOFTFONT(roman10)                           && Select 10 point Times-Roman
???  SAYIT( 4.16, 0.65, 'INV DATE',")
???  SAYIT( 4.16, 1.60, 'SALES REP',")
???  SAYIT( 4.16, 2.80, 'ORDER NO.',")
???  SAYIT( 4.16, 4.03, 'ORDER DATE',")
???  SAYIT( 4.16, 5.40, 'SHIP VIA',")
???  SAYIT( 4.16, 6.72, 'TERMS',")
???  SAYIT( 4.76, 0.58, 'QTY ORDER',")
???  SAYIT( 4.76, 1.69, 'QTY SHIP',")
???  SAYIT( 4.76, 2.70, 'ITEM NUMBER/DESCRIPTION',")
???  SAYIT( 4.76, 5.07, 'UNIT',")
???  SAYIT( 4.76, 5.55, 'UNIT PRICE',")
???  SAYIT( 4.76, 6.65, 'AMOUNT',")
???  SAYIT( 8.60, 5.60, 'SALES',")
???  SAYIT( 8.80, 5.60, 'SALES TAX',")
???  SAYIT( 9.00, 5.60, 'FREIGHT',")
???  HLINE( 9.10, 5.50, 2.00, 3 )
???  SAYIT( 9.35, 5.60, 'TOTAL',")

**  Remove the following for "real" use
???  INTERNAL(1)                                 && Selects internal Courier 10
???  SAYIT( 10.00, 0.50, 'INVOICE1.PRG - SOFT FONT DEMO'," )

**  NOTE: The following uses the DOS copy command
**  to copy an image to the printer.Remove unless you like ferrets.

!COPY FERRET.PIC /B &printport /B > NUL          && Prints cute picture

EJECT
```

A LaserJet invoice

Summary

FoxPro 2.0 affords several ways to do reports. You can use FoxReport to design a wide variety of reports with no coding. You also can write your own. Using the LaserPro library, you can design beautiful forms and reports.

12
Color

The PC screen actually consists of two bytes of information for each one that you see. In the area of memory reserved for the video display, the bytes that contain what you display on your screen are alternated with *attribute bytes*, which tell the monitor what to do with the byte beside it. Programs that dump the screen actually print a byte, skip a byte, print a byte, skip a byte, and so on. Commands that affect colors actually affect these attribute bytes—sometimes all of them at once.

Color can be one of the most powerful aspects of software design. Screens that make good use of color are informative and easy to use. Some are even little works of art to those of us who talk about such things over coffee.

The raw materials

In FoxPro, as in any screen-oriented language, color is a very complex issue. There are 8 colors:

Name	Code
Black	N
Blue	B
Red	R
Green	G
Cyan	BG
Yellow	GR
Magenta	RB
White	W

Each of these can be used either as a foreground color or a background color, in any combination. If you think of a letter, say the letter *T*, as being a pair of lines drawn on a piece of paper, the color of the two lines that form the *T* is the foreground and the color of the paper is the background. So, the usual color specification is a *color pair*—foreground and background, separated by a slash, like this:

W/B   Yellow on blue
W/BR   White on magenta

Detecting color monitors

When I write a program in FoxPro, I seldom know what type of monitor will be displaying it. For one thing, most of what I write is for Novell networks; you never know what kind of third-world hardware will be hooked up to it. Also, when users see their gorgeous new software on their dowdy monochrome screens after watching me develop it on my NEC MultiSync II, they go out and buy one.

In FoxPro, the ISCOLOR( ) function returns a logical .T. if a color monitor board is detected and .F. otherwise. You can use this to write all of your programs so that they work equally well in both environments. The same approach also will let you test your monochrome color settings on a color screen, provided you adhere to the little trick that I used back in chapter 9 (see LISTING 9-11, lines 5-8).

Intensity and blink

Each foreground color can be used in either low or high intensity. High-intensity color codes are followed by a plus sign. For example, high-intensity white on a blue background is set as follows:

    SET COLOR TO W+/B   && Bright white on blue

Each background color can be assigned high intensity by typing an asterisk after it. However, you must first SET BLINK OFF. The reason for this is that the attribute byte reserves one bit for either blinking or background intensity, so you can't have both. I seldom use blinking, so BLINK OFF is generally the preferred set of colors. Note that, when you SET BLINK OFF, it instantly changes all background colors on the screen, because it changes the way DOS looks at the attribute byte.

Putting color pairs together

Some commands, notably the @...SAY/GET command, need two pairs of colors. The first color pair determines the text color; the second determines the input field color. For example:

    SET COLOR TO GR+/B,N/W
    @ 3, 3 SAY [Name?] GET M->Name FUNCTION [!]

would display the NAME? prompt in yellow on blue, while the input field itself would be black on gray.

Monochrome screens

For monitors that don't have color capability, FoxPro can use a subset of the black and white (N and W) colors, together with underlining and blinking, to provide some contrast to distinguish types of areas on your screens. The function ISCOLOR( ) returns .T. on CGA/EGA/VGA and COMPAQ screens and .F. on black-and-white and monochrome screens. More about COMPAQ later.

For monochrome screens, an additional parameter, the U, is sometimes useful. The statements:

```
SET COLOR TO W+/N
@ 5, 5 SAY [ Name: ]
SET COLOR TO WU/N
@ 5,15 SAY M->Name
```

will display the Name? prompt in highlighted white on a black background and the input field M->Name as an underlined blank field. The subsequent statement:

```
SET COLOR TO N/W
@ 5,15 GET M->Name
```

produces a reverse video field that lets the user know that input is required.

I should say here and now that you should seldom, if ever, SET COLOR TO anything. Doing so works at cross purposes with color schemes, which means more work for you. I'll say more about this later.

Detecting monochrome VGA

Today, many monochrome VGA monitors are sold that return ISCOLOR-( )=.T. even though they are black and white. Also, Compaqs can be monochrome CGA, which also returns ISCOLOR( )=.T.

If your AUTOEXEC.BAT file includes the following statement (or if you enter it at the DOS prompt)

```
SET MONITOR=COMPAQ
```

you can write your programs to test whether the workstation actually is a monochrome Compaq by including the statements:

```
MonitorType = GETENV([MONITOR])
IF Monitor = [COMPAQ] .OR. .NOT. ISCOLOR( )
  SET COLOR TO WU/N
ELSE
```

Detecting monochrome VGA   **279**

```
    SET COLOR TO N/W
ENDIF
```

On a network, this can make your life a lot easier.

The color picker and assigned color schemes

Pressing Alt – W, then L produces the color picker. This is the official FoxPro way of doing colors on your screens. If it meets your needs, it's a lot easier than handling color on a case-by-case basis. FoxPro also comes with a program called ProColor, which was written by Blaise Mitsutama, that can give you valuable insight into color schemes. My favorite authority on color sets is Wayne Harless, who's down in Harahan, Louisiana scaring the neighbors with his high-tech wizardry. I learned more in a day from the Harless Color Sets than I did in a year of experimenting on my own. By the way, the color schemes are different than they were in 1.02.

FoxPro assigns the color schemes 1 through 12 to the following uses:

1. User windows
2. User menus (pop-ups, see chapter 7)
3. The menu bar
4. Menu pop-ups
5. Dialogs
6. Dialog pop-ups
7. Alerts
8. Windows
9. Window pop-ups
10. Browse
11. Report writer
12. Alert pop-ups

For each one of these color schemes, the 10 color pairs are assigned to a different collection of screen objects. For example, in scheme 2, the pop-up border is defined using the third color pair (SET COLOR OF SCHEME 2 TO ,,W+/R will make your pop-up borders appear as white lines on a red background).

For each color scheme, the list of objects 1 through 10 might be different. You have to look at each one to determine what to color how. Also, you might have to experiment for a while to determine the difference between, say, alerts and alert pop-ups and to determine whether you care. Schemes 1, 2, and 10 are pretty crucial. You might not need to do much with the others.

Finally, you can do a quick switch of color assignments by using, for cxamplc:

    SET COLOR OF SCHEME 2 TO SCHEME 7

which uses the alert colors for your pop-ups. If you do this, the pop-ups are assigned colors as of the color settings in effect when you DEFINE POPUP. If you change the color scheme, reissue the DEFINE POPUP statement (LISTING 12-1). If you want to save a color scheme, use this trick:

```
SET COLOR OF SCHEME 12 TO SCHEME 2
SET COLOR OF SCHEME 2 TO whatever weird colors you want
...Do your stuff... then,
SET COLOR OF SCHEME 2 TO SCHEME 12 && bring 'em back
```

That gets you through the generalities of color. The rest of this chapter deals with specific color designs and issues.

Listing 12-1

```
DEFINE    POPUP FUBAR FROM 5,5 PROMPT FIELD STATE && USES COLOR SCHEME 2
ACTIVATE  POPUP FUBAR                                && Show colors under scheme 2
SET COLOR OF SCHEME 2 TO SCHEME 7                    && Change color scheme
ACTIVATE  POPUP FUBAR                                && Notice no color change..
RELEASE   POPUP FUBAR                                && Not necessary, but safe.
DEFINE    POPUP FUBAR FROM 5,5 PROMPT FIELD STATE && Redefine popup...
ACTIVATE  POPUP FUBAR                                && Uses scheme 7 colors
```

Commands with COLOR

There are a number of commands that can include a COLOR specification:

@...SAY/GET	DEFINE BAR	EDIT
@...EDIT	DEFINE MENU	READ
@...FILL	DEFINE PAD	SHOW GET
BROWSE	DEFINE POPUP	SHOW GETS
CHANGE	DEFINE WINDOW	SHOW OBJECT

Each of these can have a parameter of the form [COLOR *ColorPair*], or occasionally [COLOR SCHEME *ExpN*]. One of the more interesting ones is the use of READ...COLOR to force the screen to display the CURRENT INPUT FIELD in a different color from other pending GETs (LISTING 12-2). If you only learn one color trick, make it this one. The result is shown in FIG. 12-1.

Listing 12-2

```
* Program-ID.....: ColoRead.PRG
* Purpose........: Demonstrates 'read loop' color input fields

SET TALK OFF
SET BLINK OFF

DEFINE    WINDOW GETNAME FROM 5, 5 TO 18, 65 COLOR N/GR* SHADOW
ACTIVATE  WINDOW GETNAME

STORE SPACE(30) TO Name,Address,Address2
STORE SPACE(12) TO Phone
CLEAR

@ 1, 19 SAY  'Patient Name and Address'
```

Listing 12-2 Continued
```
@  2, 19 TO 2, 42
@  4,  9 SAY '    Name: ' ;
         GET name      COLOR ,N/W

@  6,  9 SAY 'Address: ' ;
         GET Address   COLOR ,N/W

@  7,  9 SAY '         ' ;
         GET Address2  COLOR ,N/W

@  9,  9 SAY '   Phone: ' ;
         GET Phone     COLOR ,N/W

READ CYCLE COLOR W+/R,W+/R

SET   CURSOR OFF
WAIT WINDOW
SET   CURSOR ON

RELEASE WINDOW GETNAME

RETURN
```

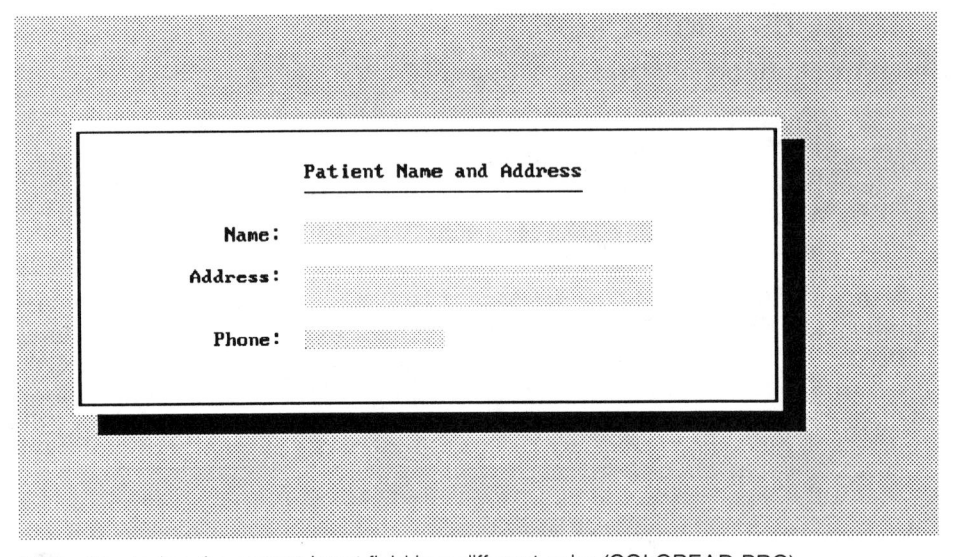

12-1 Displaying the current input field in a different color (COLOREAD.PRG).

The @ SAY...GET statements display the input fields in black on gray (N/W). As each field is processed with READ, the active field turns bold white on red (W+/R) during its read, then reverts to black on gray as the cursor moves to the next field. The resulting effect is gorgeous and users don't whine about not being able to see the cursor.

Color schemes

Listing 12-3 lets you select from among color schemes 1 through 12, so that you can get an idea of what the color assignments are. Figure 12-2 shows the user screen with the currently selected color scheme in effect.

Listing 12-3

```
* Program-ID......: Schemes.PRG
* Purpose.........: Displays color schemes

SET Bell OFF
CLEAR

SchemeNum = 1

DO WHILE SchemeNum > 0

   DEFINE WINDOW COLORWIN FROM 2, 2 TO 20, 60 ;
          COLOR SCHEME SchemeNum ;
          TITLE [Sample Window]  ;
          SHADOW

   ACTIVATE WINDOW COLORWIN

   CLEAR
   DEFINE POPUP   POPTEST   FROM 2, 5
   DEFINE BAR     1 OF POPTEST PROMPT [ First Line  ]
   DEFINE BAR     2 OF POPTEST PROMPT [ Second Line ]
   DEFINE BAR     3 OF POPTEST PROMPT [ Third Line  ] COLOR N/W,W+/R

   SHOW POPUP POPTEST

   STORE SPACE(30) TO mName
   @ 8,  5 SAY [ Enter your name:] ;
           GET mName ;
           MESSAGE [PgDn top change colors] ;
           FUNCTION [!]

   Season = 1
   @ 11, 5 SAY [           Season:] ;
           GET Season ;
           MESSAGE [PgDn to change colors] ;
           PICTURE [@^ Winter;Spring;Summer;Fall]

   WhatNext = 1
   @ 16,19 GET   WhatNext ;
           MESSAGE [PgDn to change colors]  ;
           PICTURE [@*H Save;Cancel] SIZE 1,15,3
   READ

   ACTIVATE SCREEN

   SchemeNum = 0
   @ 22, 0 SAY [Enter a scheme number from 1 to 12:] ;
           GET SchemeNum ;
           PICTURE [99]  ;
```

Listing 12-3 Continued

```
            MESSAGE [ ZERO cancels ] ;
            RANGE 0,12

   READ

   @ 24, 0 CLEAR

   RELEASE WINDOW COLORWIN

ENDDO
```

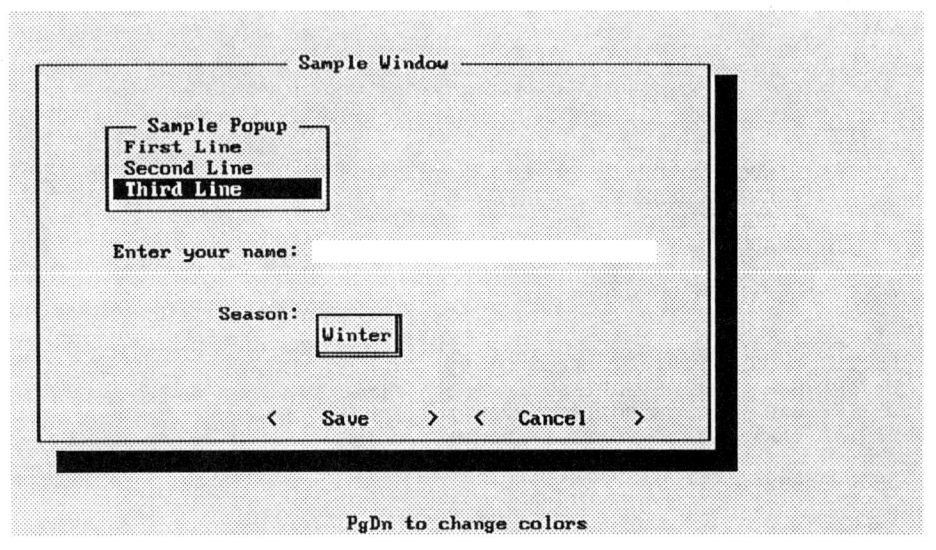

12-2 Color Schemes sampler (SCHEMES.PRG).

In some of the color schemes, the colors for screen text and input fields are exactly the same, so not all schemes can be used for data entry.

If you use color scheme 1 or 2, FoxPro allows you to assign your favorite colors to each of seven areas: normal, messages, titles, box, highlight, information, AND fields. Listing 12-4 lets you pick whatever color you want to assign to each of the seven areas, then shows you the result. The results are shown in FIGS. 12-3 and 12-4 shown on page 290.

Listing 12-4

```
* Program-ID.......: SetColor.PRG
* Purpose..........: Lets user select color settings for scheme 1

SET TALK OFF
SET BELL OFF
SET ESCAPE OFF
CLEAR

UpArrow     =   5
DownArrow   =  24
```

```
LeftArrow   = 19
RightArrow  =  4
ENTER       = 13
ESCAPE      = 27
AreaChosen  = [ ]
Bright      = .T.
Blink       = .T.

DIMENSION AREA(7)
DIMENSION PairList(64)

Area (1) = [ NORMAL      ]
Area (2) = [ MESSAGES    ]
Area (3) = [ TITLES      ]
Area (4) = [ BOX         ]
Area (5) = [ HIGHLIGHT   ]
Area (6) = [ INFORMATION ]
Area (7) = [ FIELDS      ]

DIMENSION ActColor (7)

ActColor (1) = [GR+/B]
ActColor (2) = [GR+/B]
ActColor (3) = [W+/B]
ActColor (4) = [GR+/B]
ActColor (5) = [W+/R]
ActColor (6) = [GR+/B]
ActColor (7) = [W+/BR]

FOR I = 1 TO 7
  ColorSet = [SET COLOR OF] + TRIM(Area(I)) + [ TO ] + ActColor(I)
  &ColorSet
ENDFOR

DEFINE WINDOW PICKER FROM 0, 1 TO 23, 76 ;
       [-],[-],[¤],[¤],[ø],[ñ],[Æ],[§] ;
       TITLE [ Color Picker Screen ] ;
       COLOR SCHEME 1 ;
       SHADOW

DO WHILE .T.

DEFINE WINDOW InputWin FROM 0, 2 TO 20, 55 ;
TITLE [ Sample Input Screen ] ;
COLOR SCHEME 1 SHADOW

SET COLOR TO GR+/B
@ 1, 58 SAY [1  Color Scheme 1 0]
@ 2, 58 SAY [1  Color Settings 0]
FOR I = 1 TO 7
  SET COLOR TO &ActColor(I)
  ColorInfo =  LEFT ( Area(I) + [ ] + ActColor(I) + [ ] , 21)
  @ I+ 2, 58 SAY ColorInfo
ENDFOR
SET COLOR TO GR+/B

ACTIVATE WINDOW InputWin

CLEAR
DEFINE POPUP  POPTEST   FROM 2, 5
DEFINE BAR    1 OF POPTEST PROMPT [ First Line  ]
```

Listing 12-4 Continued

```
DEFINE BAR    2 OF POPTEST PROMPT [ Second Line ]
DEFINE BAR    3 OF POPTEST PROMPT [ Third Line  ]

SHOW POPUP POPTEST

STORE SPACE(25) TO mName
@ 8,  5 SAY [ Enter your name:] ;
        GET mName ;
        MESSAGE [Press PgDn to change colors] ;
        FUNCTION [!]

Season = 1
@ 11, 5 SAY [          Season:] ;
        GET Season ;
        PICTURE [@^ Winter;Spring;Summer;Fall]

Features = 1
@ 15, 5 SAY [  Other features:] ;
        GET Features ;
        PICTURE [@*RH \<First;\<Second] SIZE 1,9,4

WhatNext = 1
@ 17,19 GET  WhatNext ;
        PICTURE [@*H \<Change Colors;C\<ancel] SIZE 1,15,2

   READ

   RELEASE WINDOW InputWin

   DO CASE
     CASE WhatNext = 1 .AND. LASTKEY() <> ESCAPE
     DO PICKER
   OTHERWISE
     EXIT
   ENDCASE

ENDDO


PROCEDURE Picker

ACTIVATE WINDOW PICKER

SET COLOR TO GR+/B
CLEAR

SET CURSOR OFF

@ 1, 1 SAY [-------------------- F o r e g r o u n d;
            -------------------- BackGrnd]
@ 2, 1 SAY [None     Blue     Green    Cyan     Red      Magenta;
            Yellow   White                    ]
@ 3, 66 say                                                         [None    ]
@ 4, 66 say                                                         [Blue    ]
@ 5, 66 say                                                         [Green   ]
@ 6, 66 say                                                         [Cyan    ]
@ 7, 66 say                                                         [Red     ]
@ 8, 66 say                                                         [Magenta]
```

```
@ 9, 66 say                                                          [Yellow ]
@10, 66 say                                                          [White  ]

COLORS = [N    B    G    BG  R    BR  GR  W   ]
=ShoColor()

ON KEY LABEL F2 DO FGToggle
ON KEY LABEL F3 DO BGToggle

DO WHILE .T.

   SET COLOR TO GR+/B

   @ wrows()-1, 1 SAY [ F2 - Toggle Foreground Intensity;
     F3 - Toggle Background Intensity]
FOR I = 1 TO 7
   SET COLOR TO &ActColor(I)
   ColorInfo =  LEFT ( Area(I) + [ ] + ActColor(I) + [ ] , 21)
   @ I+12, 50 SAY ColorInfo
ENDFOR
SET COLOR TO GR+/B
AreaNum = 0
@ 12, 10 GET AreaNum FROM Area VALID GetArea()
READ

IF AreaNum = 0
   EXIT
ENDIF

@ AreaNum+12, 47 SAY [--0]

I = 1
J = 1
A = 0

@ I+2,((J-1)*8) SAY CHR(174)
@ I+2,((J*8)  ) SAY CHR(175)

@ wrows()-1, 1 CLEAR    && remove message
@ wrows()-1, 1 SAY [ Use arrow keys to select a color and press ENTER,;
   or press ESCAPE]

DO WHILE .NOT. ( A = ENTER .OR. A = ESCAPE )

   A = INKEY(0)

   @ I+2,((J-1)*8) SAY [ ]     && Blank out the chevrons
   @ I+2,((J*8)  ) SAY [ ]     && that marked the previous choice.

   DO CASE

      CASE A = UpArrow
         I = I - 1
         IF I = 0
            I = 8
         ENDIF
      CASE A = DownArrow
         I = I + 1
         IF I > 8
            I = 1
```

Listing 12-4 Continued

```
      ENDIF
    CASE A = LeftArrow
      J = J - 1
      IF J = 0
        J = 8
      ENDIF
    CASE A = RightArrow
      J = J + 1
      IF J > 8
        J = 1
      ENDIF
    CASE A = ENTER .OR. A = ESCAPE    && don't beep if ENTER/ESCAPE

    OTHERWISE

        ?? CHR(7)

    ENDCASE

    SET COLOR TO W+/B
    @ I+2,((J-1)*8) SAY CHR(174)
    @ I+2,((J*8)  ) SAY CHR(175)

  ENDDO

  @ AreaNum+12, 47 SAY [   ]

  @ I+2,((J-1)*8) SAY [ ]     && Blank out the chevrons
  @ I+2,((J*8)  ) SAY [ ]     && that marked the previous choice.

  IF A = ENTER    && ESCAPE wasn't pressed
    ColorPair = PairList (( I-1)*8 + J)
    ActColor (AreaNum) = ColorPair
    ColorInfo =  LEFT ( Area(areanum) + [ ] + ActColor(areanum) + [ ] , 21)
    @ areanum+12, 50 SAY ColorInfo
    SET COLOR OF &AreaChosen TO &ColorPair
  ENDIF

ENDDO

DEACTIVATE WINDOW PICKER

SET CURSOR ON

RETURN

FUNCTION GetArea
IF AreaNum <> 0
  AreaChosen = Area(AreaNum)
ENDIF
RETURN .T.

FUNCTION FGToggle
Bright = .NOT. Bright
=ShoColor()
RETURN .T.
```

```
PROCEDURE Remove
PARAMETERS char

FOR I = 1 TO 7
  Where = AT ( char , ActColor ( I ) )
  IF where > 0
    ActColor(I) = LEFT(ActColor(I),where-1) + SUBSTR(ActColor(I),where+1)
  ENDIF

ENDFOR
RETURN

FUNCTION BGToggle
Blink = .NOT. Blink
IF Blink
  SET BLINK ON
ELSE
  SET BLINK OFF
  DO Remove WITH [*]
ENDIF
=ShoColor()
RETURN .T.

PROCEDURE ShoColor

FOR I = 1 TO 8
  BG = TRIM ( SUBSTR ( COLORS , (I-1)*3 + 1 , 3 ) )
  BG = BG + IIF ( Blink , [] , [*] )
  FOR J = 1 TO 8
    FG = TRIM ( SUBSTR ( COLORS , (J-1)*3 + 1 , 3 ) )
    FG = FG + IIF ( Bright, [+] , [] )
    ColorPair = FG + [/] + BG
    PairList (( I-1)*8 + J) = ColorPair
    SET COLOR TO &ColorPair
    @ I + 2, (J-1)*8 + 1 SAY LEFT(ColorPair+"        ",7)
  ENDFOR
ENDFOR

FOR I = 1 TO 7
  SET COLOR TO &ActColor(I)
  ColorInfo =  LEFT ( Area(I) + [ ] + ActColor(I) + [ ] , 21)
  @ I+12, 50 SAY ColorInfo
ENDFOR
SET COLOR TO GR+/B
```

User-selectable colors

Lots of my users have asked for a way to redefine the colors on their screens. There's much more involved than they imagine. If your users are like some of mine, you should give them a reasonable range of choices, say, three or four, so that they can't get themselves in trouble.

The program in LISTING 12-5 takes that approach. It lets users select Colors from their menu, then lets them assign one of four available color combinations to each of the four area types. You can define six or seven areas and increase the range of color pairs to whatever fits on the screen.

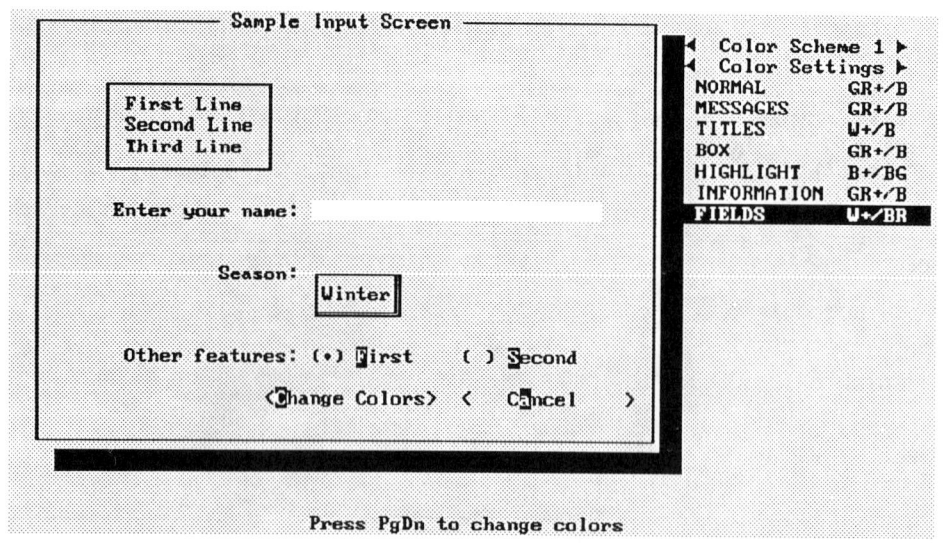

12-3 Color Pair sampler (SETCOLOR.PRG).

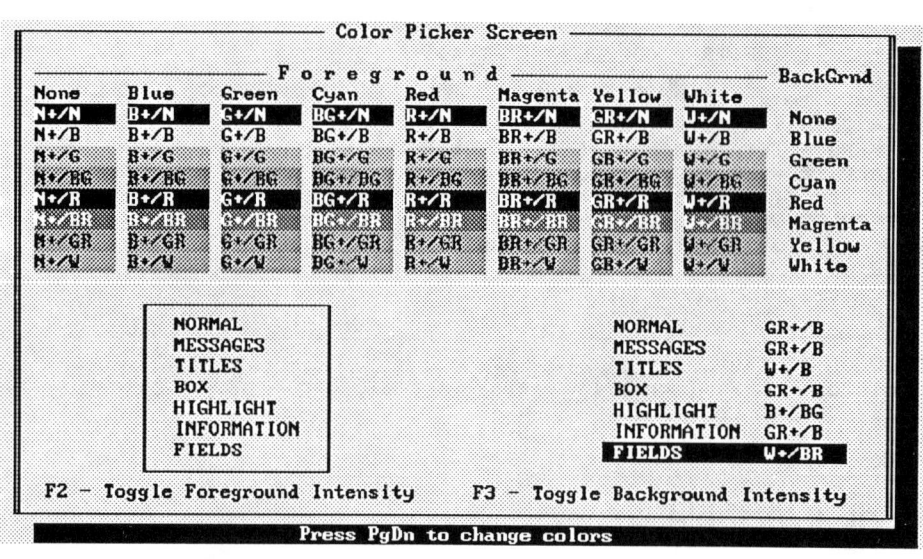

12-4 Color Pair sampler option selection (SETCOLOR.PRG).

Listing 12-5

```
* Program-ID....: UserColr.PRG
* Purpose.......: User-defined color picker with limited choices

* -- Create screen colors memory variables if not found.
if .not. file('COLORS.MEM')
   ATRSIGNON = IIF ( iscolor() , "N/W*,W+/R"  , "W+/N,N/W"  )
   ATRSCREEN = IIF ( iscolor() , "GR+/B,B/W"  , "W+/N,N/W"  )
   ATRPROMPT = IIF ( iscolor() , "N/W,W+/R"   , "W+/N,N/W"  )
```

290 Color

```
      ATRHELP  = IIF ( iscolor() , "W+/BR,N/GR" , "N/W,W+/N"  )
      ATRDATA  = IIF ( iscolor() , "N/W,W+/R"   , "N/W,W+U/N" )
      save to COLORS
endif

restore from COLORS
set color to &ATRSIGNON                    && Not changeable...

STORE 1 TO Row,Col

DO WHILE .T.

   SET COLOR TO &ATRSIGNON                 && Not changeable...
   DO TOPMENU

   DO CASE
     CASE Row = 3 .AND. Col = 1
       DO ColorSet
     CASE Row = 4 .AND. Col = 1
       EXIT
   ENDCASE

ENDDO

RETURN



procedure COLORSET

SAVE SCREEN TO ColrScrn

COLOR1 = IIF ( iscolor() , "GR+/B,B/W"  , "W+/N,N/W" )
COLOR2 = IIF ( iscolor() , "W+/R,W+/BG" , "W+/N,N/W" )
COLOR3 = IIF ( iscolor() , "W+/BR,N/GR" , "N/W,W+/N" )
COLOR4 = IIF ( iscolor() , "W+/BG,GR+/W", "N/W,W+/N")

screen = ATRSCREEN
help   = ATRHELP
prompt = ATRPROMPT
data   = ATRDATA

do while .T.

   set color to &SCREEN
   @  0, 0 clear to 24, 79

   @  1, 1,10,78 box "èë¡°ƒëà¯"
   @  5, 33 say " Color Manager "

   @ 12,10,14,20 box "Öá¢°Ìáâ° "
   @ 12,22,14,32 box "Öá¢°Ìáâ° "
   @ 12,34,14,44 box "Öá¢°Ìáâ° "
   @ 12,46,14,56 box "Öá¢°Ìáâ° "

   set color to &SCREEN
   @ 13, 11 say " Screen "
   set color to &HELP
   @ 13, 23 say " Help   "
   set color to &PROMPT
   @ 13, 35 say " Prompt "
```

Listing 12-5 Continued

```
set color to &DATA
@ 13, 47 say "   Data    "
set color to &SCREEN

@ 16,10,19,20 box "Öá¢°ìáâ° "
@ 16,22,19,32 box "Öá¢°ìáâ° "
@ 16,34,19,44 box "Öá¢°ìáâ° "
@ 16,46,19,56 box "Öá¢°ìáâ° "

@ 17, 60 say '<-Output'
@ 18, 60 say '<-Input'

set color to &COLOR1
X =          " Color1 "
@ 17, 11 say X
@ 18, 11 get X
set color to &COLOR2
X =          " Color2 "
@ 17, 23 say X
@ 18, 23 get X
set color to &COLOR3
X =          " Color3 "
@ 17, 35 say X
@ 18, 35 get X
set color to &COLOR4
X =          " Color4 "
@ 17, 47 say X
@ 18, 47 get X

clear gets

set color to &SCREEN
@ 23, 0 clear
set message to 24
@ 23,     0 prompt " \<Screen " message " Select Screen Colors"
@ 23, col() prompt " \<Help "   message " Select Help Message Colors"
@ 23, col() prompt " \<Prompt " message " Select Prompt Colors"
@ 23, col() prompt " \<Data "   message " Select Data Field Colors"
@ 23, col() prompt " Sa\<ve "   message " Save and Exit"
@ 23, col() prompt " \<Quit "   message " Exit Without Saving Changes"

GETCOL = 1
menu to GETCOL

do case

   case GETCOL = 1

      set color to &SCREEN
      @ 23, 0 clear

      @ 23, 0 say "Color for Screens" ;
      get GETCOL   ;
      picture '9'  ;
      range 0,4    ;
      message " Enter a number between 1 and 4"

      read
```

```
      if GETCOL = 0
        loop
      endif

      COLNAME = 'COLOR' + str(GETCOL,1)
      screen  = &COLNAME

case GETCOL = 2

   set color to &SCREEN
   @ 23, 0 clear

   @ 23, 0 say "Color for Help Screens" ;
   get GETCOL   ;
   picture '9'  ;
   range 0,4    ;
   message " Enter a number between 1 and 4"

   read

   if GETCOL = 0
      loop
   endif

   COLNAME = 'COLOR' + str(GETCOL,1)
   help    = &COLNAME

case GETCOL = 3

   set color to &SCREEN
   @ 23, 0 clear

   @ 23, 0 say "Color for Prompts" ;
   get GETCOL   ;
   picture '9'  ;
   range 0,4    ;
   message " Enter a number between 1 and 4"

   read

   if GETCOL = 0
      loop
   endif
   COLNAME = 'COLOR' + str(GETCOL,1)
   prompt  = &COLNAME

case GETCOL = 4

   set color to &SCREEN
   @ 23, 0 clear
   @ 23, 0 say "Color for Data" ;
   get GETCOL   ;
   picture '9'  ;
   range 0,4    ;
   message " Enter a number between 1 and 4"

   read

   if GETCOL = 0
      loop
   endif
```

Listing 12-5 Continued

```
      COLNAME = 'COLOR' + str(GETCOL,1)
      data    = &COLNAME

   case GETCOL = 5

      ATRSCREEN = screen
      ATRHELP   = help
      ATRPROMPT = prompt
      ATRDATA   = data
      ATRSIGNON = IIF ( iscolor() , "N/W*,W+/R"    , "W+/N,N/W"  )

      save to COLORS all like ATR*
      set color to &SCREEN
      @ 11, 0 clear to 24, 79
      exit

   case GETCOL = 6 .or. GETCOL = 0

      set color to &SCREEN
      @ 11, 0 clear to 24, 79
      exit

endcase

enddo

RESTORE SCREEN FROM ColrScrn

RETURN



PROCEDURE ErrBox
PARAMETERS Line,Text
DEFINE   WINDOW ErrWindo FROM Line, 4 TO Line+2, 75 SHADOW
ACTIVATE WINDOW ErrWindo
= center(Text)
RETURN


FUNCTION Center
PARAMETERS Info
@ 0,(WCOLS()-LEN(Info))/2 SAY Info
RETURN .T.


PROCEDURE TopMenu

RELEASE   TOP
DIMENSION TOP(4,2)

RELEASE   FYLES,   DATA,    UTILITY,   STOP
DIMENSION FYLES(5),DATA(4),UTILITY(2),STOP(1)

TOP = "
TOP(1,1) = '  FILES'     && offset 2 spaces
TOP(2,1) = '  DATA'
TOP(3,1) = '  UTILITY'
TOP(4,1) = '  QUIT'
```

```
FYLES(1)    = 'USE'
FYLES(2)    = '\PURGE'
FYLES(3)    = '\-'
FYLES(4)    = '\LIST'
FYLES(5)    = '\HELP'

DATA(1) = '\CREATE'
DATA(2) = '\EDIT'
DATA(3) = '\BROWSE'
DATA(4) = '\DESTROY'

UTILITY(1) = 'COLORS'
UTILITY(2) = '\GAMES'

STOP(1)     = 'EXIT'

* DO WHILE .T.

   SAVE SCREEN TO MainScrn
   MENU BAR TOP,4
   MENU 1,FYLES,5,5
   MENU 2,DATA,4,4
   MENU 3,UTILITY,2,2
   MENU 4,STOP,1,1

   READ MENU BAR TO Row,Col SAVE

*  Command = 'M_'+LEFT(LTRIM(TRIM(M_TOP(M_MNU,1))),3)
*  && DETERMINES MENU CHOICE NAME OF SORT/APPEND/EDIT ETC.
*  M_CMD = &M_CMD(M_ITM)

   RESTORE SCREEN FROM MainScrn

* ENDDO

RETURN
```

The point is that too many choices might get you and them into trouble; this reduction of freedom of choice is sometimes a better solution. Figure 12-5 contains the screen produced by this program.

You might want to confect a combination of the previous two programs, allowing your users to select from the full range of colors to define six or eight attribute variables, which your code then would use in predictable ways. You also could just buy Wayne Harless' color sets and code your screens without recourse to the SET COLOR TO *colorpair* command.

A manifestly beautiful screen

Imitation is the sincerest form of flattery. Some screens are so beautiful that they beg imitation. The following example (FIG. 12-6) is derived from the lovely QuarterDeck MANIFEST screen, which actually has been touted in the press for its creative use of colors. It rather drives home the

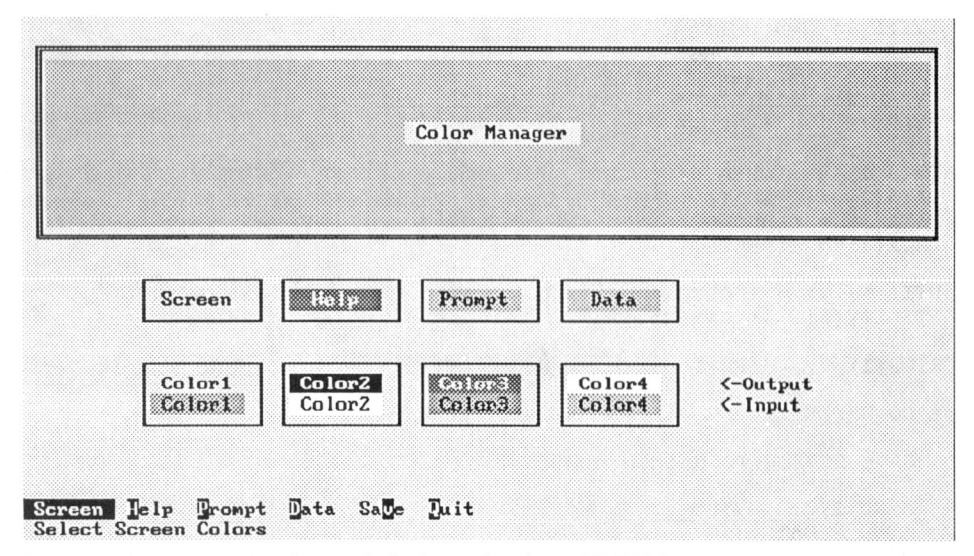

12-5 Letting users select from a limited set of options (USERCOLR.PRG).

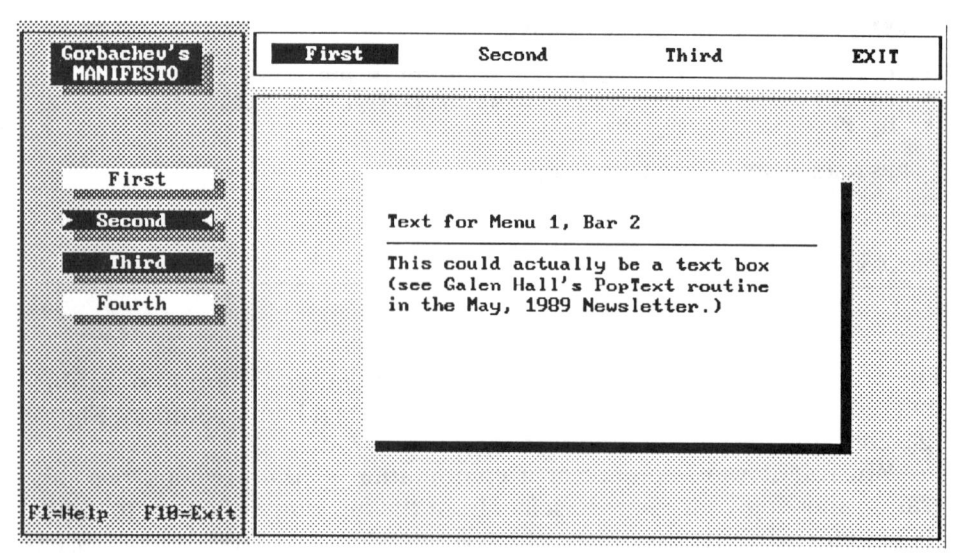

12-6 An emulation of the QD Manifest screen (MANIFEST.PRG).

point that color on white is a nice combination. Notice also the use of the half-height solid bar as a shadow character. This effect is really special. (The program code is shown in LISTING 12-6.)

Listing 12-6

```
* Program-ID....: MANIFEST.PRG
* Purpose.......: Emulate the Manifest ((C) Quarterdeck) menu system.

SET TALK OFF
```

296   Color

```
SET STAT OFF
SET SCOR OFF
SET COLOR TO GR+/B
CLEAR

SET PROCEDURE TO Manifest    && This file....

* Inkey values
leftarrow    = 19
rtarrow      =  4
home         =  1
end          =  6
uparrow      =  5
downarrow    = 24
pageup       = 18
pagedown     =  3
esc          = 27
enter        = 13
controlend   = 23
controlhome  = 29
helpkey      = 28

OptKeys      = ""
MenuNum      = 1
BarNum       = 1

NumItems     = 4
Dimension NewMenu ( NumItems , 6 )

SET COLOR     TO W/BG
@ 3, 20 CLEAR TO 24, 79
@ 3, 20       TO 24, 79

DO LoadBar1
DO BuildKey
DO WhiteBox
DO ShowBar

?? SYS(2002)    && cursor off

DO WHILE .T.

   DO CurrON    WITH BarNum

     DO CASE

        CASE MenuNum = 1 .and. BarNum = 1
        DO BlueBox with 7, 30, 19, 70
        Set Color to GR+/B
        @  9, 32 say 'Text for Menu 1, Bar 1'
        Set Color to  W+/B
        @ 10, 32 TO 10, 68

      CASE MenuNum = 1 .and. BarNum = 2

        DO BlueBox with  7, 30, 19, 70
        Set Color to GR+/B
        @  9, 32 say "Text for Menu 1, Bar 2"
        Set Color to  W+/B
        @ 10, 32 TO 10, 68
        @ 11, 32 say "This could actually be a text box"
```

A manifestly beautiful screen   297

Listing 12-6 Continued

```
       @ 12, 32 say "(see Galen Hall's PopText routine"
       @ 13, 32 say "in the May, 1989 Newsletter.)       "

   CASE MenuNum = 3

       DO BlueBox with  7, 30, 19, 70
       Set Color to GR+/B
       @  9, 32 say "Text for Menu 3"
       Set Color to  W+/B
       @ 10, 32 TO 10, 68
       @ 11, 32 say "Note that some selections have no"
       @ 12, 32 say "menu associated with them.       "

   CASE MenuNum = 4

       DO BlueBox with  7, 30, 19, 70
       Set Color to GR+/B
       @  9, 32 say "Exit"
       Set Color to  W+/B
       @ 10, 32 TO 10, 68
       @ 11, 32 say "Press ENTER to leave this program"

   OTHERWISE

       DO BlueBox with 7, 30, 19, 70

   ENDCASE

a = INKEY(0)
a = abs(a)

DO ShowButn WITH BarNum

DO CASE

   CASE a = helpkey

      DO HELP

   CASE UPPER ( CHR(a) ) $ OptKeys

      Selected = AT ( UPPER( CHR(a) ) , OptKeys )

      SET COLOR TO GR+/B
      CLEAR
      ?? SYS(2002,1)   && cursor on

      @ 24, 0 say 'Selected ' + NewMenu ( Selected , 1 )

      RETURN

   CASE a = enter .OR. a = esc

      Selected = BarNum

      IF MenuNum = 4
        SET COLOR TO GR+/B
        CLEAR
        ?? SYS(2002,1)   && cursor on
```

```
            EXIT
         ENDIF

         DO CASE

            CASE MenuNum = 1 .and. BarNum = 1
               * Do whatever this pair dictates...
            CASE MenuNum = 1 .and. BarNum = 2
               * Do whatever this pair dictates...
*              ...
*              ...
*              ...
         ENDCASE

      CASE a = downarrow

         BarNum = BarNum + 1

         IF BarNum > NumItems
            BarNum = 1              && to stop at top, use '= NumItems'
         ENDIF

      CASE a = uparrow

         BarNum = BarNum - 1

         IF BarNum = 0
            BarNum = iif(NumItems=0,1,NumItems) && to stop at bottom, use '= 1'
         ENDIF

      CASE a = rtarrow

         MenuNum = MenuNum + 1
         IF MenuNum > 4
            MenuNum = 1
         ENDIF

         BarNum = 1

         StrBar= str(MenuNum,1)
         DO LoadBar&StrBar
         DO BuildKey
         DO ShowBar

      CASE a = leftarrow

         MenuNum = MenuNum - 1
         IF MenuNum < 1
            MenuNum = 4
         ENDIF

         BarNum = 1

         StrBar= str(MenuNum,1)
         DO LoadBar&StrBar
         DO BuildKey
         DO ShowBar

   ENDCASE
```

Listing 12-6 Continued

```
ENDDO

QUIT


PROCEDURE BuildKey

OptKeys = ""

I = 1
DO WHILE I <= NumItems
  Option = NewMenu ( I, 2 )
  NewMenu ( I , 6 ) = AT ( Option, NewMenu ( I , 1 ) )
  OptKeys = OptKeys +     UPPER ( NewMenu ( I , 2 ) )
  I = I + 1
ENDDO

RETURN


PROCEDURE Center
PARAMETERS row, msg
@ row, 40 - len(trim(msg))/2 SAY trim(msg)
RETURN .T.


PROCEDURE ShowBar

DO ClearWht   && Draw left screen box

* -- Screen Title:

SET COLOR TO N+/W
@ 1, 16    SAY CHR(220)
@ 2, 16    SAY chr(219)
@ 3,  4    SAY REPLICATE(CHR(223),13)

SET COLOR TO R/R
@ 1,  3, 2, 15 BOX REPLICATE(chr(219),9)

SET COLOR TO GR+/R
@ 1,  4 SAY [Gorbachev's]
SET COLOR TO  W+/R
@ 2,  4 SAY [ MANIFESTO ]

SET COLOR TO N/W
@ 23, 1 say 'F1=Help    F10=Exit'

SET COLOR      TO W/B
@ 0, 20 CLEAR TO  2, 79
@ 0, 20         TO  2, 79

SET COLOR TO GR+/B
@ 1, 22 SAY '   First    '
@ 1, 38 SAY '   Second   '
@ 1, 53 SAY '   Third    '
@ 1, 68 SAY '   EXIT     '

SET COLOR TO W+/G
DO CASE
```

```
   CASE MenuNum = 1
     @ 1, 22 say '   First    '
   CASE MenuNum = 2
     @ 1, 38 SAY '   Second   '
   CASE MenuNum = 3
     @ 1, 53 SAY '   Third    '
   CASE MenuNum = 4
     @ 1, 68 SAY '    EXIT    '
ENDCASE

I = 1
DO WHILE I <= NumItems
  DO ShowButn with I
  I = I + 1
ENDDO

RETURN


PROCEDURE WhiteBox

SET COLOR TO N/W

@ 0, 0 CLEAR TO 24, 19
@ 0, 0       TO 24, 19

RETURN


PROCEDURE ClearWht

SET COLOR TO N/W

@ 4, 1 CLEAR TO 22, 18

RETURN


PROCEDURE ShowButn
PARAMETERS I

  IF I > NumItems
    RETURN
  ENDIF

  OptionName = NewMenu ( I, 1 )
  HighLetter = NewMenu ( I, 2 )
  Row        = NewMenu ( I, 3 )
  Column     = NewMenu ( I, 4 )
  BGColor    = NewMenu ( I, 5 )
  ButtonCol  = NewMenu ( I, 6 )
  ItemLength = len(OptionName)

  SET COLOR TO N+/W
  @ Row  , Column+ItemLength SAY CHR(220)
  @ Row+1, Column+1          SAY REPLICATE(CHR(223),ItemLength)

  SET COLOR TO &BGColor
  @ Row  , Column   SAY REPLICATE(chr(219),9)

  SET COLOR TO N/&BGColor
  @ Row, Column SAY OptionName
```

Listing 12-6 Continued

```
   SET COLOR TO W+/&BGColor
   @ Row, Column+ButtonCol-1 SAY NewMenu ( I, 2 )

RETURN


PROCEDURE CurrON
PARAMETERS I

   IF I > NumItems
      RETURN
   ENDIF
   OptionName = NewMenu ( I, 1 )
   HighLetter = NewMenu ( I, 2 )
   Row        = NewMenu ( I, 3 )
   Column     = NewMenu ( I, 4 )
   BGColor    = NewMenu ( I, 5 )
   ButtonCol  = NewMenu ( I, 6 )
   ItemLength = len(OptionName)

   SET COLOR TO N/W
   @ Row  , Column+ItemLength SAY CHR(220)
   @ Row+1, Column+1          SAY REPLICATE(chr(223),ItemLength)

   SET COLOR TO W+/&BGColor
   @ Row, Column              SAY chr(16)
   @ Row, Column+ItemLength-1 SAY chr(17)

RETURN


PROCEDURE LoadBar1

* -- These are the menu options
NewMenu (  1 ,  1 ) = '   First   '
NewMenu (  2 ,  1 ) = '   Second  '
NewMenu (  3 ,  1 ) = '   Third   '
NewMenu (  4 ,  1 ) = '   Fourth  '

* -- These are the selection letters to be highlighted in bright white
NewMenu (  1 ,  2 ) = 'F'
NewMenu (  2 ,  2 ) = 'S'
NewMenu (  3 ,  2 ) = 'T'
NewMenu (  4 ,  2 ) = 'o'

* -- These are the row locations
NewMenu (  1 ,  3 ) =  7
NewMenu (  2 ,  3 ) =  9
NewMenu (  3 ,  3 ) = 11
NewMenu (  4 ,  3 ) = 13

* -- These are the column locations
NewMenu (  1 ,  4 ) =  4
NewMenu (  2 ,  4 ) =  4
NewMenu (  3 ,  4 ) =  4
NewMenu (  4 ,  4 ) =  4

* -- Background and box colors
NewMenu (  1 ,  5 ) = 'GR'
```

```
NewMenu (  2 ,  5 ) =  'R'
 NewMenu (  3 ,  5 ) =  'R'
NewMenu (  4 ,  5 ) =  'BR'

MenuNum  = 1
NumItems = 4

RETURN

PROCEDURE LoadBar2

* -- These are the menu options
NewMenu (  1 ,  1 ) = '   Spring   '
NewMenu (  2 ,  1 ) = '   Summer   '
NewMenu (  3 ,  1 ) = '    Fall    '
NewMenu (  4 ,  1 ) = '   Autumn   '

* -- These are the selection letters to be highlighted in bright white
NewMenu (  1 ,  2 ) = 'S'
NewMenu (  2 ,  2 ) = 'u'
NewMenu (  3 ,  2 ) = 'F'
NewMenu (  4 ,  2 ) = 'A'

* -- These are the row locations
NewMenu (  1 ,  3 ) =  7
NewMenu (  2 ,  3 ) =  9
NewMenu (  3 ,  3 ) = 11
NewMenu (  4 ,  3 ) = 13

* -- These are the column locations
NewMenu (  1 ,  4 ) =  4
NewMenu (  2 ,  4 ) =  4
NewMenu (  3 ,  4 ) =  4
NewMenu (  4 ,  4 ) =  4

* -- Background and box colors
NewMenu (  1 ,  5 ) = 'GR'
NewMenu (  2 ,  5 ) = 'R'
NewMenu (  3 ,  5 ) = 'R'
NewMenu (  4 ,  5 ) = 'BR'

MenuNum  = 2
NumItems = 4

RETURN

PROCEDURE LoadBar3
MenuNum  = 3
NumItems = 0


PROCEDURE LoadBar4
MenuNum  = 4
NumItems = 0

PROCEDURE BlueBox
PARAMETERS row1, col1, row2, col2

SET COLOR TO B/B
```

Listing 12-6 Continued

```
@ row1, col1 CLEAR TO row2, col2
SET COLOR TO N/BG
@ row1+1 , col2+1 , row2 ,col2+1 BOX REPL ( CHR ( 219 ) ,                9 )
@ row1    , col2+1    SAY                  CHR ( 220 )
@ row2+1 , col1+1     SAY            REPL ( CHR ( 223 ) , col2 - col1 + 1 )

RETURN


PROCEDURE RedBox
PARAMETERS row1, col1, row2, col2

** NOTE: Generally, if box color and size change, clear the CYAN window first.
**SET COLOR     TO W/BG
**@ 4, 21 CLEAR TO 23, 78

SET COLOR TO R/R
@ row1, col1 CLEAR TO row2, col2
SET COLOR TO N/B   && note that BG color matches with box underneath.
@ row1+1 , col2+1 , row2 ,col2+1 BOX REPL ( CHR ( 219 ) ,                9 )
@ row1    , col2+1    SAY                  CHR ( 220 )
@ row2+1 , col1+1     SAY            REPL ( CHR ( 223 ) , col2 - col1 + 1 )

RETURN


PROCEDURE HELP

SAVE SCREEN

   DO RedBox with 8, 40, 17, 60

   SET COLOR TO GR+/R
   @ 10, 42 say 'Help with what?'
   @ 11, 44 to 11, 58
   @ 12, 44 say chr(249)+' Summer'
   @ 13, 44 say chr(249)+' Fall'
   @ 14, 44 say chr(249)+' Winter'
   @ 15, 44 say chr(249)+' Spring'

   a  = inkey(0)

RESTORE SCREEN

RETURN
```

Summary

Color can turn a "ho-hum" screen into a "golly gee will ya just look at that" screen. Surprisingly, it takes an inordinate amount of effort; however, life is what you make of it. If you put in the time to master color, I'm confident that your efforts will be rewarded.

13
Searching and selecting

I occasionally meet a potential client who told me something like "I want to be able to sort on anything." They almost never mean that.

Sorting appears to have a different meaning in the vernacular than it does in a strict technical sense. Users who tell me that they want to sort on anything generally mean that they want to be able to *select* any subset of their data. Just to set the record straight: *select* means to choose a subset of the data, while *sort* means to order the data alphabetically or in some other lexicographical order. Thus, you can clearly select based on one criterion and sort on some completely different set of keys.

Users select subsets of data for reporting and on-screen displays. In addition, it often is convenient to search for a particular record based on a key entered by the user. Sometimes, users guess at keys. Sometimes, they misspell them. Sometimes, they're just too darned lazy to type in the whole thing and they figure, "What do I have a computer for? Let it find the record."

This chapter deals with the many ways to search for a single record, some of which display all match candidates and let the user pick the right one from a pop-up menu. There are several ways to do searches. No single one is best; the technique should match the situation.

Desperately seeking records

After data entry, the most important feature many users look for is the ability to find subsets of their data. Customer or order inquiry depends on being able to quickly find the record you're looking for. I've had a number of projects where I spent half of my time designing the application and the other half optimizing the searching tools.

Some files have a small number of fields, one of which is clearly the choice for a key field. A key is useful if there's a high probability of duplication in the more obvious identification fields (e.g., last name) or if the key field is long and hard to remember (again, last names are a good example). If you have many records, knowing a particular key *a priori* might not be in the cards.

Also, key fields are sometimes not common knowledge. As quick tools for searching the database, they're useful to users familiar with the data. For new employees, however, keys might be confusing. So, it generally is a good idea to allow some type of near-match search. This also allows typographical errors to generate some sort of near-match list. This process can help train employees to recognize the keys actually used in your files.

In files having many fields, there can be several ways that you'd reasonably want to search for a particular record. Instead of a single key, you might want to be able to search by street name or street address, phone number, last name, or order date.

Finally, there are applications where you want to find any member of a class of records that meet a set of conditions. For these applications, the program should always expect to find and display any number of matching records in a pop-up window, often with the ability to zoom in on anyone for closer inspection.

Often, it's desirable to extract all matching records and do something else with them—a report, for example. For that reason, searching and selecting fall within the same area. I'll look first at search techniques, then move into techniques that find all matching records.

Indexed searches

Indexes can be created on every single field in the database in FoxPro 2.0. I'll use the database structure shown in TABLE 13-1.

You can create a compound index (.CDX) file using a command like:

INDEX ON UPPER(CITY) TAG CITYNAME

to create a compound index file called AIRCRAFT.CDX or to add the index tag CITYNAME to the existing AIRCRAFT.CDX file. You can also add keys involving more than one field:

INDEX ON STR(ENGINES,1)+STR(HOBBES,5) TAG TYPETIME

which would create an index that would put single engine aircraft before twins and by ascending Hobbes tachometer time within each grouping of aircraft by number of engines.

If your data is indexed on the key or keys that users want to search on, speed is dazzling. If it's not indexed—and some types of data searches are inherently not indexable—then speed will be a function of database size and might even be dreadful. However, there are techniques for making sequential searches palatable.

Table 13-1   Structure for the AIRCRAFT.DBF database.

Field	Field Name	Type	Width	Dec	Index
1	ID	Character	6		Asc
2	OWNER	Character	30		Asc
3	ADDRESS1	Character	30		
4	ADDRESS2	Character	30		
5	CITY	Character	16		
6	STATE	Character	2		
7	ZIP	Character	10		
8	HOME	Character	12		
9	WORK	Character	12		
10	CELLULAR	Character	12		
11	ANNUAL	Date	8		
12	EQUIPMENT	Character	90		
13	TYPE	Character	10		Asc
14	COLORS	Character	10		
15	ENGINES	Numeric	1		
16	SEATS	Numeric	3		
17	TACH	Numeric	5		
18	HOBBES	Numeric	5		
19	RENTAL	Numeric	6	2	
20	LEASEBACK	Logical	1		
** Total **			300		

Notes and observations

There are several commands that control the way FoxPro searches. SET EXACT ON forces searches to match as to length of strings. That is, if you issue the command:

    SET ORDER TO TYPE
    SET EXACT ON
    SEEK "'C"

and you SET EXACT ON, you won't find the Cessna 172 (Type C-172) in the database, because FoxPro will want all 6 characters to be exactly the same. On the other hand:

    SET EXACT OFF
    SEEK "C"

will indeed find the first Cessna. It will find the first C-152, which comes before C-172.

In addition, the command:

    SET NEAR ON

causes FoxPro to find the first record that would have followed the one you were searching for, if it had existed. This command occasionally can be.

used to advantage. I use it to determine where to position the record pointer after deleting a record.

You should always convert keys to uppercase upon input, using the FUNCTION [!] parameter in your GET statement. At the same time, all key fields containing alphanumerics should use something like:

INDEX ON UPPER(*name*) TAG CUSTNAME OF CUSTOMER

to ensure that searches are not case-sensitive.

Non-indexed (Sequential) searches

If your data is entered sloppily, you might have some Cessna 172s entered as C172 and others as C-172. In that case, the command:

SET ORDER TO TYPE
SEEK "172"

won't find anything, whether EXACT is on or off, because comparison always begins with the leftmost character of the current index key field. In that case, you have to use the LOCATE command and the instring dollar sign operator to find your data, as follows:

LOCATE FOR "172" $ TYPE

In this case EXACT can be on or off. It doesn't affect instring searches.

This duality of searching can add considerable complexity to your system design. In addition, the Rushmore technology developed by Fox can't optimize instring searches, so the difference in speed will be even more noticeable to your users.

The examples that follow give some ideas for how to incorporate these techniques into your programs. There are other variations on these themes that you can cook up to add even more variety to your searches.

Simple searches

The simplest case of a search looks like LISTING 13-1. I've used the program in LISTING 13-2 to provide a background for this and the next few example programs. It's an interesting use of low-level I/O to redisplay other programs' output in a format of your own choosing.

Listing 13-1

```
* Program-ID.....: Search1.PRG
* Purpose........: Demonstrates simple searches in FoxPro
CLEAR
USE AIRCRAFT ORDER ID

DO ListTags

DO WHILE .T.
```

```
    mID = SPACE(LEN(AIRCRAFT.ID))
    @ 23, 0 CLEAR
    @ 23, 0 SAY [Aircraft ID: ] GET mID FUNCTION [!]
    READ

    IF LEN(ALLTRIM(mID)) = 0
      EXIT
    ENDIF

    SEEK mID
    IF .NOT. FOUND()
      WAIT [Not found - Reenter] TIMEOUT 2
      LOOP
    ENDIF

    @ 23, 0 SAY [ID: ] + AIRCRAFT.ID + [ - Aircraft type is ] + Type
    @ 24, 0 SAY [Owner is ] + OWNER
    SET   CURSOR OFF
    WAIT WINDOW
    SET   CURSOR ON

ENDDO

CLOSE ALL
CLEAR ALL
CLEAR

RETURN
```

Listing 13-2

```
* Program-ID.....: ListTags.PRG
* Purpose........: Lists active file and index tags
SET CONSOLE OFF
LIST STATUS TO STAT.LST
SET CONSOLE ON
fh = FOPEN([STAT.LST])
FOR I = 1 TO 24
  line = FGETS(fh)
  IF UPPER(line) = [FILE SEARCH PATH]
    EXIT
  ENDIF
  IF I > 3
    ? [   ] + line
  ENDIF
ENDFOR
@ 0, 0 TO 22, 79
=FCLOSE(fh)
DELETE FILE STAT.LST

RETURN
```

Alternatively, you can take the official FoxPro approach (LISTING 13-3). Then, use SET ORDER TO ltags(l), where ltags(l) is selected from a pop-up. This command lets users choose the current index.

The program that appears in LISTING 13-1 is the simplest form of an indexed search. If the key that you typed in does not match, you get no

Listing 13-3

```
PROCEDURE settags
ltags(1) = "Record#"
FOR i = 2 to 256
  IF LEN(tag(i-1)) = 0
    i = i - 1
    DIMENSION ltags(i)
    EXIT
  ELSE
    ltags(i) = tag(i-1)
  ENDIF
ENDFOR
```

information. Because the probability of entering a key incorrectly increases with key length, this obviously could be improved.

Comparisons and searching are controlled by the SET EXACT statement. If EXACT is on, FoxPro compares two strings byte for byte. If they're not the same length, they don't match. The same is true of a SEEK with SET EXACT ON.

If EXACT is set off, the comparison only goes up the length of the last character in the string on the right side of the equals sign. If you SET EXACT OFF in FoxPro, anything that matches the length of the search key up to the number of characters in the key is considered a match. The next example (LISTING 13-4) uses SET EXACT OFF and a trimmed key, to allow a partial match to be selected.

Listing 13-4

```
* Program-ID.....: Search2.PRG

CLEAR
SET EXACT OFF
USE AIRCRAFT ORDER ID

DO ListTags

DO WHILE .T.

  mID = SPACE(LEN(AIRCRAFT.ID))
  @ 23, 0 CLEAR
  @ 23, 0 SAY [Aircraft ID: ] GET mID FUNCTION [!]
  READ

  IF LEN(ALLTRIM(mID)) = 0
    EXIT
  ENDIF

  SEEK TRIM(mID)                       && NOTE TRIMMED KEY!!!
  IF .NOT. FOUND()
    WAIT [Not found - Reenter] TIMEOUT 2
    LOOP
  ENDIF

  @ 23, 0 SAY [ID: ] + AIRCRAFT.ID + [ - Aircraft type is ] + Type
  @ 24, 0 SAY [Owner is ] + OWNER
```

```
        SET   CURSOR OFF
     WAIT WINDOW
        SET   CURSOR ON

ENDDO

CLOSE ALL
CLEAR ALL
CLEAR

RETURN
```

Tabling near-matches

This last approach was better, but it still doesn't help if several records matched. Your user might be lazy, and might want to type in only the first few letters, then pick visually. You also might have keys that are hard to spell (names, for example) so that a partial match with visual selection would make more sense. The next example addresses this need.

Another need should be addressed in dealing with partial matches. Sometimes the reason that the search fails is that the operator transposed two letters. This is a common typo; its probability of occurrence increases as more letters are typed. The truncate key function, TrunkKey( ), which is used in subsequent examples, is based on this idea. My users find it very intuitive and natural.

The pop-up in LISTING 13-5 can be made somewhat more useful by displaying not only the aircraft ID, but the owner's name as well. The only changes are that the DEFINE BAR command is expanded and the key is extracted from its position within PROMPT( ), as shown in LISTING 13-6.

Listing 13-5

```
* Program-ID.....: Search3.PRG
* Purpose........: Demonstrates partial match searches.

CLEAR
SET EXACT OFF

USE AIRCRAFT ORDER ID
SET UDFPARMS TO REFERENCE

DO ListTags

DO WHILE .T.
   mID = SPACE(LEN(AIRCRAFT.ID))
   @ 23, 0 CLEAR
   @ 23, 0 SAY [Aircraft ID: ] GET mID FUNCTION [!]
   READ

   IF LEN(TRIM(mID)) = 0
      EXIT
   ENDIF

   mID = TRIM(mID)
```

Listing 13-5 Continued

```
  SEEK mID
  IF .NOT. FOUND()
    IF .NOT. TruncKey(mID)
      WAIT [Not found - Reenter] TIMEOUT 2
      LOOP
    ENDIF
  ENDIF

  DEFINE POPUP IDS FROM 5,5 ;
         TITLE  [ Pick an ID ] ;
         FOOTER [ Press ESCAPE to cancel ]
  I = 0
  SCAN WHILE AIRCRAFT.ID = TRIM(mID)
    I = I + 1
    DEFINE BAR I OF IDS PROMPT ID
  ENDSCAN
  ON SELECTION POPUP IDS DEACTIVATE POPUP IDS
  ACTIVATE     POPUP IDS

  IF LEN(TRIM(PROMPT())) = 0
    LOOP
  ENDIF


  SEEK PROMPT()

  @ 23, 0 SAY [ID: ] + AIRCRAFT.ID + [ - Aircraft type is ] + Type
  @ 24, 0 SAY [Owner is ] + OWNER
  SET   CURSOR OFF
  WAIT WINDOW
  SET   CURSOR ON

ENDDO

CLOSE ALL
CLEAR ALL
CLEAR

RETURN


FUNCTION TruncKey
PARAMETERS mKEY
DO WHILE .NOT. FOUND() .AND. LEN(mKEY) > 1
  mKEY = LEFT(mKEY,LEN(mKEY)-1)
  SEEK mKEY
  IF FOUND()
    EXIT
  ENDIF
ENDDO
IF FOUND()
  RETURN .T.
ELSE
  RETURN .F.
ENDIF

RETURN
```

Listing 13-6

```
CLEAR
USE AIRCRAFT ORDER ID
SET UDFPARMS TO REFERENCE

DO ListTags

DO WHILE .T.

   mID = SPACE(LEN(AIRCRAFT->ID))
   @ 23, 0 CLEAR
   @ 23, 0 SAY [Aircraft ID: ] GET mID FUNCTION [!]
   READ

   IF LEN(ALLTRIM(mID)) = 0
      EXIT
   ENDIF

   SEEK TRIM(mID)
   IF .NOT. FOUND()
      IF .NOT. TruncKey(mID)
         WAIT [Not found - Reenter] TIMEOUT 2
         LOOP
      ENDIF
   ENDIF

   DEFINE POPUP IDS FROM 5,5 ;
         TITLE   [ Pick an ID ] ;
         FOOTER [ Press ESCAPE to cancel ]

   I = 0
   SCAN WHILE AIRCRAFT.ID = TRIM(mID)
       I = I + 1
       DEFINE BAR I OF IDS PROMPT ID + [ | ] + Owner
   ENDSCAN
   ON SELECTION POPUP IDS DEACTIVATE POPUP IDS
   ACTIVATE       POPUP IDS

   IF LEN(TRIM(PROMPT())) = 0
      LOOP
   ENDIF

   SEEK LEFT( PROMPT() , 6 )

   @ 23, 0 SAY [ID: ]+AIRCRAFT.ID+[ - Aircraft type is ]+Type
   @ 24, 0 SAY [Owner is ] + OWNER
   SET   CURSOR OFF
   WAIT WINDOW
   SET   CURSOR ON

ENDDO

CLOSE ALL
CLEAR ALL
CLEAR

RETURN


FUNCTION TruncKey
```

Listing 13-6 Continued

```
PARAMETERS mKEY
DO WHILE .NOT. FOUND() .AND. LEN(mKEY) > 1
   mKEY = LEFT(mKEY,LEN(mKEY)-1)
   SEEK mKEY
   IF FOUND()
      EXIT
   ENDIF
ENDDO
IF FOUND()
   RETURN .T.
   ELSE
   RETURN .F.
ENDIF
```

The pop-up in LISTING 13-7 is easier to understand, because it displays more information. You can display multiple fields in any way, subject to the ability to extract the key information for record positioning.

Listing 13-7

```
* Program-ID.....: Search4.PRG
* Purpose........: Searching with a two-field popup for near-matches.

CLEAR
SET EXACT OFF

USE AIRCRAFT ORDER ID
SET UDFPARMS TO REFERENCE

DO ListTags

DO WHILE .T.

   mID = SPACE(LEN(AIRCRAFT.ID))
   @ 23, 0 CLEAR
   @ 23, 0 SAY [Aircraft ID: ] GET mID FUNCTION [!]
   READ

   IF LEN(ALLTRIM(mID)) = 0
      EXIT
   ENDIF

   SEEK TRIM(mID)
   IF .NOT. FOUND()
      IF .NOT. TruncKey(mID)
         WAIT [Not found - Reenter] TIMEOUT 2
         LOOP
      ENDIF
   ENDIF

   DEFINE POPUP IDS FROM 5,5 ;
          TITLE  [ Pick an ID ] ;
          FOOTER [ Press ESCAPE to cancel ]

   I = 0
   SCAN WHILE AIRCRAFT.ID = TRIM(mID)
      I = I + 1
```

314 Searching and selecting

```
      DEFINE BAR I OF IDS PROMPT ID + [ | ] + Owner
   ENDSCAN
   ON SELECTION POPUP IDS DEACTIVATE POPUP IDS
   ACTIVATE       POPUP IDS

   IF LEN(TRIM(PROMPT())) = 0
     LOOP
   ENDIF

   SEEK LEFT( PROMPT() , 6 )
   @ 23, 0 SAY [ID: ] + AIRCRAFT.ID + [ - Aircraft type is ] + Type
   @ 24, 0 SAY [Owner is ] + OWNER
   SET   CURSOR OFF
   WAIT WINDOW
   SET   CURSOR ON

ENDDO

CLOSE ALL
CLEAR ALL
CLEAR

RETURN


FUNCTION TruncKey
PARAMETERS mKEY
DO WHILE .NOT. FOUND() .AND. LEN(mKEY) > 1
   mKEY = LEFT(mKEY,LEN(mKEY)-1)
   SEEK mKEY
   IF FOUND()
      EXIT
   ENDIF
ENDDO
IF FOUND()
   RETURN .T.
ELSE
   RETURN .F.
ENDIF

RETURN
```

If you want to display a pop-up that doesn't contain the key, build a separate array on the line following the DEFINE BAR command, then return the bar number—BAR( )—rather than the PROMPT( ). You then can seek KEYFIELD(BAR( )), which will contain the corresponding key field.

Databases with multiple keys

What about files with more than one key? Actually, in FoxPro 2.0, there's little if any reason not to include as many keys as you could ever make use of in a single compound index (CDX) file. The following example (LISTING 13-8) makes use of the AIRCRAFT file, which has three index tags: ID, OWNER, and TYPE. The program lets the user select a search order, then

Listing 13-8

```
* Program-ID.....: Search5.PRG
* Purpose........: User-selected search keys.

CLEAR
SET EXACT OFF

USE AIRCRAFT ORDER ID
SET UDFPARMS TO REFERENCE    && NOT *VALUE*! Key won't be modified..

TagNum = 1
Cancelled = .F.

DO ListTags

DO WHILE .T.

   DO GetTag

   IF Cancelled
      EXIT
   ENDIF

   DO CASE

      CASE ORDER([AIRCRAFT]) = [ID]

         mID = SPACE(LEN(AIRCRAFT.ID))
         @ 23, 0 CLEAR
         @ 23, 0 SAY [Aircraft ID: ] GET mID FUNCTION [!]
         READ
         IF LEN(ALLTRIM(mID)) = 0
            EXIT
         ENDIF
         mID = TRIM(mID)
         SEEK mID
         IF .NOT. FOUND()
            IF .NOT. TruncKey(mID)
               WAIT [Not found - Reenter] TIMEOUT 2
               LOOP
            ENDIF
         ENDIF

         DEFINE POPUP IDS FROM 5,5 ;
                TITLE  [ Pick an ID ] ;
                FOOTER [ Press ESCAPE to cancel ]

         I = 0
         SCAN WHILE AIRCRAFT.ID = TRIM(mID)
            I = I + 1
            DEFINE BAR I OF IDS PROMPT ID + [ | ] + Owner
         ENDSCAN
         ON SELECTION POPUP IDS DEACTIVATE POPUP IDS
         ACTIVATE       POPUP IDS
         IF LEN(TRIM(PROMPT())) = 0
            LOOP
         ENDIF
         SEEK LEFT( PROMPT() , 6 )

      CASE ORDER([AIRCRAFT]) = [OWNER]
```

```
    mOWNER = SPACE(LEN(AIRCRAFT.OWNER))
    @ 23, 0 CLEAR
    @ 23, 0 SAY [OWNER: ] GET mOWNER FUNCTION [!]
    READ
    IF LEN(ALLTRIM(mOWNER)) = 0
      EXIT
    ENDIF
    mOWNER = TRIM(mOWNER)
    SEEK mOWNER
    IF .NOT. FOUND()
      IF .NOT. TruncKey(mOWNER)
        WAIT [Not found - Reenter] TIMEOUT 2
        LOOP
      ENDIF
    ENDIF

    DEFINE POPUP OWNERS FROM 5,5 ;
           TITLE   [ Pick an Owner ] ;
           FOOTER [ Press ESCAPE to cancel ]

    I = 0
    SCAN WHILE UPPER(AIRCRAFT.OWNER) = TRIM(mOWNER)
      I = I + 1
      DEFINE BAR I OF OWNERS PROMPT ID + [ | ] + Owner
    ENDSCAN
    ON SELECTION POPUP OWNERS DEACTIVATE POPUP OWNERS
    ACTIVATE     POPUP OWNERS
    IF LEN(TRIM(PROMPT())) = 0
      LOOP
    ENDIF
    SEEK UPPER(RIGHT( PROMPT() , 30 ))

CASE ORDER([AIRCRAFT]) = [TYPE]

    mTYPE = SPACE(LEN(AIRCRAFT.TYPE))
    @ 23, 0 CLEAR
    @ 23, 0 SAY [TYPE: ] GET mTYPE FUNCTION [!]
    READ
    IF LEN(ALLTRIM(mTYPE)) = 0
      EXIT
    ENDIF
    mTYPE = TRIM(mTYPE)
    SEEK mTYPE
    IF .NOT. FOUND()
      IF .NOT. TruncKey(mTYPE)
        WAIT [Not found - Reenter] TIMEOUT 2
        LOOP
      ENDIF
    ENDIF

    DEFINE POPUP PLANES FROM 5,5 ;
           TITLE   [ Pick an Aircraft ] ;
           FOOTER [ Press ESCAPE to cancel ]

    I = 0
    SCAN WHILE UPPER(AIRCRAFT.TYPE) = TRIM(mTYPE)
      I = I + 1
      DEFINE BAR I OF PLANES PROMPT ID + [ | ] + OWNER + [ | ] + TYPE
    ENDSCAN
    ON SELECTION POPUP PLANES DEACTIVATE POPUP PLANES
    ACTIVATE     POPUP PLANES
```

Listing 13-8 Continued

```
            IF LEN(TRIM(PROMPT())) = 0
              LOOP
            ENDIF
            SET ORDER TO ID
            SEEK LEFT( PROMPT() , 6 )
            SET ORDER TO TYPE

     ENDCASE

     @ 23, 0 SAY [ID: ] + AIRCRAFT.ID + [ - Aircraft type is ] + Type
     @ 24, 0 SAY [Owner is ] + OWNER
     SET   CURSOR OFF
     WAIT WINDOW
     SET   CURSOR ON

ENDDO

CLOSE ALL
CLEAR ALL
CLEAR

RETURN
PROCEDURE GetTag

@ 23, 0 CLEAR
@ 23, 0 SAY [ Tag: ] GET TagNum PICTURE [@*H ID;OWNER;TYPE] SIZE 1,8,3
READ CYCLE

DO CASE
  CASE LASTKEY() = 27
    Cancelled = .T.
  CASE TagNum = 1
    SET ORDER TO ID
  CASE TagNum = 2
    SET ORDER TO OWNER
  CASE TagNum = 3
    SET ORDER TO TYPE
ENDCASE


FUNCTION TruncKey
PARAMETERS mKEY
DO WHILE .NOT. FOUND() .AND. LEN(mKEY) > 1
  mKEY = LEFT(mKEY,LEN(mKEY)-1)
  SEEK mKEY
  IF FOUND()
    EXIT
  ENDIF
ENDDO

IF FOUND()
  RETURN .T.
ELSE
  RETURN .F.
ENDIF

ENDCASE
```

prompts for the key information and performs the search. Near misses are tabled for selection by the user (LISTING 13-9).

Note that the statement SET UDFPARMS TO REFERENCE is required so that the called routine, TrunkKey( ), can modify the passed parameter. If set to the default value, the string isn't modified.

Listing 13-9

```
CLEAR
USE AIRCRAFT ORDER ID
SET UDFPARMS TO REFERENCE

TagNum = 1
Cancelled = .F.

DO ListTags

DO WHILE .T.

   DO GetTag

   IF Cancelled
      EXIT
   ENDIF

   DO CASE

      CASE ORDER([AIRCRAFT]) = [ID]

            mID = SPACE(LEN(AIRCRAFT->ID))
            @ 23, 0 CLEAR
            @ 23, 0 SAY [Aircraft ID: ] GET mID FUNCTION [!]
            READ
            IF LEN(ALLTRIM(mID)) = 0
               EXIT
            ENDIF
            mID = TRIM(mID)
            SEEK mID
            IF .NOT. FOUND()
               IF .NOT. TruncKey(mID)
                  WAIT [Not found - Reenter] TIMEOUT 2
                  LOOP
               ENDIF
            ENDIF

            DEFINE POPUP IDS FROM 5,5 ;
                   TITLE  [ Pick an ID ] ;
                   FOOTER [ Press ESCAPE to cancel ]

            I = 0
            SCAN WHILE AIRCRAFT.ID = TRIM(mID)
               I = I + 1
               DEFINE BAR I OF IDS PROMPT ID + [ | ] + Owner
            ENDSCAN
            ON SELECTION POPUP IDS DEACTIVATE POPUP IDS
            ACTIVATE       POPUP IDS
            IF LEN(TRIM(PROMPT())) = 0
```

Listing 13-9

```
            LOOP
        ENDIF
        SEEK LEFT( PROMPT() , 6 )
CASE ORDER([AIRCRAFT]) = [OWNER]

    mOWNER = SPACE(LEN(AIRCRAFT->OWNER))
    @ 23, 0 CLEAR
    @ 23, 0 SAY [OWNER: ] GET mOWNER FUNCTION [!]
    READ
    IF LEN(ALLTRIM(mOWNER)) = 0
        EXIT
    ENDIF
    mOWNER = TRIM(mOWNER)
    SEEK mOWNER
    IF .NOT. FOUND()
        IF .NOT. TruncKey(mOWNER)
            WAIT [Not found - Reenter] TIMEOUT 2
            LOOP
        ENDIF
    ENDIF

    DEFINE POPUP OWNERS FROM 5,5 ;
           TITLE  [ Pick an Owner ] ;
           FOOTER [ Press ESCAPE to cancel ]

    I = 0
    SCAN WHILE UPPER(AIRCRAFT.OWNER) = TRIM(mOWNER)
        I = I + 1
        DEFINE BAR I OF OWNERS PROMPT ID + [ | ] + Owner
    ENDSCAN
    ON SELECTION POPUP OWNERS DEACTIVATE POPUP OWNERS
    ACTIVATE       POPUP OWNERS
    IF LEN(TRIM(PROMPT())) = 0
        LOOP
    ENDIF
    SEEK UPPER(RIGHT( PROMPT() , 30 ))

CASE ORDER([AIRCRAFT]) = [TYPE]

    mTYPE = SPACE(LEN(AIRCRAFT->TYPE))
    @ 23, 0 CLEAR
    @ 23, 0 SAY [TYPE: ] GET mTYPE FUNCTION [!]
    READ
    IF LEN(ALLTRIM(mTYPE)) = 0
        EXIT
    ENDIF
    mTYPE = TRIM(mTYPE)
    SEEK mTYPE
    IF .NOT. FOUND()
        IF .NOT. TruncKey(mTYPE)
            WAIT [Not found - Reenter] TIMEOUT 2
            LOOP
        ENDIF
    ENDIF

    DEFINE POPUP PLANES FROM 5,5 ;
```

```
                TITLE  [ Pick an Aircraft ] ;
                FOOTER [ Press ESCAPE to cancel ]
        I = 0
        SCAN WHILE UPPER(AIRCRAFT.TYPE) = TRIM(mTYPE)
           I = I + 1
           DEFINE BAR I OF PLANES PROMPT ID+[ | ]+OWNER+ [ | ]+TYPE
        ENDSCAN
        ON SELECTION POPUP PLANES DEACTIVATE POPUP PLANES
        ACTIVATE      POPUP PLANES
        IF LEN(TRIM(PROMPT())) = 0
           LOOP
        ENDIF
        SET ORDER TO ID
        SEEK LEFT( PROMPT() , 6 )
        SET ORDER TO TYPE

   ENDCASE

   @ 23, 0 SAY [ID: ]+AIRCRAFT.ID+[ - Aircraft type is ]+Type
   @ 24, 0 SAY [Owner is ] + OWNER
   SET   CURSOR OFF
   WAIT WINDOW
   SET   CURSOR ON

ENDDO

CLOSE ALL
CLEAR ALL
CLEAR

RETURN


PROCEDURE GetTag

@ 23, 0 CLEAR
@ 23, 0 SAY [ Tag: ] GET TagNum PICTURE [@*H ID;OWNER;TYPE] SIZE 1,8,3
READ CYCLE

DO CASE
   CASE LASTKEY() = 27
        Cancelled = .T.
   CASE TagNum = 1
        SET ORDER TO ID
   CASE TagNum = 2
        SET ORDER TO OWNER
   CASE TagNum = 3
        SET ORDER TO TYPE
ENDCASE


FUNCTION TruncKey
PARAMETERS mKEY
 DO WHILE .NOT. FOUND() .AND. LEN(mKEY) > 1
    mKEY = LEFT(mKEY,LEN(mKEY)-1)
    SEEK mKEY
    IF FOUND()
```

Listing 13-9 Continued
```
        EXIT
     ENDIF
ENDDO
IF FOUND()
   RETURN .T.
   ELSE
   RETURN .F.
ENDIF
```

Sequential (non-indexed) searches

What about searches where the object of the search isn't a key field? Even with the awesome index capabilities of FoxPro 2.0, some types of searchable objects just aren't amenable to building indexes. The most common example is the instring expression—for example, looking for a last name within a name field that generally contains a first name/last name pair. Listing 13-10 demonstrates how to deal with them.

Listing 13-10
```
* Program-ID.....: Search6.PRG
* Purpose........: Demonstrates in-string searches
CLEAR
USE AIRCRAFT ORDER ID

TagNum = 1
Cancelled = .F.

DO ListTags

DO WHILE .T.

   DO GetTag

   IF Cancelled
      EXIT
   ENDIF

   DO CASE

     CASE ORDER([AIRCRAFT]) = [ID]

        mID = SPACE(LEN(AIRCRAFT.ID))
        @ 23, 0 CLEAR
        @ 22,16 SAY [ (Any ID containing your string will match)]
        @ 23, 0 SAY [Aircraft ID: ] GET mID FUNCTION [!]
        READ
        @ 22,16 say REPL([-],50)
        @ 23, 0 CLEAR
        IF LEN(ALLTRIM(mID)) = 0
           EXIT
        ENDIF

        DEFINE POPUP IDS FROM 5,5 ;
               TITLE [ Pick an ID ] ;
```

```
              FOOTER [ Press ESCAPE to cancel ]
    I = 0
    GO TOP
    SCAN
      IF TRIM(mID) $ AIRCRAFT.ID
        I = I + 1
        DEFINE BAR I OF IDS PROMPT ID + [ | ] + Owner
      ENDIF
    ENDSCAN
    ON SELECTION POPUP IDS DEACTIVATE POPUP IDS
  IF CNTBAR([IDS]) = 0
    WAIT [ Nothing matches your request ] WINDOW TIMEOUT 1
    LOOP
  ENDIF

  ACTIVATE    POPUP IDS
  IF LEN(TRIM(PROMPT())) = 0
    LOOP
  ENDIF
  SEEK LEFT( PROMPT() , 6 )

CASE ORDER([AIRCRAFT]) = [OWNER]

  mOWNER = SPACE(LEN(AIRCRAFT.OWNER))
  @ 23, 0 CLEAR
  @ 22,16 SAY [ (Any name containing your string will match)]
  @ 23, 0 SAY [OWNER: ] GET mOWNER FUNCTION [!]
  READ
  @ 22,16 say REPL([-],50)
  @ 23, 0 CLEAR
  IF LEN(ALLTRIM(mOWNER)) = 0
    EXIT
  ENDIF

  DEFINE POPUP OWNERS FROM 5,5 ;
         TITLE  [ Pick an Owner ] ;
         FOOTER [ Press ESCAPE to cancel ]

  I = 0
  GO TOP
  SCAN
    IF TRIM(mOWNER) $ UPPER(AIRCRAFT.OWNER)
      I = I + 1
      DEFINE BAR I OF OWNERS PROMPT ID + [ | ] + Owner
    ENDIF
  ENDSCAN
  ON SELECTION POPUP OWNERS DEACTIVATE POPUP OWNERS

  IF CNTBAR([OWNERS]) = 0
    WAIT [ Nothing matches your request ] WINDOW TIMEOUT 1
    LOOP
  ENDIF

  ACTIVATE    POPUP OWNERS
  IF LEN(TRIM(PROMPT())) = 0
    LOOP
  ENDIF
  SEEK UPPER(RIGHT( PROMPT() , 30 ))
  CASE ORDER([AIRCRAFT]) = [TYPE]
```

Listing 13-10 Continued

```
    mTYPE = SPACE(LEN(AIRCRAFT.TYPE))
    @ 23, 0 CLEAR
    @ 22,16 SAY [ (Any type containing your string will match)]
    @ 23, 0 SAY [TYPE: ] GET mTYPE FUNCTION [!]
    READ
    @ 22,16 say REPL([-],50)
    @ 23, 0 CLEAR
    IF LEN(ALLTRIM(mTYPE)) = 0
      EXIT
    ENDIF

    DEFINE POPUP PLANES FROM 5,5 ;
           TITLE  [ Pick an Aircraft ] ;
           FOOTER [ Press ESCAPE to cancel ]

    I = 0
    GO TOP
    SCAN
      IF TRIM(mTYPE) $ UPPER(AIRCRAFT.TYPE)
        I = I + 1
        DEFINE BAR I OF PLANES PROMPT ID + [ | ] + OWNER + [ | ] + TYPE
      ENDIF
    ENDSCAN
    ON SELECTION POPUP PLANES DEACTIVATE POPUP PLANES

    IF CNTBAR([PLANES]) = 0
      WAIT [ Nothing matches your request ] WINDOW TIMEOUT 1
      LOOP
    ENDIF

    ACTIVATE    POPUP PLANES
    IF LEN(TRIM(PROMPT())) = 0
      LOOP
    ENDIF
    SET ORDER TO ID
    SEEK LEFT( PROMPT() , 6 )
    SET ORDER TO TYPE

ENDCASE

@ 23, 0 SAY [ID: ] + AIRCRAFT.ID + [ - Aircraft type is ] + Type
@ 24, 0 SAY [Owner is ] + OWNER
SET   CURSOR OFF
WAIT WINDOW
SET   CURSOR ON
ENDDO

CLOSE ALL
CLEAR ALL
CLEAR

RETURN


PROCEDURE GetTag

@ 23, 0 CLEAR
@ 23, 0 SAY [ Tag: ] GET TagNum PICTURE [@*H ID;OWNER;TYPE] SIZE 1,8,3
READ CYCLE
```

```
DO CASE
  CASE LASTKEY() = 27
    Cancelled = .T.
  CASE TagNum = 1
    SET ORDER TO ID
  CASE TagNum = 2
    SET ORDER TO OWNER
  CASE TagNum = 3
    SET ORDER TO TYPE
ENDCASE
```

Continue loops

A final case consists of applications where sequential (non-indexed) searches of very large databases are concerned. I don't mean very large in the way that FoxPro considers databases very large—over 500,000 records. If your application has many tens of thousands of records, don't use sequential searches. If you have reasonable sized files that occasionally need to be searched sequentially, however, you might want to use the LOCATE/CONTINUE command pair to search the database.

In the past, the technique that was favored involved finding the first matching record, then displaying it on the screen with an offer to Continue or Cancel:. The following example (LISTING 13-11) demonstrates that approach (which still has applicability), as well as a tabled approach (which you might prefer). The latter reads the entire file before it lets you see what it found, but it does appeal more to some users. The choice is yours.

Listing 13-11

```
* Program-Id....: Search7.prg
* Purpose.......: Demonstrates LOCATE loop

SET TALK OFF
CLEAR
USE AIRCRAFT ORDER ID
SCATTER MEMVAR

DEFINE WINDOW MAIN FROM  0, 3 TO 20, 76 ;
       DOUBLE SHADOW GROW FLOAT ZOOM MINIMIZE TITLE [ Aircraft Database ]

DEFINE WINDOW MORE FROM 16,30 TO 18, 50 ;
       DOUBLE SHADOW GROW FLOAT ZOOM MINIMIZE TITLE [ Continue? ]

DEFINE POPUP MATCHES FROM 3,45 SHADOW TITLE [ Matches ]
ON SELECTION POPUP MATCHES DEACTIVATE POPUP MATCHES

TestColor = IsColor()
AtrNormal = IIF ( TestColor , [GR+/B,W+/R] , [W+/N,N/W] )
AtrData   = IIF ( TestColor , [,N/W]       , [,N/W]     )

DO DispRec

ACTIVATE SCREEN
@ 24, 0 SAY [Press ENTER to begin demonstration]
```

Listing 13-11 Continued

```
READ

GETEXPR [Enter an expression to search for] TO expr

IF LEN(ALLTRIM(expr)) > 0
  IF METHOD() = 1
    DO PopLoop
  ELSE
    DO LocLoop
  ENDIF
ELSE
  WAIT WINDOW [No expression entered - cancelling] TIMEOUT 2
  CLEAR WINDOWS
ENDIF

CLEAR
CLEAR ALL
CLOSE ALL

RETURN


PROCEDURE Method

ACTIVATE SCREEN
method = 1
@ 24, 0 CLEAR
@ 24, 0 SAY [Which method? ] ;
        GET method PICTURE [@*H Popup list;CONTINUE loop]
READ CYCLE
@ 24, 0 CLEAR

RETURN method


PROCEDURE LocLoop

LOCATE FOR &Expr

IF .NOT. FOUND()
  WAIT WINDOW [no match - press any key]
  RETURN
ENDIF

DO WHILE .NOT. EOF()

  IF EOF()
    WAIT WINDOW [No more matches - press any key]
    CLEAR
    CLEAR ALL
    CLOSE ALL
    RETURN
  ENDIF

  DO DispRec

  IF ShowMore()
    CONTINUE
    IF .NOT. EOF()
```

```
      SCATTER MEMVAR
    ELSE
      WAIT WINDOW [No more matches - press any key]
      EXIT
    ENDIF
  ELSE
    WAIT WINDOW [Cancelled - press any key]
    RETURN
  ENDIF
ENDDO

RETURN


PROCEDURE PopLoop

LOCATE FOR &Expr

IF .NOT. FOUND()
  WAIT WINDOW [no match - press any key]
  RETURN
ENDIF

I = 1

DEFINE BAR I OF MATCHES PROMPT AIRCRAFT.ID + [ | ] + AIRCRAFT.OWNER

DO WHILE .NOT. EOF()

  CONTINUE

  IF .NOT. EOF()
    I = I + 1
    DEFINE BAR I OF MATCHES PROMPT AIRCRAFT.ID + [ | ] + AIRCRAFT.OWNER
  ELSE
    EXIT
  ENDIF

ENDDO

ACTIVATE SCREEN
@ 24, 0 SAY PADC ( ;
STR( CNTBAR([MATCHES]),4)+' found - Select one, or press ESCape to exit',80)
DO WHILE .T.
  ACTIVATE POPUP MATCHES
  IF [] = PROMPT()
    EXIT
  ELSE
    KEY = LEFT(PROMPT(),6)
    SEEK KEY
    SCATTER MEMVAR
    DO DispRec
    HIDE POPUP MATCHES
    WAIT WINDOW
  ENDIF
ENDDO

RETURN
```

Continue loops 327

Listing 13-11 Continued
```
PROCEDURE DispRec

DO DispScrn
DO SayData
CLEAR GETS

RETURN


FUNCTION ShowMore

ACTIVATE WINDOW MORE
more = 1
@ 0, 2 GET more PICTURE [@*H Yes;No] SIZE 1,6,3
READ CYCLE
DEACTIVATE WINDOW MORE
RETURN IIF ( more = 1 , .T. , .F. )


PROCEDURE DispScrn

ACTIVATE WINDOW MAIN

CLEAR

@  0,  0 SAY PADC( [ AirCraft Information Screen ] , WCOLS() )

@  2,  3 SAY [       ID: ]
@  3,  3 SAY [    Owner: ]
@  4,  3 SAY [  Address: ]
@  7,  3 SAY [   Phones: ]

@  8,  3 SAY [     Home: ]
@  9,  3 SAY [     Work: ]
@ 10,  3 SAY [ Cellular: ]

@ 12,  3 SAY [     Last ]
@ 13,  3 SAY [   Annual: ]

@ 15,  2 SAY [Equipment:]

@  2, 51 SAY [    Type: ]
@  3, 51 SAY [  Colors: ]
@  5, 51 SAY [  Engines: ]
@  6, 51 SAY [    Seats: ]

@  8, 51 SAY [    Tach: ]
@  9, 51 SAY [  Hobbes: ]
@ 12, 51 SAY [  Hourly ]
@ 13, 51 SAY [  Rental: ]

RETURN


PROCEDURE SayData

ACTIVATE WINDOW MAIN
SET COLOR TO &AtrData
```

328 Searching and selecting

```
@  2, 13 GET M.ID         PICTURE [!!!!!!]           DEFAULT [N        ]
@  3, 13 GET M.Owner      PICTURE [!XXXXXXXXXXXXXXXXXXXXXXXXXXX]
@  4, 13 GET M.Address1   PICTURE [!XXXXXXXXXXXXXXXXXXXXXXXXXXX]
@  5, 13 GET M.Address2   PICTURE [!XXXXXXXXXXXXXXXXXXXXXXXXXXX]
@  6, 13 GET M.City       PICTURE [###.##]
@  6, 34 GET M.State      PICTURE [###.##]           DEFAULT [CA]
@  6, 37 GET M.Zip        PICTURE [#####-####]       DEFAULT [94   -      ]

@  8, 13 GET M.Home       PICTURE [415-###-####]
@  9, 13 GET M.Work       PICTURE [415-###-####]
@ 10, 13 GET M.Cellular   PICTURE [415-###-####]

@ 13, 13 GET M.Annual

@ 15, 13 EDIT M.Equipment SIZE 4, 30

@  2, 61 GET M.Type       PICTURE [!!!!!!!!!!]
@  3, 61 GET M.Colors     PICTURE [!!!!!!!!!!]
@  5, 61 GET M.Engines    PICTURE [#]               DEFAULT 1
@  6, 61 GET M.Seats      PICTURE [###]             DEFAULT 4

@  8, 61 GET M.Tach       PICTURE [#####]
@  9, 61 GET M.Hobbes     PICTURE [#####]

@ 13, 61 GET M.Rental     PICTURE [###.##]          RANGE 1,9999

@ 15, 53 GET M.LeaseBack  PICTURE [@*C LeaseBack]

@ WROWS()-1,0 SAY PADC([ Order: ]+ORDER([Aircraft]),WCOLS())

RETURN
```

In order to use this, you need to provide for a search expression that is a valid FoxPro expression of the filter variety. Figure 13-12 shows the one used to test Program Search7.

Listing 13-12
```
SET TALK OFF
CLEAR
USE AIRCRAFT ORDER ID
SCATTER MEMVAR

DEFINE WINDOW MAIN FROM  0, 3 TO 20, 76 ;
       DOUBLE SHADOW GROW FLOAT ZOOM;
         MINIMIZE TITLE [ Aircraft Database ]

DEFINE WINDOW MORE FROM 16,30 TO 18, 50 ;
       DOUBLE SHADOW GROW FLOAT ZOOM MINIMIZE TITLE [ Continue? ]

DEFINE POPUP MATCHES FROM 3,45 SHADOW TITLE [ Matches ]
ON SELECTION POPUP MATCHES DEACTIVATE POPUP MATCHES

TestColor = IsColor()
AtrNormal = IIF ( TestColor , [GR+/B,W+/R] , [W+/N,N/W] )
AtrData   = IIF ( TestColor , [,N/W]       , [,N/W]     )
```

Continue loops 329

Listing 13-12 Continued

```
@ 24, 0 SAY [Press ENTER to begin demonstration]
READ

GETEXPR [Enter an expression to search for] TO expr

IF LEN(ALLTRIM(expr)) > 0
   IF METHOD() = 1
      DO PopLoop
   ELSE
      DO LocLoop
   ENDIF
ELSE
   WAIT WINDOW [No expression entered - cancelling] TIMEOUT 2
   CLEAR WINDOWS
ENDIF

CLEAR
CLEAR ALL
CLOSE ALL

RETURN

PROCEDURE Method

ACTIVATE SCREEN
method = 1
@ 24, 0 CLEAR
@ 24, 0 SAY [Which method? ] ;
      GET method PICTURE [@*H Popup list;CONTINUE loop]
READ CYCLE
@ 24, 0 CLEAR

RETURN method

PROCEDURE LocLoop

LOCATE FOR &Expr

IF .NOT. FOUND()
   WAIT WINDOW [no match - press any key]
   RETURN
ENDIF

DO WHILE .NOT. EOF()

   IF EOF()
      WAIT WINDOW [No more matches - press any key]
      CLEAR
      CLEAR ALL
      CLOSE ALL
      RETURN
   ENDIF

   DO DispRec

DO DispRec

ACTIVATE SCREEN
```

```
      IF ShowMore()
         CONTINUE
         IF .NOT. EOF()
            SCATTER MEMVAR
          ELSE
            WAIT WINDOW [No more matches - press any key]
            EXIT
         ENDIF
       ELSE
         WAIT WINDOW [Cancelled - press any key]
         RETURN
      ENDIF

ENDDO

RETURN


PROCEDURE PopLoop

LOCATE FOR &Expr

IF .NOT. FOUND()
   WAIT WINDOW [no match - press any key]
   RETURN

ENDIF

I = 1

DEFINE BAR I OF MATCHES PROMPT AIRCRAFT.ID + [ | ] + AIRCRAFT.OWNER

DO WHILE .NOT. EOF()

   CONTINUE

   IF .NOT. EOF()
      I = I + 1
      DEFINE BAR I OF MATCHES PROMPT AIRCRAFT.ID + [ | ] + AIRCRAFT.OWNER
    ELSE
      EXIT
   ENDIF

ENDDO

ACTIVATE SCREEN
@ 24, 0 SAY PADC ( ;
STR( CNTBAR([MATCHES]),4)+' found - Select one, or press ESCape to exit',80)

DO WHILE .T.
   ACTIVATE POPUP MATCHES
   IF [] = PROMPT()
      EXIT
    ELSE
      KEY = LEFT(PROMPT(),6)
      SEEK KEY
      SCATTER MEMVAR
      DO DispRec
      HIDE POPUP MATCHES
      WAIT WINDOW
   ENDIF
```

Listing 13-12   Continued
```
ENDDO

RETURN


PROCEDURE DispRec

DO DispScrn
DO SayData
CLEAR GETS

RETURN


FUNCTION ShowMore

ACTIVATE WINDOW MORE
more = 1
@ 0, 2 GET more PICTURE [@*H Yes;No] SIZE 1,6,3
READ CYCLE
DEACTIVATE WINDOW MORE
RETURN IIF ( more = 1 , .T. , .F. )


PROCEDURE DispScrn

ACTIVATE WINDOW MAIN

CLEAR

@  0, 0 SAY PADC( [ AirCraft Information Screen ] , WCOLS() )

@  2,  3 SAY [      ID: ]
@  3,  3 SAY [   Owner: ]
@  4,  3 SAY [ Address: ]
@  7,  3 SAY [  Phones: ]

@  8,  3 SAY [    Home: ]
@  9,  3 SAY [    Work: ]
@ 10,  3 SAY [Cellular: ]

@ 12,  3 SAY [    Last  ]
@ 13,  3 SAY [  Annual: ]

@ 15,  2 SAY [Equipment:]

@  2, 51 SAY [    Type: ]
@  3, 51 SAY [  Colors: ]
@  5, 51 SAY [ Engines: ]
@  6, 51 SAY [   Seats: ]

@  8, 51 SAY [    Tach: ]
@  9, 51 SAY [  Hobbes: ]

@ 12, 51 SAY [  Hourly  ]
@ 13, 51 SAY [  Rental: ]

RETURN
```

```
PROCEDURE SayData

ACTIVATE WINDOW MAIN
SET COLOR TO &AtrData

@  2, 13 GET M->ID       PICTURE [!!!!!!]             DEFAULT [N      ]
@  3, 13 GET M->Owner    PICTURE [!XXXXXXXXXXXXXXXXXXXXXXXXXXX]
@  4, 13 GET M->Address1 PICTURE [!XXXXXXXXXXXXXXXXXXXXXXXXXXX]
@  5, 13 GET M->Address2 PICTURE [!XXXXXXXXXXXXXXXXXXXXXXXXXXX]
@  6, 13 GET M->City     PICTURE [###.##]
@  6, 34 GET M->State    PICTURE [###.##]             DEFAULT [CA]
@  6, 37 GET M->Zip      PICTURE [#####-####]         DEFAULT [94    -     ]
@  8, 13 GET M->Home     PICTURE [415-###-####]
@  9, 13 GET M->Work     PICTURE [415-###-####]
@ 10, 13 GET M->Cellular PICTURE [415-###-####]

@ 13, 13 GET M->Annual

@ 15, 13 EDIT M->Equipment SIZE 4, 30

@  2, 61 GET M->Type     PICTURE [!!!!!!!!!!!]
@  3, 61 GET M->Colors   PICTURE [!!!!!!!!!!!]
@  5, 61 GET M->Engines  PICTURE [#]                  DEFAULT 1
@  6, 61 GET M->Seats    PICTURE [###]                DEFAULT 4

@  8, 61 GET M->Tach     PICTURE [#####]
@  9, 61 GET M->Hobbes   PICTURE [#####]

@ 13, 61 GET M->Rental   PICTURE [###.##]             RANGE 1,9999

@ 15, 53 GET M->LeaseBack PICTURE [@*C LeaseBack]

@ WROWS()-1,0 SAY PADC([ Order: ]+ORDER([Aircraft]),WCOLS())

RETURN
```

A potpourri of searches

My final example (LISTING 13-13) is an application that combines various of the previous techniques, so that you can get the feel of it. The GETEXPR command used in my function SELECTS( ) is new to version 2.0, but it might drive your users nuts.

Listing 13-13

```
* Program-ID......: Aircraft.PRG
* Purpose.........: Demonstrate indexed and non-indexed searching

SET ESCAPE OFF
CLEAR
SET MESSAGES TO 24

TestColor = IsColor()
AtrNormal = IIF ( TestColor , [GR+/B,W+/R] , [W+/N,N/W] )
AtrData   = IIF ( TestColor , [,N/W]       , [,N/W]     )

FiltExpr = [ ]

IF .NOT. FILE([AIRCRAFT.CDX])
```

Listing 13-13 Continued
```
      DO INDEXIT
ENDIF

DEFINE WINDOW MAIN FROM  0, 3 TO 20, 76 ;
       DOUBLE SHADOW GROW FLOAT ZOOM MINIMIZE TITLE [ Aircraft Database ]
DEFINE WINDOW SAVE FROM 16,33 TO 18, 47 ;
       DOUBLE SHADOW GROW FLOAT ZOOM MINIMIZE TITLE [ Save? ]
DEFINE WINDOW DEL  FROM 16,33 TO 18, 47 ;
       DOUBLE SHADOW GROW FLOAT ZOOM MINIMIZE TITLE [ Delete? ]
DEFINE WINDOW SRCH FROM 16,15 TO 19, 63 ;
       DOUBLE SHADOW GROW FLOAT ZOOM MINIMIZE TITLE [ Search for what? ]
DEFINE WINDOW INDX FROM 16,15 TO 19, 63 ;
       DOUBLE SHADOW GROW FLOAT ZOOM MINIMIZE TITLE [ Report Order? ]
DEFINE WINDOW DEST FROM 16,15 TO 19, 63 ;
       DOUBLE SHADOW GROW FLOAT ZOOM MINIMIZE TITLE [ Send report where? ]

DEFINE         POPUP REPORTS FROM 12,15 SHADOW TITLE [ Available Reports ]
ON SELECTION POPUP REPORTS DEACTIVATE POPUP REPORTS
DEFINE BAR 1 OF     REPORTS PROMPT [ Owner's Directory       ]
DEFINE BAR 2 OF     REPORTS PROMPT [ Planes Due for Annual ]

USE AIRCRAFT ORDER ID

DO WHILE .T.

   DO DispScrn
   SCATTER MEMVAR
   DO DispData

   SET COLOR TO &AtrNormal
   ACTIVATE SCREEN

   @ 23, 0   PROMPT [ Add ]    MESSAGE [ Add an aircraft]
   @ 23, $+1 PROMPT [ Edit ]   MESSAGE [ Edit this plane's data]
   @ 23, $+1 PROMPT [ Delete ] MESSAGE [ Delete this aircraft]
   @ 23, $+1 PROMPT [ Find ]   MESSAGE [ Show the 'Find an aircraft' menu]
   @ 23, $+1 PROMPT [ Print ]  MESSAGE [ Print report]
   @ 23, $+1 PROMPT [ Quit ]   MESSAGE [ Exit]
   MENU TO nchoice
   @ 23, 0 CLEAR
   choice = IIF ( nchoice = 0 , [Q] , SUBSTR ( [AEDFPQ] , nchoice , 1 ) )

   DO CASE

     CASE choice = [A]

        DO AddPlane

     CASE choice = [E]

        DO EdtPlane

     CASE choice = [D]

        DO DelPlane

     CASE choice = [F]

        DO GetPlane
```

```
      CASE choice = [P]

         DO PrtPlane

      CASE choice = [Q]

         EXIT

   ENDCASE

ENDDO

CLOSE ALL
CLEAR ALL

RETURN


PROCEDURE DispScrn

ACTIVATE WINDOW MAIN

CLEAR

@  0,  0 SAY PADC( [ AirCraft Information Screen ] , WCOLS() )

@  2,  3 SAY [     ID: ]
@  3,  3 SAY [  Owner: ]
@  4,  3 SAY [ Address: ]
@  7,  3 SAY [ Phones: ]

@  8,  3 SAY [   Home: ]
@  9,  3 SAY [   Work: ]
@ 10,  3 SAY [Cellular: ]

@ 12,  3 SAY [   Last  ]
@ 13,  3 SAY [ Annual: ]

@ 15,  2 SAY [Equipment:]

@  2, 51 SAY [   Type: ]
@  3, 51 SAY [ Colors: ]
@  5, 51 SAY [ Engines: ]
@  6, 51 SAY [  Seats: ]

@  8, 51 SAY [   Tach: ]
@  9, 51 SAY [ Hobbes: ]

@ 12, 51 SAY [ Hourly  ]
@ 13, 51 SAY [ Rental: ]

RETURN


PROCEDURE DispData
DO SayData
CLEAR GETS
RETURN


PROCEDURE AddPlane
```

Listing 13-13 *Continued*

```
SCATTER MEMVAR BLANK
DO   SayData
READ COLOR N/W,W+/R

ACTIVATE WINDOW SAVE
SET COLOR TO &AtrNormal
@ 0, 1    PROMPT [ Yes ]
@ 0, $+2 PROMPT [ No ]
ok = 2
MENU TO ok
ACTIVATE WINDOW MAIN

IF ok <> 2
  GO BOTTOM
  IF ID <> [<Tilde>]
    APPEND BLANK
  ENDIF
  GATHER MEMVAR
ENDIF

RETURN


PROCEDURE EdtPlane

SCATTER MEMVAR
DO SayData
READ COLOR N/W,W+/R

ACTIVATE WINDOW SAVE
SET COLOR TO &AtrNormal
@ 0, 1    PROMPT [ Yes ]
@ 0, $+2 PROMPT [ No ]
ok = 2
MENU TO ok
ACTIVATE WINDOW MAIN

IF ok <> 2
  GATHER MEMVAR
ENDIF

RETURN


PROCEDURE SayData

ACTIVATE WINDOW MAIN
SET COLOR TO &AtrData

@  2, 13 GET M.ID        PICTURE [!!!!!!]            DEFAULT [N      ]
@  3, 13 GET M.Owner     PICTURE [!XXXXXXXXXXXXXXXXXXXXXXXXXXX]
@  4, 13 GET M.Address1  PICTURE [!XXXXXXXXXXXXXXXXXXXXXXXXXXX]
@  5, 13 GET M.Address2  PICTURE [!XXXXXXXXXXXXXXXXXXXXXXXXXXX]
@  6, 13 GET M.City      PICTURE [###.##]
@  6, 34 GET M.State     PICTURE [###.##]            DEFAULT [CA]
@  6, 37 GET M.Zip       PICTURE [#####-####]        DEFAULT [94    -    ]

@  8, 13 GET M.Home      PICTURE [415-###-####]
@  9, 13 GET M.Work      PICTURE [415-###-####]
@ 10, 13 GET M.Cellular  PICTURE [415-###-####]
```

```
@ 13, 13 GET M.Annual

@ 15, 13 EDIT M.Equipment SIZE 4, 30

@  2, 61 GET M.Type     PICTURE [!!!!!!!!!!!]
@  3, 61 GET M.Colors   PICTURE [!!!!!!!!!!!]
@  5, 61 GET M.Engines  PICTURE [#]           DEFAULT 1
@  6, 61 GET M.Seats    PICTURE [###]         DEFAULT 4

@  8, 61 GET M.Tach     PICTURE [#####]
@  9, 61 GET M.Hobbes   PICTURE [#####]

@ 13, 61 GET M.Rental   PICTURE [###.##]      RANGE 1,9999

@ 15, 53 GET M.LeaseBack PICTURE [@*C LeaseBack]

@ WROWS()-1,0 SAY PADC([ Order: ]+ORDER([Aircraft]),WCOLS())

RETURN



PROCEDURE INDEXIT

USE AIRCRAFT

INDEX ON ID             TAG ID       OF AIRCRAFT COMPACT ASCENDING
INDEX ON UPPER(OWNER)   TAG OWNER    OF AIRCRAFT COMPACT ASCENDING
INDEX ON TYPE           TAG TYPE     OF AIRCRAFT COMPACT ASCENDING

USE AIRCRAFT ORDER ID

RETURN


PROCEDURE DelPlane

ACTIVATE WINDOW DEL
SET COLOR TO &AtrNormal
@ 0, 1   PROMPT [ Yes ]
@ 0, $+2 PROMPT [ No ]
ok = 2
MENU TO ok
ACTIVATE WINDOW MAIN

IF ok = 1
  SaveID = ID
  SCATTER MEMVAR BLANK
  GATHER  MEMVAR
  REPLACE NEXT 1 ID WITH [<Tilde>], OWNER WITH [<Tilde>],TYPE WITH [<Tilde>]
  SET  NEAR ON
  SEEK SAVEID
  SET NEAR OFF
  SCATTER MEMVAR
  DO DispData
ENDIF

RETURN



PROCEDURE GetPlane
```

Listing 13-13 Continued

```
ACTIVATE SCREEN
@ 24, 0 SAY PADC([Press ESCAPE to return to the previous menu],80)

FindWhat = 1

DO WHILE .T.

   ACTIVATE WINDOW SRCH
   CLEAR
   @ 1,   2 PROMPT [ Next ]
   @ 1, $+1 PROMPT [ Previous ]
   @ 1, $+1 PROMPT [ Top ]
   @ 1, $+1 PROMPT [ Bottom ]
   @ 1, $+1 PROMPT [ Search ]

   MENU TO FindWhat
   FindWhat = IIF ( FindWhat = 0, [Q], SUBSTR ( [NPTBS] , FindWhat , 1 ) )

   DO CASE

      CASE FindWhat = [Q]

         EXIT

      CASE FindWhat = [N]

         IF .NOT. EOF()
            SKIP
            IF ID = [<Tilde>] .OR. EOF()
               =Alarm()
               SKIP -1
            ENDIF
            SCATTER MEMVAR
            DO DispScrn
            DO DispData
         ENDIF

      CASE FindWhat = [P]

         IF .NOT. BOF()
            SKIP -1
            IF BOF()
               =Alarm()
               GO TOP
            ENDIF
            SCATTER MEMVAR
            DO DispScrn
            DO DispData
         ENDIF

      CASE FindWhat = [T]

         GO TOP
         SCATTER MEMVAR
         DO DispScrn
         DO DispData

      CASE FindWhat = [B]
```

```
            SEEK [<Tilde>]                         && Look for 'deleted' records
            IF .NOT. FOUND()
               GO BOTTOM
            ELSE
               SKIP -1
            ENDIF
            SCATTER MEMVAR
            DO DispScrn
            DO DispData

         CASE FindWhat = [S]

            DO FindPlan
            SCATTER MEMVAR
            DO DispScrn
            DO DispData

      ENDCASE

ENDDO

HIDE WINDOW SRCH

RETURN


PROCEDURE FindPlan

ACTIVATE WINDOW SRCH
Data  = SPACE(LEN(&Field))
@ 0, 0 SAY [ Enter ] + Field GET Data FUNCTION [!]
READ
DEACTIVATE WINDOW SRCH

IF LEN(TRIM(Data)) = 0
   RETURN
ENDIF

SEEK UPPER(TRIM(Data))
IF ALLTRIM(DATA) == ALLTRIM(&FIELD)
   SCATTER MEMVAR
   DO DispData
   RETURN
ENDIF

* -- Either a partial match or no match....
DO WHILE .NOT. FOUND() .AND. LEN(TRIM(Data)) > 0
   Data = LEFT(Data,LEN(TRIM(Data))-1)
   SEEK UPPER(Data)
ENDDO

IF LEN(Data) = 0
   WAIT WINDOW [Nothing even remotely similar on file - Press any key]
   RETURN
ENDIF

DEFINE POPUP  FIND FROM  2,15 ;
       SHADOW TITLE [ Similar entries ]
ON SELECTION POPUP FIND DEACTIVATE POPUP FIND

I = 0
```

Listing 13-13 Continued

```
SCAN WHILE UPPER(ALLTRIM(&FIELD)) = UPPER(ALLTRIM(Data))
  I = I + 1
  DEFINE BAR I OF FIND PROMPT &Field
ENDSCAN

ACTIVATE POPUP FIND
mData = PROMPT()

RELEASE POPUP FIND

IF LEN(TRIM(mData)) = 0    && ESCAPE was pressed...
  WAIT WINDOW [ Cancelled by operator ] TIMEOUT 1
  RETURN
ENDIF

SEEK UPPER(mData)

RETURN


FUNCTION Alarm

FOR I = 1 TO 3
  SET BELL TO 800,1
  ?? CHR(7)
  SET BELL TO 1200,1
  ?? CHR(7)
ENDFOR
RETURN .T.


PROCEDURE PrtPlane

Cancelled = .F.

DO SELECTS

IF .NOT. Cancelled
  DO ORDER
ENDIF

IF .NOT. Cancelled
  DO REPORTS
ENDIF

RETURN


PROCEDURE SELECTS

ACTIVATE SCREEN
@ 23, 0 CLEAR
getfilt = 0
@ 23, 1 SAY [Select only certain aircraft? ] ;
        GET getfilt PICTURE [@*H Yes;No] SIZE 1, 8 , 3
READ
@ 23, 0 CLEAR

IF LASTKEY() = 27
```

```
    Cancelled = .T.
    RETURN
ENDIF

IF GetFilt = 1
  GETEXPR [What planes do you want included in the report?] TO expr
  IF LEN(ALLTRIM(expr)) = 0
    Cancelled = .T.
  ENDIF
  FiltExpr = [ FOR ] + expr + [ .AND. ID <> "~" ]
ELSE
  FiltExpr = [ FOR ID <> "~" ]
ENDIF

RETURN


PROCEDURE ORDER

ACTIVATE WINDOW INDX

WhichNdx = 1
CLEAR
@ 1, 3 GET WhichNdx PICTURE [@*H ID;Owner;Type] SIZE 1,10,4
READ

DEACTIVATE WINDOW INDX

IF LASTKEY() = 27        && ESCAPE WAS PRESSED
  Cancelled = .T.
  RETURN
ENDIF

Field = TAG([AIRCRAFT],WhichNdx)
SET ORDER TO &Field

DO DispScrn
DO DispData

ACTIVATE SCREEN
@ 24, 0 CLEAR

RETURN


PROCEDURE REPORTS

ACTIVATE WINDOW MAIN

Rept = 1

ACTIVATE    POPUP REPORTS
Rept = BAR()
DEACTIVATE POPUP REPORTS

IF BAR() = 0
  Cancelled = .T.
  RETURN
ENDIF

DO WhereTo
```

Listing 13-13 Continued

```
IF Cancelled
  RETURN
ENDIF

SaveRec = RECNO()

DO CASE

   CASE Rept = 1 .AND. ORDER([Aircraft]) = [ID]
     REPORT FORM OWNER &FiltExpr
   CASE Rept = 1 .AND. ORDER([Aircraft]) = [OWNER]
     REPORT FORM OWNER &FiltExpr
   CASE Rept = 1 .AND. ORDER([Aircraft]) = [TYPE]
     REPORT FORM OWNERTYP &FiltExpr    && because it has groups
   CASE Rept = 2
     SAVEORDER = ORDER ( [Aircraft] )
     SET ORDER    TO TYPE
     REPORT FORM MAINTREP &FiltExpr
     SET ORDER    TO &SaveOrder

ENDCASE

ACTIVATE SCREEN
CLEAR
ACTIVATE WINDOW MAIN
WAIT WINDOW

GOTO SaveRec

RETURN


PROCEDURE WhereTo

ACTIVATE WINDOW DEST
CLEAR
ReptDest = 1
@ 1, 1 GET   ReptDest PICTURE [@*H Screen;Printer;File] SIZE 1,10,3
READ CYCLE
CLEAR

IF LASTKEY() = 27
  DEACTIVATE WINDOW DEST
  Cancelled = .T.
  RETURN
ENDIF

IF ReptDest = 3
  mFile = SPACE(8)
  @ 1, 1 Say [File Name:] GET mFile PICTURE [!!!!!!!!]
  READ
  DO WHILE LEN(ALLTRIM(mFile)) = 0 .AND. LASTKEY() <> 27
    =Alarm()
    WAIT WINDOW [ You must enter a file name ] TIMEOUT 1
    @ 1, 1 Say [File Name:] GET mFile PICTURE [!!!!!!!!]
    READ
  ENDDO
  IF LASTKEY() = 27
    DEACTIVATE WINDOW DEST
```

```
          Cancelled = .T.
        RETURN
      ENDIF
      SET PRINTER TO &mFile
   ENDIF

   IF ReptDest = 2
      SET PRINTER TO PRN
   ENDIF

   IF ReptDest > 1
      SET PRINT ON
   ELSE
      HIDE WINDOWS ALL
      ACTIVATE SCREEN
      CLEAR
   ENDIF

   DEACTIVATE WINDOW DEST

   RETURN
```

In the following section, I'll talk about different ways to extract only selected records. The screen referred to appears in FIG. 13-14.

Listing 13-14
```
SET ESCAPE OFF
CLEAR
SET MESSAGES TO 24

TestColor = IsColor()
AtrNormal = IIF ( TestColor , [GR+/B,W+/R] , [W+/N,N/W] )
AtrData   = IIF ( TestColor , [,N/W]       , [,N/W]     )

FiltExpr = [ ]

IF .NOT. FILE([AIRCRAFT.CDX])
   DO INDEXIT
ENDIF

DEFINE WINDOW MAIN FROM  0, 3 TO 20, 76 ;
       DOUBLE SHADOW GROW FLOAT ZOOM MINIMIZE TITLE [ Aircraft Database ]
DEFINE WINDOW SAVE FROM 16,33 TO 18, 47 ;
       DOUBLE SHADOW GROW FLOAT ZOOM MINIMIZE TITLE [ Save? ]
DEFINE WINDOW DEL  FROM 16,33 TO 18, 47 ;
       DOUBLE SHADOW GROW FLOAT ZOOM MINIMIZE TITLE [ Delete? ]
DEFINE WINDOW SRCH FROM 16,15 TO 19, 63 ;
       DOUBLE SHADOW GROW FLOAT ZOOM MINIMIZE TITLE [ Search for what? ]
DEFINE WINDOW INDX FROM 16,15 TO 19, 63 ;
       DOUBLE SHADOW GROW FLOAT ZOOM MINIMIZE TITLE [ Report Order? ]
DEFINE WINDOW DEST FROM 16,15 TO 19, 63 ;
       DOUBLE SHADOW GROW FLOAT ZOOM MINIMIZE TITLE [ Send report where? ]

DEFINE         POPUP REPORTS FROM 12,15 SHADOW TITLE [ Available Reports ]
ON SELECTION POPUP REPORTS DEACTIVATE POPUP REPORTS
DEFINE BAR 1 OF    REPORTS PROMPT [ Owner's Directory    ]
DEFINE BAR 2 OF    REPORTS PROMPT [ Planes Due for Annual ]

USE AIRCRAFT ORDER ID
```

Listing 13-14 Continued

```
DO WHILE .T.

    DO DispScrn
    SCATTER MEMVAR
    DO DispData

    SET COLOR TO &AtrNormal
    ACTIVATE SCREEN

    @ 23, 0   PROMPT [ Add ]     MESSAGE [ Add an aircraft]
    @ 23, $+1 PROMPT [ Edit ]    MESSAGE [ Edit this plane's data]
    @ 23, $+1 PROMPT [ Delete ]  MESSAGE [ Delete this aircraft]
    @ 23, $+1 PROMPT [ Find ]    MESSAGE [ Show the 'Find an aircraft' menu]
    @ 23, $+1 PROMPT [ Print ]   MESSAGE [ Print report]
    @ 23, $+1 PROMPT [ Quit ]    MESSAGE [ Exit]

    MENU TO nchoice
    @ 23, 0 CLEAR

    choice = IIF ( nchoice = 0 , [Q] , SUBSTR ( [AEDFPQ] , nchoice , 1 ) )

    DO CASE

        CASE choice = [A]

            DO AddPlane

        CASE choice = [E]

            DO EdtPlane

        CASE choice = [D]

            DO DelPlane

        CASE choice = [F]

            DO GetPlane

        CASE choice = [P]

            DO PrtPlane

        CASE choice = [Q]

            EXIT

    ENDCASE

ENDDO

CLOSE ALL
CLEAR ALL

RETURN


PROCEDURE DispScrn

ACTIVATE WINDOW MAIN
```

```
CLEAR

@  0,  0 SAY PADC( [ AirCraft Information Screen ] , WCOLS() )

@  2,  3 SAY [      ID: ]
@  3,  3 SAY [   Owner: ]
@  4,  3 SAY [ Address: ]
@  7,  3 SAY [  Phones: ]

@  8,  3 SAY [    Home: ]
@  9,  3 SAY [    Work: ]
@ 10,  3 SAY [Cellular: ]
@ 12,  3 SAY [    Last ]
@ 13,  3 SAY [  Annual: ]

@ 15,  2 SAY [Equipment:]

@  2, 51 SAY [    Type: ]
@  3, 51 SAY [  Colors: ]
@  5, 51 SAY [ Engines: ]
@  6, 51 SAY [   Seats: ]

@  8, 51 SAY [    Tach: ]
@  9, 51 SAY [  Hobbes: ]

@ 12, 51 SAY [  Hourly ]
@ 13, 51 SAY [  Rental: ]

RETURN


PROCEDURE DispData
DO SayData
CLEAR GETS
RETURN


PROCEDURE AddPlane

SCATTER MEMVAR BLANK
DO   SayData
READ COLOR N/W,W+/R

ACTIVATE WINDOW SAVE
SET COLOR TO &AtrNormal
@ 0, 1    PROMPT [ Yes ]
@ 0, $+2 PROMPT [ No ]
ok = 2
MENU TO ok
ACTIVATE WINDOW MAIN

IF ok <> 2
   GO BOTTOM
   IF ID <> [~]
      APPEND BLANK
   ENDIF
   GATHER MEMVAR
ENDIF

RETURN
```

Listing 13-14 Continued

```
PROCEDURE EdtPlane

SCATTER MEMVAR

DO SayData
READ COLOR N/W,W+/R

ACTIVATE WINDOW SAVE
SET COLOR TO &AtrNormal
@ 0, 1    PROMPT [ Yes ]
@ 0, $+2 PROMPT [ No ]
ok = 2
MENU TO ok
ACTIVATE WINDOW MAIN

IF ok <> 2
   GATHER MEMVAR
ENDIF

RETURN


PROCEDURE SayData

ACTIVATE WINDOW MAIN
SET COLOR TO &AtrData

@  2, 13 GET M->ID        PICTURE [!!!!!!]           DEFAULT [N     ]
@  3, 13 GET M->Owner     PICTURE [!XXXXXXXXXXXXXXXXXXXXXXXXX]
@  4, 13 GET M->Address1  PICTURE [!XXXXXXXXXXXXXXXXXXXXXXXXX]
@  5, 13 GET M->Address2  PICTURE [!XXXXXXXXXXXXXXXXXXXXXXXXX]
@  6, 13 GET M->City      PICTURE [###.##]
@  6, 34 GET M->State     PICTURE [###.##]           DEFAULT [CA]
@  6, 37 GET M->Zip       PICTURE [#####-####]       DEFAULT [94   -

@  8, 13 GET M->Home      PICTURE [415-###-####]
@  9, 13 GET M->Work      PICTURE [415-###-####]
@ 10, 13 GET M->Cellular  PICTURE [415-###-####]

@ 13, 13 GET M->Annual

@ 15, 13 EDIT M->Equipment SIZE 4, 30

@  2, 61 GET M->Type      PICTURE [!!!!!!!!!!!]
@  3, 61 GET M->Colors    PICTURE [!!!!!!!!!!!]
@  5, 61 GET M->Engines   PICTURE [#]                DEFAULT 1
@  6, 61 GET M->Seats     PICTURE [###]              DEFAULT 4

@  8, 61 GET M->Tach      PICTURE [#####]
@  9, 61 GET M->Hobbes    PICTURE [#####]

@ 13, 61 GET M->Rental    PICTURE [###.##]           RANGE 1,9999

@ 15, 53 GET M->LeaseBack PICTURE [@*C LeaseBack]

@ WROWS()-1,0 SAY PADC([ Order: ]+ORDER([Aircraft]),WCOLS())

RETURN
```

```
PROCEDURE INDEXIT

USE AIRCRAFT

INDEX ON ID              TAG ID      OF AIRCRAFT COMPACT ASCENDING
INDEX ON UPPER(OWNER)    TAG OWNER   OF AIRCRAFT COMPACT ASCENDING
INDEX ON TYPE            TAG TYPE    OF AIRCRAFT COMPACT ASCENDING

USE AIRCRAFT ORDER ID

RETURN



PROCEDURE DelPlane

ACTIVATE WINDOW DEL
SET COLOR TO &AtrNormal
@ 0, 1    PROMPT [ Yes ]
@ 0, $+2  PROMPT [ No ]
ok = 2
MENU TO ok
ACTIVATE WINDOW MAIN

IF ok = 1
   SaveID = ID
   SCATTER MEMVAR BLANK
   GATHER   MEMVAR
   REPLACE NEXT 1 ID WITH [~], OWNER WITH [~],TYPE WITH [~]
   SET  NEAR ON
   SEEK SAVEID
   SET NEAR OFF
   SCATTER MEMVAR
   DO DispData
ENDIF

RETURN



PROCEDURE GetPlane

ACTIVATE SCREEN
@ 24, 0 SAY PADC([Press ESCAPE to return to the previous menu],80)

FindWhat = 1

DO WHILE .T.

   ACTIVATE WINDOW SRCH
   CLEAR
   @ 1,   2 PROMPT [ Next ]
   @ 1, $+1 PROMPT [ Previous ]
   @ 1, $+1 PROMPT [ Top ]

   @ 1, $+1 PROMPT [ Bottom ]
   @ 1, $+1 PROMPT [ Search ]

   MENU TO FindWhat
   FindWhat = IIF ( FindWhat = 0, [Q], SUBSTR ( [NPTBS] , FindWhat , 1 ) )

   DO CASE
```

A potpourri of searches

Listing 13-14 Continued
```
     CASE FindWhat = [Q]

          EXIT

     CASE FindWhat = [N]

          IF .NOT. EOF()
             SKIP
             IF ID = [~] .OR. EOF()
                =Alarm()
                SKIP -1
             ENDIF
             SCATTER MEMVAR
             DO DispScrn
             DO DispData
          ENDIF

     CASE FindWhat = [P]

          IF .NOT. BOF()
             SKIP -1
             IF BOF()
                =Alarm()
                GO TOP
             ENDIF
             SCATTER MEMVAR
             DO DispScrn
             DO DispData
          ENDIF

     CASE FindWhat = [T]

             GO TOP
             SCATTER MEMVAR
             DO DispScrn
             DO DispData

     CASE FindWhat = [B]

             SEEK [~]
             IF .NOT. FOUND()
                GO BOTTOM
             ELSE
                SKIP -1
             ENDIF
             SCATTER MEMVAR
             DO DispScrn
             DO DispData

     CASE FindWhat = [S]

             DO FindPlan
                SCATTER MEMVAR
                DO DispScrn
                DO DispData

     ENDCASE

ENDDO
```

```
HIDE WINDOW SRCH

RETURN


PROCEDURE FindPlan

ACTIVATE WINDOW SRCH
quit
Data  = SPACE(LEN(&Field))
@ 0, 0 SAY [ Enter ] + Field GET Data FUNCTION [!]
READ
DEACTIVATE WINDOW SRCH

IF LEN(TRIM(Data)) = 0
   RETURN
ENDIF

SEEK UPPER(TRIM(Data))
IF ALLTRIM(DATA) == ALLTRIM(&FIELD)
   SCATTER MEMVAR
   DO DispData
   RETURN
ENDIF

* -- Either a partial match or no match....
DO WHILE .NOT. FOUND() .AND. LEN(TRIM(Data)) > 0
   Data = LEFT(Data,LEN(TRIM(Data))-1)
   SEEK UPPER(Data)
ENDDO

IF LEN(Data) = 0
   WAIT WINDOW [Nothing even remotely similar on file - Press any key]
   RETURN
ENDIF

DEFINE POPUP  FIND FROM  2,15 ;
      SHADOW TITLE [ Similar entries ]
ON SELECTION POPUP FIND DEACTIVATE POPUP FIND
I = 0
SCAN WHILE UPPER(ALLTRIM(&FIELD)) = UPPER(ALLTRIM(Data))
   I = I + 1
   DEFINE BAR I OF FIND PROMPT &Field
ENDSCAN
ACTIVATE POPUP FIND
mData = PROMPT()

RELEASE POPUP FIND

IF LEN(TRIM(mData)) = 0    && ESCAPE was pressed...
   WAIT WINDOW [ Cancelled by operator ] TIMEOUT 1
   RETURN
ENDIF

SEEK UPPER(mData)

RETURN


FUNCTION Alarm
```

Listing 13-14   Continued

```
FOR I = 1 TO 3
   SET BELL TO 800,1
   ?? CHR(7)
   SET BELL TO 1200,1
   ?? CHR(7)
ENDFOR
RETURN .T.


PROCEDURE PrtPlane

Cancelled = .F.

DO SELECTS

IF .NOT. Cancelled
   DO ORDER
ENDIF

IF .NOT. Cancelled
   DO REPORTS
ENDIF

RETURN


PROCEDURE SELECTS

ACTIVATE SCREEN
@ 23, 0 CLEAR
getfilt = 0
@ 23, 1 SAY [Select only certain aircraft? ] ;
        GET getfilt PICTURE [@*H Yes;No] SIZE 1, 8 , 3
READ
@ 23, 0 CLEAR

IF LASTKEY() = 27
   Cancelled = .T.
   RETURN
ENDIF

IF GetFilt = 1
   GETEXPR [What planes do you want included in the report?] TO expr
   IF LEN(ALLTRIM(expr)) = 0
      Cancelled = .T.
   ENDIF
   FiltExpr = [ FOR ] + expr + [ .AND. ID <> "~" ]
ELSE
   FiltExpr = [ FOR ID <> "~" ]
ENDIF

RETURN


PROCEDURE ORDER

ACTIVATE WINDOW INDX

WhichNdx = 1
```

350   Searching and selecting

```
CLEAR
@ 1, 3 GET WhichNdx PICTURE [@*H ID;Owner;Type] SIZE 1,10,4
READ

DEACTIVATE WINDOW INDX

IF LASTKEY() = 27        && ESCAPE WAS PRESSED
   Cancelled = .T.
   RETURN
ENDIF

Field = TAG([AIRCRAFT],WhichNdx)
SET ORDER TO &Field

DO DispScrn
DO DispData

ACTIVATE SCREEN
@ 24, 0 CLEAR

RETURN


PROCEDURE REPORTS

ACTIVATE WINDOW MAIN
Rept = 1

ACTIVATE      POPUP REPORTS
Rept = BAR()
DEACTIVATE POPUP REPORTS

IF BAR() = 0
   Cancelled = .T.
   RETURN
ENDIF

DO WhereTo

IF Cancelled
   RETURN
ENDIF

SaveRec = RECNO()

DO CASE

   CASE Rept = 1 .AND. ORDER([Aircraft]) = [ID]
        REPORT FORM OWNER &FiltExpr
   CASE Rept = 1 .AND. ORDER([Aircraft]) = [OWNER]
        REPORT FORM OWNER &FiltExpr
   CASE Rept = 1 .AND. ORDER([Aircraft]) = [TYPE]
        REPORT FORM OWNERTYP &FiltExpr    && because it has groups
   CASE Rept = 2
        SAVEORDER = ORDER ( [Aircraft] )
        SET ORDER    TO TYPE
        REPORT FORM MAINTREP &FiltExpr
        SET ORDER    TO &SaveOrder

ENDCASE
```

Listing 13-14 Continued

```
ACTIVATE SCREEN
CLEAR
ACTIVATE WINDOW MAIN
WAIT WINDOW

GOTO SaveRec

RETURN


PROCEDURE WhereTo

ACTIVATE WINDOW DEST
CLEAR
ReptDest = 1
@ 1, 1 GET  ReptDest PICTURE [@*H Screen;Printer;File] SIZE 1,10,3
READ CYCLE
CLEAR

IF LASTKEY() = 27
   DEACTIVATE WINDOW DEST
   Cancelled = .T.
   RETURN
ENDIF

IF ReptDest = 3
   mFile = SPACE(8)
   @ 1, 1 Say [File Name:] GET mFile PICTURE [!!!!!!!!]
   READ
   DO WHILE LEN(ALLTRIM(mFile)) = 0 .AND. LASTKEY() <> 27
      =Alarm()
      WAIT WINDOW [ You must enter a file name ] TIMEOUT 1
      @ 1, 1 Say [File Name:] GET mFile PICTURE [!!!!!!!!]
      READ
   ENDDO
   IF LASTKEY() = 27
      DEACTIVATE WINDOW DEST
      Cancelled = .T.
      RETURN
   ENDIF
   SET PRINTER TO &mFile
ENDIF

IF ReptDest = 2
   SET PRINTER TO PRN
ENDIF

IF ReptDest > 1
   SET PRINT ON
  ELSE
   HIDE WINDOWS ALL
   ACTIVATE SCREEN
   CLEAR
ENDIF

DEACTIVATE WINDOW DEST

RETURN
```

Selecting records

In most applications, users also want to extract records that match some criteria. Expressions like:

```
LIST FOR STATE = [TX]
```

work fine from the command line, but teaching your users command line FoxPro probably is not in the cards. Usually, you build the expression by letting them fill in the blanks, then format the expression in native FoxPro and apply it to the job at hand.

Selecting records in FoxPro is done in one of four ways:

- Processing (usually reporting) under a filter expression.
- Copying all selected records to a work file, from which reporting or further processing is done.
- Executing a command that permits the FOR or WHILE command to include only records that match a filter expression.
- Using Relational Query By Example (RQBE) to generate the output file or even direct it to the report writer.

In all of these cases, the Rushmore technology might be able to greatly increase the speed of your data selection.

Rushmore

The Rushmore technology is a data access technique that permits sets of records to be accessed very efficiently, at speeds comparable to single-record indexed access. Rushmore can be utilized with any FoxPro index: standard (.IDX) indexes as utilized in FoxPro versions 1.*xx*, compact (.IDX) indexes, or compound (.CDX) indexes. In particular, Rushmore does not depend on the new compact index format. Compact indexes can be processed faster solely because they are physically smaller.

When very large databases are being processed, Rushmore might not have sufficient memory to operate on smaller machines. In this circumstance, a warning message appears (Not enough memory for optimization) and execution proceeds as in earlier versions of FoxPro. If that happens, you might want to use the FoxPro Extended version. A good rule of thumb is to use the FoxPro Extended version if the total of all of the records in all of your databases is anywhere near 500,000 records or more.

In its simplest form, Rushmore speeds up single-database commands utilizing FOR clauses that specify sets of records in terms of existing indexes. Also, Rushmore can speed the operation of certain commands when SET FILTER is in effect and the filtering condition is specified in terms of existing indexes.

To take advantage of Rushmore with multiple databases, you must use the SQL SELECT command. FoxPro's SQL facility makes use of Rushmore as a basic tool in multi-database query optimization, utilizing Rushmore with existing indexes and even creating new ad-hoc indexes to speed queries.

Rushmore with multiple databases

When you use SELECT, the rules that you normally must follow to benefit from Rushmore are no longer in effect. SQL decides what is needed to optimize a query and does the work for you. You don't need to open databases or indexes. If SQL decides it needs indexes, it creates temporary indexes for its own use. You generally should SET ORDER TO 0 before using Rushmore.

Rushmore with single databases

With single databases, you can take advantage of Rushmore anywhere that a FOR clause appears. Rushmore is designed so that its speed is proportional to the number of records retrieved.

In addition to an optimizable FOR clause expression, the commands in TABLE 13-2 must have a scope clause of ALL or NEXT to take advantage of Rushmore. Rushmore also works when you allow the scope to default to ALL.

Table 13-2 Potentially optimizable commands with FOR clauses.

AVERAGE	EXPORT
BROWSE	LABEL
CALCULATE	LIST
CHANGE	LOCATE
COUNT	RECALL
COPY TO	REPLACE
COPY TO ARRAY	REPORT
COUNT	SCAN
DELETE	SORT
DISPLAY	SUM
EDIT	TOTAL

When optimizing, Rushmore can utilize any open indexes except for filtered and unique indexes.

For optimal performance, don't set the order of the database. You can use SET ORDER TO 0 to be sure that no order is set. Also, you can improve Rushmore's performance by setting DELETED to off, especially on queries that return a large number of records.

If you create indexes or tags, remember that this automatically sets the order. If you want to take maximum advantage of Rushmore with a large data set and you require the data in a specific order, issue SET ORDER TO to turn off index control, then use the SORT command.

Basic optimizable expressions

Rushmore technology depends on the presence of a basic optimizable expression in a FOR clause. A basic optimizable expression can form an entire expression or can appear as part of an expression.

The rules for combining basic optimizable expressions appear in the section titled "Combining basic optimizable expressions." A basic optimizable expression takes one of the following forms:

index_expression relational_operator constant_expression

or

constant_expression relational_operator index_expression

In a basic optimizable expression:

- *index_expression* must exactly match the expression on which an index is constructed and *index_expression* must not contain aliases.
- *relational_operator* must be one of the following: <, >, =, < =, > =, < >, #, !=.
- *constant_expression* can be any expression, including memory variables and fields from other unrelated databases.

For example, if you have indexes on the following expressions:

NAME
INVOICENO

then the following are basic optimizable expressions:

NAME = 'Joe'
INVOICENO > = 1000

Variables and substrings of variables can be used in place of the right-hand constants.

Combining basic optimizable expressions

Rushmore's data retrieval optimization is dependent on the FOR clause expression. With a FOR clause expression, data retrieval speeds can be enhanced if the FOR expression is optimizable.

Basic expressions can be optimizable. Basic expressions can be combined with AND, OR, and NOT to form a complex FOR clause expression that also can be optimizable.

An expression created with a combination of optimizable basic expressions is fully optimizable. If some of the basic expressions are not optimizable, the complex expression can be partially optimizable or not optimizable.

The rules that determine whether query optimization is possible are outlined in TABLE 13-3.

Table 13-3 Combining basic expressions.

Operator: AND		
	Opt.	*Not opt.*
Opt.	Fully opt.	Partially opt.
Not opt.	Partially opt.	Not opt.
Operator: OR		
	Opt.	*Not opt.*
Opt.	Fully opt.	Not opt.
Not opt.	Not opt.	Not opt.
Operator: NOT		
	Opt.	*Not opt.*
	Fully opt.	Not opt.

Combining complex expressions

You can combine complex expressions to create a more complex expression that is fully optimizable, partially optimizable, or not optimizable, as shown in TABLE 13-4. These more complex expressions can similarly be combined to create expressions that can be fully or partially optimizable or not optimizable at all.

Table 13-4 Combining complex expressions.

Operator: AND			
	Fully opt.	*Partially opt.*	*Not opt.*
Fully opt.	Fully opt.	Partially opt.	Partially opt.
Partially opt.	Partially opt.	Partially opt.	Partially opt.
Not opt.	Partially opt.	Partially opt.	Not opt.
Operator: OR			
	Fully opt.	*Partially opt.*	*Not opt.*
Fully opt.	Fully opt.	Partially opt.	Not opt.
Partially opt.	Partially opt.	Partially opt.	Not opt.
Not opt.	Not opt.	Not opt.	Not opt.
Operator: NOT			
	Fully opt.	*Partially opt.*	*Not opt.*
	Fully opt.	Partially opt.	Not opt

The standard version of FoxPro can disable Rushmore when the total number of records in all open databases exceeds 500,000 records. The FoxPro Extended version can use Rushmore to enhance performance with database record totals of over 500,000 records, as well as with database record totals under 500,000. If you run low on memory, Rushmore can't optimize data retrieval.

Disabling Rushmore

Sometimes, you'll need to disable Rushmore. If a potentially optimizable command modifies the index key in the FOR clause, Rushmore's record set can become outdated. In a case like this, you can disable Rushmore to ensure that you have the most current information from the database.

To disable Rushmore for an individual command, include the NOOPTIMIZE keyword with the command. To globally disable (or enable) Rushmore for all commands that benefit from Rushmore, use SET OPTIMIZE. The command SET OPTIMIZE OFF disables Rushmore; SET OPTIMIZE ON enables Rushmore. The default setting is ON.

Building a filter expression

You can use the FoxPro function GETEXPR to build a filter expression, as shown in LISTING 13-15. Be advised that your users might have a question or two—and that they might call you at odd hours of the night with their questions.

Listing 13-15

```
GETEXPR [List which customers?] TO expr
SET FILTER TO &expr
GO TOP
ON KEY LABEL F10 KEYBOARD CHR(23)
WAIT WINDOW [Press F10 when done]
BROWSE NOMODIFY
ON KEY LABEL F10
IF CONFIRM ( [Print report?] )
   REPORT FORM CUSTLIST TO PRINT
ENDIF
SET FILTER TO
```

Roll your own expression builders

Writing software to build a filtered expression is an art in itself. Most users get confused very easily when building queries. There are several third-party products that offer good approaches to building filter expressions. Galen Hall of HallOGram Software has a generic expression builder that's fast and easy to use. The AppGen that comes with Luis Castro's STAGE product builds *sui generis* expression builder screens that look good and are easy to use.

The one built by STAGE consists of a screen that's very user-friendly, and saves previously generated expressions in a file. Subsequently, users can select a previously saved expression from a screen that includes a short name and a brief explanation of the filter expression.

In particular, the expression builder screen can be customized to reflect more meaningful names for your fields, without being restricted to the 10-character FoxPro field name limitation. You can add your own or system variables into the list of available expressions (FoxPro puts them into a second list window). You also can force uppercase comparison without ever telling your users. Your users might find this sort of facility easier to work with.

The GETEXPR command

FoxPro includes a unique function to build filtering expressions. The syntax is:

GETEXPR *prompt* TO *variable_name*

The GETEXPR function is FoxPro's method of building a filter expression. Your users will want to be able to select only part of their database; you need to provide them with the ability to do so—preferably in a form they can learn in a normal life span.

FoxPro's RQBE screen is powerful but complex. Unfortunately, there probably is no better way to do the job, due to the inherent complexity in multi-file queries.

Copying to a work file

Once you've built a filter expression, you might want to use it to copy records to an intermediate file. In the past, because indexing or reindexing in a multiuser environment isn't always possible, I sometimes copy all matching records to a work file, which I then can do whatever I want with (LISTING 13-16).

Listing 13-16

```
WorkFile = SYS(3)
COPY TO (WorkFile) FOR &expr
currarea = SELECT()
SELECT 0
USE (WorkFile) EXCLUSIVE
INDEX ON DTOC(DATE,1) + CUSTOMER TO (WorkFile)
GO TOP
REPORT FORM HEADING [Overdue accounts for ]+DTOC(DATE) TO PRINT
USE
DELETE FILE &WorkFile.DBF
DELETE FILE &WorkFile.IDX
SELECT (CurrArea)
```

Scope and condition selection

The expression LIST TO PRINT FOR STATE = [TX] will run extremely fast if a compound index tag exists that Rushmore can take advantage of. This is the equivalent of:

```
SEEK [TX]
LIST TO PRINT WHILE STATE = [TX]
```

On the other hand, LIST TO PRINT FOR [MOUNTAIN] $ CITY won't be speeded up at all by Rushmore, because there's no way to take advantage of an index.

Commands that can take advantage of Rushmore using the FOR expression were listed in TABLE 13-2.

SQL Select

SQL SELECT (RQBE) is a book all by itself. As an alternative to the expression builder, RQBE can be used to build select expressions that make full use of the Rushmore technology. It also might be more appealing to your users. On the other hand, they might find it a bit overwhelming.

As a programmer, you'll find many uses for RQBE. You can build SQL expressions and ask FoxPro to show you the resulting expression, thus using RQBE as a tool for learning the syntax of SQL SELECT. You can build SQL SELECT code directly into your applications. In cases where you know in advance what you want to select and where you want to write the results of the query to a file for further processing or reporting, it probably is the way to go.

There are some other very important capabilities in RQBE. In the LaserDisk example, you saw how SQL SELECT can be used to build an array of the unique values of an indexed field for use in a pop-up or list field. This might mean that you can dispense with table files for validation in your applications.

All in all, SQL is highly touted as the user-friendly feature of the future. Whether or not it's the feature of the present is unclear. If users are afraid of it, you might need to bridge the gap with some code of your own.

You can either write your own extraction logic or use the RQBE feature in FoxPro. Where possible, you should use features that support the Rushmore technology. Where you can't, speed will be greatly reduced. RQBE uses Rushmore; the results are amazing. You literally can't code a program that can do the same query in anywhere near the time that it takes Rushmore to do it.

Summary

FoxPro provides a huge array of choices of programming techniques for searching databases and extracting matching records. For searching, a number of techniques can be used to streamline and smooth out your search dialogs. For selecting data, you can let your users use the SQL SELECT facility or you can write your own select screens. Using tools like those presented in this chapter, your applications can do their own searching in very simple and powerful ways within a user interface that's under your control.

A pitch for the source code on disk: You'll save yourself a heap of time if you get these routines into your hard disk, then run them until you see something you like. At that point, you can extract the code that works and patch it into your own programs.

A pitch for the Newsletter: My monthly newsletter will continue to produce code on topics like those seen in this book. If you can save yourself even a couple of hours of head-scratching, you're money ahead. I'm always looking for articles on topics of general interest to FoxPro programmers. We all are out there trying to accomplish pretty much the same things; we might as well help each other out if we can.

Index

&& command, 9
= sign operator (*see* EVALUATE)

@...EDIT, 130
   COLOR specification, 281
@...FILL, COLOR specification, 281
@...GET, 10, 134-135
   @...GET FROM, 128-129
   @...GET POPUP, 128-129
   check boxes, 126
   invisible buttons, 126
   pop-ups, 126-128, 179
   push buttons, 129-130
   radio buttons, 128
@...GET FROM, 128-129
@...GET POPUP, 128-129
@...SAY/GET, 125-126
   color pairs, 278-279
   COLOR specification, 281
   K PICTURE code, 125-126
   SIZE clause, 125-126

_MFIRST, 156
_MLAST, 156
_PDPARMS (*see* printers and printing)

A

ACOPY, 43
ACTIVATE clause, 57, 82-83
ACTIVATE WINDOW, 6, 90-92, 94-95
ADD, 172
ADEL, 43
ADIR, 43
AELEMENT, 43
AFIELDS, 43
AINS, 43
Aircraft.PRG search/select example, 333-352
Airline Seating pop-ups example, 196, 197-199
ALEN, 43
aliasing, data file, 2
AND logical expression, 20, 355-357
Anthology, 160
APP format, 21, 22
APPEND FROM ARRAY, 43
AppGen, 357
application writing, 21-25
   APP format, 21, 22
   compact EXE format, 21, 22
   directory structure, 24
   FXP (tokenized) format, 21, 22
   main program designation, SET MAIN, 22
   pathing, PATH, 25
   screen builder files (SCX), 23-24
   standalone EXE format, 21-22
   structure, internal program structure, 22
Applications Programming Interface, functions library, 48, 51
arrays, 20-21, 43-46
   add database data to array, APPEND FROM ARRAY, 43
   commands, array commands, 43
   copy element, ACOPY, 43
   create, DECLARE, 43
   create, DIMENSION, 43
   delete element, ADEL, 43
   field names in array, AFIELDS, 43
   filenames in array, ADIR, 43
   functions, array functions, 43
   insert element, AINS, 43
   location of element, AELEMENT, 43
   location of element, ASUBSCRIPT, 43
   looping, 44
   menu arrays, 44
   move database fields to arrays, SCATTER, 44
   number of elements, ALEN, 43
   procedure use, SET UDFPARMS TO, 21
   search for expression, ASCAN, 43
   sort elements, ASORT, 43, 45-46
   store elements in database, GATHER, 44
ASCAN, 43
ASORT, 21, 43-46
ASUBSCRIPT, 43
attribute bytes, 277

B

bands, reports, 249
BELL.PRG, 55
Bitstream, 267
blinking screen, SET BLINK, 278
Bookstore-Inventory screen
  field positioning, SELECT ALL FIELDS, 162-163
  file structure, 161
  finding files, FIND, 174
  listing files, LIST, 163-164
  menu added to screen, 164-165, 171
  operation of screen, 164-177
  ordering files, ORDER, 165, 174
  storing screen, 163
  user-input fields, ADD and SHOW GETS, 166, 172
borders, windows
  DOUBLE, PANEL, NONE, SYSTEM, 90-91
  WnBorder.PRG, 91
BREAK, 253
BROWSE, 5, 6
  BROWSE windows, 101-106, 196, 199-206
  BrowSkip.PRG, 102
  COLOR specification, 281
  input screens, BrowWind.PRG, 103-105
  invoice model, 103
  one-to-many browse, SET SKIP, 101, 102
  table lookup use, 105-106, 199-206
BrowSkip.PRG, 102
BrowWind.PRG, 103-105
Buerg, Vern, 1
buffers, 28-29
  flushing, 2
  high memory area, QEMM386, 29
Build Application dialog, 16
BUILD PROJECT, 213

C

calling programs and functions, 9
CaseTest.PRG, 72
Castro, Luis, 106, 119, 357
CenTest.PRG, 54
CHANGE, COLOR specification, 281
check boxes, @...GET, 126
child files, 33, 35
CIRCLE.SPR, 122-124
CIRCLE1.PRG, 120-122

CLEAR, 5
CLEAR READ, 174
CLEAR WINDOW, 92
Clipper, 142
code generators, 142
color use, 277-304
  assigning color schemes, SET COLOR OF, 280-281
  attribute bytes, 277
  available FoxPro colors, 277-278
  blinking screen, SET BLINK, 278
  color pairs, 278-279
  color picker, Alt-W, 280
  color schemes, Schemes.PRG, 283-289
  commands with COLOR specification, 281-282
  detecting color monitors, ISCOLOR, 278
  detecting monochrome VGAs, 279-280
  Harless Color Sets program, 9, 280
  intensity setting, SET COLOR, 278
  monochrome screens, 279
  pop-ups, 184-185
  ProColor program, 280
  QuarterDeck MANIFEST screen example, 295-304
  READ, 164
  user-preferences file (FOXUSER.DBF), 9
  user-selectable colors, UserColr.PRG, 289-295
COLOR clause, READ, 87
color pairs, 278-279
ColoRead.PRG, 281-282
command line, xiv
command trees, 18
command window, 12-13
commands, 5-6
  command trees, 18
  metacommands, 6
  operands, 5
comments, && command, 9
compact EXE format, 21, 22
compilers and compilation process, 16
  compact EXE format files, 16
  formats, 21
  library support, 16
complex logical expressions, 20, 355-357
compound index files (CDX), 2

CONFIG.FP file, 26-27, 41
CONFIG.SYS, 26
Confirm1.PRG, 185-186
Confirm2.PRG, 187-188
continue loops, searching, 325-333
control structures, 18, 65-88
  DO CASE...ENDCASE, 69-72
  DO loops, 65
  DO WHILE...ENDDO loops, 65-67, 144
  event handlers, 78, 80
  FOR...ENDFOR loops, 69
  IF...ENDIF loops, 67
  loops, 65-72
  menus, 73-78
  READ command and clauses, 80-88
  SCAN...ENDSCAN loops, 67-69
CREATE REPORT, 248
CREATE SCREEN, 161
CREATE TABLE, 33, 39
CREATE VIEW, 253
Customer Database report example, 248-259
customizing FoxPro, 27-28
CYCLE clause, READ, 81-82, 208, 218-219

D

data files, 28-29
  aliasing, 2
  buffer flushing, 2
  delete, DELETE, 5
  delete, PACK, 4-5
  delete, record recycling techniques, 5
  delete, SET DELETED ON, 4-5
  header, 1
  hex viewers, 1
  naming, 2
  open, limitations on number simultaneously open, 4
  open, USE and USE AGAIN, 2
  packing, 4-5
  records, writing records to disk, 2
  selecting for work, SELECT, 2
  structural changes and recompilation, 2
  X-based standard, 1
data modeling, 35-38
  dependent data, secondary dependencies, 36-38
  redundant data, 35
  repetitious data, 35

362 Index

DEACTIVATE clause, 57, 82-83
DEACTIVATE WINDOW, 7, 92, 94-95
debugging program code
  recompilation, SET DEVELOPMENT OFF/ON, 15
  screen builder, ON ERROR, 174
  step, SET STEP OFF/ON, 15
  TRACE window, 15
  viewing process, SET DISPLAY TO, 15
DECLARE, 43
DEFINE BAR, COLOR specification, 281
DEFINE MENU, 143, 206
  COLOR specification, 281
DEFINE PAD, 156, 206
  COLOR specification, 281
DEFINE POPUP, 143, 156, 179, 180, 182-183, 185-188, 206
  COLOR specification, 281
DEFINE POPUP PROMPT FIELD, 189-191
DEFINE WINDOW, 6, 90-92
  COLOR specification, 281
DELETE, 5
dependent data, secondary dependencies, 36-38
Developer's Kit, 16
dialog boxes, 106-115
  Print-to-Where?, PrinCon2.PRG, 106-107
  Print-to-Where?, PrinCon3.PRG, 107-115
DIMENSION, 43
directory structure, 24
disk space requirements, 29
Distribution Kit files, 16
DO, 9, 22, 164
DO CASE...ENDCASE, 18, 69-72
DO loops, 65
DO WHILE...ENDDO loops, 18, 65-67, 144
DoLoop2.PRG, 68

E

EDIT
  COLOR specification, 281
  windows, EDIT windows, 101
editing and editor use, 17-18
  carriage returns, CHR(13), 18
  copy text, Ctrl-C, 18
  cut text, Ctrl-X, 18
  highlight text, Shift key use, 18
  invoke, MODIFY COMMAND, 17

paste text, Ctrl-V, 18
  word-wrap, MODIFY FILE, 17
Elliott, Rich, 267
environmental settings for FoxPro
  CONFIG.FP file, 26-27
  customizing FoxPro, SET commands, 27
  toggle controls, SET CONFIRM OFF/ON, 27
ErrMenu.PRG, 78, 79-80
error trapping
  ON ERROR, 57-59
  pulldown-menu type, ErrMenu.PRG, 78, 79-80
ERRTRAP.PRG, 58-59
escape routines
  escape trapping, SCAN...ENDSCAN, 62
  ON ESCAPE, 58, 60-61
EscTest.PRG, 60-61
EVALUATE, 19-20, 53-57
event handlers, 7, 78, 80
event loops, xvi-xvii, 72, 78, 144
event-driven programming, 18-19, 72, 78
EX1.PRG, 99-100
expanded memory (EMS), 28-29
exporting data, 39
extended FoxPro vs. standard FoxPro, 30
Extended Support Library, 16
extracting records from searching, 306, 343-353

F

files (see also data files; index files), 28-29
  child files, 33, 35
  create file within program, CREATE TABLE, 33
  data files (see data files)
  data modeling techniques, 35-38
  dependent data, secondary dependencies, 36-38
  file-management utilities, 64
  flat files, 32
  hierarchical sequential data structures, 32-33
  importing/exporting data, 39
  index files (see index files)
  memo fields, 38
  memory variables, 39
  parent files, 33
  primary files, 33-35
  redundant data, 35
  repetitious data, 35

secondary files, 33-35
  segment IDs, 32, 33
  sequential access, 34
  structure of files, 32-33
filter expressions, 357
  Relational Query By Example (RQBE), 6
FIND, 174
fixed-length pop-ups, 179, 180
flat files, 32
FLOAT data types, 39
fonts, 267
FOR...ENDFOR loops, 69
foundation reads, xvi-xvii
FOXUSER.DBF user-preference file, 9
FUNCTION, 212
function keys
  hot keys, ON KEY LABEL, 19
  reassign, ON KEY LABEL, 13-14
  reassign, SET FUNCTION TO, 13
functions, 5-6, 47-57
  API library functions, 48, 51
  array-specific functions, 20-21
  built-in functions, 48
  calling functions, 9, 51-57
  calling functions, evaluation with = operator, 53-57
  calling functions, execute-as-programs, 52
  calling functions, regular expressions, 52
  calling functions, returning values, 52-53
  duplicated function names, FoxPro solution, 124
  hot keys, 19
  library building, SET LIBRARY TO, 16, 48
  menu-option use, 143
  naming functions, 47
  parameter modification, SET UDFPARMS TO, 47, 52
  parameter passing, WITH, 47-48
  parameters, 5
  screen builder placement, 219-222
  terminate, RETURN, 47, 48
  test operation, EVALUATE, 19-20, 53-57
  user-defined (UDF), 8, 48, 52-53
  VALID, WHEN, ACTIVATE/DEACTIVATE, SHOW clauses, 57
FXP (tokenized) format, 21, 22

Index   363

G

GATHER, 44
GENIFER, 142
GetaCode.PRG, 182-183
GETEXPR, 357-358
GO TO screens, 209, 222-231

H

Hall, Galen, 20-21, 78, 357
HALLoGRAM Software, 78, 357
Harless Color Sets, 9
Harless, Wayne, 9, 280
headers, data file, 1
HIDE WINDOW, 7, 92
hot keys, 19, 143, 150-151

I

IF...ENDIF loops, 67
IfNest.PRG, 71
importing data, 39
IN WINDOW clause, 92-93
index files, 2-4, 28-29
   compound index files (CDX), 2
   create, INDEX ON, 34
   create, TAG, 2-3
   find records, LOCATE, 4
   find records, SEEK, 3, 4
   find records, SET RELATION TO, 3
   inverting, fully inverting the file, 3
   reading, Rushmore use, 3-4, 133, 353-357
   searching, INDEX ON, 20, 34, 306-307
   structural index files, 2-3
   types, data types, 3
INDEX ON, 34, 161, 306-307
indirection, 19
InkeyTst.PRG, 67
InsMode, 5
installing FoxPro 2.0, 30
inverting, index files, 3
invisible buttons, @...GET, 126
invoice model, 103
Invoice.PRG, 273-275
invoices, LaserJet example, 267-269, 273-275
ISCOLOR, 278, 279-280

K

K PICTURE code, @...SAY/GET, 125-126
key fields, searching and selecting, 305-306
   multiple key fields, 315-322
keyboard macros, 12

Korenthal Associates, 16

L

label forms (LBX), 9, 38
laser printers
   invoices, 267-269, 273-275
   reports, 259-265
LASER.SPR screen builder demo program, 130-142
LaserDisk library screen builder example, 208-247
LaserJet invoice, 267-269, 273-275
LaserPro.PRG, 260-265
libraries
   build, SET LIBRARY TO, 16, 48
   Extended Support Library, 16
   procedure libraries, 63-64
   standard library files, 16
   Support Library files, 16
LIST, 106, 163-164, 179, 353
LIST TO PRINT FOR, 359
LIST.COM, 1
lists (see pop-ups)
LOADHI, 29
LOCATE, 4
logical expressions, complex:AND, OR, NOT, 20, 355-357
loops, 18, 65-72
   arrays, 44
   continue loops, searching, 325-333
   DO loops, 65
   DO WHILE...ENDDO loops, 65-67, 144
   event loops, xvi-xvii, 72, 78, 144
   FOR...ENDFOR loops, 69
   IF...ENDIF loops, 67
   SCAN...ENDSCAN loops, 67-69
   SKIP command, 69

M

macros, 19
   define macro, Shift-F10, 12
   indirection, 19
   keyboard macros, 12
MANIFEST.PRG, 296-304
MEM files, 40-41
memo fields, 4, 38, 215
memory management
   allocation of memory, 29
   disk space requirements, 29
   expanded memory (EMS) and FoxPro, 28-29

FoxPro requirements, 29
   high memory area, LOADHI, 29
   memory variables, allocating memory for, 41
   networking requirements, NETROOM, 29
memory variables, 39
   allocating memory for, 41
   copy fields as memory variables, SCATTER MEMVAR, 39
   copy memory variables as fields, GATHER MEMVAR, 39
   create, SAVE SCREEN, 39
   hidden memory variables, 39-40
   number of, MVCOUNT, 41
   procedures, assigning memory variables, SETUDFPARMS TO, 40
   space available for, MVARSIZ, 41
   storing, MEM files, 40-41
MENU, 44, 179, 180-182
menu arrays, 44
MenuBar.PRG, 74-77
MENULOOP.PRG, 66
menus and menu builder files (MNX) (see also pop-ups), 9, 10-11, 38, 73-78, 143-159
   bar number options, 150
   check mark option, SET MARK and MRKBAR, 157
   code generation, 151-153
   command options, 149
   create, DEFINE MENU, 143
   create, DEFINE POPUP, 143
   error-trapping routine, ErrMenu.PRG, 78, 79-80
   event-loop programming, SampMenu.PRG, 145-146
   first and last items in menu, _MFIRST and _MLAST, 156
   FoxPro menu design, 146-149
   functions as options, 143
   hot keys, 143, 150-151
   menu bar menus, 73-78
   Menu menu, Alt-M, 150
   multi-column menus using pop-ups, 193-196
   options, alphabetize, ASORT, 21
   options, bar number options, 150
   options, command options, 149
   options, hot keys, 143, 150-151

options, names, SYS(2013), 11, 153
options, procedure options, 150
options, submenu options, 149
pads, DEFINE PAD, 156
pads, remove, RELEASE PAD, 156
pads, restore, SET SYSMENU TO DEFAULT, 156
pop-up, DEFINE POPUP, 156
pop-up, remove, RELEASE BAR, 159
procedure options, 150
Program menu, Alt-P, 151
return to default, POP_MSYSMENU, 11, 148-149
return to default, SET SYSMENU TO DEFAULT, 11, 144
sample session, 149-151
save existing menu, PUSH_MSYSMENU, 11, 146, 147-148
screen building using menus, 164-165, 212-213, 237-245
System menu emulation, 11, 144
System menu pads and names, 153-156
traditional menu structure, 144-146
trapping routines, ON SELECTION BAR, 143
use new menu, ACTIVATE MENU_MSYSMENU, 11
uses for menus, 143-144
using parts of FoxPro System menu, 153-159
metacommands, 6
Mitsutama, Blaise, 280
MODAL clause, READ, 118
MODIFY COMMAND, 17
MODIFY FILE, 17
MODIFY PROJECT, 210
modular programming, 18
MOVE, 116
MOVE WINDOW, 92
MRKBAR, 157
MultProm.PRG, 194-196
MVARSIZ, 41
MVCOUNT, 41
MyLookup.PRG, 200-206

N

NearMiss.PRG, 192-193
NETROOM, 29
NewWindo.PRG, 90
NODEBUG, 22
NOMOUSE clause, READ, 87
Norton Utilities, 1
NOT logical expression, 20, 355-357

O

OBJECT clause, READ, 86
OldWindo.PRG, 89-90
ON ERROR, 57-59, 78, 174
ON ESCAPE, 58, 60-61, 78
ON KEY, 78
ON KEY LABEL, 13-14, 19, 78
ON PAD, 78
ON SELECTION BAR, 143
ON SELECTION PAD, 78
ON SELECTION POPUP, 78, 143
one-to-many relationship reports, 251-253
OnePage.PRG, 266-267
operands, command, 5
optimization techniques, 25-26
OR logical expression, 20, 355-357
ORDER, 174
OVERLAY file, 26

P

PACK MEMO, 38
PACK, 4-5
parameters, function, 5
parent files, 33
PATH, 25, 26
PCTOOLS, 64
pop-ups (see also menus), 115-116, 179-207, 217
@...GET, 126-128
Airline Seating example, PROMPT, 196, 197-199
BROWSE windows, 196, 199-206
color control in pop-ups, 184-185
confirmation-windows, special-use pop-ups, 185-188
create, @...GET, 179
create, DEFINE POPUP, 156, 179, 182-183
create, LIST, 179
create, MENU, 179, 180-182,
create, POPUP, 179
create, PROMPT, 183-184
custom-designed, 196, 199-206
finding and popping up near misses, 191-193
fixed-length pop-ups, 179, 180
multi-column menus, PROMPT, 193-196
multi-field display pop-ups
multi-value selection from pop-ups, MULTI, 207
remove pop-up, RELEASE BAR, 159
scrolling information displays, 188-189
uses and applications, 179
variable-length pop-ups, 179, 189-191
PopList.PRG, 129
PopNames.PRG, 127
POPUP, 179
POP_MSYSMENU, 11, 148-149, 208
primary files, 33-35
PrinCon2.PRG, 106-107
PrinCon3.PRG, 107-114
PrintCon.PRG, 101
printers and printing, 56-57
creating printer-driver files, 256-257
dialog boxes, Print-to-Where?, 106-115
font libraries, 267
laser printers and reports, 259-265
overriding driver routines, 257-258
printer control codes, 255-256
reports, 253-259
saving modified printer-driver setup, 258
style of type (bold, italic, etc.), 255
two-column reports, 265-267
_PDPARMS code assignment, 259
PRINTFUN.PRG, 56-57
private variables, 41, 42
procedures (see also functions), 57-64
arrays used in procedures, SET UDFPARMS TO, 21
duplicated procedure names, FoxPro solution, 124
error trapping, ON ERROR, 57-59
escape routines, ON ESCAPE, 58, 60-61
escape trapping, SCAN...ENDSCAN, 62
library building, 63-64

procedures (*Cont.*)
   naming, SET PROCEDURE TO, 63-64
   screen builder placement, 219-222
ProColor, 280
PRODUCT.PRG, 70-71
programming in FoxPro (*see also* application writing), xiv-xv, 18-21
   APP, EXE, FXP file formats, 21, 22
   application writing, 21-25
   arrays, array-specific functions, 20-21
   arrays, procedure use, SET UDFPARMS TO, 21
   characters-per-line limitations, 9
   command trees, 18
   compilation formats, 21
   CONFIG.FP file, 26-27
   control structures, 18
   customizing FoxPro, SET commands, 27
   debugging, 14-16
   directory/subdirectory structures, 24
   EVALUATE-ing functions, 19-20
   event loops, xvi-xvii, 72
   event-driven programming concepts, 18-19, 72, 78
   foundation reads, xvi-xvii
   hot keys, 19
   indirection, 19
   logical expressions, complex: AND, OR, NOT, 20
   loops, 18
   macros, 19
   modular programming, 18
   optimization, 25-26
   pathing, PATH, 25
   running programs, DO, 9
   screen builder as design tool, 23-24
   snippets, screen builder, 119
   structure of program, 18-19, 22
   testing, 14-16
project builder files (PJX) and project manager, 9, 11, 16-17, 38
   system variables, 11
   screen builder use, 246-247
PROMPT, 180, 183-184, 193-196, 197-199
PrtTest, 129-130
public variables, 41, 42
pulldowns (*see also* menus; pop-ups), 12, 179

push buttons, @...GET, 129-130
PUSH_MSYSMENU, 11, 146, 147-148, 208, 215

Q
QEMM386, 29
QuarterDeck MANIFEST screen, color-use example, 295-304
QuickScreen, Alt-SQ, 161-162

R
radio buttons, @...GET, 128
READ command, 80-88
   ACTIVATE/DEACTIVATE clauses, 82-83
   COLOR clause, 87, 164, 281
   CYCLE clause, 81-82, 208, 218-219
   exiting READ CYCLE, CLEAR READ, 174
   MODAL clause, 118
   NOMOUSE clause, 87
   OBJECT clause, 86
   order of processing clauses, 87-88
   SAVE clause, 86-87
   SHOW clause, 83-84, 141-142, 166, 221
   TIMEOUT clause, 86
   VALID clause, 84-85
   WHEN clause, 85-86
   window-access control, MODAL clause, 118
ReadAct.PRG, 82-83
ReadShow.PRG, 83-84
ReadVal.PRG, 84-85
ReadWhen.PRG, 85-86
RECCOUNT, 5
record recycling, 5
records, writing records to disk, 2
redundant data, 35
regional variables, 41, 42-43, 213-214
Relational Query By Example (RQBE), 6
   filter expressions, 6
   report writer, 259
   searching, SQL SELECT, 6, 20, 359
RELEASE BAR, 159
RELEASE PAD, 156
RELEASE WINDOW, 7
repetitious data, 35
REPORT FORM, 3
Report screens, 209, 231-237
reports and report forms, 9, 248-276
   bands, 249

   create, CREATE REPORT, 248
   Customer Database report example, 248-259
   font libraries, 267
   FoxReport, 11
   inserting items in reports, 251
   invoices, LaserJet example, 267-269, 273-275
   laser printers, special considerations, 259-265
   moving items in reports, 250-251
   one-to-many relationships, 251-253
   overriding printer driver routines, 257-258
   printer control codes, 255-256
   printer drivers, 253-259
   printer-driver file creation, 256-257
   report forms, 248
   RQBE and report writer, 259
   saving modified printer-driver setup, 258
   screen builder use, 246
   two-column reports, 265-267
   type styles (bold, italic, etc.), 255
   variable definition, 249-250
   _PDPARMS code assignment, printer drivers, 259
RESTORE WINDOW, 92
Rettig, Tom, 21
RETURN, 47, 48
Rushmore, 3-4, 133, 353-357
   complex logical expressions, 355-357
   disabling, 357
   index-file reading, 3-4, 133, 353-357
   multiple database searching, 354
   optimizable expressions, 355-356
   single database searching, 354-355
   SQL SELECT use, 359

S
SampMenu.PRG, 145-146
SAVE clause, READ, 86-87
SAVE SCREEN, 39
SAVE WINDOW, 92
SCAN...ENDSCAN loops, 62, 67-69
ScanTst2.PRG, 69
SCATTER, 44
SCATTER MEMVAR, 39

Schemes.PRG, 283-289
screen builder, 9, 10, 23-24, 38, 119-142, 160-178, 208-247
  @...GET FROM, 128-129
  @...GET POPUP, 128-129
  @...GET, 10, 134-135
  @...SAY/GET control, 125-126
  activating screen, READ, 218-219
  Bookstore Inventory example, BOOKS.SPR, 160-178
  check boxes, @...GET, 126, 217
  Circle Diameter example, 119-124
  CLEANUP code window, 138-139
  code generator use, 142
  color use, 131
  cursor movement, 131
  debugging, ON ERROR, 174
  field positioning, SELECT ALL FIELDS, 162-163
  file structures, 161
  finding files, FIND, 174
  function placement, 219-222
  GET initialization, 215
  GO TO screens, 209, 222-231
  invisible buttons, @...GET, 126
  LASER.SPR demonstration program, 130-142
  LaserDisk library example, 208-247
  listing files, LIST , 163-164
  local variables, 133
  memo fields, 215
  menus and screens, 164-165, 171, 212-213, 215, 237-245
  options, 211-212
  ordering files, ORDER, 165, 174, 217
  pop-ups, @...GET, 126-128, 131, 217
  procedure placement, 219-222
  project manager use, 246-247
  push buttons, @...GET, 129-130
  QuickScreen, Alt-SQ, 161-162
  radio buttons, @...GET, 128
  READ SHOW clause, 141-142
  regional variables, REGIONAL, 213-214
  report forms, 246
  Report screens, 209, 231-237
  select area, 133
  setup code, 215
  SHOW GETS statements, 139, 141
snippets, 119
storing screens, 163
studio codes, 133
text editing regions, @...EDIT, 130
user-input fields, 166, 172
validation fields, 133
viewing screens, 211
windows defined, 214
windows used in screen design, PrintCon.PRG, 100-101
yes/no variables, 136-137
ScrlText.PRG, 188-189
scrolling pop-ups, 188-189
Search1.PRG through Search7.PRG, 308-333
searching/selecting, 20, 305-360
  continue loops, Search7.PRG, 325-333
  exact match, SET EXACT OFF/ON, 307, 310
  extracting records, 306, 343-353
  filter expressions, copying to work file, 358
  filter expressions, GETEXPR, 357-358
  indexed searches, INDEX ON, 306-307
  key fields, 305-306
  key fields, displaying, Search4.PRG, 314-315
  key fields, multiple key fields, 306, 315-322
  key fields, truncating for accuracy, TrunkKey, 311
  LOCATE, 4
  logical expressions, complex: AND, OR, NOT, 20, 355-357
  multiple databases, Rushmore use, 354
  near-match searches, 191-193, 306, 307-308, 311-315
  Relational Query By Example (RQBE), 6
  RQBE, SQL SELECT, 20, 359
  Rushmore , 3-4, 353-357
  sample applications, Aircraft.PRG, 333-352
  scope and condition selection, LIST TO PRINT FOR, 359
  SEEK, 3, 4
  sequential searches, 308, 322-325
  SET RELATION TO, 3
  simple search, Search1.PRG and Search2.PRG, 308-311
single databases, Rushmore use, 354-355
  SQL SELECT use, 20, 359
Seasonal.PRG, 184
Seasons.PRG, 126
Seating.PRG, 197-199
secondary files, 33-35
SEEK, 3, 4
segment IDs, 32, 33
SELECT, 2
SELECT ALL FIELDS, 162-163
semicolon use, 12-13
sequential searches, 308, 322-325
SET BELL OFF/ON, 27
SET BLINK, 278
SET COLOR, 278
SET COLOR OF, 280-281
SET commands, 27
SET CONFIRM OFF/ON, 27
SET CONSOLE OFF/ON, 62
SET DELETED ON, 4-5
SET DEVELOPMENT OFF/ON, 15
SET DISPLAY TO, 15
SET EXACT OFF/ON, 307, 310
SET FILTER, 353
SET FUNCTION TO, 13
SET LIBRARY TO, 16, 48
SET MAIN, 22
SET MARK, 157
SET NEAR OFF/ON, 307-308
SET ODOMETER TO, 62
SET ORDER TO, 354-355
SET PROCEDURE TO, 22, 63
SET RELATION, 3, 253
SET SKIP, 101, 102, 253
SET STEP OFF/ON, 15
SET SYSMENU TO DEFAULT, 11, 144, 156
SET TALK OFF/ON, 62
SET UDFPARMS TO, 21, 40, 47, 52
SET VIEW TO, 253
SHOW clause, 57, 83-84, 166
SHOW GET, COLOR specification, 281
SHOW GETS, 139, 141, 172, 221 COLOR specification, 281
SHOW OBJECT, COLOR specification, 281
SHOW WINDOW, 92
SIZE clause, @...SAY/GET, 125-126
SKIP, 69
SMART TEMPLATES, 142
snippets, 119
SofCraft, 267

sorting (see also
   searching/selecting), 253
   array elements, ASORT, 45-46
   menu-options, ASORT, 21
SpeeDisk, 64
SQL SELECT, 6, 359
StateVal.PRG, 189-191
structural index files, 2-3
subdirectories, 24
Support Library files, 16
SWATCH program, 16
SWFTE, 267
SYS(2013), 11, 153
System menu, 11, 144, 153-156
   display, F10, 12
   pulldown menus, 12
systems analysis, xv-xvi

T

table lookups, BROWSE use,
   105-106, 199-206
TAG, 2-3
testing code (see also debugging
   program code), 14-16
text editing regions, @...EDIT, 130
TIMEOUT clause, READ, 86
toggle controls, set, SET
   CONFIRM OFF/ON, 27
tokenized (FXP) format, 21, 22
TRACE window, 15
trees, command treeds, 18
TrunkKey, 311
two-column reports, 265-267
TwoCol.PRG, 270-273

U

UI2, 142
upgrading FoxPro 1.02 to 2.0, 30
USE, 2, 161
USE AGAIN, 2
user interface, xiv
user-defined functions (UDF), 8,
   48, 52-53
   calling, 9
UserColr.PRG, 290-295

V

VALID clause, 57, 84-85
validation pop-up windows, 115-116
   + ValWind.PRG, 115-116
VanZoeren, Pei-shan, 160
variable-length pop-ups, 179,
   189-191
variables
   private variables, 41, 42
   public variables, 41, 42
   regional variables, 41, 42-43,
      213-214
ViewGen, 119
VOPT, 64

W

WHEN clause, 57, 85-86
WhereTo.PRG, 180-181
WINDEX.PRG, 117-118
windows, 6-8, 89-118
   access control, READ MODAL,
      118
   activate, ACTIVATE WINDOW,
      94-95
   borders, DOUBLE, PANEL,
      NONE, SYSTEM, 90-91
   borders, WnBorder.PRG, 91
   BROWSE windows, 101-106,
      196, 199-206
   BROWSE windows, table
      lookup use, 105-106, 199-206
   command window, 7, 12-13
   commands, window-related, 92
   confirmation-windows, pop-ups,
      DEFINE POPUP, 185-188
   create, ACTIVATE WINDOW, 6,
      90-92
   create, DEFINE WINDOW, 6,
      90-92
   create, NewWindo.PRG, 90
   create, OldWindo.PRG, 89-90
   delete, DEACTIVATE WINDOW,
      7, 94-95
   delete, HIDE WINDOW, 7
   delete, RELEASE WINDOW, 7
   demonstration program,
      WINDEX.PRG, 117-118
   dialog boxes, 106-115
   EDIT windows, 101
   functions, window-related, 92
   IN WINDOW clause use, 92-93
   input fields, WININPUT.PRG,
      97-98
   list available windows, Alt-W, 7
   mouse use, 95-98
   moving between windows, 7,
      98-100
   moving windows, MOVE, 116
   open, GET, 7
   program use of windows, 94
   pulldown menu, Wwindows,
      7-8
   screen design using windows,
      PrintCon.PRG, 100-101
   select, Ctrl-F1, 19
   sequential activation,
      WindSet1.PRG, 94-95
   sequential deactivation,
      WindSet2.PRG, 95
   size, ZOOM, FLOAT, GROW,
      MINIMIZE, 90, 116
   split screens, 101
   validation pop-up windows,
      115-116
WindSet1.PRG through
   WindSet3.PRG, 94-96
WININPUT.PRG, 97-98
WnBorder.PRG, 91
WONTOP, 92, 98, 100
WITH, 47